20, 94

Risk

**evaluation, management
and sharing**

Yours sincerely,

Louis

(also for Christian)

(I hope to see you in Roms
for FUR).

Risk

evaluation, management and sharing

Louis Eeckhoudt
*Catholic Universities of Mons, Lille
and Louvain*

Christian Gollier
*University of Toulouse and HEC School
of Management (Paris)*

Translated by Val Lambson
Brigham Young University

Preface by Denis Kessler
*President of the French Federation of
Insurance Companies*

HARVESTER
WHEATSHEAF

New York   London   Toronto   Sydney   Tokyo   Singapore

First published in French in 1992 by
Ediscience international, Paris

This translation published 1995 by
Harvester Wheatsheaf
Campus 400, Maylands Avenue
Hemel Hempstead
Hertfordshire, HP2 7EZ
A division of
Simon & Schuster International Group

Typeset in 10/12 pt Sabon
by Mathematical Composition Setters Ltd, Salisbury, Wiltshire.

Printed and bound in Great Britain by
T. J. Press (Padstow) Ltd

British Library Cataloguing in Publication Data

A catalogue record for this book is available from
the British Library

ISBN 0-7450-1592-1

1 2 3 4 5   98 97 96 95 94

Contents

Foreword

Subjective expected utility is my favourite theory. Its compelling axioms and beautiful derivations yield genuine insights and widely useful models and guidance. To find it at the core of a book on risk by two experts of the coming generation is a great pleasure – such a pleasure that I agreed, against character, to write a Foreword. I then began to ponder what purposes a pundit of the passing generation could serve in doing so. Three came to mind: historical review, grand-manner futurism and entertainment. Having little talent for any of these, I decided instead to indulge in a bit of personal reminiscence, taking advantage of my rare freedom from the censorship (or is it discipline?) of editors and referees – an opportunity unlikely to be offered me again, I dare say.

When I completed my PhD in statics in 1955, subjective expected utility, also known as Bayesian decision theory, had not yet carried the day. In fact, it was barely out of the starting blocks. From today's perspective one might wonder why, since Ramsey presented a clear and decisive argument for its unique rationality before 1930. Although this was always remembered at his university (Cambridge) and he did other significant work, he had little influence in economics and statistics; apparently the world wasn't ready, and he died too young to proselytise. Cogent arguments were given for subjective probability by De Finetti in Italy in the 1930s and for expected utility by von Neumann and Morgenstern in America in the 1940s. Blackwell and Girshick's 1954 book, *Theory of Games and Statistical Decisions*, a centrepiece of my graduate education, contains a complete and rigorous argument but presents it almost incidentally, in the midst of objectivistic exotica, and the clincher appears only in an exercise with no interpretation. Neyman–Pearson statisticians were developing elegant and useful methods apace, even as their own examples exposed irremediable cracks in their philosophical foundations. It was Savage's 1954 book, *The Foundations of Statistics*, that finally forced Bayesian inference and decision theory out of theoreticians' amusement parks and smoke-filled tea-rooms (life was different then) and into the mainstream of statistics and, from what I read, of economics. His argument was so clear, cogent, rigorous, careful, complete, honest and beautifully wrought as to be irresistible. (Read the relevant parts of it, remembering its historical context, before you read any revisionists or dare to write on foundations of decision theory.) Bayesian inference has not prevailed in practice because it does too little to discipline the wishful thinking and special pleading that poison statistics in public discourse. Economists must account for the unaccountable irrationality of real people. However, the unassailable position of Bayesian inference and decision theory as the dominant paradigm on the intellectual high ground has been recognised for many years. As Savage says of a taxonomy of probability concepts in his introduction, that commentary 'is bound to infuriate any expert on the foundations of probability, but I trust it may do the less learned more good than harm'.

In 1961, when I joined Howard Raiffa and Robert Schlaifer at the Harvard Business School, they were embarked on a programme and campaign to get Bayesian decision theory taken seriously in business education and business decisions. They also had a wonderful research seminar going, with memoranda appearing thick and fast from all sides. A more exciting atmosphere could not be hoped for – nor, alas, could its long continuation. One idea which profoundly affected the rest of my professional life came from Schlaifer in a memo of 13 November, 1961. He suggested that the probability of a favourable outcome required to make a cautious person indifferent between the lottery $x \pm h$ and x for certain should decrease as the base wealth x increases (with h fixed). He then derived the local approximation $\frac{1}{2} - \frac{1}{4} h u''(x)/u'(x)$ for the indifference probability $\pi(x, h)$ and concluded that $r(x) = -u''(x)/u'(x)$ is 'a natural measure of risk avoidance' which should be decreasing in x. Through my good fortune and Schlaifer's enterprise in assembling colleagues, I was the right person in the right place at the right time; within the month I had proved the converse (by Cauchy's theorem – still my favourite proof, but limited to this case) and the natural generalisation to certainty equivalents of arbitrary gambles. Schlaifer's motivation is interesting and is suggested by his statement,

> It seems to me that the *cautious* person sets $\pi(x, h) > \frac{1}{2}$, not because he has any dislike for uncertainty (or entrepreneurial activity) as such, but because he feels that he can expect to do better in the long run by playing it safe for the present and thus increasing the probability that he will have the funds available to take advantage of more favorable deals which may arise in the future.

We attempted to derive cautiousness (decreasing risk aversion) or other good behaviour of immediate utility from conditions on ultimate utility and intervening opportunity sets, but obtained only negative results except for constant absolute and relative risk aversion. This, and work on his 1969 text, may explain why Schlaifer never published his thinking separately apart from what appears in his books.

Although some nice results were obtained in the 1960s and 1970s using nothing stronger than decreasing risk aversion, it seems that further progress requires further properties. There have been impressive developments along these lines in recent years. This book on the theory of risk by major contributors to the field is thus most timely and welcome. So let me stop here and urge you to get on with reading it.

John W. Pratt
William Ziegler Professor of
Business Administration,
Harvard University

Preface

This is a timely work. It fills a great void. For three hundred years, mathematicians, statisticians and economists have attempted to understand the decisions made by economic agents faced with risk and uncertainty.

During the last forty years – thanks to the considerable work of such esteemed economists as M. Allais, K. Arrow, H. Markowitz, J. Pratt, J. Mossin, J. Stiglitz, M. Rothschild, K. Borch, M. Yaari, S. Grossman, J. Drèze, M. Machina, J. J. Laffont and, more recently, H. Schlesinger, N. Doherty and G. Dionne – new tools have been forged and the original models have been extended to finally allow the development of a rigorous economic theory of risk and uncertainty. It is this theory that is majestically presented to us – or, better said, dissected for us – in this book, which is based on the most fundamental and recent work in the field.

Microeconomics – and for that matter macroeconomics – have been too long satisfied with treating only the cases of certainty. This has resulted in models that are rather 'mechanical', abstracting from that 'spice of economic life' which is risk and uncertainty. Yet uncertainty characterises all activities, be they in production or exchange. It affects all the fundamental variables that determine behaviour, explain choices and bring about decisions.

This work is comprised of three equally important parts, dealing respectively with evaluation of risky situations, individual decisions under uncertainty and markets for risk.

Above all, one should not wish to skip immediately to the second part: certainly the study of risk situations is fascinating, and the rigorous presentation that is made of the key concepts of the analysis deserves to be read carefully. These concepts are the following: lotteries, expected utility, risk aversion, the measurement of risk and stochastic dominance.

The reader will gain, particularly from this section, an excellent characterisation of lotteries, as well as a very interesting distinction between absolute, relative and partial risk aversion. It is obvious that individual preferences vary widely, and that there coexist in society risk averters, risk lovers and those who are 'risk neutral'. Furthermore, there are many degrees within each of these categories. The authors take these preferences as given. One should – but this is not the goal of this work – enquire as to the formation of these preferences. The reader will also appreciate the very clear presentation of the complex problems that are posed by the measurement of risk: how can one determine whether a given situation becomes riskier? It is evident from reading this chapter that the authors fully accept the concept of expected utility and reject the alternative approaches that have been attempted during past years. It is difficult to reproach them, but epistemology has taught us that paradigms themselves have finite life expectancies, and the authors' implicitly severe attitude towards those who have attempted to explore alternative paths is perhaps excessive. It is true that the expected utility hypothesis is canonical, and that heretics are seldom the popes of the future.

After this explanation of the concepts, the authors deal in the second part with individual decisions under uncertainty. The arguments are formulated in a partial equilibrium setting – it is assumed that the agents' decisions do not fundamentally affect the environment in which they evolve (for example, investment choices do not change the interest rate) and that their actions do not interact with each other. The authors consider three cases in turn: portfolio choices under uncertainty, insurance decisions and production decisions.

It is in this part that one sees the richness of the tool box presented in the first. The first case deals with a question which seems simple: the allocation of a portfolio between a risky asset and a risk-free asset. The difficulty of this problem is due to the endogeneity of the risk to which investors – who could be placed in an entirely risk-free situation if so desired – expose themselves. The authors present, in turn, the various criteria which might explain the choice of the investor, and carry out comparative statics exercises to study the effect of an increase in initial wealth, in the rate of return or in the level of risk. They thus make clear the central nature of the concept of risk aversion.

The demand for insurance constitutes the second area of application. Why, and under what conditions, will an economic agent decide to divest all or part of the risk that is faced? How can the decisions as to the level of coverage be explained? Once again the question appears simple, but becomes more complex after closer study. One must take into account the costs, the prices charged by the insurer, the information that the insurer and the insured respectively have access to, and so on. The most innovative developments concern the case where the agent faces several risks that may or may not be interdependent. In this case as well, risk aversion explains the agent's decisions, particularly when prices rise or initial wealth increases.

Christian Gollier and Louis Eeckhoudt conclude the second part by dealing with the problem of production decisions under uncertainty. On the one hand, producers face technological risks that can affect their level of production, and on the other hand, producers face market risks that affect prices or the level of demand. The authors study the behaviour of producers who choose their level of production in order to maximise their profits. This introduction of the risks that are inherent in business activity enriches the classical microeconomic approach under certainty. They continue with an interesting discussion on futures markets, whose role is formally very close to the role of traditional insurance markets. There is no doubt that in future years there will be much research done on the behaviour of producers who face technological and market risk (and why not social risk as well?).

The third and final part deals with markets for risk. Can markets correctly evaluate the price of risk? How is the allocation of risk decided and who finally bears it? Transferring risk from one agent to another or sharing risk collectively does not, of course, make the risk disappear. Thus one can legitimately enquire about the benefits of the mechanisms of transfer or sharing. Louis Eeckhoudt and Christian Gollier prove, in Part Three, that these mechanisms increase the welfare of all, under certain conditions. The reallocation of risk by the market has real effects that suggest the conclusion that the final welfare of the different agents, as a general rule, is higher when the possibility of risk reallocation exists. The concepts of risk sharing, risk pooling, risk tolerance and incompleteness of markets then naturally appear. Risk sharing, after market reallocation, is Pareto efficient if the reallocation is the result of perfectly competitive mechanisms. The authors conclude the third part by presenting, as an illustration, the capital asset pricing model (CAPM) of valuing financial assets. This permits the reader to understand how a market evaluates risks and redistributes them across agents. It is assumed that the agents use a mean variance model to determine their decisions under uncertainty: they attempt to maximise the return for a given level of risk, or to minimise the level of risk for a given return. They are guided *de facto* to diversify their risks by constructing a stock portfolio. This model of valuing financial assets depends on certain restrictive hypotheses, but the authors make those explicit. Finally, the authors deal with situations where there is asymmetric information between economic agents – especially between the insurer and the insured. These developments are fascinating to the extent that asymmetric information seems a more realistic hypothesis than the hypothesis that all agents have the same quantity and quality of information.

I hope there will be a sequel to this work. I would like to see a complementary discussion on the nature of risks (depending on whether they are diversifiable, transferable, insurable, etc.), on the phenomena of moral hazard and adverse selection, as well as on the nature and the role of insurance companies. Certainly the first three topics are already well treated in the text that Louis Eeckhoudt and Christian Gollier offer us, but it seems that the concepts that result in perverse coverage incentives might be explored more fully. As for the insurance industry, it remains rather mysterious. Beyond the concept of insurance markets, we must further understand the role and functioning of insurance companies themselves. And since I am permitting myself to suggest the areas of research that I think it would be desirable to pursue further, without requiring of myself the prudence that all insurers should adopt, I will suggest three paths: multiple risks, depending on whether they are interdependent or not; multiperiod analysis, where agents receive new information each moment which compares the realisation to the prediction;

and game theory, for the phenomena of risk-sharing are not always as co-operative as one may think.

This book is a success. Louis Eeckhoudt and Christian Gollier completely master their subject. Furthermore, they have both contributed to the enrichment of the stock of theorems and proofs over the years. Their own contributions to this theory of risk should be valued at their just price, and that is high. This work, which is supposed to be a textbook − as is seen by the very clear examples that accompany the arguments − is really much more. Although it allows students to discover the fundamental aspects of the economics of risk and uncertainty, it will also allow researchers to rediscover known results and to uncover new ones, always proven with rigour and clarity. It should also allow practitioners − whether in the world of finance or insurance − to become familiar with the theoretical developments that should guide them to better understand the foundations of their practices, the nature of the contracts that they write and the functioning of the markets that they create.

This work motivates the reader to take only calculated risks and, if possible, to share them. I believe that I am taking no risk in affirming that this work will soon become a classic. Those who read it will rapidly discover that I need not insure myself or share the risk that this assertion will be contradicted!

Denis Kessler

Director of Studies,
School of Graduate Studies in the Social Sciences

President,
French Federation of Insurance Companies

Introduction

The severity of unemployment problems in the heart of the industrialised economies in recent years has made public opinion sensitive – from time to time – to the question of 'job sharing'. At about the same time, we have seen a prodigious development of new financial instruments. These testify, notably, to the great need that modern economies have to create efficient instruments for 'risk-sharing'.

The growth in the number and importance of different kinds of risk will make the question of optimal risk-sharing more and more important in the social and collective contexts.

This textbook attempts to survey the current state of economic knowledge about these issues. Of course, to share risks efficiently, it is first necessary to evaluate them and to consider methods of managing them. This is why the title and the contents of this work make explicit reference to these indispensable steps, which ultimately provide the foundation for a discussion of the problem of risk-sharing.

In the interest of simplicity, we have limited ourselves to the examination of risks for which the consequences can be uniquely expressed in monetary units. (We might call these 'financial risks'.) Of course, there exist many risks (of accident, of illness, of failure, etc.) for which the consequences are not only monetary. Nevertheless, the tools developed in the financial sector perform well (though not perfectly) in the examination of other risk situations.

Since the question is both recent[1] and difficult, the reader should not be surprised to find the arguments somewhat technical sometimes. We hope the reader will not hold that against us (too much). We have attempted throughout to keep the arguments as intuitive as possible.

We have always tried to tie together rigour and intuition so that the book might be accessible to any student who has received basic economics training in mathematics, statistics and microeconomics. Consequently, this textbook should be appropriate for graduate students in economics as well as for advanced undergraduates. Furthermore, as we have restricted ourselves as much as possible to the subjects of finance and insurance, the text could also be used in business and management schools.

Since the text contains three parts and results from the efforts of two authors, the reader may speculate as to the 'division of labour' between the two 'factors of production'. Those of our colleagues who know us and who, in spite of this, make the effort to read our work will have no difficulty discovering which of us has – in one section or another – written the first draft. We must say, however, that from the perspective of optimal risk-sharing, we share all responsibility. Criticisms and suggestions can thus be addressed to the 'pool' that will distribute them thereafter to each of its members. Indeed, one of the great pleasures we enjoyed while writing this book (yes, there were some pleasures!) was the constant exchange that we engaged in concerning practically every page of the text.

It goes without saying that a large number of colleagues, by their teaching, advice and encouragement, or simply by their friendship, have indirectly lent an appreciated helping hand over the years to the preparation of this manuscript and its editing. We have chosen to mention only three because otherwise the list would be too long. Louis Eeckhoudt wishes especially to express gratitude to his statistics and decision theory professors: J. Kmenta, then at Michigan State University (now at the University of Michigan) and P. Capéraà at Laval University (Quebec). Christian Gollier, for his part, has benefited greatly from the teaching and advice of J. Drèze, his professor and thesis supervisor at the Catholic University of Louvain. The brevity of our acknowledgements 'covaries' positively and perfectly with the intensity of our gratitude.

In the shorter term, we are pleased to acknowledge that the first version of the manuscript was read with great care by two colleagues: G. Dionne (University of Montreal) and P. Roger (University of Strasbourg). Their detailed and precise comments proved to be very useful many times.

Two assistants, P. Scarmure and N. Meskens, collaborated very efficiently while carefully overseeing the polishing of different aspects of the text. Finally, the secretarial skills of D. Raulier and I. Doison were much appreciated, even if the dexterity of one of the authors in the utilisation of the modern technologies of word processing largely compensated for the inaptitude of the other!

All of these inputs contributed to the production of the finished product, which is now left in the care of our readers.

Note

1. Indeed, the systematic development of the analysis of risk in economic theory dates to the mid-1960s.

One
The evaluation of risk situations

Framework of analysis and basic notation

Part One is naturally dedicated to the presentation of the basic tools of analysis that will be applied throughout the text. In addition to this introductory role, Part One also introduces a fundamental subject in economics, that of evaluation. One often hears, in the political arena, for example, about the evaluation of public policies or about the evaluation of a troubled corporation. The reader may also remember the lengthy debate in France over how to assign values to the companies that were to be privatised. In Part One we will discuss the evaluation of that good which constitutes the theme of this book: a lottery.

Throughout the book, unless otherwise stated, we assume that the individual or corporation – or more generally, the 'decision-maker' – is only interested in one thing: the level of final wealth (or some function thereof). For some economists this assumption seems too strong because they have a tendency to think that the methods employed to achieve wealth, as well as the resulting wealth, ought to be incorporated in the evaluation. For others, influenced no doubt by the contributions of modern financial theory, the criterion of final wealth really is the only one to consider. Besides, they sometimes argue, those who do otherwise will disappear from the scene, if not physically, in any case economically!

We do not intend to engage in a debate that tends towards the 'theological'. Indeed, as we will often have occasion to assert, the economic theory of risk is already sufficiently complex and – in some ways – ambiguous in the one-dimensional framework of final wealth, that one can be satisfied with a pragmatic approach to evaluation which is limited to this single variable.

The final wealth of the decision-maker is denoted w_f and, since there is final wealth, one can suppose that there is also initial wealth, denoted w_0. In the case of a firm, for example, w_0 represents the initial value of assets minus the initial value of debts to third parties and w_f equals w_0 plus the undistributed profits of the period. If these are certain – for example, if one invests *ex post* (that is, after observing the undistributed profits of the period) – then neither w_f nor w_0 is random.

Of course, in practice, when investing before the fact, no one can predict with certainty what will happen to their wealth even over an extremely short time. Uncertainty, not certainty, is our daily lot! To reflect this state of affairs, we adopt the following definition:

$$\tilde{w}_f \equiv w_0 + \tilde{x} \tag{1.1}$$

where $\tilde{x}$ is the random element that is added to the certain component of wealth (w_0) thus making final wealth random as well. Notice that the definition in Equation (1.1) is restrictive in the sense that the lottery is additive with respect to w_0. This definition of $\tilde{w}_f$ formalises the example of the firm mentioned above where undistributed profits (a random variable) are added to a certain initial wealth to constitute final wealth. As we will have the occasion to say later, other situations are possible. Thus risk $\tilde{x}$ could very well be multiplicative with respect to initial wealth and one would have:

$$\tilde{w}_f \equiv w_0(1 + \tilde{x}) \tag{1.2}$$

An obvious example of such a situation is the investment of a given amount of initial capital (w_0) when the rate of return, $\tilde{x}$, is random in such a way that $\tilde{w}_f$ obeys the definition given in Equation (1.2).

Even though we will tend to focus on situations that can be modelled by Equation (1.1), lotteries that can be modelled by Equation (1.2) as well as intermediate cases are also of interest.

The lottery $\tilde{x}$, whether additive or multiplicative, can be represented either by a discrete or a continuous random variable. In the discrete case, the possible outcomes are denoted $x_i (i = 1, ..., n)$ and their respective probabilities are denoted $p_i (i = 1, ..., n)$ where, of course, $\Sigma_i p_i = 1$ and $0 \leqslant p_i \leqslant 1$. This somewhat cumbersome notation is sometimes condensed into the vector representation $[\mathbf{p}; \mathbf{x}]$ where $\mathbf{p}$ is the vector of probabilities p_i *and* $\mathbf{x}$ is the vector of corresponding outcomes x_i^1. In the continuous case, the random $\tilde{x}$ is characterised by a density function $f(x)$ and/or a distribution function $F(x)$.

Attention is often restricted to a subset of discrete lotteries known as 'binary lotteries'. This subset contains lotteries composed of only two possible outcomes to which the probabilities p and $1 - p$ are respectively assigned. These lotteries are sometimes called 'bets'. In light of their obvious pedagogical value, we will often refer to them even though, due to their very simple structure, they have some properties that do not generalise.

Now that the framework of analysis has been described, Chapter 2 presents an overview of the criteria for evaluating lotteries which, at various times, have had their moment of glory. In addition to their obvious historical interest, study of these criteria allows the natural introduction, in Chapter 3, of the fundamental concept of expected utility from which have been derived, in turn, the notions of a certainty equivalent, asking price and risk premium of a lottery.

Chapter 4 uses these notions to immediately present two others: relative and partial risk aversion. It also presents several reasonable assumptions concerning the properties of different kinds of risk aversion and, in light of these, considers various utility functions commonly used in literature.

Chapter 5 concentrates on the other ingredient of risk premium revealed by the Arrow–Pratt formula: the quantity of risk. It examines some possible definitions of the notion of a change in risk and discusses their internal consistency. The chapter concludes by exploring the limits (but also the uses) of variance as an indicator of the quantity of risk.

Chapters 6 and 7 deviate somewhat from the general thrust of the others without, however, being unrelated. Thus Chapter 6 suggests some potential extensions of the concepts considered earlier in Part One. Finally, Chapter 7 introduces another approach, different in form but not in content, from the notion of risk aversion. In the literature this approach is called 'state-claim analysis' and it proves very useful for the study of risk-sharing.

Note

1. The probabilities p_i and the outcomes x_i may come from objective studies (as do mortality tables in the actuarial sciences) or from the subjective evaluation of the decision-maker. Depending on the case, one speaks of objective or subjective probability. Recently some debates, which are sometimes rather obscure, have once again begun to revolve around these two concepts. We will ignore these issues.

2 : Criteria for evaluating lotteries: a (very brief) overview

The evaluation of risks is a difficult and controversial subject. For just one of many possible examples, consider the vast and complex literature on 'the value of human life'. Lotteries are no exception to this rule. Of course, evaluation is easy when it comes to lotteries that trade on large competitive markets. No one will deny that a share of stock in a company listed on a stock exchange is a lottery because its value tomorrow is perceived today as being random. Yet if the stock trades on an active exchange where new information is made available instantaneously, then its market price today unambiguously reflects its value. In this case, the market is the perfect vehicle for the evaluation of lotteries, and this is one of its well-understood roles in decentralised economies.[1] These comfortable situations (for the purposes of evaluation) are, however, the exception. In many cases, there is not a perfect market for the lotteries held by a decision-maker and one cannot escape the need to adopt one or several criteria of evaluation. For this reason, the theory of risk offers a large number of such criteria.[2] We will mention a few here before focusing more deeply in succeeding chapters on the criterion that we emphasise: the expected utility of final wealth.

Meanwhile, before beginning a rigorous discussion, we point out an interesting paradox. By a strange irony, very common in science, the criteria developed here, which clearly apply to lotteries that are not tradable on an efficient market, have been very useful in the analysis of efficient markets. Thus the study of evaluation criteria is useful even when these criteria are unnecessary.

Finally, as is the case for decision theory under certainty, an evaluation criterion implies a decision criterion: lottery $\tilde{x}$ is preferred to lottery $\tilde{y}$ if and only if the value attached to $\tilde{x}$ and denoted $V(\tilde{x})$ exceeds the value attached to $\tilde{y}$ $(V(\tilde{y}))$. This notion will often be applied in Part Two when we study choice under uncertainty; at that time we will characterise the action which, among all possible actions, maximises the value function.

We now consider several evaluation criteria that have been and continue to be widely employed.

2.1 The expected value criterion

By this criterion, one evaluates the lottery $\tilde{x}$ simply by calculating its expected value, namely,

$$V(\tilde{x}) = E(\tilde{x}) \tag{2.1}$$

where $V(\tilde{x})$ denotes the value of $\tilde{x}$ and where $E(\tilde{x})$ is the usual expected value, which we sometimes represent more compactly by μ. By way of reminder, we indicate that:

$$E(\tilde{x}) = \mu = \sum_{i=1}^{n} p_i x_i$$

for discrete distributions and that

$$E(\tilde{x}) = \int_{a}^{b} x f(x) \, \mathrm{d}x$$

for continuous distributions on the interval $[a, b]$.

We remark that instead of evaluating $\tilde{x}$ by the expected value criterion, one could equivalently evaluate $\tilde{w}_\mathrm{f}$. Then one would write:

$$V(\tilde{w}_\mathrm{f}) = V(w_0 + \tilde{x}) = E(w_0 + \tilde{x}) = w_0 + E(\tilde{x}) \tag{2.2}$$

Since of course $V(w_0) = w_0$, Expressions (2.1) and (2.2) are equivalent.

The expected value criterion is the oldest and is completely reasonable in some contexts but insufficient in others. To illustrate a case where the expected value criterion is adequate, consider an individual who faces a risk of disaster described as follows:

x	$p(x)$
0	0.9
−1 000	0.1

where $\tilde{x}$ is the loss from the potential disaster. Simple calculations establish that:

$$E(\tilde{x}) = -100$$
$$\sigma^2(\tilde{x}) = (0.9)\,(100)^2 + (0.1)\,(900)^2 = 90\,000$$
$$\sigma(\tilde{x}) = 300$$

and, of course, $\sigma(\tilde{x})$ is far from negligible. Suppose now that, in the country where this individual resides, 10 000 people face the same risk and that the disasters are independent. If these 10 000 people form an insurance company with the idea of reimbursing the losers from the contributions of everyone,[3] how much must each person contribute? To finance all of the losses, each member must make a contribution of

$$\tilde{p} = \left[\frac{1}{10\ 000}\right] (\tilde{x}_1 + \tilde{x}_2 + \ldots + \tilde{x}_{10\ 000})$$

where $\tilde{p}$ is the average loss and where $\tilde{x}_i$ refers to the loss suffered by the ith individual. Employing well-known results from mathematical statistics establishes that:

$$E(\tilde{p}) = -100$$
$$\sigma^2(\tilde{p}) = 90\ 000/10\ 000$$
$$\sigma(\tilde{p}) = 3$$

The risk of disaster is very small relative to its expected value and it would be zero for all practical purposes if n, the number of individuals, approached $+\infty$. In this case, where there is a large portfolio of independent risks, each risk can be evaluated – without risk – by its expected value. This would not be acceptable if each risk were considered in isolation.

The reader will not be surprised to learn that one of the branches of economic activity where the expected value criterion has been most utilised (consciously) is the area of life insurance. There the 'pure premium' (that is, the premium net of administrative costs) is none other than the expected value of the obligations of a company that enters into a large number of independent contracts. This idea has been understood for a long time. In a 'prospectus' addressed to Louis XVI in 1788 to justify life insurance (!), Clavière (1788) wrote that:

> One can determine, without danger of great miscalculation (that is, without much risk) the average life span for a large number of individuals of a given age; but it is impossible to assign with any certainty the life span of each of the individuals.

In addition to allowing a review of some statistical notions, this example and the accompanying discussion illustrate the usefulness and the limits of the expected value criterion. This criterion is completely reasonable for evaluating lotteries that are part of a large portfolio of identical and independent risks. For a single lottery or when there is dependence among the lotteries, this criterion is not a very good indicator of value. To understand better, consider another example. Compare two situations. In the first situation (Situation A) the individual receives 10 000 F[4] with certainty. The fact that the payment is certain implies that the probability of receiving 10 000 F equals one and that Situation A is represented by the vector:

$$(1; 10\ 000)$$

In Situation B, there are 3 chances out of 10 that the individual will have to pay 4 000 F and 7 chances out of 10 that the individual will receive 18 000 F. The vector representation of Situation B is:

$$(0.3, 0.7; -4\,000, +18\,000)$$

Offered a choice between A and B, many individuals would naturally prefer A, worried no doubt by the non-negligible chance ($p = 0.3$) of losing 4 000 F. Yet, if one considered only the expected values, then:

$$E(\tilde{x} \mid A) = 10\,000 \text{ F}$$

$$E(\tilde{x} \mid B) = -1\,200 + 12\,600 = 11\,400 \text{ F}$$

Anyone who declares a preference for A thus implicitly rejects the expected value criterion, because otherwise they would have to choose B!

Since we have cited the relatively unknown Clavière, we also note that the inadequacy of the expected value criterion seems to have already been mentioned in 1738 (!) by the famous scientist D. Bernoulli in a widely cited (if not widely read) article. In addition to a proof of the inadequacy of this criterion,[5] Bernoulli also had the intuition for another criterion, that of expected utility, which we use most in this text. Curiously, and interestingly for the historians of science, the expected utility criterion took about two centuries to establish itself. When finally established, it had the unhappy experience of seeing several competitors – of which we say little here – flourish under the name of 'non-expected utility models'! In the meantime, there have been many other approaches that are of great interest, either because of their own properties or because they illustrate the advantages and shortcomings of the expected utility model. We will briefly examine some of these.

2.2 The 'mean variance' criterion

This criterion, of which the promoter was H. Markowitz, recognises the role of expected value in the evaluation of a lottery while supplementing it very appropriately with a notion of risk. Since, consistent with a long tradition, risk seems to be well described by the notion of variance,[6] it is quite natural to write:

$$V(\tilde{w}_f) = f[E(\tilde{w}_f), \sigma^2(\tilde{w}_f)] \tag{2.3}$$

This expression[7] formalises very well the intuition that the value of a lottery depends on both its 'return' (captured by $E(\tilde{w}_f)$) and its 'risk' (measured by σ^2). In addition, the form of function f provides some important information about the preferences of the decision-maker.

Since a higher return is always appreciated, it is completely natural to assume that the partial derivative of f with respect to $E(\tilde{w}_f)$ is strictly positive, that is,

$$f_1 \equiv \partial f / \partial E > 0 \tag{2.4}$$

This means that, for a given level of variance, an individual facing a risk situation is made better off by an increase in $E(\tilde{w}_f)$. Although the positive sign of the partial derivative of f with respect to its first argument poses no problem, the sign of $\partial f / \partial \sigma^2$, which will be denoted more compactly by f_2, is more controversial. There are three possibilities.

1. f_2 always equals zero. This means that in evaluating the lottery, the decision-maker is not influenced by the level of risk. The only thing that is of concern is $E(\tilde{w}_f)$ and we have once again the expected value criterion discussed previously. Thus, it is clear that the mean variance criterion incorporates the expected value criterion as a special case. Specifically, to generate the latter it suffices to assume that function f in Equation (2.3) has everywhere a zero partial derivative with respect to σ^2. If this is the case, we say that the decision-maker is 'risk neutral', that is, that risk – represented by the notion of variance – does not influence evaluation of the lottery.

2. From the comparison of Situations A and B at the end of Section 2.1, it seems natural to suppose that, for individuals who prefer A, f_2 is negative. If we calculate the variances of lotteries A and B, we obtain:

   $$\sigma^2(\tilde{x} \mid A) = 0$$

   since, in Situation A, the individual receives 10 000 with certainty, and

   $$\sigma^2(\tilde{x} \mid B) = (0.3)(15\ 400)^2 + (0.7)(6\ 600)^2 = 101\ 640\ 000$$

   If, despite the fact that $E(\tilde{x} \mid B)$ exceeds $E(\tilde{x} \mid A)$, an individual (using the mean variance criterion) declares a preference for A, it can only be explained by a negative weight on variance in the evaluation of a lottery. This phenomenon is captured mathematically by a negative value for the partial derivative f_2. If f_2 is everywhere negative, we say that the decision-maker is 'risk averse'. This implies that, faced with two lotteries exhibiting the same mean, a risk-averse individual will choose the one with smallest variance.

3. By symmetry with Possibility 2, we say that a positive value of f_2 indicates 'risk loving' behaviour since an increase in the variance of a lottery (*ceteris paribus*) makes the decision-maker better off.

The reader who is familiar with the notion of indifference curves under certainty will easily guess that the function (2.3) defines a marginal rate of substitution (MRS) between return $(E(\tilde{w}_f))$ and risk $(\sigma^2(\tilde{w}_f))$. Indeed, given constant V, one finds by fully differentiating Equation (2.3) that

$$\text{MRS}_{E,\sigma^2} = - \, dE/d\sigma^2 = f_2/f_1 \tag{2.5}$$

Intuitively, the ratio of the two partial derivatives indicates how much E must increase to compensate the decision-maker for an increase in σ^2 if V is to remain constant.

Expression (2.5) suggests how to construct indifference curves in mean variance space. The discussion concerning the signs of f_1 and f_2 shows that indifference curves are upward-sloping, downward-sloping or horizontal depending on whether the individual has risk-averse, risk-loving or risk-neutral preferences. Indeed, since f_1 is always positive, the sign of MRS is completely determined by the sign of f_2.

For a risk-averse individual (who could be called a 'riskophobe'[8]), indifference curves are upward-sloping, but are they concave or convex? This question resulted in several debates in the literature following the appearance of an article published by a pioneer in the area, James Tobin. We do not explore this question here partly because it is too narrow and partly because it is not necessary for the study of a major application of the mean variance model: the evaluation of financial assets (see Part Three). Indeed, for all questions concerning portfolio management it is sufficient to consider a special case of Equation (2.3), namely,

$$V = E(\tilde{w}_f) - k\sigma^2(\tilde{w}_f) \tag{2.6}$$

where k is a constant. In this case f is linear with $f_1 = 1$ and $f_2 = -k$. It is easy to interpret coefficient k. If it is positive, there is risk aversion, and the larger it is the higher is the level of aversion. To better grasp this assertion, consider an individual, S, who adopts Equation (2.6) to evaluate lotteries and declares an indifference between Lotteries I and II described below:

I		II	
$x = -6$	$p = 1/2$	$x = -10$	$p = 1/2$
$x = +10$	$p = 1/2$	$x = +20$	$p = 1/2$

As can be confirmed by calculating the variances, Lottery II is riskier than Lottery I (because $\sigma^2(\tilde{x}\,|\,\text{II}) = 225$ while $\sigma^2(\tilde{x}\,|\,\text{I}) = 64$). If S is indifferent between I and II, this means that the same value is assigned to each and hence for S,

$$2 - k(64) = 5 - k(225)$$

Thus k_S, the value of the coefficient k for S, is $3/161 = 0.018\,63$.

Now imagine that Individual T, faced with the same two lotteries has a preference for I. One then suspects, since T rejects the riskier lottery, that T is more risk averse than S. By calculating k_T one can quantify the higher level of risk aversion. If T said, 'I would consider I and II to be equivalent if each of the outcomes in II were increased by 2, then k_T could be evaluated. The addition of a constant does not change the variance so T's indifference between unchanged I and modified II implies:

$$2 - k(64) = 7 - k(225)$$

and thus,

$$k = 5/161 = 0.031\ 06$$

Thus T is more risk averse than S. The simple (linear) version of the mean variance criterion even allows us to say that this risk aversion is 1.667 times greater.

To conclude this brief presentation of the mean variance model, we mention that it is the subject of much recurring controversy in the theory of risk. We will later have the opportunity to discuss some of its weaknesses. This section has brought to light two of its advantages – and none of its disadvantages – namely, its great simplicity and its very intuitive nature.

2.3 The 'safety first' criteria

There are many criteria of the 'safety first' type; a good reference is Arzac's paper (1976). We will consider only one example here in order to give the reader a basic idea of this very appealing but nevertheless very little used approach. We note, however, that this criterion has begun to make its way timidly into the financial realm, as reflected in a recent article by Moshe Hagigi and Brian Kluger (1987).

The safety-first criteria, and especially the one we discuss here, are analogous to the linear form of the mean variance model (see Equation (2.6)). They also evaluate lotteries by weighing risk and return, but the level of risk is not measured by variance. Rather, the safety-first criteria assume that the decision-maker distinguishes between the realisations of w_f according to whether they exceed a threshold (t) that is taken by the decision-maker to be the level below which, 'if possible', the outcome must not fall.

Determination of the critical threshold has been the subject of much discussion. There are cases, however, where the threshold is naturally imposed. We will give an example of this below. We point out to the reader enamoured by history that the first application of the safety-first concept was in 1786[9] by Tetens, who wanted to measure the risks run by an insurance company underwriting a contract. That author defined risk as the situation where the indemnity paid by the company, that is the realisation of the random variable, surpasses the natural threshold given by the premium and thus results in a loss for the contract. In a sense, individuals tend to measure risk by the probability of receiving a value of w_f that is less than the tolerable threshold, t, and by the negative spread between the actual outcome and that threshold. When unconcerned about the variability of w_f for realisations above t, the decision-maker will focus on the variability of w_f below t. A statistical concept that reflects this approach toward risk is the 'semi-variance' with respect to t, that is defined as follows for continuous distributions:

$$\sigma^{2-}(t) = \int_a^t (w_f - t)^2 f(w_f) \, dw_f \qquad (2.7)$$

where a is the lowest value that w_f can take on.

This semi-variance is, in a sense, a doubly truncated variance since, on the one hand, the integral goes from a to t (and not to b, the upper bound of w_f) and on the other the deviations are not expressed relative to the mean μ but rather relative to the tolerable threshold, t.

Once $\sigma^{2-}(t)$ is calculated, lottery $\tilde{w}_f$ is valued at:

$$V(\tilde{w}_f) = E(\tilde{w}_f) - k\sigma^{2-}(t) \qquad (2.8)$$

To better grasp the difference between the mean variance criterion and the safety-first criterion, consider the following example. Let there be two lotteries characterised as follows:

A		B	
x	p	x	p
-1	0.2	-20	0.01
$+4$	0.3	$+7$	0.49
$+10$	0.5	$+8$	0.50

In addition, let $w_0 = 3$ and $k = 1$.

If the individual evaluates these lotteries by the mean variance criterion, the choice is easy. Indeed, Lottery B has a higher return than A because $E(\tilde{x}|B) = 7.23$ while $E(\tilde{x}|A) = 6$, and it is less risky because $\sigma^2(\tilde{x}|B) = 7.737$ while $\sigma^2(\tilde{x}|A) = 19$. A risk-averse decision-maker who measures risk by the variance and adopts the mean variance criterion need not even consider the trade-off between risk and return (the value of k) because, as long as k is positive, Lottery B dominates Lottery A in the sense that it yields more that is good (return, E) and less that is bad (risk σ^2). Thus, if $k = 1$ (or any other positive number) then $V(\tilde{x}|A) < V(\tilde{x}|B)$.

What happens now if one adopts a safety-first approach? Suppose the decision-maker fixes the 'wealth threshold' at $t = 0$, this indicates worry over the possibility that the final fortune could be negative and especially over the variability of wealth below that threshold. Under these conditions, the individual considers Lottery A to be risk-free because, regardless of the outcome, the final wealth will never fall below the threshold (here $t = 0$).

Indeed, even if the worst outcome is realised ($x = -1$), the final wealth will remain above the critical level. In contrast, with Lottery B the decision-maker perceives a level of risk measured by:

$$\sigma^{2-}(t = 0) = 0.01(-17 - 0)^2 = 2.89$$

where -17 corresponds to the final wealth when $x = -20$ is realised. For $k = 1$,

$$V(w_f \mid A) = 9 - 1(0) = 9$$
$$V(w_f \mid B) = 10.23 - 1(2.89) = 7.34$$

so that, for an equal rate of substitution between risk and return ($k = 1$) the shift from the mean variance criterion to the safety-first criterion reverses the ranking of the two lotteries.

This example makes clear the difference in 'philosophy' between the two criteria. By using variance to measure risk, the mean variance criterion appeals to the notion of global variability across a lottery's outcomes. It gives equal weight to both positive and negative deviations from μ, because it uses $(x - \mu)^2$ to calculate σ^2. The safety-first criterion uses t in place of μ and differentiates between 'good' deviations ($x > t$) and 'bad' ones ($x < t$). The latter are the only ones to enter into the definition of a lottery's risk under the safety-first criterion.

2.4 Some brief remarks on other criteria

The criteria just discussed have one point in common: when calculating the expected value of a lottery they take into account *all* possible outcomes and their respective probabilities.

Several other criteria that have been proposed do not impose this condition. For example, there is the 'maximin' criterion. This applies to extremely pessimistic individuals who, even though they are well informed as to the probabilities of the results of a lottery, assume that fate will necessarily choose the least favourable outcome. Decision-makers who employ this criterion are in some sense believers in the 'law of universal vexation'. They are extreme pessimists. Indeed if, following J. Hey (1984), one defines a pessimist as one who overestimates (underestimates) the probability of unfavourable (favourable) events, then one finds the limiting case of pessimism to be that which is modelled by the maximin criterion.

In practice, then, when applying the maximin criterion, decision-makers replace the vector of possible outcomes by the single number that corresponds to the minimal value of the different x_i and assign to it a probability equal to unity. The chosen lottery is the one that, from among all these numbers (these *minima*), furnishes the best outcome (the *maximum*). The name of the

criterion of course comes from this sequence of operations which consists first of determining the minima over x_i of the different vectors $\mathbf{x}$ and then choosing the maximum of these minima. As an example, consider the lotteries:

I		II		III	
x	$p(x)$	x	$p(x)$	x	$p(x)$
+ 5	0.3	+ 2	0.3	+ 6	0.1
+10	0.2	+ 70	0.2	+ 7	0.1
+ 20	0.2	+ 80	0.2	+ 8	0.1
+ 30	0.3	+ 90	0.3	+ 9	0.7

Intuition suggests that many individuals would prefer Lottery II given the structure of the possible outcomes and their probabilities. However, someone who adopts the maximin criterion ignores all but the worst outcomes and summarises the different vectors as follows:

I		II		III	
x	$p(x)$	x	$p(x)$	x	$p(x)$
5	1	2	1	6	1

Thus Lottery III is preferred because it maximizes the minimum, to which the decision-maker assigns a probability weight of unity (that is, the minimum is considered to be a certain outcome).

Of course, in the same way that the maximin criterion reflects an outrageously pessimistic attitude, one can construct a criterion corresponding to an overflowing optimism (the maximax criterion) and one can even take a weighted average of the two extreme attitudes (this is Hurwicz's criterion).

In this text, we do not delve deeply into this kind of criterion because they contradict two basic axioms of the criterion that we emphasise (namely, expected utility): they do not consider all possible outcomes and they deform the actual probabilities. This choice does not in any way reflect disdain for these different approaches. Today they enjoy a renewed interest indirectly through the 'non-expected utility' models. Furthermore, they very elegantly allow modelling of the fundamental psychological attitudes of optimism and pessimism, whereas the expected utility model focuses on risk aversion.

After this quick overview of different methods of evaluating risky situations, we can now dedicate an important chapter to the criterion of expected utility. In what follows we will regularly revisit the criteria discussed in Sections 2.1–2.3 because we will show that they are special cases of the expected utility criterion.

Exercises

2.1 Besides a certain wealth of 500, an individual – Investor 1 – faces a lottery $\tilde{x}_1$ defined by

x_1	$p(x_1)$
0	0.80
-100	0.20

Questions
(a) Compute the mathematical expectation and the variance of $\tilde{x}_1$ (as well as its standard deviation).
(b) Express the probability distribution of final wealth $\tilde{W}_1$ and compute its mathematical expectation and its variance (as well as its standard deviation).

2.2 Besides Investor 1, consider now Investor 2 who lives in the same country. Investor 2 has an initial wealth of 500 and faces a lottery $\tilde{x}_2$ which is identical to $\tilde{x}_1$ (same possible outcomes with the same probabilities). The lotteries $\tilde{x}_1$ and $\tilde{x}_2$ are independent.

Investors 1 and 2 agree to share their total risk on a 'fifty-fifty' basis which means that each bears one-half of the total result $\tilde{x}_1 + \tilde{x}_2$.

Questions
(a) What are the possible outcomes of $\tilde{x}_1 + \tilde{x}_2$ and their respective probabilities?
(b) Express the density function of $\tilde{p}_1 = (\tilde{x}_1 + \tilde{x}_2)/2$ and compute its mathematical expectation and its variance (as well as its standard deviation).
(c) If the utility function of Investor 1 is written as:

$$V_1 = E(\tilde{W}_1) - k_1\sigma^2(\tilde{W}_1) \qquad (k_1 > 0)$$

show that the welfare is greater after the risk-sharing arrangement (that is with $\tilde{p}_1$) than before (with $\tilde{x}_1$). Show that the same result holds for Investor 2 with utility function:

$$V_2 = E(\tilde{W}_2) - k_2\sigma^2(\tilde{W}_2) \qquad (k_2 > 0)$$

2.3 Assume now that Investors 1 and 2 share the total risk $(\tilde{x}_1 + \tilde{x}_2)$ according to the following rule:

$$\alpha(0 < \alpha < 1) \qquad \text{for Investor 1}$$
$$1 - \alpha \qquad \text{for Investor 2}$$

Questions

(a) Express V_1 and V_2 as functions of α (this generalises what you have done in Exercise 2.2: instead of using $\alpha = \frac{1}{2}$, you can now use any value of α).

(b) If collective welfare (V) is defined by the sum of individual values, that is, if

$$V = V_1 + V_2$$

express the value of α that maximises collective welfare (compute $\mathrm{d}V/\mathrm{d}\alpha$ and equate this derivative to zero).

You should obtain, in accordance with intuition, that α is inversely related to Investor 1's degree of risk aversion (k_1), (indeed the optimal α is $k_2/(k_1 + k_2)$).

2.4 Let us consider two lotteries $\tilde{X}$ and $\tilde{Y}$. $\tilde{X}$ has a uniform density defined on $[-12, +20]$, while $\tilde{Y}$ has a uniform density on $[-11, +4]$. Assume the individual has an initial wealth equal to 40.

Questions

(a) Compute for each lottery $E(\tilde{W}_f)$, $\sigma^2(\tilde{W}_f)$ and the semi-variance if the wealth threshold t amounts to 35.

(b) If the wealth threshold is 29, which lottery becomes more risky in the sense of the safety-first criterion?

Notes

1. This theme will be revisited in detail in Section 2.3.
2. Some day someone should construct a multi-criterion model with which to evaluate the different criteria of evaluation that have been proposed!
3. The motto of Lloyd's is 'The contribution of the many to the misfortunes of the few.' See D. Kessler (1990)
4. In the absence of a common world currency, let us agree without chauvinism to use French francs.
5. Daniel Bernoulli (1738) had 'proved' the inadequacy of the criterion of mathematical expectation by proposing a solution to the 'Saint Petersburg Paradox'. This problem had already been discussed by Montmort (1708), Nicolas Bernoulli, Daniel's cousin and by Cramer (1728).
6. See Chapter 5 for further discussion.
7. Instead of referring to the 'mean variance' model some authors evaluate lotteries by the 'mean standard deviation' criterion and thus write:

$$V(\tilde{w}_f) = f[E(\tilde{w}_f), \sigma(\tilde{w}_f)]$$

Since σ^2 is a monotonic transformation of σ, it is clear that the two methods are fundamentally equivalent even though their geometric presentations highlight different aspects of the results (see the article by Meyer (1987)).

8. This very practical expression seems to have been coined (in French) by our colleagues at the University of Montreal, M. Boyer and G. Dionne (1983).

9. It is interesting to note how fertile the eighteenth century was for contributions in the areas of risk and insurance. We cite as examples the works of Clavière (1788) and Bernoulli (1738).

10. Although it builds upon the previous ones, this exercise is slightly more difficult. In fact, it is an intuitive introduction to Chapter 13.

References

Arzac E. (1976), Profits and safety in the theory of the firm under price uncertainty, *International Economic Review*, vol. 17, 163–171.

Bernoulli D. (1738), Specimen theoriae novae de mensura sortis, *Proceedings of the Imperial Academy*, 5, 175–192, St. Petersbourg. Translated into English as: Exposition of a new theory on the measurement of risk, *Econometrica*, (1954), vol. 22, 23–36.

Boyer M. and G. Dionne (1983), Riscophobie et étalement à moyenne constante, *L'Actualité économique*, vol. 59, 208–229.

Clavière E. (1788), Prospectus de l'établissement des assurances sur la vie. Republished in *Risques. Les Cahiers de l'assurance*, (1990), vol. 1, 123–126.

Cramer G. (1728) Letter to Nicolas Bernoulli. Republished in *Econometrica*, (1954), vol. 22, 33–35.

Hagigi M. and B. Kluger (1987), Safety-first: An alternative performance measure, *The Journal of Portfolio Management*, vol. 13, 34–40.

Hey J. (1984), The economics of optimism and pessimism: a definition and some applications, *Kyklos*, vol. 37, 181–205.

Kessler D. (1990), Très petit dictionnaire d'économie de l'assurance, *Risques: Les Cahiers de l'assurance*, vol. 1, 29–51.

Meyer J. (1987), Two-moment decision models and expected utility maximization, *American Economic Review*, vol. 77, 421–430.

Montmort P.-R. de (1708), *Essai d'analyse sur les jeux de hasard*, Paris.

Tetens J. (1786), *Einleitung Zur Berechnung Der Leibrenten Und Anwartschaften*, Leipzig.

3: The expected utility criterion and its implications

Of all the chapters of a textbook on risk, this is without a doubt the most difficult to write. Indeed, relevant work on the concept of expected utility can be found in philosophy, psychology, statistics, mathematics, history, operations research, marketing, and even in economics and finance.

Our feeling is that this criterion deserves its own textbook (perhaps in two volumes if its extensions are to be included!) and that, in the absence of this, it is necessary to abstain as much as possible from entering into the details of the axioms upon which the criterion is founded and especially of the controversies that surround them. In some sense, we will minimise the presentation of the concept itself in order to better highlight its implications. These implications are extremely useful and pertinent for economic analysis and for modern financial theory.

3.1 Some reflections on expected utility

The first criterion that we presented in Chapter 2 was the expected value criterion. This values a lottery by weighting its possible outcomes by their respective probabilities and summing over all of them. In some sense, this criterion takes the raw data (x_i and p_i) without transformation and applies a linear operation that defines the central value of the distribution. Unfortunately, as we have seen, this procedure successfully captures the 'return' of the lottery but is completely unable to judge its risk, thus leading to the consideration of other criteria such as 'mean variance' and 'safety first'.

As a first rough approximation – but one that is sufficient for understanding what follows – one can say that with the expected utility criterion it is possible to retain the notion of expected value, the return, while also taking risk into account. In this spirit – and still as a first approximation – we allude to a well-known principle of psychology which asserts that changes in stimulus do not necessarily induce similar changes in sensation or perception.[1] This simple idea is reflected here in the notion of utility, by which given changes in stimulus (the level of wealth) do not necessarily induce similar modifications in perception (the satisfaction derived from that wealth). We will thus assume that in evaluating risk situations the decision-maker replaces the monetary values of final wealth by the utility (a function) of final wealth. Utility can thus be interpreted as a method of passing from a more objective level to a more subjective[2] or psychological level: that of the amount of satisfaction achieved.

The transformation performed by the notion of utility requires some structure, however. Specifically, the greater the stimulus (the level in wealth) the more the perception (the utility of final wealth) must rise. Technically speaking, utility is an increasing monotonic transformation of wealth. Many transformations that obey this restriction are possible, and their combination with the notion of expected value (of utility) will allow us to characterise attitudes towards risk.

Before concluding this brief introductory paragraph, we shall quickly mention one last point. The expected utility criterion modifies the values of w_f by replacing them with $U(w_f)$, but it does not transform the probabilities in any way. Thus, this criterion is said to be linear in the probabilities. This approach has been followed for such a long time and with such zeal by researchers that they have not, until recently, entertained the possibility of transforming the probabilities (see Demers and Demers (1990), Quiggin (1982) or Yaari (1987)). Today there is a very active research programme consisting of models collectively referred to as 'non-expected utility models' and to which we have already made (and will continue to make – see Chapter 6) occasional and brief reference. It is interesting to note that numerous developments in the domain of 'non-expected utility models' have their origin in an old contribution by M. Allais (1953), Nobel laureate in economics. The importance of Allais' writing on the economic theory of risk has recently been put in perspective by B. Munier (1989).

3.2 The notion of the certainty equivalent

In the one-dimensional case (where only final wealth matters), and consistent with the expected utility framework, we will assume that each individual has a utility function that allows evaluation of the lotteries. If a lottery over final wealth is evaluated by its expected utility then it follows from the definition of expected value that:

$$V(\tilde{w}_f) = \int_a^b U(w_0 + x)f(x)\,\mathrm{d}x \tag{3.1}$$

where $U(w_0 + x) = U(w_f)$ is the utility of final wealth, $U' = \mathrm{d}U/\mathrm{d}w_f$ (that is, the marginal utility of w_f) is strictly positive, and the right-hand side of Equation (3.1) represents an expected value in which a and b, respectively, are the minimal and maximal values attainable by the random variable $\tilde{x}$.

In the discrete case,

$$V(\tilde{w}_f) = \sum_{i=1}^{n} p_i U(w_0 + x_i) \tag{3.1a}$$

Here it is easily seen that V is a linear function of the probabilities p_i but not of the values of final wealth represented by $w_0 + x_i$. Once this evaluation criterion is adopted, it is natural to ask the question: how much certain wealth (without the lottery) would yield a decision-maker with utility function U the same level of satisfaction as an original endowment of the certain sum w_0 and lottery $\tilde{x}$? If one denotes this certainty equivalent by w^* then its formal definition is:

$$U(w^*) = \int_a^b U(w_0 + x)f(x)\,\mathrm{d}x \tag{3.2}$$

Taking advantage of the fact that U, being monotonic, has an inverse function, we can also write:

$$w^* = U^{-1}(U(w^*)) = U^{-1}\left(\int_a^b U(w_0 + x)f(x)\,\mathrm{d}x\right) \tag{3.2a}$$

Although this last expression is rather formidable, its interpretation is rather simple as we will show using two examples.

Let there be an individual whose utility function is 'piece-wise linear' so that globally it is non-linear.[3] More precisely, let the utility function be of the following algebraic form:

$U(w_f) = 2w_f$	if $w_f \leqslant 100$
$U(w_f) = 100 + w_f$	if $100 \leqslant w_f \leqslant 200$
$U(w_f)200 + (\frac{1}{2})w_f$	if $200 \leqslant w_f$

This utility function is increasing and continuous but not everywhere differentiable. Its graph is shown in Figure 3.1, where it is clear that the marginal utility of w_f is non-increasing (it is piece-wise constant and globally decreasing).

If this individual faces the lottery:

x	$p(x)$
-80	0.3
$+40$	0.4
$+120$	0.3

and if their initial wealth is 100, then what is the lottery's certainty equivalent?

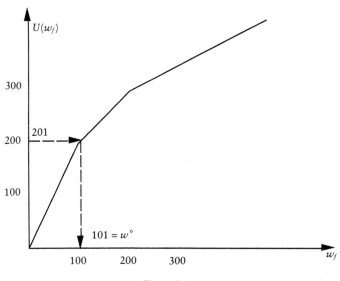

Figure 3.1

Beginning at $w_0 = 100$, the characteristics of $\tilde{x}$ imply that the random variable $\tilde{w}_f$ has the following distribution:

x_f	$p(w_f)$
$+20$	0.3
$+140$	0.4
$+220$	0.3

The individual can thus evaluate the lottery by the expected utility criterion and find that:

$$E\,[U(\tilde{w}_f)] = V(\tilde{w}_f) = (0.3)(U(20)) + (0.4)(U(140))$$
$$+ (0.3)(U(220))$$
$$= (0.3)(40) + (0.4)(240) + (0.3)(310)$$
$$= 201$$

One can then ask what certain level of w_f (w_f^*) yields the same level of satisfaction. One easily obtains $w_f^* = 101$ as the certainty equivalent by starting with $E\,[U(\tilde{w}_f)] = 201$ on the vertical axis and finding the value of w_f on the horizontal axis that yields this level of satisfaction. This result is illustrated in Figure 3.1.

Our decision-maker therefore seems indifferent between a wealth of 101 obtained with certainty and the risk situation composed of w_0 and lottery $\tilde{x}$.

Now consider another decision-maker characterised by the utility function:

$$U(w_f) = (w_f)^2$$

but who – except for this difference in psychological nature – is in exactly the same situation as the first decision-maker. With this utility function one obtains:

$$E[U(\tilde{w}_f)] = V(\tilde{w}_f)$$
$$= (0.3)(400) + (0.4)(19\ 600) + (0.3)(48\ 400)$$
$$= 22\ 480$$

To find the certainty equivalent, one must find the value of w_f^* that, when run through the utility function, yields a level of satisfaction of 22 480. More specifically, one must solve:

$$(w_f^*)^2 = 22\ 480$$

or, applying the notion of the inverse function described in Equation (3.2a):

$$w_f^* = (22\ 480)^{1/2} = 149.93$$

This operation is illustrated in Figure 3.2. What may we conclude? Beginning with two identical situations in terms of initial wealth and lottery, a change in the utility function induces a different certainty equivalent. In other words, though the expected value of the lottery is the same (and, more generally, so is its association probability distribution), its perception by the

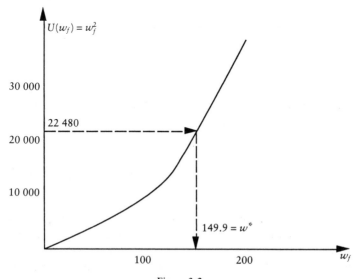

Figure 3.2

individual differs. This suggests that a difference in the utility function reflects in some sense a difference in attitude toward risk. This assertion will serve as a point of departure for the measurement of the 'degree of risk aversion' that is the subject of the next few sections.

Before broaching this subject, it is important to state a result, which is more important than it seems, concerning the transformations that one may apply to a utility function without changing the certainty equivalent or, in other words, without changing the decision-maker's appraisal of the situation. Obviously the transformation that produced the second example from the first was highly non-linear and it induced, as we saw, a change in the certainty equivalent. However, we must call the attention of the reader to the following result.

Theorem 3.1 If a utility function R is an increasing linear transformation of another utility function U, that is, if $R(w_f) = d + gU(w_f)$ with $g > 0^4$, then the certainty equivalent is unchanged.

Proof Call w_U^* the certainty equivalent given U and w_R^* the certainty equivalent given R. From the definition of w^* have:

$$U(w_U^*) = \int_a^b U(w_0 + x)f(x)\,\mathrm{d}x \qquad (3.3)$$

$$R(w_R^*) = \int_a^b R(w_0 + x)f(x)\,\mathrm{d}x \qquad (3.4)$$

From the definition of R, Equation (3.4) can also be written as:

$$d + gU(w_R^*) = \int_a^b (d + gU(w_0 + x))f(x)\,\mathrm{d}x$$

$$= d + g \int_a^b U(w_0 + x)f(x)\,\mathrm{d}x$$

Subtracting d from both sides and then dividing by g yields:

$$U(w_R^*) = \int_a^b U(w_0 + x)f(x)\,\mathrm{d}x \qquad (3.5)$$

Comparing Equations (3.5) and (3.3) reveals immediately that $w_U^* = w_R^*$. Q.E.D.

Although increasing linear transformations never change the certainty equivalent, this is not the case for non-linear transformations. The invariability of the certainty equivalent with respect to increasing linear transformations implies that, in the theory of risk, utility is *cardinal* and that it is thus analogous to a measure of distance, time or temperature.[5]

3.3 The asking price (bid price) and the risk premium: notions of risk aversion, risk loving and risk neutrality

Having defined the certainty equivalent, we now compare two other previously introduced variables: w_0 and $E(\tilde{w}_f)$. This comparison will lead us to definitions of the asking price and the risk premium associated with a lottery. While analysing the asking price we will also quickly define the bid price.

One way of interpreting Equation (3.2) is to say that the individual's initial endowment is comprised of w_0 and lottery $\tilde{x}$. Valued by the expected utility criterion, this endowment yields a level of satisfaction determined by the right-hand side of Equation (3.2). The individual then considers how much certain wealth (instead of the lottery) would give the same level of welfare. The individual is asking, in fact, what are the fair terms (to themselves) of exchange between uncertainty $(w_0 + \tilde{x})$ and certainty (w^*). It is then very natural to define the asking price of a lottery (p_a) by:

$$p_a = w^* - w_0 \tag{3.6}$$

Indeed, for any good or service (book, theatre ticket) the asking price equals the seller's cash balance after the transaction minus the initial cash balance. Here the good that the individual sells is a lottery and the initial and final cash balances are respectively w_0 and w^*. The definition in Equation (3.6) thus applies the natural definition of an asking price to a lottery. We emphasise that the asking price as defined in Equation (3.6) is actually the *minimum* price demanded by the individual to sell the lottery. If a buyer was found who was prepared to pay more than p_a, then the owner of $\tilde{x}$ would jump at the chance to engage in the transaction. In contrast, if there were no buyers in the market willing to pay p_a, then the owner would keep $\tilde{x}$. These aspects can be presented more formally by noting that the asking price can also be defined as follows by combining Equations (3.2) and (3.6):

$$U(w_0 + p_a) = \int_a^b U(w_0 + x)f(x)\,\mathrm{d}x \tag{3.6a}$$

It follows that if the price p at which an individual can sell their lottery is less than p_a, then $U(w_0 + p)$ is less than the expected value from keeping lottery $\tilde{x}$. Thus, by employing the expected utility criterion the individual refuses to sell the lottery if the price offered is only $p < p_a$. In contrast, and by identical reasoning, if $p > p_a$, the individual increases welfare by selling the lottery at price p. In summary, the asking price p_a is the minimum price at which an individual is prepared to sell a lottery. One can easily imagine the applications that can be made of such a concept, for example, in finance and in insurance.

In the two examples considered above, the asking prices were respectively +1 (101 − 100) and +49.93 (149.93 − 100). The two individuals assign a positive asking price ($p_a > 0$) to a lottery that has a positive effect on their welfare: they positively value the lottery $\tilde{x}$. It can be the case, however, for some lotteries and some utility functions, that the asking price will be negative. Here is an example[6]:

$$U = (w_f)^{1/2} \qquad w_0 = 100$$

and

x	$p(x)$
− 50	$\frac{1}{2}$
+ 50	$\frac{1}{2}$

$$E[U(\tilde{w}_f)] = (\tfrac{1}{2})(7.071) + (\tfrac{1}{2})(12.247) = 9.659$$

From the definition of the certainty equivalent, $(w_f^*)^{1/2} = 9.659$ and, by squaring both sides, one obtains:

$$w_f^* = 93.296 \qquad \text{which implies } p_a = -6.699$$

A negative asking price means that the individual is prepared to pay (subsidise) anyone who is willing to take the lottery off their hands.

The notion of the asking price of a lottery corresponds to the idea of insurance (for the buyer of an insurance policy) since it gets rid of an initially held risk on payment of a sum of money. In other spheres of economic activity, such as finance, one tends to think more of the opposite situation: the decision-maker has a certain initial wealth and considers purchasing a lottery (for example, a risky stock). This notion of a bid price is also applicable to the case of an insurance company (that is, a seller of insurance) when, for example, having raised a (certain) initial amount of capital it begins acquiring risks, that is, underwriting policies. One can thus legitimately wonder about the maximum amount of money that an individual would pay to acquire a lottery and define in this way the bid price (p_b). More formally, p_b is the solution to:

$$U(w_0) = \int_a^b U(w_0 + x - p_b)f(x)\,\mathrm{d}x \qquad (3.7)$$

The value of p_b that satisfies this equation makes the buyer indifferent about purchasing $\tilde{x}$. If the price of $\tilde{x}$ exceeds p_b, the transaction will not be acceptable to the prospective buyer, and if the price of $\tilde{x}$ is less than p_b then the buyer will realise a profit, implying that the price is less than the maximum acceptable price. Just as p_a, defined in Equation (3.6) is a minimum price, the value of p_b satisfying Equation (3.7) is, in some sense, an upper bound for the prospective buyer.

Intuitively, it would be natural to guess that $p_a = p_b$ for given U, w_0 and $\tilde{x}$. In reality this is not necessarily true. However, to analyse the relationship between the two concepts we will need a precise measure of risk aversion and an assumption about its properties. We will thus postpone this discussion until Chapter 4. Below, we develop the notion – well known but sometimes poorly understood – of the risk premium. This follows very naturally from the certainty equivalent and the asking price. Nevertheless, to grasp the logical tie between these concepts, we must first state and prove an important theorem.

Theorem 3.2 If an individual's utility function is linear in final wealth, the asking price of a lottery is equal to its expected value $E(\tilde{x})$.
Proof Since U is linear:

$$U(w_f) = g + dw_f \qquad \text{with } d > 0$$

It follows that:

$$E[U(\tilde{w}_f)] = E[g + d(w_0 + \tilde{x})]$$
$$= g + dw_0 + dE(\tilde{x})$$

To derive the certainty equivalent apply Equation (3.2) to write:

$$g + dw_f^* = g + dw_0 + dE(\tilde{x})$$

so that $w_f^* = w_0 + E(\tilde{x})$. Hence from the definition of p_a in Equation (3.6),

$$p_a = w_f^* - w_0 = E(\tilde{x})$$

Q.E D.

This means that a decision-maker with a linear utility function values the lottery exclusively by the expected value of the result. We are already familiar with this attitude: it corresponds to the first evaluation criterion discussed at the beginning of Chapter 2. The expected value criterion is thus – as asserted above – a special case of expected utility: it is observed when utility takes on a particular form, that of a linear function.

It is sometimes said that the linearity of U implies *risk neutrality*. This follows from the following fact: if U is linear and if the individual is faced with two lotteries that have the same expected value but are otherwise very different (in their variance and/or their other moments) the same asking price is assigned to both nevertheless. In some sense the individual only cares about the central tendency of the distribution without considering the other characteristics such as risk. To reflect risk neutrality, we say that the risk premium (π) is zero, where π is defined by:

$$\pi = E(\tilde{x}) - p_a \tag{3.8}$$

When U is linear there is risk neutrality because $p_a = E(\tilde{x})$ as a result of Theorem 3.2, from which it follows that π is zero.

The case of risk neutrality serves as a foundation on which to build a precise definition of the concepts of risk aversion and risk loving.

There is risk aversion if $\pi > 0$. Specifically, $\pi > 0$ implies that $p_a < E(\tilde{x})$ where $E(\tilde{x})$ would be the asking price of the lottery *if* the individual were risk neutral. Since $\pi > 0$ implies that p_a is less than the asking price that would result from risk neutrality, it follows that the individual does not value the risk implicit in the lottery.

In contrast, $\pi < 0$ is a sure indication of a taste for risk. Specifically, $\pi < 0$ implies that $p_a > E(\tilde{x})$ and thus that the asking price exceeds the asking price that would arise in the case of risk neutrality. The individual assigns a higher value to the lottery (relative to the case of risk neutrality) and thus reveals a positive appraisal of the risk that it embodies.

As an exercise, reconsider the lottery used as an example in Section 3.2. Its expected value is:

$$E(\tilde{x}) = (0.3)(-80) + (0.4)(40) + (0.3)(120) = +28$$

The first individual (who had the piece-wise linear utility function illustrated in Figure 3.1) assigns to this lottery a p_a of +1. This risk premium is thus positive ($\pi + 28 - 1 = 27$). The asking price of the lottery for the second individual (whose utility function is $U = w^2$, as illustrated in Figure 3.2) is 49.93 and thus π is $28 - 49.93 = -21.93$. What may we conclude? The utility function in Figure 3.1 is concave and π is positive. In contrast, in Figure 3.2, U is convex and π is negative. There exists, in fact, a relationship between the concavity (convexity) of U and the positivity (negativity) of π, somewhat in the same way as the linearity of U implies $\pi = 0$. This is established by Theorem 3.3

Theorem 3.3 If the utility function of an individual is strictly increasing and strictly concave (convex) then the risk premium assigned to any lottery is strictly positive (negative).

The proof of this theorem is based on a famous inequality that is often used in the theories of finance and of risk – Jensen's inequality – which is stated as follows:

> If $\tilde{y}$ is a random variable and $f(y)$ is a strictly concave transformation then $E[f(\tilde{y})] < f[E(\tilde{y})]$. The direction of the inequality is reversed if f is convex.[7]

It is important that the reader grasp the intuition behind this result. It is well known that a strictly concave function never rises above a line that is tangential to it at any point. Formal proof of this assertion can be found in numerous textbooks (for example, K. Lancaster (1968)), but Figure 3.3 gives

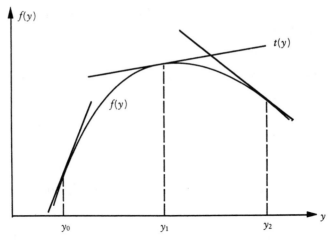

Figure 3.3

a rather convincing illustration, since it clearly shows that the concave function $f(y)$ is everywhere below the three tangential lines that have been chosen for the purposes of illustration.

Recall that the equation of the tangent $t(y)$ at a point – for example, y_1 in Figure 3.3 – is:

$$t(y) = f(y_1) + (y - y_1)f'(y_1)$$

where $f'(y_1)$ is the derivative (the slope) of $f(y)$ at y_1. One can apply this notion at that point $E(\tilde{y})$ to obtain:

$$t(y) = f[E(\tilde{y})] + [y - E(\tilde{y})]f'[E(\tilde{y})] \tag{3.9}$$

Since at each point y (here treated as a realisation of the random variable $\tilde{y}$) $t(y) \geq f(y)$, this relationship must also hold on average, namely,

$$E[t(\tilde{y})] > E[f(\tilde{y})] \tag{3.10}$$

Now, by applying operator E to Equation (3.9) one obtains:

$$\begin{aligned} E[t(\tilde{y})] &= E[f(E(\tilde{y})] + f'[E(\tilde{y})] E[\tilde{y} - E(\tilde{y})] \\ &= f[E(\tilde{y})] \end{aligned} \tag{3.11}$$

Combining Equations (3.11) and (3.10), one may write:

$$f[E(\tilde{y})] > E[f(\tilde{y})]$$

which is Jensen's inequality. Having provided 'proof' of Jensen's inequality, we are now ready to apply this result in the proof of Theorem 3.3.

Let there be a decision-maker with utility function $U(w_f)$, that is strictly increasing $(U'(w_f) > 0)$ and strictly concave $(U''(w_f) < 0)$ where U'' is the second derivative of U). This individual evaluates the pair $\langle\langle w_0, \tilde{x} \rangle\rangle$ by the expected utility criterion, that is, by:

$$E[U(\tilde{w}_f)] = E[U(w_0 + \tilde{x})]$$

From Jensen's inequality, we know from the concavity of U that:

$$E[U(w_0 + \tilde{x})] < U[E(w_0 + \tilde{x})] = U[w_0 + E(\tilde{x})]$$

Applying the definition of the certainty equivalent to the left-hand side of this inequality yields:

$$U(w_f^*) < U[w_0 + E(\tilde{x})]$$

Given that U is increasing, the last inequality can only hold if:

$$w_f^* < w_0 + E(\tilde{x})$$

or, equivalently, $w_f^* - w_0 < E(\tilde{x})$. Thus, $p_a < E(\tilde{x})$ from Equation (3.6) or, put another way, $0 < E(\tilde{x}) - p_a = \pi$ from Equation (3.8).

Combining this result with the previous discussion makes clear that there is a perfect correlation between the concavity of U, risk aversion and a positive risk premium. Similar reasoning establishes that there is an equally perfect correlation between the convexity of U, risk loving and a negative risk premium.

Before proceeding to a graphical interpretation of the somewhat technical results presented so far, we must emphasise a point that our experiences as teachers tells us is often a source of confusion. Though risk aversion implies a positive risk premium it does *not*, contrary to a widely held belief, imply the rejection of all lotteries. In other words, individuals who are 'riskophobes' can demand a strictly positive asking price in order to get rid of a lottery that they hold. Their positive risk premium implies only that this asking price is less than the expected value of the lottery, which is the price that would be demanded by a risk neutral neighbour.

Of course, $p_a < E(\tilde{x})$ for the riskophobe implies $\pi > 0$ but not necessarily $p_a < 0$, especially, of course, if $E(\tilde{x})$ is large. Risk aversion does not imply the frantic[8] rejection of all risk; it is a question of recognising that risk is not valued and so it must be offset by a greater return as represented by higher $E(\tilde{x})$. There thus exist lotteries that are sufficiently attractive in terms of $E(\tilde{x})$ for the risk-averse decision-maker to assign them a positive value despite the element of risk that they contain. Securities traded on stock exchanges are good examples of lotteries that increase the welfare of their owners.[9]

These observations illustrate the importance of the notion of risk premium. An individual who has concave utility can assign a positive asking price to some lotteries and a negative asking price to others. In contrast, the risk premium will *always* be positive. There is thus a perfect correlation between the (positive) sign of π and the concavity of U (but not between the sign of p_a and the concavity of U). It is this perfect equivalence that makes the concept of risk premium important.

As promised, we conclude this rather dense section with a graphical illustration based on a numerical example. We construct it in such a way as to make concrete the results that we have just derived. To this end we consider once again Cramer's utility function, $U = (w_f)^{1/2}$, and an initial wealth of 5 along with a lottery defined by:

x	$p(x)$
-4	0.2
$+4$	0.8

This lottery is 'actuarially favourable' – following the usual expression from risk theory – because $E(\tilde{x})$ is strictly positive and equal to $+2.4$. The utility function, drawn in Figure 3.4, is concave, from which it follows that the decision-maker is risk averse.

The expected utility the individual assigns to this situation is:

$$E[U(\tilde{w}_f)] = (0.2)(+1)^{1/2} + (0.8)(+9)^{1/2} = 2.6$$

and its certainty equivalent w_f^* satisfies:

$$(w_f^*)^{1/2} = 2.6 \qquad \text{that is, } w_f^* = 6.76$$

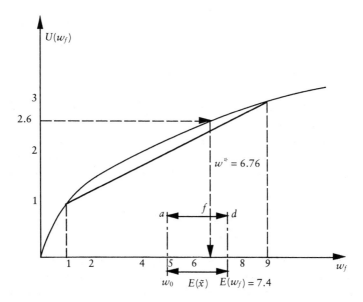

Figure 3.4

This operation is illustrated in Figure 3.4 by the 'arrows' beginning at 2.6 on the vertical axis and ending at 6.76 on the horizontal axis.

Since w_0 is equal to 5, the asking price of this lottery is $+1.76$ which is thus positive (and even large in relative terms because it represents 35 per cent of the certain component of wealth!). The positive value of p_a is due to the very large average return to the lottery $(+2.4)$ that appears in the graph as the distance ad, that is, the difference between $E(\tilde{w}_f)$ on the one hand and w_0 on the other. The difference between ad (which equals $E(x)$) and af (the asking price) is the amount of risk premium, namely, fd. This risk premium $(2.4 - 1.76 = 0.64)$ is a spread between two asking prices: that which a risk-neutral individual would demand $(+2.4)$ and that which would be demanded by an individual when $U = (w_f)^{1/2}$, namely, $+1.76$.

3.4 The Arrow–Pratt approximation and the notion of absolute risk aversion

In Section 3.3 we discussed in depth the notion of risk premium and we hope that the reader has acquired good intuition at this stage. In addition, thanks to some simple mathematical tools, K. Arrow (1965) and J. Pratt (1964) have been able to show in two famous articles that the risk premium is the product of two elements that are easily interpreted. They accomplished this through the clever use of approximation formulas for continuous and differentiable functions at each point of their domain of definition. We present here an overview of their reasoning.

Using the definition of the certainty equivalent along with that of the asking price we write:

$$U(w_0 + p_a) = \int_a^b U(w_0 + x)f(x)\,\mathrm{d}x \tag{3.12}$$

Given U, w_0 and the random variable $\tilde{x}$ as characterised by $f(x)$, Equation (3.12) constitutes one (non-linear) equation in one unknown: p_a. Thus Equation (3.12) implicitly defines p_a. Our goal is to make p_a explicit. To this end, we begin with a first-order approximation of $U(w_0 + p_a)$ around $(w_0 + \mu)$ – recall that $\mu \equiv E(\tilde{x})$ – and, using a well-known mathematical result, we write:

$$U(w_0 + p_a) \cong U(w_0 + \mu) + (w_0 + p_a - (w_0 + \mu))U'(w_0 + \mu)$$
$$\cong U(w_0 + \mu) + (p_a - \mu)U'(w_0 + \mu) \tag{3.13}$$

where the tilde above the equal sign denotes an approximation.

Similarly, we construct a second-order approximation of $U(w_0 + x)$, which appears in the integral, around $(w_0 + \mu)$. It is natural to ask the reason for this difference in treatment of the two sides of Equation (3.13) as to the order of approximation. The reason is found implicitly in Figure 3.4: $w_0 + \mu$ ($= 7.4$) and $w_0 + p_a$ ($= 6.76$) are relatively close together while $w_0 + \tilde{x}$, which in one case takes on the value of 1 in the example, is clearly farther from $w_0 + \mu$. Given that the precision of the approximation diminishes with the distance between points on the horizontal axis, it is necessary to compensate by approximating the right-hand side to a higher order. This brings us to:

$$U(w_0 + x) \cong U(w_0 + \mu) + (x - \mu)U'(w_0 + \mu)$$
$$+ ((x - \mu)^2/2!)U''(w_0 + \mu) \qquad (3.14)$$

Substituting this result into the right-hand side of Equation (3.12) and recalling that

$$\int_a^b (x - \mu)f(x)\, dx = 0$$

from the definition of $E(\tilde{x})$) and that

$$\int_a^b (x - \mu)^2 f(x)\, dx = \sigma^2$$

(from the definition of variance) allows the right-hand side to be approximated by:

$$U(w_0 + \mu) + (\sigma^2/2)U''(w_0 + \mu) \qquad (3.15)$$

Setting Equation (3.13) equal to Equation (3.15) – since they approximate, respectively, the left- and right-hand sides of the definition in Equation (3.12) – we obtain, after some obvious simplifications:

$$p_a - \mu \cong (\tfrac{1}{2})\sigma^2 [U''(w_0 + \mu)/U'(w_0 + \mu)]$$

or, from the definition of π,

$$\pi \cong (\tfrac{1}{2})\sigma^2 [- U''(w_0 + \mu)/U'(w_0 + \mu)] \qquad (3.16)$$

As promised, this formulation makes the components of π clear:

1. π depends on the variance of $\tilde{x}$, which can be interpreted as a measure of the level of risk embodied in the lottery[10];
2. π also depends on the expression $(- U''/U')$, which reflects in some sense the nature of the utility function, which is fundamentally subjective and specific to the individual. This expression bears the name of 'the degree of absolute risk aversion' and we denote it by A_a. Since A_a is a *local* measure of risk aversion, it is a function of wealth: $A_a(w) = - U''(w)/U'(w)$.

Expression (3.16) explains why individuals in objectively identical situations have different risk premia. Indeed, if two individuals have the same wealth and hold the same lottery (that is, if μ and σ^2 are the same), they can have different values of π because their risk aversion, measured by A_a, differs.

Expression (3.16) is very important. It will be seen often in Chapters 4 and 5 where the components of π are studied in more depth: in the measures of risk aversion (Chapter 4) and in the measures of risk (Chapter 5). Before continuing, however, we will first make a few somewhat disorganised remarks about Pratt's formula.

3.4.1 Some remarks

1. The expression for π, Equation (3.16), is not the true value of the risk premium but it is a 'good' approximation of it. To understand this recall the example from the end of Section 3.3. for which the exact value of the risk premium ($\pi = 0.64$) was derived. What value of risk premium is implied by the approximation? We already know that $\mu = 2.4$ and a simple calculation shows that $\sigma^2 = 10.24$. Furthermore, since $U = (w_f)^{1/2}$, it follows that:

$$U' = (\tfrac{1}{2})w_f^{-1/2} \quad \text{and} \quad U'' = -(\tfrac{1}{4})w_f^{-3/2}$$

so $A_a = \tfrac{1}{2}w_f^{-1}$. Evaluated at $w_f = w_0 + \mu = 7.4$, Pratt's formula assigns π the approximate value of $(0.5)(10.24)(1/14.8) = 0.35$.

It must be admitted that 0.35 is quite far from 0.64, and therefore in this case the approximation is not very good. This comes from the fact that the lottery includes possible outcomes that are large relative to initial wealth. It must not be forgotten that an approximation formula works best when applied to small changes. Since, in the example, the values of final wealth can be very different from the value of initial wealth, Pratt's formula cannot yield very good results. To convince the reader of this assertion, it suffices to consider a less risky lottery, for example:

x	$p(x)$
-1	0.2
$+1$	0.8

For this lottery, where the variance is only 0.64, the true value of π is 0.0323 whereas Pratt's formula estimates it at 0.0286. While in the first example, the relative error was $(0.64 - 0.35)/0.64 = 0.4531$, in this example it is only $(0.0323 - 0.0286)/0.0323 = 0.1146$. As predicted, the precision of Pratt's formula is better when the lottery is 'small' relative to the certain component of the initial endowment.

2. If an individual is risk neutral, Pratt's formula gives an exact answer. Owing to Theorem 3.2, linear U implies the true value of $\pi = 0$. This is also the result given by the approximation formula of Equation (3.16). In short, if U is linear, U'' is zero and the application of Equation (3.16) furnishes the true result.

3. Even though Pratt's formula can, as we have seen, result in approximation errors, it never makes a mistake as to the sign. Indeed, Theorem 3.3, which concerns the sign of π, is fully consistent with Equation (3.16). If U is concave, U'' is negative and the approximate value of π is positive as is its true value. Conversely, if U is convex, U'' is positive and the approximate value and true value of π are both negative.

4. Although in Parts One and Two of this text we refer mainly to the notion of risk aversion, in Part Three we will more frequently see a related notion: risk tolerance. While risk aversion measures the intensity with which a riskophobe rejects risk, it is natural to define risk tolerance by the ease with which risk is accepted. There is thus an inverse relationship between risk aversion and risk tolerance: the larger the former the smaller the latter. To illustrate this idea, define risk tolerance (T_a) by:

$$T_a = 1/A_a \qquad (3.17)$$

Note that, consistent with intuition, risk neutrality implies an infinite risk tolerance.

5. Absolute risk aversion provides indirect support for Theorem 3.1. Specifically, consider the utility function $L(w_f) = a + bU(w_f)$ with $b > 0$ and note that

$$L'(w_f) = bU'(w_f)$$

$$L''(w_f) = bU''(w_f)$$

from which it follows that $-(L''/L') = -(U''/U')$, that is, the two functions exhibit the same degree of absolute risk aversion. Decision-makers with utility functions L and U have the same attitude toward risk. Thus these utility functions are actually identical in spite of their different appearance at first glance.

Having concluded this long chapter dealing with the expected utility criterion and several of its immediate implications, of which the least important is certainly not the notion of the risk premium, we now begin the in-depth study of its two elements: measuring the attitude towards risk (its 'subjective' element) and measuring the degree of risk (its 'objective' element).

Exercises

3.1 A decision-maker is endowed with initial wealth $W_0 = 100$ and with a lottery $\tilde{x}$ defined by:

x	$p(x)$
-10	0.25
$+10$	0.75

The utility function is written as:

$$U = 2W_j \qquad \text{for} \qquad W_j \leqslant 100$$

$$U = W_j + 100 \qquad \text{for} \qquad W_j > 100$$

Questions
(a) Compute the certainty equivalent, the asking price of $\tilde{x}$ and the risk premium (use a graphical illustration besides numerical developments).
(b) What happens to these values if U becomes V, another utility function defined by:

$$V = 2W_j \qquad \text{for} \qquad W_j \leqslant 100$$

$$V = 0.5W_j + 150 \qquad \text{for} \qquad W_j > 100$$

Interpret in intuitive terms the change that you observe in the certainty equivalent, asking price and risk premium of $\tilde{x}$.
Hint: draw the utility curves U and V, and figure out which one is 'more concave', that is, 'more risk averse'.[11]

3.2 Returning to the utility function U of Exercise 3.1, and the initial wealth of 100, consider now lottery $\tilde{y}$:

y	$p(y)$
-16	0.25
$+12$	0.75

Compute the certainty equivalent, asking price and risk premium attached to $\tilde{y}$ and compare with the results for $\tilde{x}$ under U.

You should observe that the certainty equivalent and asking price fall while the risk premium increases. As you will see in Chapter 5 it must be so because $\tilde{y}$ is 'riskier' than $\tilde{x}$.

3.3 Consider the negative exponential utility function[12]

$$U = -e^{-2w_f}$$

and assume an initial wealth of 1 associated with a lottery $\tilde{x}$ defined by a uniform density on $[-0.4, +0.6]$.

Questions
(a) Compute the certainty equivalent, asking price and risk premium attached to $\tilde{x}$.
(b) Compare the exact risk premium with its approximation obtained from the Arrow–Pratt formula

3.4 Applying the same utility function as in Exercise 3.3, consider now the random variable $\tilde{y}$ with normal density characterised by $E(\tilde{y}) = +1$ and

$$\text{Var}(\tilde{y}) = \sigma_{\tilde{y}}^2 = \frac{25}{3}$$

Solve questions (a) and (b) of Exercise 3.3 for lottery $\tilde{y}$.
Hint: Remember that for a normal density $f(y)$,

$$\int -e^{ty}f(y)\, dy = -e^{-tE(\tilde{y})+.5t^2\sigma_{\tilde{y}}^2}$$

Notes

1. The interested reader is referred to the excellent work (too little known in our opinion) of H. Sinn (1983).
2. We emphasise that the interpretation proposed here is only intuitive and makes no pretence of rigour. Indeed, there exists an abundant and difficult literature that adopts a completely different point of view (see Machina (1987a and b)).
3. This sort of utility function seems to have been proposed for the first time by M. Richter (1959–1960).
4. d may be positive, zero or negative. In contrast, g must be positive because, like U, the utility function R must be increasing in final wealth.
5. Recall that under certainty, utility functions that characterise preferences over consumption bundles are ordinal.
6. This utility function has a famous history. It seems to have been proposed for the first time in 1728 by the Swiss mathematician G. Cramer (1728) who carried on a correspondence with Bernoulli concerning the evaluation of lotteries.
7. We point out in addition that if f were linear then the inequality would be an equality.

8. Lexicographic, one would say in more scientific terms.
9. As we will see in Chapter 15, a stock represents for its owner the right to a random flow of revenue (dividends plus capital gains). The expected value of this lottery exceeds its risk premium and thus the sale price demanded by the stockholder is strictly positive.
10. In Chapter 5 we will be much more precise concerning this subject.
11. These topics are discussed in more detail in Section 4.1.
12. Its properties are analysed in detail in Chapter 4.

References

Allais M. (1953), Le comportement de l'homme rationnel devant le risque, critique des postulats et axiomes de l'école américaine, *Econometrica*, vol. 21, 503–546.

Arrow K. (1965), *Aspects of the theory of risk-bearing*, Yrjo Jahnsson Saatio, Helsinki.

Cramer G. (1728), Letter to Nicolas Bernoulli. Republished in *Econometrica*, (1954), vol. 22, 33–35.

Demers F. and M. Demers (1990), Price uncertainty, the competitive firm and the dual theory of choice under risk, *European Economic Review*, vol. 34, 1181–1200.

Lancaster K. (1968), *Mathematical Economics*, Macmillan, New York. See especially section R.8.5, pp. 331–334.

Machina M. (1987a), Expected utility hypothesis, in *The New Palgrave. A Dictionary of Economics*, J. Eatwell, M. Milgate and P. Newman (eds), Macmillan Press, London, vol. 2, 232–239.

Machina M. (1987b), Choice under uncertainty: problems solved and unsolved. *The Journal of Economic Perspectives*, vol. 1, 121–154.

Munier B. (1989), Portée et signification de l'œuvre de M. Allais, *Revue d'économie politique*, vol. 99, 1–27.

Pratt J. (1964), Risk aversion in the small and in the large, *Econometrica*, vol. 32, 122–136.

Quiggin, J. (1982), A theory of anticipated utility, *Journal of Economic Behavior and Organization*, vol. 3, 323–343.

Richter M. (1959–1960), Cardinal utility, portfolio selection, and taxation, *Review of Economic Studies*, vol. 27, 152–166.

Sinn H. (1983), *Economic Decisions under Uncertainty*, North-Holland, Amsterdam.

Yaari M. (1987), The dual theory of choice under risk, *Econometrica*, vol. 55, 95–116.

4 **Other measures of risk aversion and some associated assumptions**

We begin this chapter by developing two concepts that are similar to absolute risk aversion: relative risk aversion and partial risk aversion. Once these concepts have been presented, we will discuss some reasonable assumptions that can be made concerning them. In Section 4.4, we put these concepts and assumptions to work by applying them to some specific utility functions. Using certain utility functions, we reconstruct the 'mean variance' and 'safety first' criteria presented in Chapter 2 as special cases of the expected utility model.

4.1 The notions of relative and partial risk aversion

The alert reader will have noticed that all of the discussion in Chapter 3 was in a specific context: that of lotteries that are additive with respect to wealth. Now, as noted in Chapter 1, one can also imagine multiplicative lotteries. The concept of relative risk aversion and its generalisation (partial risk aversion) were invented for this kind of situation.

4.1.1 Relative risk aversion

If a decision-maker places a fortune w_0 in an asset for which the rate of return $\tilde{y}$ is random and if the risk is to be resolved quickly, then the final wealth is defined by:

$$\tilde{w}_f = w_0(1 + \tilde{y})$$

As a result, if the decision-maker adopts the expected utility criterion, the situation is evaluated before resolution of the risk by $E[U(w_0(1 + \tilde{y}))]$.

Imagine now that someone offers to relieve our decision-maker of this (multiplicative) risk in return for a fraction of w_0[1]. To see whether the offer is advantageous, it must be compared with the fraction π' defined by:

$$U(w_0(1 - \pi')) = E[U(w_0(1 + \tilde{y})] \qquad (4.1)$$

In other words, if the decision-maker must give up exactly $\pi'w_0$ (in monetary units) there would be indifference between this outcome and simply holding lottery $\tilde{y}$. Of course, if there is an organisation (for example, an insurance company) in the market that offers to take on this risk for a fraction that is less than π', then the decision-maker will accept quickly in order to enjoy an (*ex ante*) increase in welfare.

To define relative risk aversion, apply Pratt's method of approximation to each side of Equation (4.1). To keep the notation simple (and also to avoid some minor technical problems that are not of fundamental interest), assume that the lottery $\tilde{y}$ is 'actuarially fair', that is, that $E(y) = 0$.

The first-order approximation of the left hand-side around w_0 is:

$$U(w_0(1 - \pi')) \cong U(w_0) - \pi' w_0 U'(w_0) \tag{4.2}$$

The second-order approximation of $U(w_0(1 + y))$ is:

$$U(w_0(1 + y)) \cong U(w_0) + y w_0 U'(w_0) + (y^2 w_0^2/2) U''(w_0)$$

Taking the expected value of both sides finally yields:

$$E[U(w_0(1 + \tilde{y}))] \cong U(w_0) + (w_0^2 \sigma^2/2) U''(w_0)$$

Because $E(\tilde{y}) = 0$ by assumption, $E(\tilde{y}^2)$ is the variance of $\tilde{y}$ (σ^2). Equating these approximations of the two sides of Equation (4.1) yields:

$$U(w_0) - \pi' w_0 U'(w_0) \cong U(w_0) + (w_0^2 \sigma^2/2) U''(w_0)$$

which implies that:

$$\pi' \cong (\tfrac{1}{2}) \sigma^2 [-w_0 U''(w_0)/U'(w_0)] \tag{4.3}$$

The fraction of fortune that an individual is prepared to give up in order to avoid the amount of risk is a function of two elements:

(a) the quantity of risk as measured by σ^2;
(b) a psychological element reflecting the nature of the utility function and measured by $A_r(w_0) = -w_0 U''(w_0)/U'(w_0)$, a coefficient that is called the degree of relative risk aversion.

The terms 'absolute aversion' and 'relative aversion' are tied to the nature of the lottery. Absolute risk aversion applies to additive lotteries that are expressed in monetary units while relative risk aversion applies to multiplicative lotteries expressed in rates or fractions.

It is interesting to note an obvious connection between relative risk aversion (A_r) and absolute risk aversion (A_a). If we return to the definition of A_a derived from Equation (3.15) and assume that the additive lottery is actuarially fair $(E(x) = \mu = 0)$, then $A_a = -U''(w_0)/U'(w_0)$. It is then obvious that we can write:

$$A_r = w_0 A_a \tag{4.4}$$

The relationship between the two approaches developed thus far is made clearer by the following. Begin with a multiplicative lottery $\tilde{y}$ and note that

$\tilde{w}_f$ can be written as:

$$\tilde{w}_f = w_0(1 + \tilde{y}) = w_0 + \tilde{y}w_0$$

If we agree to write $\tilde{x} = \tilde{y}w_0$, then we also have:

$$\tilde{w}_f = w_0 + \tilde{x}$$

and this permits us to shift from the multiplicative case to the additive case. We note in addition that:

$$E(\tilde{x}) = w_0 E(\tilde{y}) = 0$$

due to the assumption on $E(\tilde{y})$. The two lotteries $\tilde{x}$ and $\tilde{y}$ are thus actuarially fair. Furthermore,

$$\mathrm{Var}(\tilde{x}) = w_0^2 \mathrm{Var}(\tilde{y})$$

Although they have the same expected values (namely, zero), lotteries $\tilde{x}$ and $\tilde{y}$ have very different variances (unless $w_0 = 1$).

The definitions of the basic concepts imply:

$$\begin{aligned}
U(w_0 - \pi) &= E[U(w_0 + \tilde{x})] \\
&= E[U(w_0 + w_0\tilde{y})] \\
&= U(w_0(1 - \pi'))
\end{aligned}$$

from which it follows that:

$$\pi = \pi' w_0 \qquad\qquad (4.5)$$

If the multiplicative risk is sufficiently small for Pratt's approximation to be valid, then it can be verified that expression (4.5) implies:

$$\begin{aligned}
(\tfrac{1}{2})\sigma^2(\tilde{x})A_a &= \pi \\
&= w_0\pi' \\
&= w_0(\tfrac{1}{2})\sigma^2(\tilde{y})A_r
\end{aligned}$$

Since $\sigma^2(\tilde{x}) + w_0^2\sigma^2(\tilde{y})$, this implies that $A_r = w_0 A_a$.

All of these manipulations may have made the reader a bit dizzy, but we only wished to show that there is a close relationship between the different results. Furthermore, we hope to leave a message that is not always clear from many articles: to every multiplicative lottery there corresponds an additive lottery. This explains the strong connection between absolute risk aversion and relative risk aversion on the one hand, and between π and π' on the other. Thus, as we will argue again in Section 4.2, assumptions about the behaviour of one of these two concepts automatically implies assumptions about the behaviour of the other.

4.1.2 Partial risk aversion

In finance theory, the concept of relative risk aversion is well known and quite natural given that one is often confronted with random rates of return. Surprisingly, an interesting generalisation of relative risk aversion, namely, partial risk aversion, is practically unknown. Apparently this notion was proposed independently by two pairs of researchers at about the same time.[2] The basic idea is very simple. Let there be a given total wealth w_0 composed of two elements. The first, w_0', is completely certain, while the second, w_0'', is subject to a multiplicative risk that is assumed to be actuarially fair. Of course $w_0 = w_0' + w_0''$.

The initial situation is characterised by $E[U(w_0' + w_0''(1 + \tilde{y}))]$ and the individual considers what fraction of w_0'' would be willingly paid in order to avoid the risk and maintain welfare. The problem then is to determine the fraction π'' that satisfies:

$$U(w_0' + w_0''(1 - \pi'')) = E[U(w_0' + w_0''(1 + \tilde{y}))] \tag{4.6}$$

It follows immediately from Equation (4.6) that π'' includes π' as a special case. Specifically, if $w_0' = 0$ so that $w_0'' = w_0$ (i.e. all wealth is subject to risk), then Equation (4.6) reduces to Equation (4.1) and $\pi' = \pi''$.

In order to make π'' explicit, we take approximations of both sides of Equation (4.6) around w_0. Using the by now well-known technique, we find that:

$$\pi'' \cong (\tfrac{1}{2})\sigma^2[-w_0'' U''(w_0)/U'(w_0)] \tag{4.7}$$

where the expression in square brackets is called partial risk aversion; it is denoted A_p or sometimes $A_p(w_0'', w_0)$ to indicate that it depends on total wealth and its division between its risky and certain components. It is interesting (and comforting) to note again that if $w_0'' = w_0$, then A_p equals A_r. Furthermore, simple algebraic manipulation establishes a simple and intuitive link between A_p and A_r. Multiply the definition of A_p by w_0 and then divide it by w_0 to write:

$$A_p = -(w_0''/w_0)w_0[U''(w_0)/U'(w_0)]$$

Using the definition of relative risk aversion then yields:

$$A_p(w_0'', w_0) = (w_0''/w_0)A_r(w_0) \tag{4.8}$$

Partial risk aversion is thus proportional to relative risk aversion and it is interesting to note that the factor of proportionality equals the fraction of total wealth that is subject to risk.

4.1.3 An illustration

Returning to Cramer's utility function $U = w_f^{1/2}$, assume that an initial wealth of 10 is divided as follows: 2 is 'invested' in a safe security and the balance ($w_0'' = 8$) is 'invested' in a risky security with a random rate of return $\tilde{y}$ represented by a uniform distribution on $[-1, 1]$, so $f(y) = \tfrac{1}{2}$ while $E(\tilde{y}) = 0$

and $\sigma^2(\tilde{y}) = \frac{1}{3}$. This lottery includes extremely spectacular outcomes since if $y = -1$ is realised then all of the risk capital is lost, while if $y = 1$ is realised then the amount of risk capital doubles. The final wealth of the individual will thus fall between a minimum of 2 and a maximum of 18 if this lottery, that is about to be played, is retained. The expected utility from this lottery is:

$$E[U(\tilde{w}_f)] = \int_{-1}^{+1} [2 + 8(1 + y)]^{1/2} (\tfrac{1}{2}) \, dy$$

By applying a change of variable technique, which is naturally suggested by economic intuition since it makes the substitution:

$$w_f = 2 + 8(1 + y)$$

one can deduce that:

$$E[U(\tilde{w}_f)] = (1/16) \int_2^{18} w_f^{1/2} \, dw_f$$

$$= (1/16) [(\tfrac{2}{3}) w_f^{3/2}]_2^{18} = 3.0641$$

Given the definition of π'', it is now a matter of solving:

$$(2 + 8(1 - \pi''))^{1/2} = 3.0641$$

which, after the obvious manipulations, yields:

$$\pi'' = 0.0764$$

This means that the individual is indifferent between giving up 7.64 per cent of the risk capital to avoid the lottery or, conversely, retaining the lottery and awaiting its result.

We now compare this 'exact' result with its approximation in Equation (4.7). It was established above that, for Cramer's utility function, $-U''/U' = \frac{1}{2} w$ and thus, with $w_0 = 10$,

$$-U''(w_0)/U'(w_0) = \tfrac{1}{20}$$

So the approximation formula gives as a result:

$$\pi'' \cong (\tfrac{1}{2})(\tfrac{1}{3})(\tfrac{8}{20}) = 0.0666$$

This result is a very good approximation to the true value.

To pursue this example, consider Cramer's neighbour, whom we will call Dr Barrois. Imagine that Barrois has the same utility function and anticipates the same distribution of $\tilde{y}$ but that the total fortune $w_0 = 10$ is invested differently, namely, with $w_0' = 6$ and $w_0'' = 4$. A few calculations furnish the following results:

$$\pi'' = 0.0343 \text{ (the exact value)}$$
$$\pi'' = 0.0333 \text{ (the approximate value)}$$

Notice that the approximation is even better than before. Of course the risk inherent in $\tilde{y}$ has not changed, but since it affects a smaller fraction of the wealth, there is a smaller dispersion of possible values of $\tilde{w}_f$ which, as we have seen, improves the quality of the approximation.

We also point out that an intermediate step in deriving these results establishes that, for Dr Barrois, $E[U(\tilde{w}_f)] = 3.145$, which is larger than the similar value for Cramer. This is not surprising. Given that the utility function that both scientists have in common exhibits risk aversion, it is to be expected that Dr Barrois will be more 'comfortable' in facing less risk than Cramer while having the same expected final wealth. Specifically, $E(\tilde{w}_f) = 10$ for both individuals because $E(\tilde{y}) = 0$; but Barrois has a smaller fraction of wealth invested in the risky asset. Thus the position is necessarily less risky and, since $E(\tilde{w}_f)$ is the same, the risk-averse decision-maker prefers this. This simple assertion will be formalised in Chapter 5 when we study the notion of 'greater risk' and in Chapter 9 we will show that no risk-averse decision-maker should buy that risky security with a zero mean.

4.2 Assumptions about the properties of the measures of risk aversion

The three measures of risk aversion (A_a, A_r, A_p) that we have defined overlap, as has been shown. It could not be otherwise because the difference between the concepts is due not to the nature of the risk, but to the way that the risk is presented to the individual (additive or multiplicative). Under these conditions, it is not surprising that an assumption made about the properties of one of the measures reduces the number of plausible assumptions that can be imposed on the behaviour of another of the measures. We will not ignore these issues. The assumptions to be made will revolve around the following question: what happens to the measures of risk aversion when, *ceteris paribus*, wealth increases? This kind of question is relevant for individuals who are risk averse or, at most, are risk neutral.

4.2.1 The degree of absolute risk aversion and changing wealth

Long before the modern version of risk theory was well developed, there existed in the business world a widely held idea that a firm with a higher net worth could handle a given risk more successfully. Somewhat more precisely, it was said that an increase in wealth allows companies to retain their risk. This means that the risk premium of an additive risk must be a decreasing function of wealth, if it is to be the case that a wealthier individual has a higher propensity to accept risk. Technically, this intuitive idea is captured by Hypothesis 4.1.

Hypothesis 4.1 An individual whose wealth increases fears a given additive lottery less (or at least not more), that is,

$$dA_a/dw_0 \leqslant 0 \tag{4.9}$$

This assumption states that A_a, and thus the risk premium of any given additive risk, is a non-increasing function of wealth.[3] In terms of risk tolerance, Equation (4.9) means that, if the level of risk is unchanged, an increase in w_0 does not reduce the tolerance for this risk because T_a is inversely related to A_a. In some sense, the richer the decision-maker the better able they are to handle a given additive risk.

4.2.2 The degree of relative risk aversion and changing wealth

We now ask the same question about multiplicative risk that we asked about additive risk: given a multiplicative risk $\tilde{y}$, will an increase in wealth reduce the propensity of an individual to sell this risk? The answer requires an examination of how A_r reacts to a change in w_0, as implied by Pratt's approximation Equation (4.3) which links π' and A_r. First, it is interesting to recall the unifying relationship between absolute and relative risk aversion described by Equation (4.4), namely,

$$A_r(w_0) = w_0 A_a(w_0)$$

where the dependence of each of these coefficients on w_0 is made clear. By differentiating this expression with respect to w_0 one obtains:

$$dA_r/dw_0 = A_a + w_0(dA_a/dw_0) \tag{4.10}$$

Since A_a is non-negative, it is obvious that if A_a is increasing in w_0 then A_r will be as well. In other words, if there were increasing absolute risk aversion,[4] it would not be consistent with decreasing relative risk aversion. Furthermore, if absolute risk aversion is constant (an assumption that is perfectly consistent with Hypothesis 4.1) then dA_a/dw_0 is zero but dA_r/dw_0 is strictly positive. It follows that decreasing A_r is inconsistent with constant A_a. The most difficult case (and certainly the most likely, according to Hypothesis 4.1) is where absolute risk aversion is decreasing in wealth. In this case two opposite effects arise in Equation (4.10) and dA_r/dw_0 can be positive, negative or zero.

It is important to note the parallel between Equation (4.10) and its equivalent in terms of the risk premium. Specifically, since:

$$\pi' \cong (\tfrac{1}{2})\sigma^2(\tilde{y})\,[-w_0 U''(w_0)/U'(w_0)] = (\tfrac{1}{2}w_0)\sigma^2(\tilde{x})A_a(w_0)$$

where $\tilde{x} = w_0\tilde{y}$ is the corresponding additive risk, we have:

$$d\pi'/dw_0 \cong (\tfrac{1}{2}w_0)\sigma^2(\tilde{x})(dA_a/dw_0) + (\tfrac{1}{2})A_a[d(\sigma^2)(\tilde{x})/w_0)\,dw_0] \tag{4.10a}$$

Similar reasoning about the ambiguity of the sign of $d\pi''/dw_0$ can be stated: the first term on the right-hand side of Equation (4.10a) represents the effect on the risk premium for a given additive risk. It is negative by Hypothesis 4.1. The second term, in contrast, is positive since $\sigma^2(\tilde{x})/w_0 = w_0\sigma^2(\tilde{y})$. It represents the increase in the risk premium due to the implicit increase in additive risk.

A deeply entrenched tradition in risk theory tilts the balance in favour of a non-negative derivative as summarised in Hypothesis 4.2.

Hypothesis 4.2 If wealth increases, relative risk aversion does not decrease, that is,

$$dA_r/dw_0 \geqslant 0 \tag{4.11}$$

Since π' and A_r are proportional for small risks, Hypothesis 4.2 is equivalent to assuming that $d\pi'/dw_0 \geqslant 0$ for every lottery $\tilde{y}$.

It is important to understand this assumption well. When w_0 rises given a multiplicative lottery, there are two effects that appear clearly in the decomposition of $d\pi'/dw_0$ provided by Equation (4.10a):

(a) since w_0 increases, the individual feels wealthier and if the risk remained constant their risk aversion would have to decrease due to Hypothesis 4.1. This is the first term (which is negative) of the right-hand side of Equation (4.10a);

(b) however, since the lottery is multiplicative, the increase in w_0 implies a greater risk for final wealth because $\sigma^2(\tilde{w}_f) = \sigma^2(\tilde{y})w_0^2$, and this tends to increase aversion to the risk inherent in $\tilde{y}$. This effect is captured by the second term (which is positive) on the right-hand side of Equation (4.10a).

In imposing Hypothesis 4.2, we assume that the second effect (the 'risk' effect) is never dominated by the first effect (the 'wealth' effect). One can more easily accept the assumption of increasing relative risk aversion in w_0 by considering that when w_0 increases in a multiplicative lottery, $\sigma^2(\tilde{w}_f)$ increases much more quickly (to the second power, as we saw above), and thus the 'risk' effect quickly becomes very large. In light of the above discussion of the two effects, assuming that A_r is constant in w_0 is equivalent to asserting that the 'risk' effect exactly offsets the 'wealth' effect. This case is analysed in more detail in Appendix 1.

4.3 The common utility functions

Every increasing and concave utility function implies risk aversion (see Theorem 3.3). However, it would also be desirable for a utility function to satisfy some *a priori* reasonable properties such as those alluded to in Section 4.2. For this reason we consider various utility functions that are commonly employed in risk theory and we judge them by various criteria.

4.3.1 The quadratic utility function

This is a very popular utility function because it is easily manipulated and it provides good intuition for several specific results from finance theory. Unfortunately, it has a very undesirable property, as we shall see.

The quadratic utility function is given by:

$$U = w_f - \beta w_f^2 \tag{4.12}$$

from which it follows that $U' = 1 - 2w_f$ and $U'' = -2\beta$.

For U to be concave, it is sufficient for coefficient β to be strictly positive.[5] Note that for function U to be increasing everywhere in w_f, β should not be too large. Let w_M be the largest value of w_f, then $1 - 2\beta w_M$ must be positive if U' is positive everywhere in its domain of definition. This implies that β must be less than $\frac{1}{2}w_M$.

When β is chosen to satisfy this legitimate constraint, one easily obtains:

$$A_a(w_f) = 2\beta/(1 - 2\beta w_f) > 0$$

and it is apparent that absolute risk aversion is increasing in wealth. This result contradicts the seemingly reasonable assumption, Hypothesis 4.1. Hence, to accept the quadratic utility function is to assume that the richer an individual is the more they fear a given additive lottery. Since A_a is increasing in wealth given a quadratic utility, so is A_r, which is consistent with Hypothesis 4.2.

The balance sheet for this utility function is thus rather unimpressive, which is all the more regrettable because quadratic utility provides a justification for the intuitive 'mean variance' criterion discussed in Chapter 2. Specifically, we will show that if U is quadratic then individuals evaluate their situation exclusively by the mean and variance of final wealth. From Equation (4.12) we can derive:

$$V(\tilde{w}_f) = E[U(\tilde{w}_f)] = E[\tilde{w}_f - \beta\tilde{w}_f^2]$$

$$= E(\tilde{w}_f) - \beta[(E(\tilde{w}_f))^2 + \sigma^2(\tilde{w}_f)] \tag{4.13}$$

where the last equality follows from the well-known result that:

$$\sigma^2(\tilde{x}) = E(\tilde{x}^2) - (E(\tilde{x}))^2$$

It follows from Equation (4.13) that if U is quadratic then the value of the individual's situation is a function of $E(\tilde{w}_f)$ and of $\sigma^2(\tilde{w}_f)$ alone, as is postulated by the 'mean variance' model. Furthermore, notice that:

$$\partial V/\partial E(w_f) = 1 - 2\beta E(\tilde{w}_f) > 0$$

and

$$\partial V/\partial\sigma^2(w_f) = -\beta < 0$$

This corresponds to the situation where $f_1 > 0$ and $f_2 < 0$ and thus results in upward sloping indifference curves in mean variance space as long as $\beta > 0$.

The mediocre performance of the quadratic utility relative to Hypothesis 4.1 on the one hand and its natural association with the mean variance criterion on the other have often provided an argument against the latter. For completeness we point out that this evaluation criterion can be justified without quadratic utility. For example, the mean variance criterion is adequate if $\tilde{w}_f$ is normally distributed.[6] More recently, in a very interesting article, J. Meyer (1987) showed that the criterion is appropriate for comparing lotteries that differ only by a location parameter and a spread parameter (which includes normal distributions as a special case).

In summary, we have reservations concerning the ability of a quadratic utility to validly represent risk-averse individuals. However, these are not sufficient to reject the mean variance model despite its association with quadratic utility because it can be justified in other ways.

We point out that the 'safety-first' criterion (see Chapter 2) also has foundations in expected utility that are not far from those underlying the mean variance model. Specifically, if one writes[7]:

$$
\begin{aligned}
U &= w_f && \text{if } w_f \geq t \\
U &= w_f - k(t - w_f)^2 && \text{if } w_f \leq t \text{ and } k > 0
\end{aligned}
\tag{4.14}
$$

then one easily derives the safety-first criterion. To see this, it is sufficient to calculate $E[U(\tilde{w}_f)]$ using this utility function, that is,

$$
\begin{aligned}
E[U(\tilde{w}_f)] &= \int_t^{+\infty} w_f f(w_f)\, dw_f + \int_{-\infty}^t (w_f - k(t - w_f)^2) f(w_f)\, dw_f \\
&= \int_{-\infty}^{+\infty} w_f f(w_f)\, dw_f - k \int_{-\infty}^t (t - w_f)^2 f(w_f)\, dw_f \\
&= E(\tilde{w}_f) - k\sigma^{2-}(t)
\end{aligned}
$$

where the reader will have recognised t as the threshold above which the decision-maker is risk neutral and below which the decision-maker is risk averse.

Unfortunately, the utility function proposed in Equation (4.14) does not satisfy Hypotheses 4.1 and 4.2. For example, consider the behaviour of absolute risk aversion. For $w_f < t$ one obtains:

$$U' = 1 + 2k(t - w_f) > 0$$
$$U'' = -2k$$
$$-U''/U' = 2k/(1 + 2k(t - w_f))$$

from which it follows that the degree of risk aversion is strictly positive and growing for $w < t$. Above t it is zero because risk neutrality prevails. A similar situation arises for A_r, which is increasing below t and zero above.

4.3.2 The logarithmic utility function

We now consider a utility function that is famous because it was proposed by Bernoulli himself to resolve the 'Saint Petersburg Paradox' by demonstrating the inadequacy of the expected value criterion. This utility function is given by:

$$U = \ln w_f$$

which implies $w_f > 0$ if the function is well defined. For additive lotteries this means that if the worst possible outcome, denoted x_m, is negative, then it must be smaller in absolute value than w_0.[8] We thus implicitly assume that the lottery can never result in a loss greater than the individual's initial wealth. This assumption is very reasonable in many cases, but it can nevertheless fail to be satisfied (more and more frequently, by the way) for certain risks faced by firms when the notion of legal liability for damages is introduced.

For this utility function we have:

$$U' = 1/w_f > 0 \text{ (because } w_f > 0\text{)}$$
$$U'' = -1/w_f^2$$

and hence $A_a = 1/w_f$ is a decreasing function of wealth. Thus the logarithmic utility function satisfies Hypothesis 4.1. Furthermore, $A_r = 1$ is a non-decreasing function of wealth for which the derivative is everywhere zero. So the logarithmic utility function also satisfies Hypothesis 4.2.

4.3.3 The power function

We have already seen a special case of this function in $U = w^{1/2}$. Here we generalise the special case to write:

$$U = \text{sgn}(\beta)w^\beta$$

from which it follows that $U' = \text{sgn}(\beta)\beta w^{\beta - 1}$. It is clear that this utility function is increasing in wealth because $\text{sgn}(\beta)\beta > 0$.

Furthermore, $U'' = \text{sgn}(\beta)\beta(\beta - 1)w^{\beta - 2}$, so risk aversion implies that $\beta < 1$. Of course $\beta = 0.5$ yields the utility function attributed to Cramer, while $\beta = 1$ implies risk neutrality.

The above results imply that $A_a(w) = (1 - \beta)/w$ and $A_r = 1 - \beta$, which shows that if $\beta = 0$ then the power function exhibits the same coefficients of risk aversion as does the logarithmic.

It is easily demonstrated that the power function satisfies Hypotheses 4.1 and 4.2.

4.3.4 The negative exponential function

This function is written as:

$$U = -e^{-\beta w_f} \tag{4.15}$$

and the resulting negative values of U sometimes baffle newcomers to risk theory. In reality, the sign of U has no particular significance. Indeed, as stated in Theorem 3.1, one can apply any increasing linear transformation to a utility function without altering its properties. Thus, if one wishes to make U positive, it suffices to add a sufficiently large constant − 1 is large enough if w_f is positive − to Equation (4.15) and the result will be a positive utility function with the same interpretation as before. Although one should not worry about the sign of U, the sign of U' must be absolutely positive. Here this is guaranteed when β is positive because $U' = \beta e^{-\beta w_f}$. Furthermore, $U'' = -\beta^2 e^{-\beta w_f}$ and thus $A_a = \beta$.

We thus have, for the first time, a utility function with a constant degree of absolute risk aversion. It follows that Hypothesis 4.1 is satisfied. Hypothesis 4.2 is also satisfied because, with exponential utility, $A_r(w) = \beta w$ is an increasing function of w. Nevertheless, since relative risk aversion increases without bound in w, it can be the case for large values of w_f that π' exceeds 1, which means that the individual is prepared to abandon with certainty more than 100 per cent of the initial wealth rather than face an actuarially fair multiplicative lottery (see Appendix 2 for an example). Since such a situation is difficult to imagine in practice, the exponential function has an inherent weakness in that in certain cases it generates 'abnormal' phenomena.

This weakness aside, the utility function has many interesting properties. For example, when the utility function is a negative exponential, it turns out that individuals who maximise expected utility, given normally distributed final wealth, behave as if they were using the mean variance criterion. We will prove this result in Chapter 9 (see also Exercise 3.4). In addition, in the case of exponential utility and a normal distribution, the Arrow−Pratt approximation formula for the risk premium is exact, even for large risks. This is one of the consequences of the derivations found in Appendix 2.

4.3.5 A generalisation and summary

It is interesting to note that practically all of the utility functions presented thus far can be derived as special cases of a class of functions known as 'hyperbolic absolute risk aversion utility functions'. This generalisation is as follows:

$$U(w_f) = \frac{1 - \gamma}{\gamma} \left\{ \frac{aw_f}{1 + \gamma} + b \right\}^{\gamma} \tag{4.16}$$

where the domain of definition of the function is those values of w_f that make the expression in parentheses positive, that is, w_f satisfying $aw_f + b(1 - \gamma) > 0$.

Applying the rules of differentiation gives us:

$$U'(w_f) = a \left\{ \frac{aw_f}{1 - \gamma} + b \right\}^{\gamma - 1}$$

$$U''(w_f) = -a^2 \left\{ \frac{aw_f}{1 - \gamma} + b \right\}^{\gamma - 2}$$

from which it follows that:

$$A_a = -U''/U' = a / \left\{ \frac{aw_f}{1 - \gamma} + b \right\} \tag{4.17}$$

The name given to this class of utility functions is easily understood by noticing that, as is the case with all hyperbolic functions, w_f appears linearly in the denominator of A_a. Notice also that if one were interested in risk tolerance then it could be written as:

$$T_a = 1/A_a = w_f/(1 - \gamma) + b/a$$

which is linear in w_f. For this reason utility functions in this class are also called 'linear risk tolerance utility functions'.

The importance of the functional form in Equation (4.16) is that it furnishes an interesting generalisation of all the utility functions so far discussed. It also provides a method of remembering them. To illustrate how Equation (4.16) is a generalisation, it is sufficient to compare the absolute risk aversion of each utility function with that found in Equation (4.17). As shown in Table 4.1, a specific utility function corresponds to particular values of the parameters a, b and γ.

It is unnecessary to comment in detail on Table 4.1. The middle column (A_a) lists the results obtained for the specific utility functions. The last column lists the values that a, b and γ must take on to generate the middle column from Equation (4.17). Thus there is a perfect equivalence between the general utility function with appropriate parameter values and the corresponding specific utility functions, since they yield the same value for the

Table 4.1

Utility	A_a	Value of parameters		
Quadratic	$2\beta/(1 - 2\beta w_f)$	$b = 1$	$a = 2\beta$	$\gamma = 2$
Logarithmic	$1/w_f$	$a = 1$	$\gamma = 0$	$b = 0$
Power	$(1 - \beta)/w_f$	$a = 1 - \beta$	$b = 0$	$\gamma = \beta$
Negative exponential	$-\beta$	$\gamma = -\infty$	$a/b = \beta$	

degree of absolute risk aversion and thus reflect the same psychological attitude of a decision-maker facing risk.

To the careful reader who would like to derive the utility functions (and not their coefficients of absolute risk aversion) by substituting the parameters from the last column into Equation (4.16), we point out that this exercise is not very interesting. It poses some interesting mathematical questions but it reveals no new economic intuition.

Finally, to conclude this section, we point out that even the linear utility function is a special case of Equation (4.17). It is derived by setting $\gamma = 1$. In this case, the denominator of Equation (4.16) is infinite and thus the value of A_a is zero. Since the formulation in Equation (4.17) can generate linear or quadratic utility, it can, of course, also be used to construct the utility function that implies 'safety first' behaviour (see Chapter 2) which is a mixture of quadratic utility up to a point and linear utility thereafter.

4.4 Two extensions

Our study of measures of risk aversion now permits us to introduce two somewhat advanced subjects. The first concerns the comparison of degrees of risk aversion and it allows an elegant transition into Chapter 5, which is dedicated to the measurement of the 'degree of risk'. The second deals with the relationship between the asking price and the bid price of a lottery, a theme that was furtively approached previously.

4.4.1 The comparison of degrees of absolute risk aversion

The question can – as is often the case in microeconomics – arise in two different contexts and yet have the same kind of answer.

The first context can be called 'cross-sectional', using the language of econometrics. In this context, one compares two decision-makers at the same point in time who are in every way similar but one: their attitude toward risk.

In the second context, one adopts the philosophy of time series. One focuses on an individual and asks how their risk aversion changes over time if, for example, the initial wealth changes.

In what follows, we will adopt the first point of view but, as was seen in the discussion surrounding Hypothesis 4.1, this can be easily translated in terms of the second approach.

How can one compare two decision-makers' attitudes toward risk at a point in time? Can one make a precise comparison so as to be able to make statements like 'A is 3.42 times as risk averse as B'?

It turns out that if two individuals have utility (or evaluation) functions that belong to the same family, then in some cases one can develop precise comparisons of the kind discussed below. We already saw one such case when we presented the linear version of the mean variance model of evaluation (see Chapter 2). Here is another that belongs to the class of expected utility models. If the first decision-maker, A, is characterised by:

$$U_A(w_f) = -e^{-6.82w_f}$$

and if the second decision-maker, B, also has a negative exponential utility function:

$$U_B(w_f) = -e^{-3.41w_f}$$

then one can say that A is twice as risk averse as B. Specifically, the degree of absolute risk aversion for A is 6.82 and for B it is 3.41. In this case it is thus possible to assert without ambiguity that one decision-maker is more risk averse than the other, independently of their wealth, and one can make the intensity of the difference precise.

Now consider two individuals characterised by the power functions

$$U_A = w_f^{1/2} \text{ and } U_B = w_f^{1/3}$$

Their degrees of absolute risk aversion are respectively $\frac{1}{2}w_f$ and $\frac{2}{3}w_f$. If the two individuals have the same level of wealth, then B is more risk averse than A and one can say, for a given level of wealth, that the ratio of their degrees of risk aversion is $(\frac{2}{3})/(\frac{1}{2}) = \frac{4}{3}$. B is thus '1.33 times' as risk averse as A when they have the same wealth. While for exponential utility comparison of intensity was possible independently of the wealth of each individual, with the power function we must be careful to make comparisons of individuals with the same wealth. It is intuitively clear that the precise comparison in relative terms of the degrees of risk aversion is very difficult if not impossible when the decision-makers have utility functions that do not belong to the same family. The problem comes from the fact that absolute risk aversion is a local concept. At this higher level of generality comparison of the degrees of risk aversion can only be made 'ordinally' by saying that one individual is more risk averse than another at every level of wealth but without being able to express the intensity of the difference. This 'ordinal' definition was proposed by Pratt – once again! – in his remarkable article of 1964. One says that the utility function $L(w_f)$ exhibits more risk aversion than another utility function $U(w_f)$ at every level of wealth[9] if L can be written as an increasing concave transformation of U, that is, if there exists a function k with $k' > 0$ and $k'' < 0$ such that:

$$L(w_f) = k[U(w_f)] \text{ for all } w_f$$

An application of the chain rule yields:

$$L'(w_f) = k'[U(w_f)]U'(w_f)$$
$$L''(w_f) = k''[U(w_f)][U'(w_f)]^2 + k'[U(w_f)]U''(w_f)$$

from which it follows that:

$$-L''(w_f)/L'(w_f) = -(k''/k')U'(w_f) - U''(w_f)/U'(w_f) \quad (4.18)$$

From the assumptions that have been imposed on k'' and k', and since U' is necessarily positive, the first term on the right-hand side of Equation (4.18) is strictly positive and thus:

$$-L''(w_f)/L'(w_f) > -U''(w_f)/U'(w_f)$$

which can be interpreted as saying that for all w_f the degree of absolute risk aversion is higher for L than for U. This is denoted by $A_a^l(w_f) > A_a^u(w_f)$ where A_a^l is the degree of absolute risk aversion given the utility function L and A_a^u is the corresponding expression given U.

For brevity it is sometimes said that if the utility function L of an individual is 'more concave' than the utility function U of another individual, then the first decision-maker exhibits more risk aversion than the second.

Since the above proof of this result is somewhat abstract, we illustrate it with three examples.

The comparison of linear U to concave L

If an individual is risk neutral, their utility function is linear (see Theorem 3.2) and can thus be written as[10]:

$$U(w_f) = w_f$$

If their neighbour has a utility function, L, that can be expressed by $L = k(U) = U^{1/2}$, then $k' = (0.5)U^{-1/2} > 0$ and $k'' = (-0.25)U^{-3/2} < 0$. But $L = U^{1/2}$ and $U = w_f$ obviously imply that:

$$L = w_f^{1/2}$$

Our previous results show that $A_a^u = 0$ and $A_a^l = \frac{1}{2}w_f > 0$, (for $w_f > 0$, which corresponds to the domain of definition of L) and thus we have $A_a^l > A_a^u$.

In some sense the change from risk neutrality to risk aversion implies a concave transformation of an initially linear utility and thus a higher degree of absolute risk aversion than initially observed, and this holds for all w_f.

The transformation of one power function into another

Initially, Investor U is a riskophobe and has utility function of $U = w_f^{1/2}$. A neighbour, Investor L, has a utility function that is a concave transformation of U – indeed a power function of U – namely,

$$L = k(U) = U^{1/3}$$

from which it follows that $k' = (\frac{1}{3})U^{-2/3} > 0$ and $k'' = (-\frac{2}{9})U^{-5/3} > 0$.

Since $L = U^{1/3}$ and $U = w_f^{1/2}$, one can write $L = w_f^{1/6}$ and, using the results from the previous section (see Table 4.1),

$$A_a^l(w_f) = \tfrac{5}{6} w_f > A_a^u(w_f) = \tfrac{1}{2} w_f$$

for all $w_f > 0$, which corresponds to the domain of the functions.

We have thus reconstructed with the help of transformation k an example that had been given previously to motivate the notion of an increasing and concave transformation of U.

The transformation of logarithmic U

Let $U = \ln w_f$ and consider $L = k(U) = U^{1/2}$. It is easily shown that this transformation is increasing and concave, and thus $A_a^l(w_f)$ must exceed $A_a^u(w_f)$. Note that L can be written as $L = [\ln(w_f)]^{1/2}$ and thus the function L is only defined if $\ln w_f > 0$, that is, if $w_f > 1$.

To derive A_a^l, we calculate in turn:

$$L'(w_f) = (\tfrac{1}{2})(\ln w_f)^{-1/2}(1/w_f)$$
$$L''(w_f) = (-\tfrac{1}{2}w_f^2)(\ln w_f) - (\tfrac{1}{4}w_f^2)(\ln w_f)^{-3/2}$$

from which it follows that:

$$-L''(w_f)/L'(w_f) = (1/w_f) + (\tfrac{1}{2}w_f)(\ln w_f)^{-1}$$

Recalling that $U = \ln w_f$ implies $A_a = 1/w_f$ (see Table 4.1) and noting that $1/(2w_f \ln w_f)$ is strictly positive for $w_f > 1$, one obtains as predicted:

$$A_a^l > A_a^u$$

4.4.2 Bid and asking prices of a lottery

We briefly alluded to the difference between these two notions in Chapter 3 and we will now consider this theme in more detail. Surprisingly, the difference between the two concepts is little analysed and yet it is not uninteresting. The discussion here owes much to the excellent article by I. La Vallée (1968) which is, however, written for a mathematically sophisticated group. As usual we begin with two examples that we then generalise.

To derive the asking price of a lottery (p_a) for an individual, one assumes that initially the decision-maker holds a lottery that is intended for disposal. Thus one passes from uncertainty toward certainty when calculating the asking price. If, for example, $U = w_f^{1/2}$ with $w_0 = 5$ and a lottery characterised by:

$$x = -4 \qquad p = \tfrac{1}{4}$$
$$x = +4 \qquad p = \tfrac{3}{4}$$

then the asking price is the solution to:

$$(5 + p_a)^{1/2} = (\tfrac{1}{4})(1)^{1/2} + (\tfrac{3}{4})(9)^{1/2} = 2.50$$

It follows that $p_a = 1.25$, implying a risk premium equal to 0.75 since $E(\tilde{x}) = 2$.

To derive the bid price, one must consider the situation where initially the decision-maker does not own the lottery (certainty) but is considering acquiring the lottery by paying a price, p_b, that will be disbursed in any case independently of the realisation of $\tilde{x}$. The bid price implies a shift from certainty toward uncertainty and, in the case considered here, it is the solution to:

$$(5)^{1/2} = (\tfrac{1}{4})(1 - p_b)^{1/2} + (\tfrac{3}{4})(9 - p_b)^{1/2} \tag{4.19}$$

as is seen by applying the general definition proposed in Equation (3.7). The left-hand side represents the decision-maker's appraisal of the initial certain situation. The right-hand side is an expected utility of final wealth composed of the 'receipts' w_0 and $\tilde{x}$, and the 'expenditure' p_b that must be paid independently of the outcome of $\tilde{x}$.

To begin, we prove that in general the asking price does not equal the bid price. If it did one could substitute $p_b = p_a = 1.25$ into (4.19) and verify the equality. Yet this is absolutely impossible since it would require taking the square root of a negative number (-0.25). So it is immediately obvious from Equation (4.19) that p_b cannot exceed unity.[11] With $p_b = 1$,

$$(5)^{1/2} = 2.236\ 07 > \tfrac{1}{4}(0)^{1/2} + (\tfrac{3}{4})(8)^{1/2} = 2.121\ 32$$

So since the right-hand side is a decreasing function of p_b, there will exist a value of p_b less than 1 that will achieve the equality of the two terms. A search procedure establishes that $p_b = 0.8541$. Observe also that with the power utility function, for which absolute risk aversion is decreasing, the lottery considered here exhibits the following relationship:

$$0 < p_b < p_a$$

Consider now, in the context of the same lottery, the attitude of the decision-maker characterised by the negative exponential utility function. We have, respectively,

$$-e^{-\gamma(5 + p_a)} = -(\tfrac{1}{4})\,e^{-\gamma(1)} - (\tfrac{3}{4})\,e^{-\gamma(9)}$$

to define p_a and

$$-e^{-\gamma(5)} = -\left(\tfrac{1}{4}\right) e^{-\gamma(1 - p_b)} - \left(\tfrac{3}{4}\right) e^{-\gamma(9 - p_b)}$$

to determine p_b.

Using the well-known property that $e^{a+b} = e^a e^b$, and carrying out some obvious simplifications, one can rewrite these two equations as follows:

$$e^{-5\gamma} e^{-\gamma p_a} = \left(\tfrac{1}{4}\right) e^{-\gamma} + \left(\tfrac{3}{4}\right) e^{-9\gamma}$$
$$e^{-5\gamma} = e^{\gamma p_b} \left[\left(\tfrac{1}{4}\right) e^{-\gamma} - \left(\tfrac{3}{4}\right) e^{-9\gamma}\right]$$

and it follows, from multiplying both sides of the first equation by $e^{\gamma - p_a}$ and comparing the result with the second equation, that $e^{\gamma p_b} = e^{\gamma p_a}$, which implies $p_b = p_a$. In this case, with exponential utility characterised by constant absolute risk aversion,

$$p_b = p_a$$

The two examples just considered suggest that the relationship between the bid price and the asking price of the same lottery is determined by the behaviour of absolute risk aversion. This conclusion from the examples can be generalised in the following theorem.

Theorem 4.1 If absolute risk aversion is decreasing then:

$$\text{either } 0 < p_b < p_a$$
$$\text{or } \quad 0 > p_b > p_a$$

If absolute risk aversion is increasing then:

$$\text{either } 0 < p_a < p_b$$
$$\text{or } \quad 0 > p_a > p_b$$

Finally, in the case of constant absolute risk aversion $p_b = p_a$. After proving the first part of the theorem, we will give an intuitive justification and propose a few applications.

We consider the case where A_a is decreasing and we prove the result for $p_a > 0$, that is, we assume the lottery is favourably perceived by the risk-averse decision-maker. After the formal proof, we will provide some intuition for the result. The proof is somewhat peculiar. Thus we develop it in two steps using a somewhat cumbersome but precise notation.

Step 1 (If $p_a > 0$ then $p_b > 0$). From the usual definitions

$$U[w_0 + p_a(w_0, \tilde{x})] = E[U(w_0 + \tilde{x})] \tag{1a}$$

$$U(w_0) = E[U(w_0 + \tilde{x} - p_b(w_0, \tilde{x}))] \tag{1b}$$

where the notation $p_a(w_0, \tilde{x})$ and $p_b(w_0, \tilde{x})$ reflect that p_a and p_b refer to the prices calculated for an individual with initial wealth w_0 who owns (or considers buying for p_b) lottery $\tilde{x}$. If p_a is positive, it follows from $U' > 0$ that $U(w_0 + p_a) > U(w_0)$ and hence that $E[U(w_0 + \tilde{x})] > E[U(w_0 + \tilde{x} - p_b(w_0, \tilde{x}))]$. This implies that $p_b(w_0, \tilde{x})$ is also positive. Notice that Step 1 does not rely on the behaviour of A_a, which will play a decisive role in Step 2.

Step 2 By inspection of Equation (1b) – especially its right-hand side – we observe that it evaluates the expected utility of a lottery $\tilde{x}$ combined with a certain (non-random) amount of wealth equal to $w_0 - p_b(w_0, \tilde{x})$. We can thus ask what would be the asking price for $\tilde{x}$ associated with this wealth $w_0 - p_b(w_0, \tilde{x})$. Applying to this case the definition of the asking price we can write:

$$U[w_0 - p_b(w_0, \tilde{x}) + p_a(w_0 - p_b(w_0, \tilde{x}), \tilde{x})]$$
$$= E[U(w_0 - p_b(w_0, \tilde{x}) + \tilde{x})] \tag{2a}$$

Combining Equations (2a) and (1b) we can write:

$$p_b(w_0, \tilde{x}) = p_a(w_0 - p_b(w_0, \tilde{x}), \tilde{x}) \tag{2b}$$

Since $p_a > 0$ implies $p_b > 0$ from Step 1, if absolute risk aversion is decreasing then we have:

$$p_a(w_0 - p_b(w_0, \tilde{x}), \tilde{x}) < p_a(w_0, \tilde{x}) \tag{2c}$$

because the richer an individual is the less the fear of lottery $\tilde{x}$ and the higher will be the price demanded for it. It follows, of course, from Equations (2b) and (2c) that:

$$p_b(w_0, \tilde{x}) < p_a(w_0, \tilde{x})$$

To obtain this result we assumed that p_a is positive and that A_a is decreasing in w.

The other parts of Theorem 4.1 are proven in exactly the same way. Readers can approach them theoretically or convince themselves by example. In the case where $U = w_f^{1/2}$ and $w_0 = 5$, consider a lottery $\tilde{y}$:

y	$p(y)$
-4	$\frac{1}{2}$
$+4$	$\frac{1}{2}$

It can be seen that $p_a < 0$ implies $p_b < 0$ and that, consistent with Theorem 4.1, $0 > p_b > p_a$.

We now turn to the intuition underlying Theorem 4.1. In some sense, it allows us to better grasp the notion of decreasing risk aversion. Specifically, the theorem essentially says this: an individual exhibiting decreasing A_a who is endowed with w_0 and a favourable lottery $\tilde{x}$, will demand a higher price to sell $\tilde{x}$ than they would be willing to invest in order to buy it if there was only w_0. With decreasing A_a, the risk aversion, given only w_0, is relatively larger than it is given w_0 augmented by a favourable lottery, and the person will thus invest less to buy favourable lotteries ($p_b < p_a$) when endowed with only w_0. The assumption of decreasing absolute risk aversion implies that an individual will demand a higher price to sell a favourable lottery that they own than they are prepared to invest in its bid if this is not the case.

Surprisingly, the concept of the bid price of a lottery and its relationship with the asking price have received little attention in the literature dedicated to the economic theory of risk. We hope that these few pages will whet the appetite of researchers because we think that these concepts are important since they distinguish the strategies of risk reduction (sale of a lottery, purchase of insurance) from strategies of risk acquisition (purchase of a lottery, financial investment, physical investment). Furthermore, we think that these concepts would be useful in the study of markets for risk. Indeed, for a trade to be beneficial to two parties (and thus realised) it must be that the (minimum) asking price demanded by the owner of the risk be less than the (maximum) bid price that the potential purchaser or purchasers are prepared to pay. To our knowledge, the literature so far has little used the notions of asking price and bid price.

These few reflections complete our long study of the measures of risk aversion and of their properties. We now turn to a complementary subject: the measurement, or at least the comparison, of levels of risk.

Exercises

4.1 In a highly stimulating paper D. Bell (1988) has convincingly argued in favour of a utility function that combines linear and negative exponential utility functions, that is:

$$U = aW_j - be^{-cW_j} \qquad a \geqslant 0, b, c > 0$$

Questions
(a) Show that absolute risk aversion is decreasing.
(b) Does Bell's utility function belong to the class of hyperbolic utility functions?
(c) In the same fashion as in (a), show that the combination of two exponentials,

$$U = -ae^{-bW_j} - ce^{dW_j} \qquad a, b, c, d > 0$$

exhibits decreasing absolute risk aversion.

(d) More generally, define:

$$U_3(W) \equiv U_1(W) + U_2(W)$$

Show that U_3 exhibits decreasing absolute risk aversion if U_1 and U_2 do.
Hint: See Pratt (1964), Equation (29).

4.2 Consider Bell's utility function defined at the beginning of Exercise 4.1 together with utility:

$$L(W) = -e^{-eW_i}$$

Questions
(a) Show that L is more concave than U.
(b) More generally, define $U_3 \equiv U_1 + U_2$, where U_2 is more concave than U_1. Show that U_3 is more concave than U_1, and less concave than U_2.

4.3 Return to the data of Exercises 3.1 and 3.2, and compute the various bid prices.

4.4 Now apply Exercise 4.3 to the data of Exercises 3.3 and 3.4. Are you surprised that the bid price is always equal to the asking price?

4.5 Derive the analytical expression of the fraction r' of wealth that one is prepared to give up in order to avoid rate risk $\tilde{y}$ when $V = \text{sgn}(\beta) W_1^\beta$, $\beta \leqslant 1$. Show that this expression is larger than $-E(\tilde{y})$.

4.6 So far, we have strongly emphasised the certainty equivalent, the asking price and the risk premium of a lottery. However, in many applied fields (health economics, safety at the working place, radiological risk management, etc.) people often refer to the willingness to pay (WTP) for the reduction in the probability of an accident. The purpose of this exercise is to illustrate this notion and relate it to those you already know. Consider an individual with utility:

$$U = \ln W$$

endowed with certain wealth equal to 14 and a binary lottery $\tilde{x}$ representing the change in wealth in the states of 'no accident' and of 'accident':

x	$p(x)$
-3	0.25
$+6$	0.75

The outcome $+6$ is the increase in wealth if no accident (or illness) occurs and the outcome -3 is the reduction in wealth when an accident occurs. Hence $+9$ is the total opportunity cost of the accident.

First compute the traditional notions mentioned above (this should be no problem). Then consider the following question: how much money would you be willing to pay for a safety design that would reduce to zero the probability of an accident. If you denote this amount of money by r, you have to solve:

$$\ln(20 - r) = (0.25)\ln 11 + (0.75)\ln 20$$

since with the new safety system and the price paid for it you obtain $(20 - r)$ with certainty.

Compare the values and the definitions of p_a, π and r. You should observe that p_a measures how much you would pay (or how much you would require) to get rid of the lottery while r indicates how much you are ready to pay in order to obtain with certainty the best outcome of the lottery. The notion of WTP is also very close to that of the risk premium which measures how much one is willing to pay to obtain with certainty the expected value of the lottery. Hence WTP (as defined so far) and π are very close notions that differ only by the gap between the expected value of a binary lottery and its best outcome. As a result, WTP so far looks like a rather uninteresting notion. Its interest lies in the following (rather realistic) consideration. In practice, it is almost impossible to reduce to zero the probability of an accident. Hence, wonder now how much you would invest (r') in a system that would reduce from 0.25 to 0.10 the probability of an accident.

Hint: solve by successive approximations

$$(0.10)\ln(11 - r') + (0.90)\ln(20 - r') = (0.25)\ln 11 + (0.75)\ln 20$$

How do r and r' compare? Explain intuitively why one of them is necessarily larger than the other.

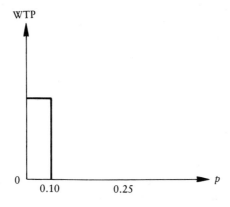

Figure 4.1

By selecting a few other values of the probability of an accident smaller than 0.25 and different from 0 or 0.10, complete Figure 4.1 that relates WTP to various levels of p when the initial probability of an accident amounts to 0.25.

While the WTP notion adds something to what you already knew, you should realise that it uses the same basic ingredients as the previous concepts: a utility function and the description of a lottery (as well as of its transformation).

Remark: A pioneering article in the field is that of Jones-Lee (1974). Notice that this author discusses WTP in the more general framework of 'state dependent' utilities which include as a special case our discussion in this book.

Notes

1. Since the risk is expressed as a rate, the premium must be expressed in the same way, that is, as a fraction. While absolute risk aversion expresses results in monetary units and is thus sensitive to changes in the units of measurement, relative risk aversion is not affected by the choice of monetary unit because it is expressed exclusively as a percentage.

2. The two pairs are C. Menezes and D. Hanson (1970) and R. Zeckhauser and E. Keeler (1970).

3. Another way to express this assumption is to assert that if a lottery is accepted by an individual with wealth w_1 then it will be accepted by an individual with wealth $w > w_1$ (see Yaari (1969) and D. Bell (1988) for a nice extension).

4. We use the conditional clause deliberately, since this case is ruled out by Hypothesis 4.1.

5. Note that if $\beta = 0$ then there is risk neutrality and the expected utility criterion reduces once again to the expected value criterion.

6. This will be examined in more detail when we study the capital asset pricing model (CAPM) in Chapter 15.

7. $k = 0$ would lead once again to risk neutrality.

8. The analogous condition for multiplicative lotteries is $y_m > -1$.

9. The converse result can be proved: if, for all w_f, absolute risk aversion is higher for L than for U then $L = k(U)$ with the properties of k stated below (see Appendix 3).

10. It is not necessary to use the more general form $U = a + bw_f$ because these utility functions are equivalent (see Theorem 3.1 or Remark 5 at the end of Chapter 3).

11. If the positive outcome of the lottery is increased without changing the negative outcome, it turns out nevertheless that the purchase price can not be larger than 1. This upper bound on p_b may seem surprising at

first sight. However, it is a result of the specific character of the utility function considered here. Specifically, U' approaches $-\infty$ as w approaches zero, and thus the decision-maker is relatively much more concerned by negative results than by positive results no matter how large they are.

References

Bell D. (1988), One switch utility functions and a measure of risk, *Management Science*, vol. 34, 1416–1424.

Jones-Lee M. (1974), The value of changes in the probability of death or injury, *Journal of Political Economy*, vol. 99, 235–849.

La Vallée I. (1968), On cash equivalence and information evaluation in decisions under uncertainty, part I, basic theory, *Journal of the American Statistical Association*, vol. 63, 252–275.

Menezes C. and D. Hanson (1970), On the theory of risk aversion, *International Economic Review*, vol. 11, 481–487.

Meyer J. (1987), Two-moment decision models and expected utility, *American Economic Review*, vol. 77, 421–430.

Pratt J. (1964), Risk aversion in the small and in the large, *Econometrica*, vol. 32, 122–136.

Yaari M. (1969), Some remarks on measures of risk aversion and on their use, *Journal of Economic Theory*, vol. 1, 315–329.

Zeckhauser R. and E. Keeler (1970), Another type of risk aversion, *Econometrica*, vol. 38, 661–665.

5 The notion of changing risk (with constant mean)

All of Chapter 4 was oriented toward the study of one ingredient in the risk premium: the notion of risk aversion. In the interest of equal time we now dedicate an entire chapter to the other element constituting the risk premium: the quantity of risk.

For a long time variance has been accepted as the risk measure. This intuition was, in some sense, reinforced by Pratt's approximation formula which implies that if σ^2 increases, other things being equal, the risk premium must increase as well and, furthermore, it must increase proportionally.

We are indebted to two colleagues, M. Rothschild and J. Stiglitz (1970, 1971), for their reconsideration of this well established idea and for their suggestion of a more solid measure of the notion of risk.

It is interesting to ask why it took so long to dethrone variance as a risk measure. In our opinion, there are two reasons for this.

The first is that if one introduces risk to a risk-free situation, then the variance, initially zero, becomes strictly positive. Conversely, if the variance of a random variable is initially positive and becomes zero, then the initial uncertainty is replaced by certainty. In this special case variance is a good indicator of risk because one may construct Table 5.1.

Thus variance is a good indicator of the presence of risk when one makes what may be called a 'global' comparison, that is, a comparison between the presence and absence of risk. The good performance of variance in this limiting case might have caused people to believe that it would also perform well in the comparison of two risk situations, that is, in the analysis of 'marginal' changes in risk. Unfortunately, as we shall see, this is not the case.

Another reason for the popularity of variance as a risk measure is the acceptance – very widespread at one time – of the 'mean variance' model (see Section 2.2) as a behavioural criterion under uncertainty. In the particular framework of this model, variance is *the* measure of risk since it is the only element other than the expected value that enters into the evaluation of the lottery. Furthermore, the sign of the partial derivative of the evaluation function of the lottery with respect to variance by itself indicates the attitude toward risk exhibited by the decision-maker. Once again, as we shall see, the shift to the more general expected utility model robs variance of (a large?) part

Table 5.1

Situation	Variance of the random variable
Certainty	$\sigma^2 = 0$
Uncertainty	$\sigma^2 > 0$

of its importance. It does, however, open new paths for reflection that we will exploit abundantly.

Let us return for a moment to the framework of the 'mean variance' model and consider the comparison of two lotteries with the same mean for different variances. It is obvious that all riskophobes ($f_1 > 0$, $f_2 < 0$; see Chapter 2) will unanimously prefer the lottery with the smallest variance. In the more general framework of the expected utility model, we will search for a definition that is similarly based on the unanimity of appraisals: between two random variables with the same expected value, one will be said to be 'less risky' if all riskophobes ($U'' < 0$) unanimously prefer it. Once one extends the point of view of the mean variance criteria to the expected utility criterion, it turns out that variance is no longer sufficient for measuring risk.

The analysis of the subject of this chapter is difficult. Also, we will try to reconcile a little bit of rigour with a maximum of intuition. For this reason we will first base our discussion on the special case of a discrete random variable. Then we will explain how the results generalise to continuous distributions.

5.1 The case of a discrete distribution: the notion of 'white noise' and the integral condition

Let there initially be a lottery $\tilde{x}$ characterised by:

x	$p(x)$
-2	0.09
$+4$	0.30
$+10$	0.40
$+16$	0.21
	1.00

Can we create examples of transformations of $\tilde{x}$ which keep $E(\tilde{x})$ constant while resulting in a random variable that is riskier[1] than $\tilde{x}$?

A first result can be stated in terms of the notion of 'white noise' that is familiar from statistics. Lottery $\tilde{x}$ contains potential outcomes (from -2 to $+16$), one of which which will be realised and thereafter will become certain (a *fait accompli*) for the decision-maker. Imagine now that, for at least one (and perhaps several or all) of the potential outcomes, the certainty of the outcome, after its realisation, disappears and is replaced by a lottery with the same expected value as the outcome that it replaces. It seems then that the new distribution will be riskier than the initial distribution because there is 'noise' added to at least one of the possible outcomes, that is, some certainty has been replaced with uncertainty.

If, for example, in the distribution of $\tilde{x}$, one replaces the realisation '+4' with the random variable:

$+3$ with probability $\frac{1}{2}$

$+5$ with probability $\frac{1}{2}$

then it is clear that the risk surrounding the outcome $+4$ has increased since it has been replaced by a random variable $\tilde{z}$ such that $E(\tilde{z}) = 4$.

If one does the same for the outcome $+16$, substituting for it the lottery

$+12$ with probability $\frac{1}{3}$

$+18$ with probability $\frac{2}{3}$

then once again the risk surrounding $+16$ increases. With the increase in risk surrounding several of the possible outcomes, a globally riskier situation is created. This is characterised by a new probability distribution for a new random variable $\tilde{y}$ that is defined as follows:

y	$p(y)$
-2	0.09
$+3$	0.15
$+5$	0.15
$+10$	0.40
$+12$	0.07
$+18$	0.14
	1.00

What connection can one establish between $\tilde{x}$ and $\tilde{y}$? Note that in the first place the two discrete distributions have certain common outcomes, with the same probability. These are the possible values of $\tilde{x}$ to which no noise has been added, namely, $x = -2$ and $x = +10$. In contrast, $x = +4$, for which the probability was 0.30, is replaced by $+3$ and $+5$ which each have a probability equal to 0.15 (that is, 0.5×0.30). Similarly, $x = +16$ with probability 0.21, has been replaced by $+12$ and $+18$ which together have a probability of 0.21 $(0.07 + 0.14)$ with a heavier weight on $+18$, since if $x = +16$ is realised then the event '$y = +18$' is twice as likely to arise as the event '$y = +12$' (it has probability $\frac{2}{3}$ rather than $\frac{1}{3}$). Given that at several points $\tilde{y}$ is riskier than $\tilde{x}$ and that at no point is it less risky, overall random variable $\tilde{y}$ represents a greater risk than random variable $\tilde{x}$. This intuition is reinforced if one calculates the expected utilities corresponding to $\tilde{x}$ and $\tilde{y}$ with a strictly increasing and strictly concave utility function, that is, a utility function that exhibits risk aversion. If $\tilde{y}$, which has the same expected value as $\tilde{x}$ ($E(\tilde{y}) = E(\tilde{x}) = +7.30$), is riskier than $\tilde{x}$ then it must be that all riskophobes prefer $\tilde{x}$. We now show that this is indeed the case. To simplify the notation we assume that initial wealth is zero so that $\tilde{w}_f = \tilde{x}$ or $\tilde{y}$. Then,

$$E[U(\tilde{x})] = 0.09U(-2) + 0.30U(+4) + 0.40U(+10)$$
$$+ 0.21U(+16)$$
$$E[U(\tilde{y})] = 0.09U(-2) + 0.30[0.50U(+3)$$
$$+ 0.50U(+5)] + 0.40U(+10)$$
$$+ 0.21[(\tfrac{1}{3})U(+12) + (\tfrac{2}{3})U(+18)]$$

These two expressions have some common elements that cannot be sources of differences between them (for example, $0.09U(-2)$ is common to the two expressions). We must thus concentrate on the elements that differ. In $E[U(\tilde{x})]$ we find $0.30[U(+4)]$; the corresponding term in $E[U(\tilde{y})]$ is $0.30[0.5U(+3) + 0.5U(+5)]$. It is easy to show that the expression in brackets is less than $U(+4)$ if U is concave. If, for purposes of illustration, one employs $U = x^{1/2}$, then one can see that the following inequality holds:

$$(4)^{1/2} = 2 > 0.5(3)^{1/2} + 0.5(5)^{1/2}$$

Rather than illustrate the result, one can prove it with the help of the famous Jensen's inequality (see Chapter 3). Specifically, if U is concave we know that $U[E(\tilde{z})] > E[U(\tilde{z})]$. Here $\tilde{z}$ can take the values $+3$ and $+5$ with probability $\tfrac{1}{2}$ so $E(\tilde{z}) = +4$, which implies that $U(+4)$ exceeds $E[U(\tilde{z})]$. We can thus assert that for all concave utility functions the second term in $E[U(\tilde{x})]$ exceeds the corresponding term in $E[U(\tilde{y})]$. Similarly, one can show, again thanks to Jensen's inequality, that the fourth term of $E[U(\tilde{x})]$, that is $0.21[U(+16)]$, is also greater than the corresponding term in $E[U(\tilde{y})]$. Specifically, from Jensen's inequality,

$$U(+16) > (\tfrac{1}{3})U(+12) + (\tfrac{2}{3})U(+18)$$

if U is concave since

$$16 = (\tfrac{1}{3})12 + (\tfrac{2}{3})18$$

If we collect the various results we notice that each element of $E[U(\tilde{x})]$ is either equal to or greater than the corresponding element of $E[U(\tilde{y})]$. It is clear that, for all concave utility functions, $\tilde{x}$ is preferable to $\tilde{y}$, and since the two lotteries have the same expected value this confirms that $\tilde{x}$ is less risky than $\tilde{y}$ because it is unanimously preferred by riskophobes.

Before formalising (and then generalising) this result, it is worth showing that the notion of 'greater risk' resulting from the addition of white noise to at least one of the outcomes of $\tilde{x}$ has a rather 'spectacular' interpretation in terms of distribution functions.

Figure 5.1 illustrates the cumulative distributions of $\tilde{x}$ and $\tilde{y}$, labelled respectively $F(t)$ and $G(t)$ where upper case F and G denote distribution functions (as opposed to the lower case f and g reserved for density functions) and where the distribution functions are calculated from the lowest possible value of $\tilde{x}$ and $\tilde{y}$ (say a) up to a number t common to both random variables.

The two distribution functions have many intervals where they coincide as is the case for all t less than 3. For $3 < t < 4$, the distribution function for $\tilde{y}$ is above the one for $\tilde{x}$ and, at $t = 4$, it has 'accumulated' an area that is greater than that associated with $\tilde{x}$ by the area of rectangle $abcd$. Between $t = 4$ and $t = 5$ the advantage achieved by G in terms of the greater area under G is progressively won back by the distribution function F which, for $4 \leqslant t \leqslant 5$ lies above G. At $t = 5$, F has completely overcome the advantage conceded to G between $t = 3$ and $t = 4$. This is reflected by the equality of the rectangles $abcd$ and $defg$.[2] Note that at $t = 5$, the areas under the function from $-\infty$ to $t = 5$ are equal, and nowhere is the area under F greater than the area under G. From $t = 5$ to $t = 12$ the equality between the areas under the distribution functions continues because the two functions coincide once again. On the interval $[12, 16]$ the advantage in terms of the area under the curves is again captured by G and at $t = 16$ this advantage is equal to the area of the rectangle $hijk = (16 - 12)(0.87 - 0.080)$. When t is between 16 and 18, F begins again to progressively nibble away at its 'deficit' and at $t = 18$ equality is once again established since the rectangles $hijk$ and $jlmn$ have the same area but opposite sign. This equality is maintained forever after because, at $t = 18$, the two

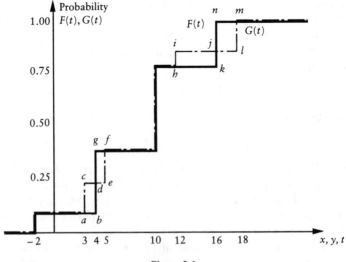

Figure 5.1

distribution functions attain their ceiling of 1 and do not diverge again. They thus coincide until $t = +\infty$, thus accumulating equal area.

The reader no doubt wonders why we linger in discussing the comparison of areas under the distribution functions. It is because we are presenting, with the aid of these calculations, a third method of comparing the level of risk, known by the name of the 'integral condition'. This rather strange term is easily explained if one remembers that a (definite) integral is nothing more than the area under a curve. In this context, it is the area under a distribution function. Since the area under G between a (that is, -2, the smallest possible realisation of $\tilde{y}$) and a certain point, say s, is always at least equal to the area under F between a and s, the 'integral condition' is written as:

$$\int_a^s G(t)\,dt \geqslant \int_a^s F(t)\,dt \qquad \text{for all } s \leqslant b \qquad (5.1)$$

where b is the largest possible value[3] of $\tilde{y}$.

When $s = b$ one necessarily has:

$$\int_a^b G(t)\,dt = \int_a^b F(t)\,dt \qquad (5.2)$$

As shown in Appendix 4, this last equality is fundamentally due to the fact that $E(\tilde{x}) = E(\tilde{y})$. It is proved using the technique of integration by parts.

Before formalising these results for a continuous distribution, we ask the reader to undertake an exercise, the object of which is to illustrate the fact that the notion of 'riskier' is transitive, that is, if random variable $\tilde{z}$ is riskier than $\tilde{y}$ and if $\tilde{y}$ is riskier than $\tilde{x}$ then $\tilde{z}$ is riskier than $\tilde{x}$. To this end assume that the random variable $\tilde{x}$ is characterised as follows:

x	$p(x)$
3	$\frac{1}{3}$
9	$\frac{2}{3}$
	1.00

Now add some noise to each possible outcome of $\tilde{x}$ to generate $\tilde{y}$, for example:

y	$p(y)$
1	$\frac{1}{6}$
5	$\frac{1}{6}$
8	$\frac{1}{3}$
10	$\frac{1}{3}$
	1.00

Finally, add some noise to some of the outcomes of $\tilde{y}$ to define $\tilde{z}$:

z	$p(z)$
1	$\frac{1}{6}$
4	$\frac{1}{12}$
6	$\frac{1}{12}$
7	$\frac{1}{6}$
9	$\frac{1}{6}$
10	$\frac{1}{3}$
	1.00

We now ask the reader to construct three graphs of cumulative distribution functions each comparing one pair of random variables. In the first graph, draw the distribution functions of $\tilde{x}$ and $\tilde{y}$, in the second the distribution functions of $\tilde{y}$ and $\tilde{z}$ and in the third the distribution functions of $\tilde{x}$ and $\tilde{z}$. It will then be easy to verify that in each of these graphs the 'integral conditions' of Equations (5.1) and (5.2) are satisfied and, as is to be expected, $\tilde{z}$ is riskier than $\tilde{y}$, $\tilde{y}$ is riskier than $\tilde{x}$, and $\tilde{z}$ is riskier than $\tilde{x}$.

To verify these relationships in another way, one can take a concave utility function and convince oneself that $E[U(\tilde{x})] > E[U(\tilde{y})] > E[U(\tilde{z})]$. For example, with $U = w_f^{1/2}$ one obtains:

$$E[U(\tilde{x})] = (\tfrac{1}{3})3^{1/2} + (\tfrac{2}{3})9^{1/2} = 2.577\ 35$$
$$E[U(\tilde{y})] = (\tfrac{1}{6})1^{1/2} + (\tfrac{1}{6})5^{1/2} + (\tfrac{1}{3})8^{1/2} + (\tfrac{1}{3})10^{1/2} = 2.536\ 25$$
$$E[U(\tilde{z})] = (\tfrac{1}{6})1^{1/2} + (\tfrac{1}{12})4^{1/2} + \ldots + (\tfrac{1}{3})10^{1/2} = 2.532\ 50$$

If the reader uses other concave functions instead ($\ln w, w - \beta w^2$, $-e^{-\beta w}, w^{1/4}$, etc.) the same relationship will always be found between the expected utilities of $\tilde{x}$, $\tilde{y}$ and $\tilde{z}$.

5.2 Generalisation to continuous distributions

If $\tilde{x}$ is continuous on the interval $[a,b]$ and if one adds white noise $\tilde{\varepsilon}$ such that $E[\tilde{\varepsilon} \mid \tilde{x} = x] = 0$ to some of the realisations of $\tilde{x}$, then a new random variable $\tilde{y}$ is generated. This new random variable $\tilde{y}$ has two properties.

5.2.1 $E(\tilde{y}) = E(\tilde{x})$

From the definition of white noise:

$$E_\varepsilon(x + \tilde{\varepsilon} \mid \tilde{x} = x) = x$$

This relationship holds for all x, so taking the expected value of both sides preserves the equality, that is,

$$E_x[E_\varepsilon(\tilde{x} + \tilde{\varepsilon} \mid \tilde{x})] = E_x(\tilde{x})$$

Applying a fundamental property of conditional expectations,[4] one also obtains

$$E[\tilde{x} + \tilde{\varepsilon}] = E(\tilde{x})$$

and, since $\tilde{y} = \tilde{x} + \tilde{\varepsilon}$, it follows that $E(\tilde{y}) = E(\tilde{x})$.

5.2.2 $\tilde{y}$ is riskier than $\tilde{x}$

This result, which is intuitively appealing, can be verified by showing that all risk-averse decision-makers unanimously prefer $\tilde{x}$ to $\tilde{y}$. Using reasoning similar to that found in Section 2.1, but beginning with Jensen's inequality, we have,

$$E_\varepsilon[U(x + \tilde{\varepsilon} \mid \tilde{x} = x)] \leqslant U(x)$$

since $E(\tilde{\varepsilon}) = 0$ and U is concave. The notation E_ε denotes the expected value with respect to the random variable $\tilde{\varepsilon}$. This inequality holds for all x, so

$$E_x[E_\varepsilon(U(x + \tilde{\varepsilon} \mid \tilde{x}))] \leqslant E_x[U(x)]$$

Applying a property of conditional expectations yields:

$$E[U(\tilde{x} + \tilde{\varepsilon})] \leqslant E[U(\tilde{x})]$$

or, by the definition of $\tilde{y}$,

$$E[U(\tilde{y})] \leqslant E[U(\tilde{x})]$$

In summary of what has been done up to now, it can be said that three definitions of greater risk – all of which are intuitively appealing – are consistent with each other.

1. If all risk-averse agents prefer $\tilde{x}$ to $\tilde{y}$ when the expected returns of the two lotteries are the same $[E(\tilde{x}) = E(\tilde{y})]$, then $\tilde{x}$ must be less risky than $\tilde{y}$.
2. If, when drawing the distribution functions of $\tilde{x}$ and $\tilde{y}$, the cumulative area under $\tilde{y}$ is never less than the cumulative area under $\tilde{x}$ and if, at the extreme point of $\tilde{y}$, the cumulative areas are equal, then $\tilde{y}$ is riskier than $\tilde{x}$.
3. If $\tilde{y}$ is obtained by adding white noise to at least one of the outcomes of $\tilde{x}$, $\tilde{y}$ is riskier than $\tilde{x}$.

In the following section, we suggest another definition that is equally 'plausible' in the sense that it would be acceptable to a person who is not well versed in risk theory and we show – more precisely, we suggest! – that it is also consistent with the preceding definitions.

5.3 The increase in risk viewed as a 'transfer of weight'

In this section, we exploit (yet) another simple idea. It is not hard to believe at an intuitive level that if one removes weight from one part of the density of $\tilde{x}$ [$f(x)$] and places it to the right and left of the interval where it was removed in such a way as to preserve the same expected value, then the new random variable thus defined, $\tilde{y}$, will be riskier than $\tilde{x}$.

To illustrate this, suppose for simplicity that $\tilde{x}$ has a uniform distribution on the interval [0,20] so that $f(x) = 1/20$. To construct $\tilde{y}$ with density function $g(y)$ remove a constant weight α from the interval [6, 10] and place part of it to the left in the interval [2, 4] and part of it to the right in the interval [16, 18]. There is no reason that these intervals should be of the same length or that they should lie in the support[5] of $\tilde{x}$. In contrast, other constraints, which are very binding, must be imposed on the transfer of probability weights.

1. The weight α taken from an interval of $\tilde{x}$ to construct $\tilde{y}$ must not be too large because $g(y)$ must be a density function and so can never take negative values. Since $f(x) = 1/20$ in the interval [6, 10], a first constraint is

$$0 \leqslant \alpha \leqslant \tfrac{1}{20} \tag{5.3}$$

2. Since $g(y)$ is a density function, the weight taken from one part must be compensated by adding weight elsewhere so that

$$\int_0^{20} g(t)\, \mathrm{d}t = \int_0^{20} f(t)\, \mathrm{d}t = 1$$

where t stands for y or x, as appropriate, and represents the values along the horizontal axes of the graphs of the density functions. If the constant weights, say β and γ, are added to the intervals [2, 4] and [16, 18], respectively, then they must satisfy:

$$\int_2^4 \beta\, \mathrm{d}t + \int_{16}^{18} \gamma\, \mathrm{d}t = \int_6^{10} \alpha\, \mathrm{d}t$$

or, after evaluating the integrals and simplifying,

$$\beta + \gamma = 2\alpha \tag{5.4}$$

If β and γ are chosen in this way (with both β and γ strictly positive), $g(y)$ will be a density function as is $f(x)$. Note that the constraints in Equations (5.3) and (5.4) leave many degrees of freedom in the choice of the pair $[\beta, \gamma]$. For example, $[\beta, \gamma] = [\alpha, \alpha]$ or $[\beta, \gamma] = [\alpha/2, 3\alpha/2]$ satisfy the constraints. One might suspect, then, that to determine the pair $[\beta, \gamma]$, another constraint is necessary. It is furnished by equating the expected values of $\tilde{x}$ and $\tilde{y}$.

3. Since we wish to compare risks given a constant expected value, we
    require $E(\tilde{x}) = E(\tilde{y})$. To this end the weights β and γ added to the
    density of $\tilde{y}$ must be exactly compensated by the subtraction of α.
    Mathematically, this condition is:

$$\int_2^4 \beta t \, dt + \int_{16}^{18} \gamma t dt = \int_6^{10} \alpha t dt \qquad (5.5)$$

which, evaluating the integrals, is equivalent to:

$$6\beta + 34\gamma = 32\alpha \qquad (5.6)$$

Combining Equations (5.4) and (5.5) and solving the system of
two linear equations in two unknowns (β and γ) yields:

$$\beta = (\tfrac{9}{7})\alpha \qquad \gamma = (\tfrac{5}{7})\alpha \qquad (5.7)$$

Thus, in the context of the intervals chosen for the example
([2, 4], [6, 10] and [16, 18]), and given α, the values of β and γ given
by Equation (5.7) will generate a random variable $\tilde{y}$ such that
$E(\tilde{x}) = E(\tilde{y})$, and $\tilde{y}$ will be said to be riskier than $\tilde{x}$.

Before convincing the reader that $\tilde{y}$ is indeed riskier than $\tilde{x}$ (a result which
so far is only intuitively plausible), we illustrate the method of constructing $\tilde{y}$
with the help of Figure 5.2.

We chose $\alpha = 1/40$ so that $\beta = 0.032\ 143$ and $\gamma = 0.017\ 857$. The initial
density function (of $\tilde{x}$) is represented by the horizontal line at 2/40. The new
density function (of $\tilde{y}$) of course coincides with the initial density on some

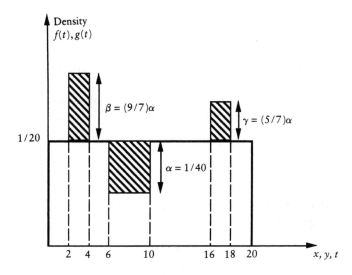

Figure 5.2

intervals, such as [4, 6], but it is distinct from the initial density at the places characterised by a 'hole' and two 'humps'. Note that the new density is not uniform. Note also that if β and γ were not chosen to satisfy Equation (5.4) then $E(\tilde{y})$ would not have been equal to $E(\tilde{x})$. For example, if $\beta = 0.5\alpha$ and $\gamma = 1.5\alpha$ then $\tilde{y}$ is a density function but its expected value exceeds[6] that of $\tilde{x}$ because too much weight is added to large values of t and too little is added to the small values.

Having intuitively presented this new definition of an increase in risk, we must now prove that it 'holds the road' in the sense that it is consistent with the other definitions suggested above. We first establish that all riskophobes ($U' > 0$ and $U'' < 0$) will prefer $\tilde{x}$ to $\tilde{y}$; that is, we prove that $E[U(\tilde{y})] < E[U(\tilde{x})]$ for all strictly increasing concave functions U. To this end, we exploit that fact that $E[U(\tilde{x})]$ and $E[U(\tilde{y})]$ have many common elements (in intervals such as [0, 2], [4, 6], etc.) and we express only their difference, that is,

$$E[U(\tilde{y})] - E[U(\tilde{x})] = \int_2^4 (\tfrac{9}{7})\alpha U(t) \, dt + \int_{16}^{18} (\tfrac{5}{7})\alpha U(t) \, dt - \int_6^{10} \alpha U(t) \, dt$$

or equivalently, noting that

$$\int_{2+e}^{4+e} U(t) \, dt = \int_2^4 U(t+e) \, dt$$

for all $e > 0$,

$$E[U(\tilde{y})] - E[U(\tilde{x})]$$

$$= \int_2^4 \{(\tfrac{9}{7})\alpha U(t) + (\tfrac{5}{7})\alpha U(t+14) - \alpha U(t+4) - \alpha U(t+6)\} \, dt$$

To prove that this expression is negative when U is concave, it is sufficient to show that the integrand is negative for all t between 2 and 4. To illustrate this result, we graphically represent the situation for some concave utility function and consider, without loss of generality, $t = 3$. The bracketed expression is thus:

$$(\tfrac{9}{7})\alpha a + (\tfrac{5}{7})\alpha b - \alpha[c' + d']$$

where a, b, c' and d' are the vertical co-ordinates of the points appearing in Figure 5.3. To prove that this expression is negative, we show that another, necessarily larger expression,[7]

$$(\tfrac{9}{7})\alpha a + (\tfrac{5}{7})\alpha b - \alpha[c + d] \tag{5.8}$$

is zero.

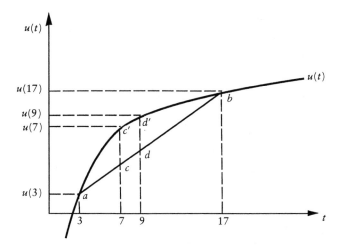

Figure 5.3

This is easy to prove using the fact that c and d lie on the line ab whose slope is $(b - a)/14$. This allows us to write Equation (5.8) as:

$$(\tfrac{9}{7})\alpha a + (\tfrac{5}{7})\alpha b - \alpha \left[\left(a + 4\,\frac{(b-a)}{14} \right) + \left(a + 6\,\frac{(b-a)}{14} \right) \right]$$

which simplifies to zero.

Of course this proof applies to any value of t, so if U is concave then the 'transfer of weight' described here indeed results in increased risk.

For the benefit of the sceptical reader (which in this context is an admirable quality) we now show that the transformation of $\tilde{x}$ to $\tilde{y}$ also satisfies the integral condition. To this end we draw the distribution functions of $\tilde{x}$ and $\tilde{y}$ in Figure 5.4.

The distribution function of $\tilde{x}$ corresponds to the thick line drawn in bold from $t = 0$ to $t = 20$. The distribution function of $\tilde{y}$ coincides with that of $\tilde{x}$ until $t = 2$. From that point the slope of G becomes steeper because

$$g(y) = \mathrm{d}G/\mathrm{d}y = (1/20) + (9/280)$$

is greater than

$$f(x) = \mathrm{d}F/\mathrm{d}x = 1/20$$

Between $t = 4$ and $t = 6$ the slopes are once again equal since $f = g = 1/20$ and then the slope of G becomes smaller from $t = 6$. Between $t = 6$ and $t = 10$, G intersects F because at $t = 10$, $G(10)$ is less than $F(10)$. From $t = 10$, G and F have the same slope. At $t = 16$, the slope of G is greater than that of F so that at $t = 16$ the curves G and F can once again coincide.

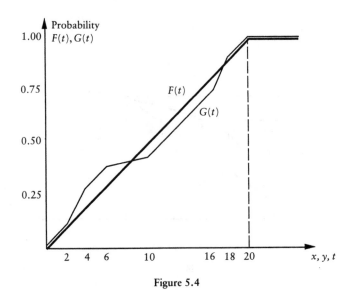

Figure 5.4

With a little patience, we can easily show that:

(a) for all $0 \leqslant t \leqslant 20$, the cumulative area under G is never smaller than the cumulative area under F – in some sense the lead gained by the area under F after $t = 2$ is never overcome by the area under F;
(b) at $t = 20$ (and thereafter) the cumulative areas under the two curves are equal.

Of course the reader recognises the characteristics of the integral condition previously presented, and this confirms again – if it is necessary – that the intuition underlying the definition of an increase in risk by the transfer of weight is well founded.

Before offering a brief summary, we present another example suggested by the excellent article of J. Meyer and M. Ormiston (1985) which we will study more deeply in Part Two. Let $f(x) = 1/20$ for $0 \leqslant x \leqslant 20$ as before. If we remove a thickness of $1/80$ everywhere between 0 and 20, and if we transfer this weight symmetrically to the two extremes of the density of $\tilde{x}$ then a new random variable $\tilde{z}$ is defined which is clearly riskier than $\tilde{x}$. Specifically, weight has been transferred from the interior to the exterior of the density as illustrated in Figure 5.5a. The distribution functions, represented in Figure 5.5, confirm that $\tilde{z}$ is indeed riskier than $\tilde{x}$.

Since the areas under the distribution functions are easily evaluated, we characterise them explicitly in order to make clear the equivalence between the

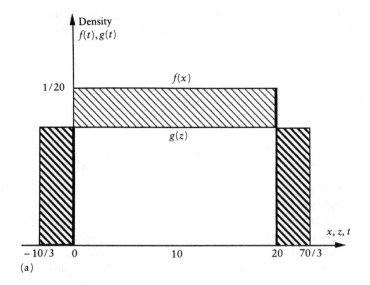

(a)

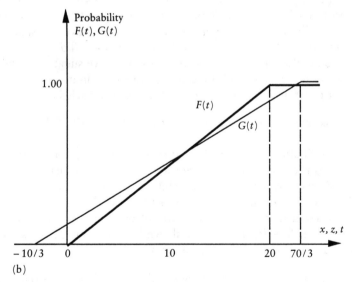

(b)

Figure 5.5

'transfer of weight' and the integral condition. Given that f and g are constant, the equations for F and G are linear:

$$F = (1/20)x \qquad \text{for } 0 \leqslant x \leqslant 20$$

and

$$G = 10/80 + (3/80)z \qquad \text{for } -10/3 \leqslant z \leqslant 70/3$$

The areas under the distribution functions are definite integrals of first-degree polynomials, and thus fundamentally second-degree polynomials, namely,

$$\int_0^s \frac{1}{20} t \, dt = \frac{1}{40} s^2$$

and

$$\int_{-10/3}^s \left(\frac{10}{80} + \frac{3}{80} t \right) dt = \frac{3}{160} s^2 + \frac{10}{80} s + \frac{100}{480}$$

It is thus easy to verify that, for all s between $-10/3$ and $+70/3$, the area under G exceeds the area under F. As an example, if $s = 18$ then the cumulative area under G is $4096/480$ while that under F is only $3888/480$.

For simplicity, we illustrated the Meyer–Ormiston definition in a situation where the initial distribution (of $\tilde{x}$) and the final distribution (of $\tilde{z}$) were uniform. In reality, the definition holds as long as the weight taken from the interior of the support of $\tilde{x}$ is transferred to the exterior or the boundary of the support (see Chapter 9) while preserving the expected value. It is thus not necessary that the initial and final random variables have the same type of distribution for the Meyer–Ormiston definition to be valid.

More generally, and by way of summary, we have suggested[8] above that there are several plausible and, indeed, equivalent, definitions of an increase in risk with constant expected value. These are, in conclusion:

1. If all risk-averse agents prefer $\tilde{x}$ to $\tilde{y}$ with $E(\tilde{x}) = E(\tilde{y})$ then $\tilde{y}$ is riskier than $\tilde{x}$.
2. If the distribution function of $\tilde{y}$ satisfies the 'integral conditions' relative to the distribution function of $\tilde{x}$ then $\tilde{y}$ is riskier than $\tilde{x}$.
3. If $\tilde{y}$ is derived from $\tilde{x}$ by adding white noise $\tilde{\varepsilon}$ such that $E(\tilde{\varepsilon} \mid \tilde{x} = x) = 0$ for all x, then $\tilde{y}$ is riskier than $\tilde{x}$.
4. If $\tilde{y}$ is derived from $\tilde{x}$ by a succession of transfers of weight from an interval to each side of the interval (while maintaining a constant expected value) then $\tilde{y}$ is riskier than $\tilde{x}$.

These conditions satisfy transitivity in the sense that if $\tilde{y}$ is riskier than $\tilde{x}$ and $\tilde{z}$ is riskier than $\tilde{y}$, then $\tilde{y}$ is riskier than $\tilde{x}$.

5.4 And the variance?

Having described the modern approaches to the notion of 'greater risk', we now return to the notion of variance which, historically, preceded it. The situation can be summarised in two statements.

1. Greater risk, as described in Sections 5.1, 5.2 and 5.3, necessarily implies higher variance. To show this it is sufficient to consider the 'white noise' approach. Since $\tilde{y} = \tilde{x} + \tilde{\varepsilon}$ and $E(\tilde{\varepsilon} \mid \tilde{x} = x) = 0$ for all x, the covariance between $\tilde{\varepsilon}$ and $\tilde{x}$ is zero, and thus:

$$\mathrm{Var}(\tilde{y}) = \mathrm{Var}(\tilde{x}) + \mathrm{Var}(\tilde{\varepsilon})$$

So $\mathrm{Var}(\tilde{y})$ exceeds $\mathrm{Var}(\tilde{x})$.

2. Greater variance need not imply greater risk. For an increase in variance to always imply an increase in risk, the third derivative of the utility function must be zero[9] (so that all higher order derivatives are also zero). This can be illustrated by comparing two lotteries with the same expected value (say zero[10]) for a risk-averse individual endowed with certain wealth of w_0, using for each lottery the second-order expansion:

$$E[U(w_0 + \tilde{x})] = U(w_0) + (\sigma_{\tilde{x}}^2/2) U''(w_0)$$
$$E[U(w_0 + \tilde{y})] = U(w_0) + (\sigma_{\tilde{y}}^2/2) U''(w_0)$$

Since the derivatives of order greater than or equal to 3 are all zero, these formulas are exact and the negativity of U'' immediately implies:

$$\sigma_{\tilde{x}}^2 < \sigma_{\tilde{y}}^2 \quad \text{if and only if} \quad E[U(w_0 + \tilde{x})] > E[U(w_0 + \tilde{y})]$$

where the right-hand inequality corresponds to the general notion of comparing risks.

In fact, we see reflected here, in a somewhat more elegant form, the result stated at the beginning of the chapter: that variance is a perfect indicator of risk when individuals are characterised by quadratic utility. In these cases derivatives of third order and higher are all zero.

When the third- (and/or higher) order derivatives are not zero, the expansions of expected utility contain higher moments than that of second order (such as $E(\tilde{x}^3)$) and then the sign of $\sigma_{\tilde{x}}^2 - \sigma_{\tilde{y}}^2$ is insufficient to determine that of $E[U(w_0 + \tilde{x})] - E[U(w_0 + \tilde{y})]$. A very interesting example is furnished by J. E. Ingersoll Jr. (1987):

x	$p(x)$	y	$p(y)$
0	0.50	+1	$\frac{7}{8}$
+4	0.50	+9	$\frac{1}{8}$

These two lotteries have the same expected value and $\sigma_{\tilde{y}}^2 > \sigma_{\tilde{x}}^2$. Nevertheless, if $U(w_f) = (w_f)^{1/2}$, it is easy to show that $E[U(w_0 + \tilde{y})]$ is greater than $E[U(w_0 + \tilde{x})]$. The reason can be seen immediately by noticing that with $U = (w_f)^{1/2}$ both U''' and U'''' are non-zero. Now these probability distributions have different coefficients of *skewness* and *kurtosis*; for example, the distribution of $\tilde{y}$ is very asymmetric while that of $\tilde{x}$ is not. Thus the higher order terms intervene and overturn the ranking that results from the variance.

This chapter essentially concludes the first part, but there remain two steps that complement what has been done so far:

1. In Chapter 6 we mention some potential extensions to which we will allude in later parts.
2. In Chapter 7 we describe a different approach to the notions seen so far. This other approach has two advantages: it allows a better grasp of the basic concepts and it is often used in certain applications linked above all to the study of risk-sharing.

Exercises

5.1 Besides a certain wealth of 100, A owns one house the value of which is 80. The probability of full loss (due to fire) for this house is equal to 0.10 for a given time period and A has no access to an insurance market. In the absence of fire the value of the house remains equal to its initial value. B has the same initial wealth but owns two houses valued at 40 for each. The probability of full loss for each house is 0.10 and the fires are assumed to be independent random variables (e.g. because one house is in Provo (Utah) and the other one in East-Lansing (Michigan)).

Questions
(a) Draw the cumulative distribution functions of final wealth for A and B and compute the expected final wealth for each of them.
(b) Can you show with the help of the integral condition that A has a riskier portfolio of houses (because it is less diversified)?

5.2 Convince yourself that A is in a riskier position by drawing the distribution function of final wealth for A and B and by showing that B can be obtained from A through a shift from the tails of B towards the centre.

You can get the same conviction by selecting three (or more!) concave utility functions and computing the expected utility for A and B. If you do not make mistakes, the expected utility of B must be systematically higher than that of A for each utility curve you have selected.

5.3[11] A has a certain wealth of 100 and owns N houses each of value L with the probability of full loss equal to p. The losses are independent random variables. B has the same initial wealth and owns N' houses of values L' such that $N'L' = NL$. The probability of full loss is also p.

Show that if N is smaller than N', A has a riskier situation (with the same expected final wealth). The basic reason for this outcome is that A's portfolio of houses is less diversified. (You will find in Rothschild–Stiglitz (1971) a nice proof of the intuitive fact that 'diversification pays' for those who are risk averse.)

5.4 Among others, J. Hadar and W. Russell (1969) have generalised the notion of 'greater risk' by allowing the mean not to be preserved: $\tilde{x}$ is 'second-degree stochastically dominated' by $\tilde{y}$ ($\tilde{y}$ SSD $\tilde{x}$) if all risk-averse individuals prefer $\tilde{y}$ to $\tilde{x}$.

Questions
(a) Show that a necessary condition for $\tilde{y}$ SSD $\tilde{x}$ is $E\tilde{x} \leqslant E\tilde{y}$.
    Hint: Consider the limiting case of a risk-neutral agent.
(b) Show that $\tilde{y}$ SSD $\tilde{x}$ if and only if $\tilde{x}$ is obtained from $\tilde{y}$ by the combination of a mean-preserving increase in risk and a sure reduction in pay-off.
    Hint: Sufficiency is obvious: necessity is shown by contradiction.

5.5 Suppose that you have the opportunity to gamble in a lottery $\tilde{x}$. The price of a ticket is 10. There is a potential gross pay-off of 110, with probability 0.10 and of 0 with probability 0.90.

Questions
(a) Will all riskophobes accept the gamble? To answer the question, show that the lottery $\tilde{x}$ is not second-degree stochastically dominated by the degenerate random variable $\tilde{y}$ that takes value 0 with probability 1 (that is, the pay-off if you do not gamble).
(b) Find a concave utility function U such that gambling is preferred (i.e. $EU(\tilde{x}) > U(0)$).
(c) Find a concave utility function V such that $\tilde{x}$ is rejected (i.e. $EV(\tilde{x}) < V(0)$). Do we necessarily have that V is more risk-averse than U?
(d) This is an open question: suppose that you are individual V and you prefer not to play the lottery. Would you nevertheless accept a gamble on 100 independent replicas of $\tilde{x}$? Some, as risk-managers and academicians, would invoke the law of large numbers to accept the deal. This is the famous 'Fallacy of the law of Large Numbers'. 'It is not by adding i.i.d. risks but rather by subdividing i.i.d. risks that one diversifies the aggregate risk.' (For more details, see Samuelson (1963), and Pratt and Zeckhauser (1987).

Notes

1. In asking the question in this way, we admit that the comparison is ordinal. There does not exist a measure of the intensity of change but only of its direction.

2. The area of *abcd* is $(4 - 3)(0.24 - 0.09) = 0.15$ and it is to G's advantage. The area of *defg* is $(5 - 4)(0.39 = 0.24) = 0.15$ and it is to F's advantage.

3. Since $\tilde{y}$ is riskier than $\tilde{x}$ its extreme values are at least as extreme as those of $\tilde{x}$, that is, $\text{Max}\{\tilde{x}\} \leqslant \text{Max}\{\tilde{y}\}$ and $\text{Min}\{\tilde{x}\} \geqslant \text{Min}\{\tilde{y}\}$.

4. This property is stated as follows: for two random variables (say $\tilde{j}$ and $\tilde{k}$) $E_{\tilde{j}}[E_{\tilde{k}}(\tilde{k} \mid \tilde{j})] = E(\tilde{k})$.

5. Indeed, we will later consider situations where the weight taken from the interior of the support of $\tilde{x}$ is placed outside of the initial support of $\tilde{x}$.

6. It is easy to show that in this case:

$$E(\tilde{y}) = E(\tilde{x}) + \int_{2}^{4} (1/20)t \ dt - \int_{6}^{10} (1/40)t \ dt + \int_{16}^{18} (3/80)t \ dt$$

$$= 10.8 > E(\tilde{x}) = 10.$$

7. It is larger because the terms affected by the negative sign are smaller in absolute value.

8. A rigorous proof of these results is furnished by Rothschild and Stiglitz (1970) but it is difficult. We hope that our examples give the reader sufficient intuition to accept as 'truth' our incomplete proofs.

9. We consider here restrictions on U. Restrictions on the density function $[f(x)]$ can also be considered: when comparing two normal distributions or two uniform distributions, variance is always a perfect indicator of risk.

10. If the expected value were not zero then the expansion below would be around $w_0 + E(\tilde{x}) = w_0 + E(\tilde{y})$.

11. This exercise is technically more difficult and can be skipped. It generalises the two previous ones.

References

Hadar J. and W. Russell (1969), Rules for ordering uncertain prospects, *American Economic Review*, vol. 59, 25–34.

Ingersoll J.E. Jr. (1987), *Theory of Financial Decision Making*, Rowman and Littlefield, Savage, Maryland. See especially Chapter 5, pp. 114–139.

Meyer J. and M. Ormiston (1985), Strong increases in risk and their comparative statics, *International Economic Review*, vol. 26, 425–437.

Pratt J. and R. Zeckhauser (1987), Proper risk aversion, *Econometrica*, vol. 55, 143–54.

Rothschild M. and J. Stiglitz (1970), Increasing risk: I. A definition, *Journal of Economic Theory*, vol. 2, 225–243.

Rothschild M. and J. Stiglitz (1971), Increasing risk: II. Its economic consequences, *Journal of Economic Theory*, vol. 3, 66–84.

Samuelson L.A. (1963), Risk and uncertainty: A fallacy of large numbers, *Scientia*, vol. 98, 108–13.

6 A smorgasbord of subjects

6.1 First-order stochastic dominance

Stochastic dominance is an important notion not only in risk theory but more generally in economic analysis because it is directly related to efficiency measures in the theory of production.

Just as Monsieur Jourdain[1] wrote prose, we have implicitly broached questions of stochastic dominance without saying so, especially in Chapter 5. Specifically, in that chapter we compared probability distributions with the same expected value and found conditions under which all decision-makers characterised by a utility function exhibiting $U' > 0$ and $U'' < 0$ would be unanimous in preferring one lottery to another. In that chapter are all the basic ingredients of a stochastic dominance relationship: one focuses on a 'class' of decision-makers and examines the properties of the lotteries (or classes of lotteries) that guarantee the unanimity of preferences on the part of those decision-makers.

In this section, we will essentially discuss one of the notions of stochastic dominance, that said to be of first order, and at the end of the section we rapidly mention second-order stochastic dominance.

The question posed in the context of first-order stochastic dominance is the following: when faced with two lotteries which do not necessarily have the same expected value,[2] under what conditions can one say that all decision-makers exhibiting $U' > 0$ will unanimously prefer one of the two lotteries? Note that we are considering a larger class of decision-makers than in Chapter 5 because here we allow U'' to have either sign, that is, we also consider 'risk-loving' agents. To introduce the notion precisely, consider three lotteries $\tilde{x}$, $\tilde{y}$, and $\tilde{z}$ defined as follows:

\multicolumn{2}{c}{$\tilde{x}$}		\multicolumn{2}{c}{$\tilde{y}$}		\multicolumn{2}{c}{$\tilde{z}$}	
x	$p(x)$	y	$p(y)$	z	$p(z)$
+6	0.2	+6	0.1	+7	0.2
+10	0.5	+10	0.4	+13	0.5
+14	0.3	+14	0.5	+16	0.3

If we compare $\tilde{x}$ and $\tilde{y}$, which have the same possible outcomes, we note that $\tilde{y}$ is derived from $\tilde{x}$ by taking part of the probability assigned to the relatively poor outcomes ($+6$ and $+10$) and transferring it to the best outcome ($+14$) which is thus more likely to be realised under lottery $\tilde{y}$. It is natural to guess that any decision-maker who 'prefers more to less' ($U' > 0$) will feel that the change from $\tilde{x}$ to $\tilde{y}$ is to their advantage and thus it is said that $\tilde{y}$ dominates $\tilde{x}$ in the sense of first-order stochastic dominance; this is denoted $\tilde{y} >_1 \tilde{x}$.

The comparison of $\tilde{x}$ and $\tilde{z}$ leads to a similar conclusion. Moving from $\tilde{x}$ to $\tilde{z}$ does not entail any change in the probabilities, but a positive number is added to each possible outcome of $\tilde{x}$. Once again, anyone who prefers more to less will inevitably declare that this change improves their welfare, so one can write $\tilde{z} >_1 \tilde{x}$.

The distribution functions of $\tilde{x}$, $\tilde{y}$ and $\tilde{z}$ are shown in Figure 6.1a and b, where it is clear that for all t in the support of the random variables we have:

$$F(t) \geqslant G(t)$$

$$F(t) \geqslant H(t)$$

where F, G and H are the distribution functions of the random variables $\tilde{x}$, $\tilde{y}$ and $\tilde{z}$, respectively. This is not an accident: indeed we have just illustrated the general notion of first-order stochastic dominance that is stated in the following theorem.

Theorem 6.1 All decision-makers with increasing utility functions unanimously prefer $\tilde{y}$ to $\tilde{x}$ if and only if, for all t in the support of $\tilde{x}$ and $\tilde{y}$,

$$F(t) \geqslant G(t) \tag{6.1}$$

with strict inequality for at least one value of t, where F and G are the cumulative distribution functions of the random variables $\tilde{x}$ and $\tilde{y}$.

We will soon prove this important theorem. First, we explain why the result is a sensible one. When Equation (6.1) holds, one can write:

$$1 - F(t) \leqslant 1 - G(t)$$

or

$$\text{Prob}\{\tilde{x} \geqslant t\} \leqslant \text{Prob}\{\tilde{y} \geqslant t\}$$

This means that the probability of receiving more than any given outcome is higher for random variable $\tilde{y}$ than for random variable $\tilde{x}$. It follows that any individual exhibiting $U' > 0$ will prefer $\tilde{y}$ because it increases the likelihood of better outcomes.

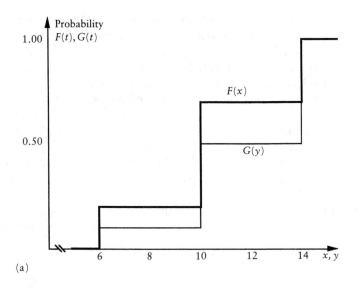

(a)

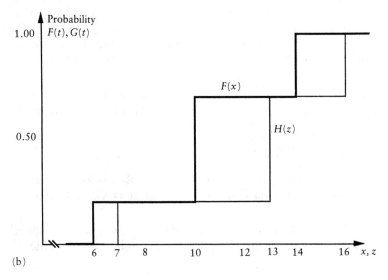

(b)

Figure 6.1

The formal proof of Theorem 6.1 is accomplished in two steps.

1. It is first shown that if $F(t) \geqslant G(t)$ then, for any utility function U such that $U' > 0$, $\tilde{y}$ is preferred to $\tilde{x}$ by the expected utility criterion. If $\tilde{y}$ is preferred to $\tilde{x}$ by this criterion, that is, if:

$$E[U(\tilde{y})] > E[U(\tilde{x})]$$

then, equivalently,

$$\int_a^b U(t)\,[\,g(t) - f(t)]\,\mathrm{d}t > 0 \tag{6.2}$$

where the limits of integration correspond to the smallest value (a) and the largest value (b) taken on by the random variables $\tilde{x}$ and $\tilde{y}$.

Applying the principles of integration by parts to Condition (6.2) it becomes:

$$U(t)\,[\,G(t) - F(t)]_a^b - \int_a^b U'(t)\,[\,G(t) - F(t)]\,\mathrm{d}t > 0 \tag{6.2a}$$

Given[3] that $G(b) = F(b) = 1$ and that $G(a) = F(a) = 0$, it is clear that Condition (6.2a) holds if, for all t, $F(t)$ is at least equal to $G(t)$ with strict inequality for at least one value of t.

2. Next it is shown that if all individuals with increasing utility prefer $\tilde{y}$ to $\tilde{x}$, then $F(t) - G(t) > 0$ for all t.

The proof is by contradiction. It is shown that, if $F(t) < G(t)$ on some interval, then it is possible to find an individual with increasing utility who prefers $\tilde{x}$ to $\tilde{y}$. To construct such an example it is sufficient to choose a utility function that increases slowly (U' small) except in the interval where $G(t)$ exceeds $F(t)$, where U' takes on very large values. Under these conditions, it is clear that $E[U(\tilde{y})]$ can be less than $E[U(\tilde{x})]$.

At this stage of the discussion it is important to note that many distributions cannot be compared using the first-order stochastic dominance criterion. Thus, if one were to draw the distribution functions of random variables $\tilde{y}$ and $\tilde{z}$ described above in a graph similar to Figure 6.1a or b, one would see that neither dominates the other in the sense of first-order stochastic dominance. Specifically, since the distribution functions intersect, it is impossible to assert that one is always at least as large as the other, and thus neither function has first-order stochastic dominance over the other. This means that within the large set of decision-makers who 'prefer more to less' ($U' > 0$) some will manifest a preference for $\tilde{y}$ while others will reveal an inclination towards $\tilde{z}$.

This discussion highlights the method of comparing two lotteries in terms of first-order stochastic dominance by drawing their distribution functions and comparing them. Although this operation is easy for lotteries such as those presented in this chapter, it can be tedious for other probability distributions. For this reason one must define necessary conditions under which one lottery dominates another in the first-order sense. One such necessary condition is presented in Theorem 6.2.

Theorem 6.2 For a random variable $\tilde{y}$ to dominate another $\tilde{x}$ in the sense of first-order stochastic dominance, it is necessary (but not sufficient) that $E(\tilde{y}) > E(\tilde{x})$.

Proof Since $\tilde{y}$ dominates $\tilde{x}$, the expected utility of $\tilde{y}$ is greater than the expected utility of $\tilde{x}$ for any increasing utility function. This is true in particular for the function $U(t) = t$. One can thus deduce in this special case that:

$$E(\tilde{y}) = \int_a^b yg(y)\, dy = \int_a^b U(y)g(y)\, dy$$

$$> \int_a^b U(x)f(x)\, dx = \int_a^b xf(x)\, dx = E(\tilde{x})$$

Q.E.D.

This theorem can be equivalently stated as follows: if a random variable has a smaller expected value than another then it cannot possibly dominate it in the sense of first-order stochastic dominance. If one considers a given lottery $\tilde{y}$ and represents the set of other lotteries in the rectangular diagram A, one can divide A into two disjoint sets (see Figure 6.2). The set on the left, denoted B, contains all lotteries with expected value less than that of $\tilde{y}$. Its complement, denoted C (and shaded) contains all lotteries with expected value greater than $E(\tilde{y})$. The border between the two contains the lotteries with the same expected value of $\tilde{y}$. Then the set of lotteries that dominate $\tilde{y}$ in the sense of first-order stochastic dominance are found in the subset of C denoted D. Similarly, there is a subset of B, denoted E, that contains the lotteries dominated by $\tilde{y}$. This partition of the set of lotteries illustrates that condition $E(\tilde{y}) > E(\tilde{x})$ is necessary but not sufficient for $\tilde{y} >_1 \tilde{x}$.

In Part Two, we consider a special case of first-order stochastic dominance, namely, the case that results from the uniform translation of

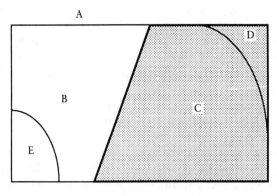

Figure 6.2

probability distributions. To illustrate this case here, we consider a random variable $\tilde{x}$ that can be written as follows:

$$\tilde{x} = E(\tilde{x}) + \tilde{\varepsilon}$$

where $\tilde{\varepsilon}$ represents the random component of $\tilde{x}$ and has zero expected value while $E(\tilde{x})$ represents the central tendency of $\tilde{x}$.

If another random variable $\tilde{y}$ can be written as:

$$\tilde{y} = E(\tilde{y}) + \tilde{\varepsilon}$$

then $\tilde{y}$ and $\tilde{x}$ only differ in their central tendencies. If $E(\tilde{y}) > E(\tilde{x})$, the difference $E(\tilde{y}) - E(\tilde{x})$ reflects the size of the uniform displacement of $\tilde{x}$ to the right that is necessary to generate $\tilde{y}$. It is then clear that $\tilde{y} >_1 \tilde{x}$. Specifically,

$$F(t) = \text{Prob}\{\tilde{x} \leqslant t\} = \text{Prob}\{\tilde{\varepsilon} \leqslant t - E(\tilde{x})\}$$

and

$$G(t) = \text{Prob}\{\tilde{y} \leqslant t\} = \{\tilde{\varepsilon} \leqslant t - E(\tilde{y})\}$$

Since by assumption $E(\tilde{y}) > E(\tilde{x})$, $t - E(\tilde{y}) < t - E(\tilde{x})$ for all t, which implies that $\text{Prob}\{\tilde{\varepsilon} < t - E(\tilde{y})\} \leqslant \text{Prob}\{\tilde{\varepsilon} < t - E(\tilde{x})\}$ and thus $G(t) \leqslant F(t)$. It also follows, as predicted, that the first order-stochastic dominance relationship favours $\tilde{y}$.

Before concluding this section dedicated to first-order stochastic dominance, we point out that there are also concepts of second- and third-order stochastic dominance in the literature. We do not treat them in this textbook because we really only need a special case of second-order stochastic dominance that has already been mentioned, the one defined by an increase in risk at a constant mean. This is actually the case of second-order stochastic dominance restricted to probability distributions having the same expected value. (See Exercises 5.4 and 5.5 for an illustration of second-order stochastic dominance when expected values are not equal.)

6.2 The notion of prudence

A significant part of the preceding chapters was dedicated to the notions of certainty equivalence and risk premium. These are based in a sense on the idea of compensation: if an individual takes on a risk, how much monetary compensation is necessary in order to maintain the same welfare? This question was easily answered by equalising the total utility and/or total expected utility before and after the liquidation of a lottery. Until now our attention has been focused on the total utility one wished to preserve by monetary compensation. This approach will be seen to be very useful in Part Two for the comparative static analysis of elementary risk management problems. We will show that the notions of absolute and relative risk aversion[4] which follow from an initial equality between total utilities, can make sense of many comparative statics results which would otherwise remain ambiguous.

It turns out, however, that in more complex problems, these notions are no longer sufficient, especially when there are multiple risks. In these cases one must apply not only the risk premium but also the prudence premium proposed by M. Kimball (1990) in an article dedicated to savings choices and applied similarly to the problem of multiple risks by Eeckhoudt and Kimball (1991).

The intuition underlying the notion of prudence can be stated as follows. In the decision problems that arise in all economic analysis, marginal notions play a much more important role than do their average or total analogues. So instead of asking about the effect of lotteries in terms of total utility, we will ask the same question in terms of marginal utilities.

If a decision-maker is endowed with w_0 and $\tilde{x}$, the expected marginal utility is $E[U'(w_0 + \tilde{x})]$. To see how $\tilde{x}$ affects this marginal utility, compare this quantity to the marginal utility obtained in the absence of $\tilde{x}$, that is, $U'(w_0)$. If, for simplicity, it is assumed that $\tilde{x}$ is actuarially fair,[5] then Jensen's inequality implies:

$$E[U'(w_0 + \tilde{x})] > U'(w_0)$$

if U' is convex and

$$E[U'(w_0 + \tilde{x})] < U'(w_0)$$

if U' is concave. If U' is linear, the actuarially neutral lottery does not affect marginal utility. In contrast, if U' is convex (concave) then the addition of lottery $\tilde{x}$ increases (reduces) marginal expected utility.

It is very natural to ask what sum of money, denoted ψ, is necessary to maintain the same level of marginal utility when the individual gives up the lottery. Formally, ψ is defined by:

$$U'(w_0 - \psi(w_0, \tilde{x})) = E[U'(w_0 + \tilde{x})] \tag{6.3}$$

where it is assumed without loss of generality that $E(\tilde{x}) = 0$.

While π indicates how much the individual must be compensated to maintain welfare, that is, total utility, ψ measures the compensation that preserves the same expected marginal utility. Since expected marginal utility directly affects choices (in contrast to total utility which explains preferences) the prudence premium permits definition of the monetary compensation that must be granted to risk-averse decision-makers so that their decision will remain unchanged when the uncertainty of the environment is modified. This tool along with the more classical notions of risk premium and risk aversion is very useful for comparative static analysis.

The prudence premium has several desirable properties. We mention two here.

The first is derived by decomposing ψ into its component parts in the same way that we previously decomposed π. To this end, we apply a Taylor series approximation to each side of Equation (6.3), to the first order on the left-hand side and to the second order on the right-hand side. Using techniques that the reader by now understands well, we derive:

$$\psi \cong (\tfrac{1}{2})\sigma_x^2(-U'''(w_0)/U''(w_0)) \tag{6.4}$$

where the expression in parentheses is called the degree of absolute prudence (DAP). For a risk-averse individual ($U'' < 0$) prudence will be positive (negative) if U''' is positive (negative). Thus, there is a behavioural interpretation of the sign of the third derivative of utility: a positive third derivative of U corresponds to prudent behaviour.[6] Note that if U is quadratic then $U''' = 0$, which implies that expected marginal utility is not affected by an increase in risk given a constant mean. Thus an individual exhibiting utility of this type is made worse off by an actuarially neutral lottery ($\pi > 0$) but is not willing to take action, such as precautionary saving, as a result.

A second property of ψ deals with its relationship to π. It is stated here as a theorem.

Theorem 6.3 If the risk premium π is positive and decreasing in w (Hypothesis 4.1) then $\psi > \pi$.

Before proving this theorem, we note that it highlights an important fact: given a perfectly reasonable assumption on the behaviour of π (Hypothesis 4.1), the monetary sum ψ exceeds π and thus, in financial terms, prudence is as important to consider as risk aversion. Indeed, the small amount of space dedicated in this textbook to the notion of prudence is due only to the newness of the concept in literature.

Proof Consider an actuarially fair lottery $\tilde{x}$. Using the definitions of risk premium, asking price and certainty equivalent, we can write:

$$U[w_0 - \pi(w_0, \tilde{x})] = E[U(w_0 + \tilde{x})] \tag{6.5}$$

where the risk premium is denoted $\pi(w_0, \tilde{x})$ to reflect that it depends both on w_0 and the properties of $\tilde{x}$.

Differentiating each side of Equation (6.5) with respect to w_0 yields:

$$(1 - \partial\pi/\partial w_0)U'(w_0 - \pi) = E[U'(w_0 + \tilde{x})] \tag{6.6}$$

and from Equation (6.3), one can equivalently write:

$$(1 - \partial\pi/\partial w_0)U'(w_0 - \pi) = U'(w_0 - \psi(w_0, \tilde{x})) \tag{6.6a}$$

where it should be noted that the number ψ – like π – depends on w_0 and the properties of lottery $\tilde{x}$.

If $\partial \pi / \partial w_0$ is negative (Hypothesis 4.1), then it obviously follows that $1 - \partial \pi / \partial w_0$ exceeds 1 and thus:

$$U'(w_0 - \psi(w_0, \tilde{x})) > U'(w_0 - \pi(w_0, \tilde{x}))$$

Since marginal utility is decreasing for a risk-averse individual, it follows that:

$$w_0 - \psi < w_0 - \pi$$

and thus that $\psi > \pi$. Q.E.D.

Of course it is easy to show that if π is increasing in w (increasing absolute risk aversion in wealth) then $\psi < \pi$. We implicitly provided an example above when remarking that $\psi = 0$ for a quadratic utility because – as we know – π exceeds zero for this utility function.

At this stage the reader is undoubtedly somewhat sceptical as to the importance of this concept. It is right to be sceptical: its importance (as is the case with all of the concepts presented here) will not be apparent until Parts Two and Three. More specifically, the prudence premium and its properties will be examined in Part Two when we discuss the effect of a non-insurable external risk on the demand for insurance for a good that can be covered by an adequate insurance policy.

6.3 Machina's triangle

Machina's triangle[7] is an ingenious graphical tool that allows characterisation of the essential difference between the expected utility model and its successors, the 'non-expected utility models'. Furthermore, it yields new and interesting insights into the results achieved within the framework of the expected utility model. It thus turns out that 'Machina's triangle' allows us to summarise in a few pages the large number of notions so far seen. This section will also play the role of synthesising the previous ones.

More precisely, we will compare lotteries exhibiting three monetary outcomes, W_1, W_2 and W_3 such that $W_1 < W_2 < W_3$. This triple of outcomes will never change in the course of analysis and thus the lotteries will differ only in the probabilities (p_1, p_2, p_3) they assign to the three outcomes. Since $p_1 + p_2 + p_3 = 1$, it follows that in Figure 6.3, where the horizontal and vertical axes are respectively labelled p_1 and p_3, the p_2 associated with any point of the triangle $0ab$ can be inferred. As a result, each point of the triangle – for example, c – represents a triple of probabilities, for example, $p_1 = 0.40$, $p_2 = 0.30$, $p_3 = 0.30$.

Of course along ab (the 'eastern' border of the triangle) p_2 is zero, while at the origin $p_2 = 1$. Also note that p_2 is constant along each line that is parallel to ab. Thus, along ed, p_2 is always equal to 0.3 while the change in

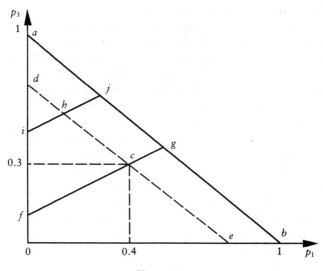

Figure 6.3

p_1 is exactly compensated by a contrary change in p_3 because the slopes of ab and ed are -1. It follows that $dp_2 = 0$ along ed. Specifically, since $p_2 = 1 - (p_1 + p_3)$, we have:

$$dp_2 = 0 - (dp_1 + dp_3) \qquad (6.7)$$

and given that dp_1 and dp_3 compensate each other along ed, it follows that $dp_2 = 0 - 0$ along ed.

In the same way that a point in the triangle represents a vector of three probabilities, it also characterises the expected value of the outcome of the corresponding lottery, essentially because W_1, W_2 and W_3 are fixed. At c, for example, the expected value of the lottery $[E(\tilde{w}_c)]$ is:

$$[E(\tilde{w}_c)] = 0.4W_1 + 0.3W_2 + 0.3W_3$$

and, more generally, for an arbitrary point of the triangle,

$$[E(\tilde{w})] = p_1W_1 + p_2W_2 + p_3W_3$$

Since the W_i are fixed, totally differentiating $E(\tilde{w})$ yields:

$$dE(\tilde{w}) = W_1\,dp_1 + W_2\,dp_2 + W_3\,dp_3 \qquad (6.8)$$

$$= (W_1 - W_2)\,dp_1 + (W_3 - W_2)\,dp_3 \qquad (6.8a)$$

using Equation (6.7). If the expected value is kept constant then $dE(\tilde{w}) = 0$ and thus

$$(dp_3/dp_1)\,|\,_{dE(\tilde{w}) = 0} = (W_2 - W_1)/(W_3 - W_2) \qquad (6.9)$$

The left-hand side of Equation (6.9) defines a marginal rate of substitution (MRS) between p_1 and p_3 to maintain a constant expected outcome. The entire equation says that this MRS is equal to a constant represented by the ratio of the differences between final wealths. Since the MRS is constant, due to the constancy of W_i, the 'iso-expected value' curves are lines. Thus an 'iso-expected value' line, denoted fcg, passes through point c. All lotteries lying on this line have the same expected value of outcome, namely, $E(\tilde{w}_c)$. Once again the constancy of the outcomes W_i guarantees that all of the iso-expected value lines are parallel to each other. Moreover, the further a line lies from the horizontal axis, the higher is the associated expected outcome. Specifically, $E[\tilde{w}_h] > E[\tilde{w}_c]$ because at h the probability of the most favourable result (p_3) is higher and the probability of the least favourable result (p_1) is lower than at c, while the probability of the intermediate result (p_2) is the same. It follows that the expected value of the outcome is the same for all points on ihj and it is greater than the expected value of the outcome at any point along fcg.

Also note that any movement from c towards f along fcg (or from h towards i along ihj) represents a 'decrease in risk with constant mean' in the sense of Rothschild and Stiglitz. Specifically, as one moves from c towards f one increases the probability of the intermediate outcome p_2 and decreases the probabilities of the extreme outcomes without affecting the expected value. There is thus a 'transfer of weight' from the extreme outcomes to the intermediate outcome. Thus we have the third definition of a decrease in risk. Of course the movement from c towards g induces an increase in risk at constant mean. Any risk-averse decision-maker would be made better off by shifting from a lottery situated to the south-west along fcg towards a lottery situated more toward the north-east along the same line. This result will also be confirmed by the following example, previously discussed in Chapter 5, of the equivalence between two definitions of an increase in risk.

Since the three values of W_i are fixed, the same is true of their associated utilities, denoted $U(W_1)$, $U(W_2)$ and $U(W_3)$. As a result, at each point of Machina's triangle one can express not only the vector of probabilities and the associated expected value of the outcome at that point, but also the expected utility at the same point. Thus, at point c,

$$E[U(\tilde{w}_c)] = 0.4U(W_1) + 0.3U(W_2) + 0.3U(W_3)$$

and, more generally, at an arbitrary point

$$E[U(\tilde{w})] = p_1U(W_1) + p_2U(W_2) + p_3U(W_3) \tag{6.10}$$

Totally differentiating Equation (6.10) and applying Equation (6.7) one can write

$$dE[U(\tilde{w})] = [U(W_1) - U(W_2)]dp_1 + [U(W_3)$$
$$- U(W_2)]dp_3 \tag{6.11}$$

from which it follows that if expected utility is constant, then:

$$(dp_3/dp_1) \mid _{dE[U(\tilde{w})] = 0}$$
$$= [U(W_2) - U(W_1)] / [U(W_3) - U(W_2)] \qquad (6.12)$$

The left-hand term in Equation (6.12) defines MRS along an 'iso-expected utility' curve and, since both the numerator and the denominator of the right-hand side of Equation (6.12) are constants, the MRS is also constant. From this it follows that the probability combinations (p_1, p_2, p_3) that maintain a constant level of welfare for a risk-averse decision-maker lie along a line with positive slope. All of these iso-expected utility lines are parallel to each other and the farther they lie from the horizontal axis the higher the expected utility, because the probability of the best outcome is higher. The question that arises then is to know how the MRS along an iso-expected utility line compares with the MRS along an iso-expected value line.

It is easy to show that if U is concave then the slope of the iso-expected utility line is always steeper than that of the iso-expected value line. Specifically, it follows from the concavity of U that:

$$[U(W_2) - U(W_1)]/(W_2 - W_1)$$
$$> [U(W_3) - U(W_2)]/(W_3 - W_2)$$

which yields the required result for all concave U.

The more concave the utility function in question is, the steeper is the iso-utility line. The iso-expected value line can be interpreted as the limiting case of an iso-expected utility line where the decision-maker is risk neutral.

One thus obtains Figure 6.4 where the solid parallel lines represent constant expected utility and the dashed parallel lines correspond to constant expected wealth. Moving from the south-east towards the north-west entails an increase in both the expected wealth and the expected utility.

This characteristic will allow us to prove in an alternative way the previously stated result that movements from left to right along an iso-expected value line are associated with increasing risk and a constant mean. Consider specifically the points r and s. At these two points the expected value of wealth is constant. However, point r lies on an iso-expected utility line uv that corresponds to higher welfare than does $u'v'$, which is the iso-expected utility line containing s.

This must be the case for all risk-averse decision-makers because, for them, the slope of the iso-expected utility lines is greater than that of the iso-expected value lines. Risk-averse agents thus unanimously reject movements toward the right on an iso-expected value line. This illustrates once again one of the definitions of a mean-preserving increase in risk presented in Chapter 5. Our analysis confirms the equivalence between the following two definitions of increased risk: a transfer of weight towards extreme outcomes and unanimity among the class of risk-averse agents.

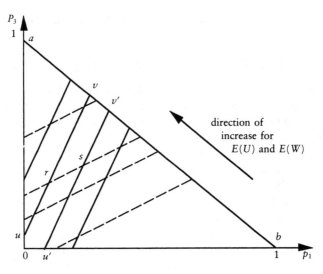

Figure 6.4

At this stage, the reader might believe that Machina's triangle brings nothing new to the understanding of these questions other than a clever presentation of already known results. In reality, the importance of the triangle rests on a property that we will now briefly mention because it distinguishes clearly between the expected utility model and its successors.

As Equation (6.10) clearly shows, the expected utility model deforms wealth (W_i is replaced by $U_{(i)}$) but it leaves the initial probabilities intact. It is sometimes said that $E(U)$ is non-linear in W_i but linear in p_i. It is essentially because of this property that we were able to generate Equation (6.12), which confirms that the iso-utility curves are really lines in the expected utility model. Fundamentally, when one moves to the 'non-expected utility models', the evaluation criterion can also entail a deformation of the probabilities, and it follows that the decision-maker's iso-objective curves are no longer lines. Their curved nature explains some choices under uncertainty that have been made by individuals in experimental situations.

Exercises

6.1 Consider a uniform density function on an interval $[a, b]$ with $a > 0$. Show that all other uniform densities on an interval $[c, d]$ with $c \geqslant d$ and $d \geqslant b$ (with at least one strict inequality) first-order stochastically dominate the initial density. Construct an example of a uniform density on $[e, f]$ that does not first-order dominate the initial density and is not dominated by it.

This amounts to proving that the first-degree stochastic dominance-ordering is a partial ordering.

6.2 Considering the 'hyperbolic absolute risk aversion utility' (see Equation (4.16)) show that for this class of utility function, the degree of absolute prudence u'''/u'' is related to the degree of absolute risk aversion by:

$$-\frac{u'''(w)}{u''(w)} = A_a(w)\,\frac{2-\beta}{1-\beta}$$

6.3 Show that if a utility function exhibits decreasing (constant) absolute risk aversion, the coefficient of absolute prudence will be greater than (equal to) that of absolute risk aversion. As you will notice, this property is (without surprise) very similar to the statement made in Theorem 6.3.

6.4 Consider the following three lotteries:

x	$p(x)$	y	$p(y)$	z	$p(z)$
0	0.50	−1	0.25	0	0.50
+10	0.50	+1	0.25	+9	0.25
		+10	0.50	+11	0.25

Questions
(a) Show that all risk-averse individuals prefer $\tilde{x}$ to any of the other two random variables. Show also that there is no unanimity among the risk averters about the choice between $\tilde{y}$ and $\tilde{z}$.
(b) Consider two different utility functions U_1 and U_2 with $U_1''' > 0$ and $U_2''' = 0$ respectively.[8] Show that with U_1 $\tilde{z}$ is preferred to $\tilde{y}$ while with U_2 there is indifference between $\tilde{z}$ and $\tilde{y}$.
(c) Observe that $\tilde{y}$ is 'downside riskier'[9] than $\tilde{z}$ in the sense that $\tilde{y}$ is obtained from $\tilde{x}$ by adding white noise around outcome $x = 0$ while $\tilde{z}$ is obtained from $\tilde{x}$ by adding the same noise to outcome $x = 10$. Can you show in general that any prudent person ($u''' > 0$) prefers $\tilde{z}$ to $\tilde{y}$ whenever $\tilde{y}$ is 'downside riskier' than $\tilde{z}$?

6.5 If an individual becomes more risk averse (U is transformed into $k(U)$) how does this change affect the slope of iso-expected utility curves in Machina's triangle?
Hint: Without loss of generality assume that $U(W_1) = k(U(W_1))$ and that $U(W_3) = k(U(W_3))$. Then draw the curves U and $k(U)$ in terms of W. This will give the answer almost immediately.

Notes

1. A character in *Le Bourgeois Gentilhomme* by Molière, who suddenly realised that he had spoken in prose all of his life without knowing it. (Translator)
2. It is important to emphasise the fact that we are departing from Chapter 5 where we compared lotteries with the same expected value. Indeed, as we shall see, first-order stochastic dominance implies that the expected values are different.
3. To avoid problems of indefiniteness, assume that $U(+\infty)$ is a finite number.
4. Without forgetting the assumptions imposed on their behaviour.
5. If $\tilde{x}$ is not actuarially fair, one would write $\tilde{x} = \mu + \tilde{\varepsilon}$ where $\mu \equiv E(\tilde{x}) \neq 0$. The analysis would then be done in terms of $w_0 + \mu + \tilde{\varepsilon}$ where $w_0 + \mu$ would play the same role as w_0 in the text.
6. Note in addition that $U''' > 0$ is a necessary (but not sufficient) condition for absolute risk aversion to be decreasing in wealth. To see this, it is sufficient to differentiate the function $A^a(w)$ with respect to w.
7. This strange term, currently used in literature, results from the combination of the triangular shape of the graphical tool and the name of its inventor, M. Machina. See Machina (1982, 1984).
8. Hint: Refer to Table 4.1 to find many examples of utility functions with $U''' > 0$ and one example with $U''' = 0$.
9. For a detailed discussion of this interesting notion see Menezes, Geiss and Tressler (1980).

References

Eeckhoudt L. and M. Kimball (1991), Background risk, prudence and the demand for insurance, in *Contributions to Insurance Economics*, G. Dionne (ed.), Kluwer Academic Press, Boston.

Kimball M. (1990), Precautionary saving in the small and in the large, *Econometrica*, vol. 58, 53–78.

Machina M. (1982), Expected utility analysis without the independence axiom, *Econometrica*, vol. 50, 277–323.

Machina M. (1984), Temporal risk and the nature of induced preferences, *Journal of Economic Theory*, vol. 33, 199–231.

Menezes C., C. Geiss and J. Tressler (1980), Increasing downward risk, *American Economic Review*, vol. 70, 921–931.

7 : Uncertainty and contingent claims

In the preceding chapters, we have constructed a framework of analysis for the behaviour of a 'rational' individual facing uncertainty. In Part Two of this book we will use this approach to derive optimal strategies in the context of the demand for insurance or for risky assets as well as in the context of supply decisions of firms facing uncertainty. In all of these models, the price (of insurance, of assets, etc.) will be taken as exogenously fixed, with the goal of showing how to manage individual risks in a given environment.

In a more general framework, it is interesting to consider how equilibrium prices are established in markets for risk (insurance markets, stock markets, etc.). Specifically, it is a question of determining how the risks faced by some influence the behaviour of others, or in other words, how markets co-ordinate individual choices by fixing market prices. One can then ask about the way risks faced by a group of individuals – or by society as a whole – are transferred and allocated. These problems are analysed in Part Three. However, we are still poorly equipped to broach these questions after the first six chapters. For this reason we dedicate this chapter to building a foundation for this approach by successively analysing the notions of a state of the world, a contingent claim and diversification. We conclude by presenting a simple graphical analysis of the problem in two dimensions.

7.1 Description of uncertainty and states of the world

When analysing the allocation of risks in a group and the interaction between these different risks, the characterisation of uncertainty is more complex than in the case considered up until now, that is, the case of one individual facing one risk. In an economy composed of n individuals, the allocation of risk can be described completely, by extending the previous work for $n = 1$, using the joint distribution function $G(\tilde{w}_{f_1}, \tilde{w}_{f_1}, ..., \tilde{w}_{f_i}, ..., \tilde{w}_{f_n})$ of n random variables $\tilde{w}_{f_i}$ representing the individual wealths $i = 1, ..., n$. Although this method is internally consistent and justifiable, it has long been surpassed by a method of modelling that is more elegant in the sense that it allows a generalisation of economic theory under certainty, as we will see more precisely in Chapter 13.

We now consider what determines the final wealth of an individual. There are of course, the choices made by individuals themselves concerning insurance, investment and portfolio management, among other things. Insurance reduces the variability of final wealth. The purchase of a risky asset, if it is not negatively correlated with other assets in the portfolio, increases this variability. Another element that influences individual i's final wealth is the set of actions chosen by other individuals: e.g. the accountant who embezzles funds, the company in which there is an investment goes bankrupt because of a bad sales strategy, etc. These are examples of human factors, that is, factors that are entirely under the control of one or other of the individuals.

There is also a set of variables that influence final welfare,[1] but that cannot be controlled by any member of society. These factors are many and varied. They run from meteorological factors (storms, droughts, sunspots, etc.) to technological factors (innovations, discoveries of new mineral sources, technical failures, etc.) to political factors (civil war, international crisis, etc.) to accidents. In short, this covers everything that is due to the intrinsic uncertainty in 'nature': it is thus said that the state of nature (or state of the world) that will prevail tomorrow is random.

When uncertainty that influences the final wealth of more than one individual at a time is considered, there arises the problem of describing this 'macroeconomic' uncertainty. In particular, the method employed so far, which consists of defining a distribution function for individual final wealth, is no longer useful. Following G. Debreu (1959), a description of this uncertainty can be made on the list of all possible states of the world that could be realised tomorrow. A particular state is thus defined by the value that each of the above-mentioned factors takes on in that state. The letter s is used to denote a particular state of the world; $\tilde{s}$ represents the corresponding random variable with distribution function $F(s)$. If there is a finite number S of possible states, then s takes on the values $1, 2, ..., S$ with probability p_s. We define these states in such a way that they take into account all of the random variables influencing human activities[2] and in such a way that they are mutually exclusive.[3]

Consider a simple example of an economy composed of three citrus producers. The first chooses to produce in a greenhouse while the others produce in fields. The first two are in Region A, while the third is in Region B, with a different climate. For simplicity, assume that there are only two possible meteorological conditions in each region: either the weather is 'good' or it is 'bad'. Production in a particular region is completely determined once the meteorological conditions in that region are known. It follows that the uncertainty is defined by four states of nature. The first ($s = 1$) corresponds to good weather in both regions. It is denoted (good, good) or (g, g). The others correspond respectively to the pairs (good, bad), (bad, good) and (bad, bad), where the first (or second) element of the pair represents the weather that prevails in Region A (or B). The probabilities of each state depend on the frequencies of weather conditions observed in each region over a long period of time, as well as on their correlation between A and B. Taking the individuals' decisions – such as the choice of land and the methods of cultivation – as exogenously given, one can represent the final wealths contingent on the states as shown in Table 7.1.

It is clear that agent $i = 1$ has succeeded in being protected from the vicissitudes of nature by cultivating in greenhouses; this wealth is independent of the states. The neighbour, agent $i = 2$, does not have this advantage since wealth is doubled when the event[4] 'good weather in A' is realised. The producer in B faces the same kind of risk in that country. By not paying the costs of maintaining greenhouses, a higher net profit is achieved in good states. In contrast, it is more profitable to have a greenhouse in bad states. In a sense, Producer 1 has protection against the uncertainty of nature.

We see that this kind of representation of uncertainty allows all the relevant cases to be considered relatively simply in terms of their risk. Once the possible different states of nature and their probabilities as given by function F are known, the individual risks are characterised by a function w_{f_i} of the random variable $\tilde{s}$. The allocation of risks across the group is thus defined by a vector of n functions of the states of the world: $[\tilde{w}_{f_1}(\tilde{s}), ..., \tilde{w}_{f_i}(\tilde{s}), ..., \tilde{w}_{f_n}(\tilde{s})]$. In this way all the non-human factors that affect welfare are taken into account. One speaks of wealth as being contingent on the state of nature.

This last function can, of course, also depend on individual choices, as is seen clearly in the above example where a farmer who chooses to produce in greenhouses does not face the same risk as one who does not. Another way of analysing the numerical example considers the problem of a farmer who has not yet determined where to produce or with what technique. The different rows in the table then correspond to different possible choices the individual can make and the entries in the matrix measure $w_f(a, \tilde{s})$ where a represents the action chosen by the individual in question. This can be thought of as a 'game against nature' in the playful jargon of game theory. This model is thus useful in determining the optimal action of an individual in an uncertain situation (see Part Two).

Table 7.1

	s = 1 (g, g)	s = 2 (g, b)	s = 3 (b, g)	s = 4 (b, b)
w_{f_1}	900	900	900	900
w_{f_2}	1 000	1 000	500	500
w_{f_3}	1 000	500	1 000	500

7.2 Contingent claims

Given the risk aversion of the members of the group in question and the risk that they face, we can ask how the allocation of risks can be modified by transfers and exchanges. Our modern economies have developed numerous methods to reallocate individual risks. A simple example is a private contract whereby one party commits to paying a certain sum if a particular event occurs. This is called a 'bet' or an 'option'. In its most pure form it consists of a bet on a particular state of the world. An example would be a promise to provide something (a sum of money, for example) if the state of the world $s = 3$ is realised, that is, if the weather is foul in Region A but fair in Region B next year. This is called a 'contingent claim'. A contingent claim is defined by its physical characteristics and by the state of the world in which it is paid or received. In the one-dimensional analysis that we are carrying out, where only wealth matters, a contingent claim is the same as a monetary promise. We nevertheless use the term 'contingent claim' because it is well established in literature.

In an economy with four possible states, the existence of four contingent claims is adequate to achieve any allocation of risk across the group. Thus, for example, the allocation in Table 7.2 is derived from the initial allocation of risks presented previously by having Agent 2 promise to pay 250 F to Agent 3 in State 2 in exchange for a reciprocal promise in State 3. These two individuals have exchanged *ex ante* 250 units of two contingent claims, claims contingent on the states $s = 2$ and $s = 3$. The reader is asked to understand carefully this element of the analysis whereby the definition of a good is extended to the case of uncertainty by taking into account the state in which it is delivered and consumed. This extension of economic theory to uncertainty constitutes the cornerstone of the 'theory of complete markets'. This theory is studied in Part Three: it attempts to determine the price of these rather special goods.

Fortunately, today there exist methods of transferring risks other than to make private bets. There are specialised markets in this industry: insurance markets, stock markets, futures markets and options markets. In fact, a stock, just like an option contract or an insurance contract, is nothing more than a

Table 7.2

	$s = 1$	$s = 2$	$s = 3$	$s = 4$
	(g, g)	(g, b)	(b, g)	(b, b)
wf_1	900	900	900	900
wf_2	1 000	750	750	500
wf_3	1 000	750	750	500

set of promises for different states of the world. Specifically, a stock 'guarantees' a particular dividend (perhaps zero) in each state. It can be said that a stock is nothing other than a 'basket' of contingent claims, sometimes called 'pure assets'. Whereas a pure asset promises 1 F if a specific state is realised and nothing in all the other states, a real asset, an insurance contract or a bond promise non-zero 'payments' in more than one state of the world. One can deduce the economic value of an asset from the prices of the different pure assets that it represents, just as one calculates the value of a basket of goods from the sum of values for each of the goods in the basket.

7.3 Socially diversifiable risks

An important question is whether there exists a way of exchanging contingent claims so that each member of society is covered 100 per cent against the hazards of nature. If this is the case, it is likely that the risk-averse individuals who make up society will find a way of achieving this risk-free allocation, as we will see in the theory of complete markets. The question posed here is under what conditions can such a situation arise.

As an example, reconsider the case of an economy composed of only our three citrus producers. Since Agent 1 is already covered, we specifically focus on the other two. We wish to make transfers of contingent claims in such a way that $w_{f_2}(\tilde{s})$ and $w_{f_3}(\tilde{s})$ are both independent of the state of the world, as is the case for Agent 1. Let t_s be the monetary transfer from $i = 2$ to $i = 3$ in the state of the world s. We thus obtain the allocation of risks given in Table 7.3.

Note that we have also calculated:

$$w(\tilde{s}) = \sum_{i=1}^{n} w_{f_i}(\tilde{s}) \tag{7.1}$$

that is, the aggregate wealth in this three-agent economy. The contingent transfers do not affect the values of $w(\tilde{s})$. It soon becomes clear that it is impossible to find a set of transfers $\{t_i\}$ that makes w_{f_i} independent of s

Table 7.3

	$s = 1$ (g, g)	$s = 2$ (g, b)	$s = 3$ (b, g)	$s = 4$ (b, b)
w_{f_1}	900	900	900	900
w_{f_2}	$1\,000 - t_1$	$1\,000 - t_2$	$500 - t_3$	$500 - t_4$
w_{f_3}	$1\,000 + t_1$	$500 + t_2$	$1\,000 + t_3$	$500 + t_4$
w	$2\,900$	$2\,400$	$2\,400$	$1\,900$

because their sum $w(\tilde{s})$ itself depends on s. In contrast, it is always possible to find exchanges of contingent claims that generate complete individual coverage when $w(\tilde{s})$ is constant. Consider specifically the example given in Table 7.4. Instead of producing citrus in B, Agent 3 has gone to live in A with the two colleagues, but has decided to produce umbrellas, thus generating final wealth of $\tilde{w}_{f_3}(\tilde{s})$. When the weather is fair, business is relatively poor. In contrast, when the weather is foul, business is much better. Since the weather conditions in the uninhabited Region B do not influence any human activity, Table 7.4 is simplified to Table 7.5 where $\tilde{s}$ takes on the values g or b depending only on conditions in A. It is clear from the example that a deviation of Agent 2's wealth from its mean is always compensated by the opposite deviation of Agent 3's wealth from its mean, implying that $w(\tilde{s})$ is constant. In other words, $w_{f_2}(\tilde{s})$ is perfectly negatively correlated with $w_{f_3}(\tilde{s})$. These two risks are thus socially diversifiable, for example, by negotiating the transfer of 250 monetary units from the healthy sector of the economy toward the sector suffering from unfavourable weather. Agents 2 and 3 would thus each enjoy a constant wealth of 750.

In summary, individual risks are socially diversifiable if aggregate wealth is certain. If it isn't, there exists 'systematic' risk that individuals must inevitably face. Put simply, since there is no insurance company external to the society to accept the non-diversifiable risk, this risk must be 'tolerated' in one way or another by the members of society. Until the millennium, the Almighty has refused to play the role of insurer, despite the risk aversion of His Faithful. There is thus a problem: who should endure the risk and at what price?

Table 7.4

	$s=1$ (g, g)	$s=2$ (g, b)	$s=3$ (b, g)	$s=4$ (b, b)
w_{f_1}	900	900	900	900
w_{f_2}	1 000	1 000	500	500
w_{f_3}	500	500	1 000	1 000
w	2 400	2 400	2 400	2 400

Table 7.5

	$s=g$	$s=b$
w_{f_1}	900	900
w_{f_2}	1 000	500
w_{f_3}	500	1 000
w	2 400	2 400

We have nearly acquired the necessary tools to answer this delicate question correctly. We must first present a graphical tool of analysis. This is done in the following section.

7.4 Graphical representation by the 'states of the world'

Remember how an individual evaluates risky wealth. According to expected utility theory, $V(w_f(\tilde{s}))$ is calculated as follows[5]:

$$V[w_f(\tilde{s})] = \sum_{s=1}^{S} p_s U[w_f(s)]$$

In an economy with two possible states of nature, $s = g$ or $s = b$, the evaluation function becomes:

$$V(w_f(\tilde{s})) = v(w_{f_g}, w_{f_b}) = pU(w_{f_g}) + (1 - p)U(w_{f_b}) \qquad (7.2)$$

where p represents the probability of the state $s = g$, w_{f_g} the wealth in that state, and w_{f_b} the wealth in the other state. Function v is a function of two variables that measures *ex ante* the level of welfare of an individual with this structure of contingent wealth. The probability p of state g is assumed to be known by everyone and is not considered a variable here, but rather a parameter. Function v can be represented in a three-dimensional space, but, having a classical bent, we prefer to use a two-dimensional graph employing the notion of indifference curves.

In Figure 7.1(a), where the final wealth in the two states g and b are measured along the respective axes, it is clear that a particular configuration of contingent final wealth is represented by a point. The random wealth of the three individuals described above – the greenhouse producer, the field producer and the umbrella seller – are reproduced in the graph by points 1, 2 and 3, respectively. Individual 1 faces no risk because $w_{f_g} = w_{f_b} = 900$, that is, because their point lies on the 45° line.

Moreover, an indifference curve for a particular individual is defined in this graph as the locus of configurations of contingent final wealth that generate the same level of satisfaction *ex ante* for the individual. Two of these curves are represented in Figure 7.1(b). It is clear that the indifference curves are downward-sloping. Specifically, an agent who gives up part of their income in state $s = g$ (moving toward the left) must, in order to compensate this loss and achieve the same level of satisfaction, receive a higher income in state $s = b$ (moving upward). This is due to the fact that more is always preferred to less. The marginal rate of substitution (MRS_{bg}) between consumption in state g and consumption in state b is defined by the minimum amount of contingent claim $s = b$ that must be offered to compensate the loss of one unit of contingent claim $s = g$. The marginal rate of substitution is nothing other than the absolute value of the slope of the indifference curve.

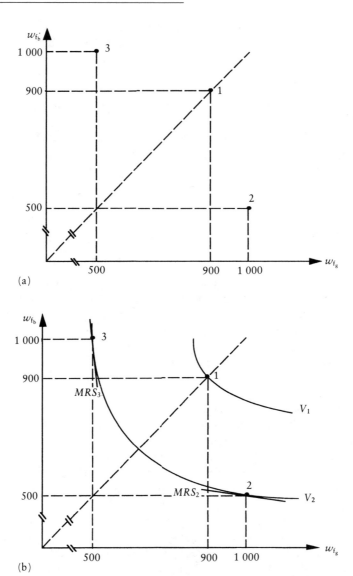

Figure 7.1

By analogy with the notion of marginal rate of substitution between two goods under certainty, it is easy to show that MRS_{bg} equals the ratio of the partial derivatives of v. Specifically, if dx and dy are the changes in the amount of the contingent claims $s = g$ and $s = b$, it must be that:

$$0 = dv = \partial v/\partial w_{f_g}\, dx + \partial v/\partial w_{f_b}\, dy$$

or, in other words, that:

$$MRS_{bg} = -(dy/dx)|_v = (\partial v/\partial w_{f_g})/(\partial v/\partial w_{f_b}) \qquad (7.3)$$

and, using the definition of v from Equation (7.2),

$$MRS_{bg} = pU'(w_{f_g})/(1-p)U'(w_{f_b}) \qquad (7.4)$$

It is useful to have good intuition for this definition. It will be used many times in what follows and especially in Part Three. The effect of the loss of 1 F if state $s = g$ is realised implies an *ex ante* expected utility loss of $pU'(w_{f_g})$. In contrast, the gain of 1 F in State b generates an increase in expected utility equal to $(1-p)U'(w_{f_b})$. It follows that the necessary sum to disburse in State b to compensate a 1 F loss in State g equals $[pU'(w_{f_g})/(1-p)U'(w_{f_b})]$ F.

Two factors influence the marginal rate of substitution: the relative probability of realising state $s = g$ and the individual's attitude toward risk. The higher the relative probability of the state $s = g$, the higher is the necessary compensation in the state $s = b$. A franc promised in a highly likely state does not have the same value as a franc promised in an unlikely state. Abstracting from the risk aversion of the individual, the expected gains from these two promises are different.

Risk aversion plays an important role in the description of the form of the indifference curves and thus in the value of MRS. Recall that under certainty the indifference curves are convex because the consumer dislikes extreme consumption bundles: if there is a choice between three baskets of goods, the third being the average of the other two which have the same utility, then the third is always preferred. Under uncertainty, risk aversion plays the same role as this preference for average consumption. The similarity is obvious, since risk aversion means that the individual prefers to 'smooth' consumption between two states; in other words, a basket containing the average of the choice of contingent claims is preferred. One way of proving the convexity of an indifference curve is to show that the marginal rate of substitution decreases as one moves to the right (and, thus, downward) along the indifference curve. Specifically, with this movement w_{f_g} increases and w_{f_b} decreases, and thus with risk aversion $U'(w_{f_g})$ falls and $U'(w_{f_b})$ rises. Using Equation (7.4), it follows that MRS will fall. Thus the indifference curves are convex.

This is easily verified in Figure 7.1(b) by comparing the random wealth of Agents 2 and 3, whom we assume are on the same indifference curve (this will be true if $p = 0.5$). For Agent 2, giving up monetary unit in state $a = g$ induces a relatively small reduction in expected utility since this state is relatively rich (1,000). As a result, the required compensation and MRS = MRS₂ is relatively small. In contrast, Agent 3 has only 500 in state $s = g$. Being relatively poor in that state, the loss of a franc is relatively costly in terms of welfare. Thus, the loss in terms of expected utility is relatively large *ex ante*, as is the required compensation and MRS = MRS$_3$. This is due to the fact that $U'(500) > U'(1000)$ because of risk aversion.

Of course, there are as many indifference curves as there are possible values of expected utility, that is, infinitely many. One thus speaks of a 'family' of indifference curves. Two curves are represented in Figure 7.1(b). A higher curve (or one further to the right) corresponds to a higher expected utility: $V_1 = v(900, 900) > V_2 = v(1000, 500)$.

The reader can verify all of the properties of indifference curves by considering particular utility functions. For example, consider the 'power' utility function seen in Chapter 4: $U(w) = w^\beta$, $\beta < 1$. Using the equation $V(w_f(\tilde{s})) = v_0$ in the two-state world, one can derive the following function $w_{f_b}(w_{f_g})$ to analytically describe an indifference curve:

$$w_{f_b}(w_{f_g}) = [(v_0 - pw_{f_g}^\beta)/(1 - p)]^{1/\beta} \tag{7.5}$$

One can also calculate the marginal rate of substitution using Equation (7.4). It is:

$$MRS_{bg} = [p/(1 - p)] (w_{f_b}/w_{f_g})^{1 - \beta} \tag{7.6}$$

It can be verified that MRS is decreasing in w_{f_g} and increasing in w_{f_b}, and thus that the indifference curves are convex.

To conclude this chapter, we show graphically that any strategy that reduces the variability of final wealth without changing its expected value will increase expected utility. The set of risky outcomes with the given expected value μ is defined by the equation:

$$pw_{f_g} + (1 - p)w_{f_b} = \mu \tag{7.7}$$

This corresponds to a line with slope $-p/(1 - p)$ in the kind of graph used above. Figure 7.2 shows a situation where $p = 0.5$ and where the random wealth corresponds to the point $(1000, 500)$. The locus of constant expected value corresponds in this case to the equation $0.5w_{f_g} = 0.5w_{f_b} = 750$, that is, to a line with slope -1. The random wealth $(900, 600)$ is on the same line. Moving from $(1000, 500)$ to $(900, 600)$, one maintains the same expected value while reducing the risk. This can be accomplished by receiving 100 units of the contingent claim $s = g$ and giving up 100 units of the contingent claim $s = b$. Note that in Figure 7.2, $(900, 600)$ lies on an indifference curve V_4 that lies above V_2. The individual's level of welfare is thus increased *ex ante*. More generally, any movement along the constant expected value locus in the direction that decreases the variability of wealth is desirable to riskophobes.

Pushing this reasoning to its limit, it is clear that any riskophobe wishes to eliminate all risk affecting their wealth if this can be done at a constant mean. The optimal solution in this case would be the point $(750, 750)$. At this point on the $45°$ line, there is a tangency between the indifference curve and the constant expected value line. Specifically, their slopes are identical and

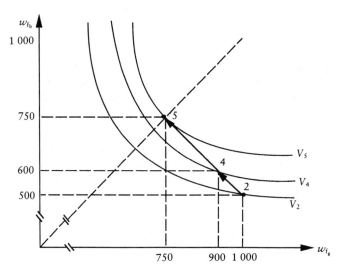

Figure 7.2

equal to $-\text{MRS} = -p/(1-p) = -1$, that is, the two curves are inclined at a $45°$ angle at that point. This result will reappear in later chapters.

This result, of course, depends exclusively on risk aversion. Indeed, if there were risk neutrality, the indifference curves would be lines with constant slope $-\text{MRS} = -pU'(w_{f_g})/(1-p)U'(w_{f_b}) = -p/(1-p) = -1$, since marginal utility would be constant. In other words, the indifference curve would lie on the line representing the locus of constant expected value. In this case, a movement along this line would not imply any change in utility. Worse, in the case of a 'risk lover', the indifference curves would be concave (the MRS would increase along an indifference curve) and a variability-reducing movement along the constant expected value locus would reduce expected utility! This is all consistent with the notions of risk aversion, risk neutrality and risk loving.

In this chapter we have outlined some common points between consumer theory under certainty and decision theory under uncertainty using the notion of contingent claims. Understanding of these common points will be useful when, in Part Three, we analyse the way risks are shared in a market economy.

Exercises

7.1 An individual is endowed with the following risk situation:

$$p = 25 \qquad W_{fb} = 10$$
$$1 - p = 75 \qquad W_{fg} = 20$$

Their utility function is:

$$U = W_j - 0.02\,W_j^2$$

Draw the indifference curve through the initial endowment in the state claims diagram. Show that this individual would agree to give up 2 units of final wealth in State g to obtain 6 units of final wealth in State b. Explain in words why such a shift is approved by this risk averter.

7.2 To build a bridge between the 'contingent claims' approach and the important notions of certainty equivalent and asking price that were developed in a different context, we offer you this exercise and guide you to its solution. Besides a wealth of 180, an individual (A) owns the following lottery $\tilde{x}$:

x	$p(x)$
-80	0.40
0	0.60

This individual has a utility function

$$U(W_f) = \ln \frac{W_f}{20}$$

First compute the certainty equivalent, asking price and risk premium of the lottery, following the approach adopted in Chapters 3 and 4. Then use a two-dimensional graph to represent the initial position of A (call it a) and draw the indifference curve through this point.[6] For the rest of this exercise it is important to locate precisely the intersection between this indifference curve and the 45° line (call this point c). Once you have located point c you should observe that its abscissa (which of course equals its ordinate) is nothing but the value of the certainty equivalent you have obtained through the 'classical' method. With some more effort you can obtain an interpretation of the asking price.

Should A have access to an insurance contract offering free of charge an indemnity of 80 if the undesirable outcome of the lottery were to occur, show that this contract would involve a transfer from initial point a to a point b located on the 45° degree line directly above a. Such a contract is, of course, 'welfare-improving' since b is on a higher indifference curve than a (draw the indifference curve through b).

Now answer the following question: how much money should A be willing to give up in *each of the two states of the world* to obtain this contract that pays money in only one state (the state of loss)? To determine this amount of money you move from b along the 45° degree line until you reach point c. You then measure this distance on the abscissa (or on the ordinate) and you recover the asking price of the lottery.

In order to illustrate the risk premium you compute $E[\tilde{W}_f]$ and locate this point on the 45° degree line. The distance between the abscissa of this point and 180 measures $E(\tilde{x})$; by comparing $E(\tilde{x})$ with the asking price you recover the risk premium.

7.3[7] We have illustrated in Exercise 7.2 our assertion that 'the notion of the asking price of a lottery corresponds to the idea of insurance' for the buyer of an insurance policy (see the example with negative asking price in Section 7.3). To be more precise and – as we will see in detail in Chapter 10 – the asking price corresponds to the idea of *full* insurance (that is, an indemnity covering 100 per cent of the loss). However, in the real world *partial* insurance coverage (e.g. through co-insurance or deductibles) is more common. Nevertheless it is easy to define the asking price for a partial insurance coverage with the help of our two-dimensional graph.

Starting from point *a* imagine now that A is offered free of charge an indemnity of 60 (i.e. cover at 75 per cent against loss of 80). There is a move from *a* in the direction of point *b* but below *b*. Call this new point *b'* (and mark it in the figure you have drawn). Also draw the indifference curve though *b'*. As expected *b'* is preferred to *a* but is dominated by *b*.

Now answer the following question: how much money should A be willing to give up in each state in order to obtain this partial insurance contract? To find the answer you start from *b'* and draw a line parallel to the 45° degree line until it intersects the indifference curve through *a* say at *c'*. Of course, you find that the asking price for a partial coverage is lower than the asking price for full coverage.

Notes

1. As before, we assume that the effects on welfare depend only on final wealth (one-dimensional analysis). There might nevertheless be other effects on welfare that cannot be measured in monetary terms: changes in health, the loss of a loved one, etc. Taking into account these effects leads economists to consider utility functions that depend on the 'state of the world'.
2. As a result, the final wealth of each individual is fully defined as soon as the individual actions and the state of nature are known.
3. This means that two states can never occur at the same time.
4. An event is technically defined as a subset of the possible states. In this case, the event 'good weather in A' is defined by the subset $\{s = 1, s\ 2\}$.
5. It is an abuse of notation to write $w_f(s)$ – representing wealth in a particular state – like function $w_f(\tilde{s})$ that represents the corresponding random variable. This should not, however, create any ambiguity in the reader's mind.

6. To do this you can compute the ordinates of a few points of the indifference curve.
7. A good understanding of the solution to Exercise 7.2 is a prerequisite for this exercise.

References

Debreu G. (1959), *Theory of Value*, Wiley, New York.
Malinvaud E. (1979), *Leçons de théorie microéconomique*, Dunod, Paris.

Two
Individual choices under uncertainty

8 · A general description of the problems

In Part One we emphasised the basic concepts. It is important now to show their usefulness in the context of microeconomic theory.

It is well known that microeconomic theory deals with two kinds of subjects.

1. The first concerns the study of individual decisions when resources are (exogenously) scarce. The individual or firm, subject to some uncontrollable forces, tries to maximise an objective subject to some constraints. The characteristics of the optimal solution are of particular interest, and we shall ask how the decisions made by a risk-averse agent under uncertainty compare with those that would have been made in a certain environment. This leads to the central exercise of microeconomics: comparative statics analysis. The analysis consists of asking how one or several changes in exogenous parameters (or sometimes, but more rarely, in the objective) modify the initial optimal solution. Comparative statics analysis attempts to predict in some sense how individuals or groups who exhibit a well-defined rationality will react – in the short or longer run – to one or more changes in their environment. In this framework, it is almost always assumed that a change in the individual's decision does not alter the environment or, at least, that the decision-maker does not anticipate the effect of the choice on the environment. In this partial equilibrium context, the environment determines the choices of households or of firms but the converse is not true, or at least is not anticipated by the decision-makers.

2. Once the optimal individual choices have been understood, it is important to see how they interact with each other. This broaches the branch of microeconomics dedicated to the study of the co-ordination of individual decisions either by markets or by government intervention, thus raising the topics of 'general equilibrium' and/or optimal modes of social organisation. These themes are the subject of all of Part Three.

In contrast, Part Two concentrates almost exclusively on optimal individual choices and their comparative statics implications. We consider essentially three subjects in increasing order of difficulty.

The first analysis is dedicated to the study of an old question in risk theory that has, by the way, strongly contributed to its diffusion to financial management specialists: the division of a portfolio of an exogenously given value between two assets, one certain and the other risky. We apply the entire arsenal of comparative statics analysis to this classical problem, and thus highlight the importance (and sometimes the limits) of the concepts discussed in Part One.

Chapter 9 is dedicated to the insurance decision of an individual or firm. First, we show that a specific insurance contract – called 'co-insurance' – shares practically all of the characteristics of the portfolio choice problem. In the second step we examine another kind of commonly practised arrangement: insurance contracts with deductibles. These introduce a non-linearity between the individual's final wealth and the outcome of the random variable.[1]

Furthermore, it will be easy to show, by applying the notion of an increase in risk, that a contract with a deductible must always – at the same premium – be preferred to a co-insurance contract (at least by the buyer).

Chapter 10 broaches in depth the question of non-linearity between final wealth and the outcome of the risk. We study this by concentrating on the output decisions of a perfectly competitive firm that is subject to a risk market price for its finished product. Because of the non-linear character of the model, the chapter provides an ideal opportunity to delve into two important subjects: the value of information – or, equivalently, the value of flexibility – and the role of futures markets as tools for risk management. We show that these markets provide the opportunity to 'separate' production decisions from risk-taking.

Of course, we present a very large part of the analysis in the framework of the expected utility model. However, we do not forget that, as mentioned in Part One, other behavioural models exist, and from time to time we allude to them.

At the end of Chapters 9, 10 and 11 dedicated to these three subjects, we discuss their common elements and mention how a uniform presentation allows their synthesis. We also take advantage of the opportunity to point out some interesting extensions.

Note

1. In contrast, for the problems of investing in risky assets and co-insurance, final wealth is a linear function of the realisation of the random variable.

9 (Simple) portfolio choices under uncertainty

9.1 The decision-maker's environment

As we shall often see, a detailed description of the decision-maker's environment facilitates a good understanding of the analysis of that environment. Thus we will invest a little effort, at the beginning of this chapter, in examining the framework.

We assume the decision-maker (firm or household) has an initial endowment which we denote, as usual, by w_0. Looking around, the decision-maker learns of only two possible investments for w_0. We assume, somewhat peculiarly, that the decision as to how to divide this w_0 between them is made without considering other possible components of wealth or their returns during the period (for a more realistic assumption see Section 10.3). The first possibility consists of investing all or part of w_0 in a 'risk-free' asset; the sum thus invested is denoted m. The investment m is risk-free in the sense that at the end of the period it yields a certain real rate of return denoted i. The contribution of m to real wealth in a period (corresponding to the time horizon of the decision-maker) is thus written as $m(1 + i)$ where i is a rate of return per monetary unit invested and is independent of the total amount invested (m). The other investment, of amount a, is risky and its return per franc invested is thus represented by a random variable denoted $\tilde{x}$ with density function $f(x)$ independent of a. This density function reflects the information gleaned by the individual about the risky asset and a (subjective) degree of optimism or pessimism concerning it. In some sense, while i is naturally assumed to be the same for all economic agents, $f(x)$ differs across agents depending on the nature of their information and their ways of subjectively translating their information into probabilities. It is equally clear that $f(x)$ can suddenly change for the same agent if new information is received or if old information is interpreted differently.

The structure of the problem facing the decision-maker can be summarised in Figure 9.1. It illustrates the initial division of w_0 between m and a, and the contributions of the two investments to final wealth, $\tilde{w}_f$, which is random if a is not zero. It is the properties of the distribution of $\tilde{w}_f$ that hold the individual's attention and define the objective as follows:

$$\tilde{w}_f = m(1 + i) + a(1 + \tilde{x}) \tag{9.1}$$

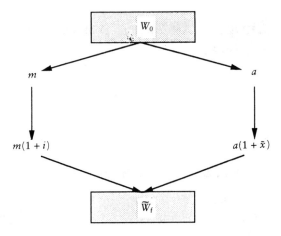

Figure 9.1

At this stage of the analysis the physical or financial nature of the asset is still vague. The reader probably imagines that a represents, for example, an investment in a stock traded on a stock exchange. This interpretation is plausible and correct, but there are others. The investment of a can be in an office building that will be sold (or at least appraised) at the end of the period. Similarly, instead of being invested in a single stock, a could stand for a basket (a portfolio) of exchange-listed stocks that will be liquidated at the end of the period. One could even think of investment a as corresponding to the acquisition of an index portfolio, that is, a portfolio containing all of the exchange-listed stocks in proportion to their market capitalisation.

Before considering possible constraints on choices, we emphasise one characteristic of this problem (and others) that distinguishes it from the approach adopted in Part One. Here risk is clearly *endogenous* while in Part One it was exogenous by nature. Specifically, very often in Part One the individual was endowed with a lottery that had been 'inherited' and the questions of how and why it was acquired were ignored. The question that was asked was under what conditions the owner would be willing to sell the lottery. Here the goal of analysis is to explain precisely why individuals deliberately hold lotteries, that is, why they take on a particular level of risk. The endogenous nature of risk is clear when one realises that at any time the individual can choose to avoid risk (by not acquiring any): it suffices in this case to set $a = 0$ in the portfolio. By varying the decision parameter a, the individual endogenously and deliberately alters their exposure to risk.

The ability to vary exposure to risk depends on the constraints that are faced. In all cases, the individual is subject to the constraint:

$$w_0 = a + m \tag{9.2}$$

that follows from the initial endowment and allocation opportunities.

It is equally possible to imagine the existence of a long list of other constraints associated for the most part with the workings of the financial markets. Two possible examples could be:

$$m \geqslant 0 \text{ and } a \geqslant 0 \tag{9.3}$$

The first constraint says that borrowing is not allowed, because borrowing would correspond to a negative value of m. The second constraint ($a \geqslant 0$) rules out short-selling. Short-selling corresponds to a negative holding of a, that is, a debt or obligation to deliver in the future an asset that one does not hold initially.

We will consider only the constraint (9.2) because it necessarily holds whereas those in (9.3) depend on circumstances. Furthermore, since they are expressed as inequalities, they require additional mathematical tools (such as the Kuhn–Tucker conditions) whose marginal cost probably exceeds their marginal benefit in terms of economic intuition. Thus, never impose inequality constraints in what follows.

9.2 Optimisation conditions for different evaluation models

Before examining the technical aspects of the optimisation condition, we point out an important characteristic of the problem, namely, the linearity of $\tilde{w}_f$ both in the decision variables (a and/or m) and in the random parameter $\tilde{x}$. This linearity will play an important role in what follows and can be expressed elegantly and intuitively by substituting the constraint (9.2) directly into the definition of $\tilde{w}_f$. Specifically, it follows from Equation (9.2) that:

$$m = w_0 - a$$

and thus that

$$\tilde{w}_f = w_0(1 + i) + a(\tilde{x} - i) \tag{9.4}$$

The first term in this definition of $\tilde{w}_f$, namely $w_0(1 + i)$, represents the final wealth that the decision-maker would have had if w_0 had been invested exclusively in the risk-free asset ($a = 0$). The second term represents the surplus (positive or negative) that results from a non-zero choice of a. The expression in parentheses ($\tilde{x} - i$) measures the economic profit (positive or negative) realised by the risky investment. Specifically, the opportunity cost of investment in the risky asset, as measured by the risk-free return, is subtracted from the gross return to the risky asset $\tilde{x}$. Essentially, if a is increased by one monetary unit this creates a new source of revenue ($\tilde{x}$) but, because of the budget constraint, it also removes a monetary unit from m and thus forfeits the return i. Expression (9.4) of course exhibits the linearity of $\tilde{w}_f$ in its arguments as well as the endogenous nature of the risk.

Having described the context within which choices are made, we may now examine the optimisation conditions under different evaluation criteria.

9.2.1 The expected value criterion

If the decision-maker uses this criterion, a value of a (and thus of m) is chosen that solves:

$$\text{Max}_a \ E(\tilde{w}_f) = w_0(1 + i) + a(\mu - i)$$

where $\mu = E(\tilde{x})$, the expected value of the return $\tilde{x}$.

The derivative of the objective function with respect to the decision variable is:

$$dE(\tilde{w}_f)/da = \mu - i$$

and three cases are possible.

1. $\mu - i > 0$ implies that a^*, the optimal value of a, tends towards infinity $(+\infty)$. Specifically, at any a, an increase in a increases the welfare of the individual and is thus undertaken. Concretely, if the expected value of the return $\tilde{x}$ exceeds i, even by a small amount, the individual dares to take an extremely risky position. Indeed, the individual goes into debt to invest an amount in the risky asset that is significantly larger than the initial endowment. The expected value criterion thus implies that, in return for a small increase in *expected* return relative to i, the decision-maker accepts a large risk of bankruptcy. Specifically, if $\tilde{x} < i$ is realised – which is far from unlikely if μ is only slightly larger than i – and if the individual has invested a lot in a, they will be unable to repay the debt and its associated interest charge. This is consistent with the logic of the criterion: by concentrating only on expected value, the decision-maker ignores all other aspects of choice, notably risk.
2. $\mu - i < 0$ implies that a^* tends towards minus infinity. The decision-maker wishes to sell short as much of the risky asset as possible because the proceeds can be invested at the risk-free rate i. *In expected value terms*, at maturity only $1 + \mu$ needs to be paid for each monetary unit's worth of the risky asset that is sold short, but $1 + i$ is received for each unit. If the expected value criterion is adopted, enormous investments are made – far larger than w_0 – that are financed by short sales. Of course if it happens that $x > i$ – which is far from impossible when μ is only slightly less than i – gigantic losses are suffered that exceed initial capital and bankruptcy results.
3. $\mu - i = 0$ implies that the individual is completely indifferent between a and m so any solution is equally acceptable.

The rather peculiar conclusions which result from the application of the expected value criterion to a basic problem in finance largely discredit the expected value model. This should not be too surprising because only one lottery is considered here and it is played only once: it is the only one because the problem entails no other source of risk and it is played only once because the decision-maker's horizon ends at the end of the period. We have already seen that in similar circumstances the expected value criterion is inadequate and our analysis here amply confirms that conclusion. Note in addition that in this application the criterion implies a discontinuity in the decision that is unlikely to be observed. Specifically, let $i = 0.10$ and let two similar distributions of $\tilde{x}$ be defined by:

I		II	
x	$p(x)$	x	$p(x)$
0.07	0.499	0.07	0.501
0.13	0.501	0.13	0.499

For these lotteries, $\mu_I = 0.100\,06 > 0.10$ and $\mu_{II} = 0.099\,94 < 0.10$. It follows that in the first case (I) a^* tends towards $+\infty$ and in the second case a^* tends toward $-\infty$: there is a complete reversal of the decision even though the change in the lottery is small. This implication of the model seems extreme because one naturally expects greater stability of optimal decisions with respect to small changes in the environment.

9.2.2 The 'mean variance' criterion

We now turn to a criterion that takes into account an attitude towards risk that differs from the one that is implicit in the previous section, namely, risk neutrality. In order to avoid complicated algebra, consider the simple version of the mean variance criterion, that is:

$$V(\tilde{w}_f) = E(\tilde{w}_f) - k\sigma^2(\tilde{w}_f)$$

where k is assumed to be positive (risk aversion).

Applying the definition of $\tilde{w}_f$ in the present case, the optimisation problem is written as:

$$\text{Max}_a \ V(\tilde{w}_f) = w_0(1 + i) + a(\mu - i) - ka^2\sigma_x^2$$

and the optimality conditions are:

$$dV/da = (\mu - i) - 2ka\sigma_x^2 = 0 \tag{9.5}$$

and

$$d^2V/da^2 = -2k\sigma_x^2 < 0 \tag{9.5a}$$

from which it follows that the solution to Equation (9.5) is indeed a maximum. When k is strictly positive, Equation (9.5) yields a unique and finite[2] solution:

$$a^* = (\mu - i)/2k\sigma_x^2 \qquad (9.5\text{b})$$

which has some very interesting properties:

1. If $(\mu - i)$ increases, *ceteris paribus*, a^* increases. This is intuitive because an increase in $(\mu - i)$ (with a constant variance of $\tilde{x}$) implies that the risky asset has become relatively more attractive for the investor than the risk-free asset.
2. If k, the degree of risk aversion, and/or σ_x^2, the level of risk, increase, the desired holdings of the risky asset diminish.

It is interesting to note that the shift from the expected value criterion to the mean variance criterion leads to much sharper and more acceptable predictions.

9.2.3 The expected utility criterion

If the investor adopts this criterion, the optimisation problem is stated as:

$$\text{Max}_a E[U(\tilde{w}_f)] = \text{Max}_a E[U(w_0(1 + i) + a(\tilde{x} - i))]$$

and the optimality conditions are:

$$dE(U)/da = E[U'(\tilde{w}_f)(\tilde{x} - i)] = 0 \qquad (9.6)$$

$$d^2E(U)/da^2 = E[U''(\tilde{w}_f)(\tilde{x} - i)^2] < 0 \qquad (9.6\text{a})$$

Before commenting in detail on the first-order condition, we note immediately that, if the investor is risk averse, the second-order condition for a maximum is automatically satisfied. Specifically, the second derivative of $E(U)$ with respect to a is nothing other than the expected value of a product of terms, one of which is always negative ($U'' < 0$ by risk aversion) and the other of which is always positive $[(x - i)^2]$. The product of these terms is thus negative for all realisations of $\tilde{x}$ and thus also in expected value. Indeed, function $E(U)$ is everywhere strictly concave in a, a property that will be seen to be extremely important in comparative statics analysis.

To analyse the first-order condition, it is first necessary to consider the sign of a at the optimum, denoted a^*. To this end, consider the value of $dE(U)/da$ at the point $a = 0$:

$$[dE(U)/da]_{a=0} = E[U'(w_0(1 + i))(\tilde{x} - i)] \qquad (9.7)$$

$$= U'(w_0(1 + i))E(\tilde{x} - i) \qquad (9.8)$$

One can derive Equation (9.8) from Equation (9.7) by moving U' outside of the expected value operator since at $a = 0$ (and only at $a = 0$) the marginal utility (U') is not random because $\tilde{w}_f$, upon which U' depends, is not random if the decision-maker owns none of the risky asset.

It follows from Equation (9.8) that the sign of $dE(U)/da$ at $a = 0$ depends exclusively on the sign of $\mu - i$. If μ exceeds i then the expression in Equation (9.8) is positive, whereas it is negative for μ less than i. This characteristic, combined with the concavity of $E(U)$ in a, allows us to conclude that:

$$a^* > 0 \text{ if and only if } \mu > i$$
$$a^* < 0 \text{ if and only if } \mu < i$$

The proof of this result is illustrated by Figure 9.2(a) and (b). In Figure 9.2(a), $dE(U)/da$ is positive at $a = 0$ and, due to the global concavity of $E(U)$, the maximum is attained at a value (denoted a^*) that is greater than 0, and thus strictly positive. The opposite occurs in Figure 9.2(b) where $E(U)$ exhibits its inevitable concavity, but since the derivative with respect to a, evaluated at $a = 0$, now takes on a negative value, the optimum is necessarily to the left of $a = 0$. In addition to being of purely technical interest, this result has an economic interpretation. It shows specifically that a risk-averse individual can very well be rational and take risks[3]! For this to happen, it is necessary and sufficient that the risky asset 'pay' more in expected value than the opportunity cost represented by i. This discussion thus provides a glimpse of the trade-off that there can be between the expected return and the level of risk.

With the help of these results, we can now better consider the significance of Equation (9.6). To this end we rewrite it as follows:

$$E[U'(\tilde{w}_f)\tilde{x}] = E[U'(\tilde{w}_f)]i$$

or, again using the definition of covariance:

$$\mu E[U'(\tilde{w}_f)] + \text{cov}(U'(\tilde{w}_f), \tilde{x}) = iE[U'(\tilde{w}_f)]$$

Given that $E[U'(\tilde{w}_f)] \equiv E(U')$ is strictly positive, both sides can be divided by $E(U')$ to finally write:

$$\mu + \frac{\text{cov}(U', \tilde{x})}{E(U')} = i \qquad (9.9)$$

The right-hand side of Equation (9.9) reflects marginal cost, the opportunity cost of acquiring an additional unit of a. Since Equation (9.9) is an equilibrium condition, elementary economic intuition suggests that the left-hand side represents a gross marginal benefit which, in equilibrium and only in equilibrium, equals marginal cost. This is indeed the interpretation to give to the left-hand side of Equation (9.9). Note that the gross marginal benefit is itself composed of two elements:

(a) the expected value of $\tilde{x}(\mu)$ which is the contribution to expected final wealth of the marginal monetary unit invested in a;

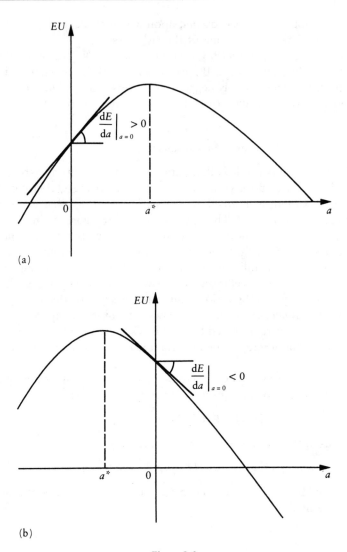

Figure 9.2

(b) another term with a negative (positive) sign for all $a > 0$ (for all $a < 0$) if the individual is risk averse.

This 'other term' deserves our attention. We first show that it is indeed negative for all $a > 0$. Specifically, in this case, when there is an increase in the realisation of $\tilde{x}$, the investor is richer and w_f is larger. Since marginal utility is decreasing in w_f (by risk aversion), an improvement in x implies, via the increase in w_f, a fall in U' and this creates a negative covariance[4] between the random variables $\tilde{x}$ and $U'(\tilde{w}_f)$. It thus turns out that, for all positive a and $U'' < 0$, the gross marginal benefit of an increase in a is less than μ. We note in passing that if the decision-maker were risk neutral then the gross marginal benefit would equal μ exactly: in the case of risk neutrality the marginal utility of U' is constant and the covariance is thus zero because U' does not react to changes in x (and in w_f).

The negative value of the second term on the left of Equation (9.9) in the case of risk aversion (and for all $a > 0$) as well as its zero value when there is risk neutrality, strongly suggests that it represents in monetary terms the psychological cost of the additional risk associated with an investment in a. This is indeed the case: one can interpret the left-hand side of Equation (9.9) as the expected value of $\tilde{x}$ minus the 'marginal cost of risk'[5] associated with an increase in a. The reader who is familiar with finance theory will undoubtedly not be surprised to see the definition of marginal cost of risk in terms of a covariance.

In Figure 9.3 we graphically represent the different terms in Equation (9.9) and show how they interact to determine a^*.

The lines at the level of μ and i are horizontal because we have assumed that these parameters are independent of the individual's decisions. When the investor is risk neutral these two lines are the only elements to consider, and if μ is greater than i, the optimal value of a tends towards $+\infty$.

With the introduction of risk aversion, an additional element must naturally be taken into account: the marginal cost of risk reflected by the covariance term in Equation (9.9). At a equal to zero, this term is zero because, with $\tilde{w}_f$ certain, U' is not random and the covariance between a constant (U') and a random variable $(\tilde{x})$ is zero. For all $a > 0$, marginal cost is strictly positive and in Figure 9.3 we have implicitly recognised that it is

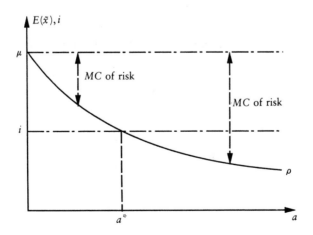

Figure 9.3

increasing with a, which is consistent with intuition.[6] Specifically, it seems clear that for a risk-averse individual it is more painful to increase a if a lot of risk has already been accepted (that is, if a is initially large) than in the opposite case. This marginal cost of risk is deducted from μ, the gross marginal benefit of a under risk neutrality, to generate the curve $\mu\rho$ which represents the true gross marginal benefit for a risk-averse individual of increasing holdings of a.

Since we attach some importance to the economic interpretation of the algebraic derivations, we now illustrate Equation (9.9) and Figure 9.3 with an example. Consider a negative exponential utility function $U(w) = -e^{-\beta w}$ where $A_a = \beta$ represents the absolute risk aversion, which is constant in this case (see Chapter 4). Assume also that the return of the risky asset is distributed normally with mean μ and variance σ_x^2, that is:

$$f(x) = \frac{1}{\sigma\sqrt{2\pi}} \exp\left(-0.5\left(\frac{x-\mu}{\sigma_x}\right)^2\right)$$

It is well known that if x is normally distributed then w_f, which is a linear function of x, is also. Now, since w_f is normally distributed with mean μ_w and variance σ_w^2,

$$E[U(\tilde{w}_f)] = -E[\exp(-\beta w_f)] = -\exp(-\beta\mu_w + 0.5\beta^2\sigma_w^2)$$

The proof of the last equality is not easy, because it requires using the moment-generating function that statisticians know well. Nevertheless, the reader can find this formula in any good table of definite integrals. The maximisation of expected utility is thus equivalent to the minimisation of the exponent of e, or, since β is positive, to:

$$\text{Max}_a \, \mu_w - 0.5\beta\sigma_w^2$$

This is particularly interesting because we have just shown that if the random variable is normally distributed and the utility function is a negative exponential, then the expected utility criterion is equivalent to the mean variance criterion with $k = 0.5\beta$. This result is intensively used in finance theory, as will be seen in Chapter 15. The first-order condition of this problem is:

$$\partial\mu_w/\partial a - 0.5\beta(\partial\sigma_w^2/\partial a) = 0$$

Now

$$\mu_w = w_0(1+i) + a(\mu - i)$$
$$\sigma_w^2 = a^2\sigma_x^2$$

It follows then from the first-order condition that:

$$(\mu - i) - \beta a^* \sigma_x^2 = 0$$

that is, that the marginal cost of risk is a linear function of a. It also follows that:

$$a^* = (\mu - i)/A_a \sigma_x^2 \qquad (9.10)$$

This solution is equivalent to the solution of Equation (9.5b) obtained in the context of the mean variance criterion. It thus turns out that, in this case, the demand for the risky asset is:

(a) a decreasing function of absolute risk aversion;
(b) an increasing function of the difference between the returns on the risky and the risk-free assets;
(c) a decreasing function of the variance of the return on the risky asset.

In the next section it is shown how these results can – or cannot – be generalised. First, we consider a numerical example. Let an investor be characterised by a negative exponential utility function $-e^{-4w_f}$. The initial wealth that can be invested is $w_0 = 10$ and there is a choice between two investment opportunities:

(a) a risk-free asset returning 12 per cent ($i = 0.12$);
(b) a risky asset represented by a tradable security whose return is normally distributed with mean $\mu = 0.16$ and standard deviation 0.06 (so that $\sigma_x^2 = 0.0036$).

One can interpret this as follows: based on the information available and taking account of 'optimism' (which translates this information into a probability distribution) the individual believes that the risky asset is likely to yield more than the risk-free asset. Specifically:

$$\text{prob}\{\tilde{x} > i\} = \text{Prob}\left\{\frac{\tilde{x} - 0.16}{0.06} > \frac{0.12 - 0.16}{0.06}\right\}$$

$$= \text{Prob}\{\tilde{z} > -\tfrac{2}{3}\}$$

where $\tilde{z}$ has a standard normal distribution. Thus, this probability is 0.7454, implying that the likelihood that the risky asset will have a better return than the risk-free asset is high.

The solution, Equation (9.10), in this case corresponds to $a^* = (0.0400/0.0144) = 2.778$, that is, the individual invests 27.78 per cent of total initial endowment of 10 in the risky asset. The derivation of this result is illustrated in Figure 9.4 where the horizontal lines corresponding to μ and i lie at levels 0.16 and 0.12, respectively.

Here the marginal cost of risk is increasing and its equation is a line with slope equal to 0.0144 which is subtracted from 0.16. It is clear from the figure

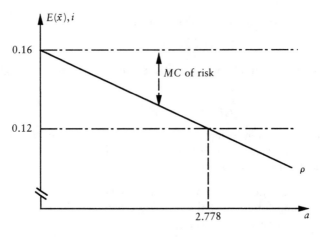

Figure 9.4

that it is not advantageous to invest more than $a = 2.778$ in the risky asset. Specifically, at point $a = 4$, the gross marginal benefit of the last franc invested in a is $0.16 - (0.0144)4 = 0.1024$ and since this rate is less than the opportunity cost (0.12) the best decision to make at $a = 4$ is to reduce the risky investment. Of course the opposite situation prevails for all $a < 2.778$.

Having listed the properties of the optimality condition, we can proceed to the different comparative statics exercises.

9.3 Comparative statics analysis

The presentation will proceed in several steps. The first, and the simplest, deals with the effect of an increase in w_0. If an investor has more initial resources will the risky investments be increased, not only in absolute value but also in relative value (a as a fraction of w_0)? We show that the assumptions made about the behaviour of absolute risk aversion and relative risk aversion are crucial for predicting the effects of an increase in w_0.

We next ask about the effect of a change in i. We show that its impact is not unrelated to that of a change in μ or a modification of the density of $\tilde{x}$ in the sense of first-order stochastic dominance. Finally, we ask how an increase in risk with a given mean for $\tilde{x}$ affects the holdings of the risky asset.

9.3.1 The effect of a change in w_0

The first question is technically stated as follows: what is the sign of da^*/dw_0? In economics terms, we ask if the risky asset is a normal good or an inferior good. The answer to this question is furnished by a well known, elegant proof, which is very useful in risk theory because it makes clear the role of assumptions on the behaviour of A_a. We present it first in its classical form and then we suggest a graphical interpretation (which is new as far as we know) based on the analysis of Figure 9.3.

Since we are essentially interested in the sign of da^*/dw_0 (and not in its magnitude) it is possible to simplify the analysis considerably by noticing that the term between the equal signs in the first-order condition (9.6) is a function of the decision variable as well as of all the exogenous variables in the problem. Specifically, $E[U'(\tilde{w}_f)(\tilde{x} - i)]$ clearly depends (explicitly) on i and on $\tilde{x}$ (and thus on its distribution). It also depends, indirectly and thus more subtly, on all of the parameters that influence $\tilde{w}_f$ namely, from the definition of $\tilde{w}_f$ in Equation (9.4), w_0 and a in addition to the variables already mentioned. As a result, one can write:

$$H(a; w_0, i, F(x)) = E[U'(\tilde{w}_f)(\tilde{x} - i)]$$

where H is a function whose properties are to be studied and in which the decision variable, a, has been set apart from the exogenous variables. Among these, the distribution function of $\tilde{x}$, $F(x)$, indicates that the nature of the function H depends on the distribution of $\tilde{x}$.

Since at the optimum $H = 0$ and, since we are interested in the effect of a change in w_0, other things equal (for example, $di = 0$), totally differentiate the left-hand side of the above equality to write:

$$dH = (\partial H/\partial a) \, da + (\partial H/w_0)w_0 = 0 \tag{9.11}$$

Given that function H is the first derivative of $E(U)$ with respect to a, the derivative of H with respect to a is itself the second derivative of $E(U)$ and thus everywhere negative. Then since:

$$da^*/dw_0 = (\partial H/\partial w_0)/(-\partial H/\partial a)$$

it follows that:

$$\text{sgn } da^*/dw_0 = \text{sgn } \partial H/\partial w_0$$

Applying the rules of differential calculus to the definition of H, we obtain:

$$\partial H/w_0 = (1 + i)E[U''(\tilde{w}_f)(\tilde{x} - i)] \tag{9.12}$$

Thus, evaluating the sign of da^*/dw_0 is the same as determining the sign of Equation (9.12) and thus the same as determining the sign of the expected value in that formula. Note that this sign is ambiguous *a priori* because, although U'' is everywhere negative, $(\tilde{x} - i)$ is sometimes positive and sometimes negative.[7] Fortunately, the assumptions on the behaviour of absolute risk aversion remove the ambiguity.

We begin by considering a case of constant absolute risk aversion. In this case:

$$-U''(w_f)/U'(w_f) = \beta$$

where β is a positive constant. It follows that one may also write: $-U''(\tilde{w}_f) = \beta U'(\tilde{w}_f)$. Consequently, it is also true that:

$$E[U''(\tilde{w}_f)(\tilde{x} - i)] = -E[\beta U'(\tilde{w}_f)(\tilde{x} - i)]$$
$$= -\beta E[U'(\tilde{w}_f)(\tilde{x} - i)]$$

The last expression is zero from the first-order condition (9.6). It follows that if A_a is constant, then $da^*/dw_0 = 0$.

What can we conclude when absolute risk aversion is positive and decreasing in wealth? In this case:

$$-U''(w_f)/U'(w_f) = \beta(w_f) \tag{9.13}$$

where $\beta(w_f)$ is a function that is everywhere positive and decreasing in w_f (and thus also in x when a is positive). Using Equations (9.13) with (9.12) yields

$$E[U''(\tilde{x} - i)] = -E[\beta(\tilde{w}_f)U'(\tilde{w}_f)(\tilde{x} - i)] \tag{9.14}$$

To find the sign of the right-hand side, note that $U'(w_f)(x - i)$ is negative for all $x < i$, positive for all $x > i$ and zero if and only if $x = i$.[8] If $\beta(w_f)$ were constant then the right-hand side of Equation (9.14) would equal zero, as we have seen. What happens when $\beta(w_f)$ is positive and decreasing? When $x < i$, and thus when $U'(w_f)(x - i)$ is negative, $U'(w_f)(x - i)$ is multiplied by a larger number, $\beta(w_f)$, than is the case for values of x that make $U'(w_f)(x - i)$ positive. This is illustrated in Figure 9.5, where the reader should compare the two sides of the vertical dashed line at $x = i$. If the weight multiplying $U'(x - i)$, namely $\beta(w_f)$, were constant, the expected value $E[U'(\tilde{x} - i)]$ would be zero. Given that $\beta(w_f)$ is 'rotated' to take on higher values when $U'(x - i)$ is negative, however, it follows that:

$$E[\beta(\tilde{w}_f)U'(\tilde{w}_f)(\tilde{x} - i)] < 0$$

so Equation (9.14) has a positive sign. We conclude that if absolute risk aversion is decreasing, then da^*/dw_0 is positive.

It is easy to show that if absolute risk aversion is increasing then the result is reversed. We summarise the above analysis in Theorem 9.1.

Theorem 9.1 Demand for a risky asset is normal (or inferior), that is $da^*/dw_0 > 0$ (or $da^*/dw_0 < 0$), if absolute risk aversion is a decreasing (or an increasing) function of wealth. Furthermore, if absolute risk aversion is constant then $da^*/dw_0 = 0$.

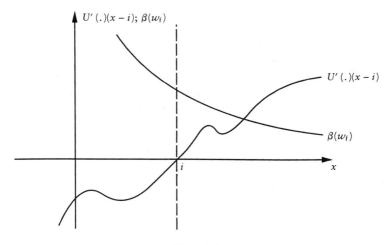

Figure 9.5

Intuition, confirmed by empirical studies, strongly suggests that risky assets are normal goods. Thus, the results contained in Theorem 9.1 lend support to the assumption of decreasing absolute risk aversion.

Before considering more deeply the results contained in Theorem 9.1, we present a graphical interpretation of the case where absolute risk aversion is decreasing in wealth. All of the essential elements for determining a^* are illustrated in Figure 9.6. Horizontal lines are drawn at μ and at i, and the marginal cost of risk is subtracted from μ to generate the curve $\mu\rho$.

To deduce how a change in w_0 affects a^*, it is necessary to know how it shifts each of the relevant curves. Since the change in w_0 is made holding all

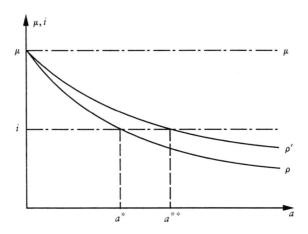

Figure 9.6

other things equal, the horizontal lines μ and i are not altered. The marginal cost of risk does change, however, and it is easy to see in which direction. Since A_a is decreasing, an increase in wealth reduces an individual's degree of absolute risk aversion and thus it decreases the subjective marginal cost of risk.[9] As a result the curve $\mu\rho$ shifts to $\mu\rho'$. For each a, $\mu\rho'$ is closer to the horizontal line μ than is $\mu\rho$, reflecting the decrease in the marginal cost of risk. Since the new curve $\mu\rho'$ is higher, it cuts the horizontal line i at a higher value of a, denoted a^{**}.

Having shown that the risky asset is indeed a normal good if A_a is decreasing, we now ask whether the risky asset is also a superior good (sometimes called a luxury good), that is, a normal good with a demand elasticity (with respect to w_0) that exceeds 1. To answer this question, first recall that this elasticity, denoted η_{w_0}, is defined by:

$$\eta_{w_0} = (\mathrm{d}a/\mathrm{d}w_0)(w_0/a)$$

Since $\mathrm{d}a/\mathrm{d}w_0 = -(\partial H/w_0)/(\partial H/\partial a)$, it follows that:

$$\eta_{w_0} = \frac{-(1+i)E[U''(\tilde{w}_f)(\tilde{x}-i)]}{E[U''(\tilde{w}_f)(\tilde{x}-i)^2]} \; \frac{w_0}{a}$$

Since we are interested in the magnitude of η_{w_0}, which is a positive number, relative to $+1$, we manipulate the last expression to write:

$$\eta_{w_0} = 1 + \frac{-(1+i)w_0 E[U''(\tilde{w}_f)(\tilde{x}-i)] - aE[U''(\tilde{w}_f)(\tilde{x}-i)^2]}{aE[U''(\tilde{w}_f)(\tilde{x}-i)^2]}$$

(9.15)

For $a > 0$ the denominator is clearly negative and thus the magnitude of η_{w_0} relative to 1 depends on the sign of the numerator, which can be written as:

$$-E[U''(\tilde{w}_f)(\tilde{x}-i)\tilde{w}_f] \tag{9.15a}$$

because $\tilde{w}_f = w_0(1+i) + a(\tilde{x}-i)$.

It turns out that the sign of this expression is determined entirely by the behaviour of relative risk aversion (A_r). Specifically, remember that $A_r = -w_f U''(w_f)/U'(w_f)$. If A_r is constant (and equal to a positive number α) then we may write:

$$-U''(w_f) = \alpha U'(w_f)/w_f$$

from which it follows that Equation (9.15a) is equivalent to:

$$\alpha E[U'(\tilde{w}_f)(\tilde{x}-i)]$$

an expression which equals zero due to the first-order condition. Thus if relative risk aversion is constant then $\eta_{w_0} = 1$.

If relative risk aversion is increasing write:

$$- [U''(w_f)/U'(w_f)] w_f = \alpha(w_f)$$

where $\alpha(w_f)$ is a positive increasing function of w_f. Then Equation (9.15a) can be rewritten as:

$$E[U'(\tilde{w}_f)(\tilde{x} - i)\alpha(\tilde{w}_f)] \qquad (9.16)$$

By reasoning similar to that used in the proof of Theorem 9.1, it can be shown that this expression is positive. Specifically, when $U'(x - i)$ is positive (that is, for all $x > i$ and thus when w_f is large), $U'(x - i)$ is multiplied by a relatively large weight $\alpha(w_f)$. In calculating the expected value, one thus weights the positive terms relatively more heavily than they are weighted when a is constant and the expected value is zero. It follows that Equation (9.16), or equivalently, (9.15a) is positive and $\eta_{w_0} < 1$. Of course, it is easy to show that if A_r is decreasing then $\eta_{w_0} > 1$.

Before summarising the results derived in this first comparative statics exercise, we provide some intuition for the above arguments. Unfortunately, it is not possible to draw a graph that is analogous to Figure 9.6 to demonstrate the different effects that play a role. The intuition for these results comes from the well-known result in microeconomics that:

$$\eta_{w_0} > 1 \qquad \text{if and only if } d(a/w_0)/dw_0 > 0.$$

To say that a is a superior good ($\eta > 1$) is the same as asserting that the fraction of the portfolio held in the risky asset increases in wealth. Yet if relative risk aversion is decreasing then we know that the individual whose wealth increases is willing to give up a smaller fraction of this wealth in return for protection against a multiplicative risk. Given that this fear of risk per monetary unit invested decreases with w_0, it is natural that, when offered a risky investment, the wealthier individual dares to invest a larger fraction of their fortune in the risky asset.

This concludes our first comparative statics exercise. The results are presented in a summary table (Table 9.1) that combines the assumptions on absolute and relative risk aversion.

Four cases correspond to impossible situations because, as was seen in Chapter 4, decreasing relative risk aversion in w_0 is inconsistent with constant or increasing absolute risk aversion in w_0 (see more specifically Equation (4.10)).

9.3.2 The effect of a change in i

We now ask how a change in i – say an increase – affects the composition of a portfolio of constant size w_0. Intuition suggests that an increase in i, by making the risk-free asset more attractive to hold, should lead to an adjustment of the portfolio towards m and away from a. The analysis to be

Table 9.1

	A_a decreasing	A_a constant	A_a increasing
A_r decreasing	$\eta > 1$	impossible	impossible
A_r constant	$\eta = 1$	impossible	impossible
A_r increasing	$0 < \eta < 1$	$\eta = 0$	$\eta < 0$

developed will allow us to see whether this intuition is well-founded. Furthermore, it will provide some opportunities for further reflection on the level and behaviour of the coefficients of risk aversion.

To study the sign[10] of da^*/di mathematically, recall the definition of H from which it is deduced by differentiation that:

$$\frac{da^*}{di} = -\frac{\partial H/\partial i}{\partial H/\partial a}$$

from which it follows that

$$\mathrm{sgn}\,\frac{da^*}{di} = \mathrm{sgn}\,\frac{\partial H}{\partial i}$$

Now it is easily shown that:

$$\frac{\partial H}{\partial i} = E\,[-U'(\tilde{w}_f) + (\tilde{x} - i)U''(\tilde{w}_f)(w_0 - a^*)] \tag{9.17}$$

The expected value in Equation (9.17) contains two terms of which the first is clearly negative. The second term may be positive or negative depending on the value of x relative to i. Note also that the sign of the second term is influenced by the sign of $w_0 - a^* = m^*$, which is positive for a net lender but negative for a net borrower. The ambiguity of the effect on a^* of a change in i is essentially due to the fact that an increase in i induces both a substitution effect and a wealth effect. Since the wealth effect can sometimes counteract the substitution effect, the net result is sometimes ambiguous. The notion of the marginal cost of risk that has already been graphically illustrated in Figures 9.3 and 9.6 is useful for understanding the different effects that are in play.

In Figure 9.7(a) the initial situation is represented by curves μ, i and $\mu\rho$, which give rise to the initial optimal point a^*. If i increases to i', the horizontal line i shifts upward. If this were the only effect then the demand for the risky asset would necessarily decrease, from a^* to $\hat{a}$. However, there is another effect to consider. If initially m^* is positive (that is, if the decision-maker is a net lender) then the increase in i is enriching him and this, as we know, affects the marginal cost of risk. When absolute risk aversion is decreasing, the investor's greater wealth reduces risk aversion and shifts the $\mu\rho$ curve to, for example, $\mu\rho'$ (see Appendix 6). This effect increases the risky investment from $\hat{a}$ to a^{**}. The net effect, illustrated in Figure 9.7, is negative because a^{**} is

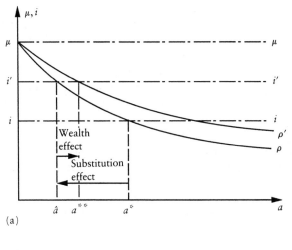

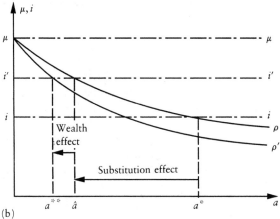

Figure 9.7

smaller than a^*. However, it is clear that if absolute risk aversion decreases quickly as wealth increases then it is possible that $a^{**} > a^*$.

This breakdown of the effect of a change in price (here, the interest rate) on the demand for a good is well-known in microeconomic theory. The change from a^* to $\hat{a}$ is called the 'substitution effect'. It consists of substituting some of the risk-free asset for some of the risky asset when the risk-free interest rate rises. The second effect is called the 'wealth (or income) effect'. It comes from the fact that an increase in interest rate implies an implicit increase in the wealth of the net lenders, inducing an increase in demand for the risky asset if $dA_a/dw_f < 0$, as we have seen previously. If the substitution effect is stronger than the wealth effect, then the net effect corresponds to basic intuition $(a^{**} < a^*)$; but the wealth effect may be stronger, implying $a^{**} > a^*$. Then it is said that the risk-free asset is a Giffen good. In classical microeconomic theory, the existence of Giffen goods cannot be excluded theoretically. Alas, things are no better under uncertainty!

It is interesting to note that, for an investor whose initial a^* exceeds w_0 $(m^* < 0)$, an increase in i causes a reduction in wealth. If absolute risk aversion decreases with wealth, then the marginal cost of risk increases when i increases. In this case, as can be seen in Figure 9.7(b), the second effect reinforces the first and a^{**} is necessarily less than a^*.

In conclusion, it must be recognised that, contrary to expectations, it is not possible to prove that da/di is always negative for a risk-averse individual. To derive this result, one must either restrict attention to the case of an individual who is initially a net borrower or one must assume − if the agent is a net lender − that the substitution effect dominates the wealth effect.

9.3.3 An improvement (in the sense of first-order stochastic dominance) in the distribution of $\tilde{x}$

In the initial situation the investor takes information about the risky asset (say stock in a company traded on a stock exchange) and, given a degree of optimism, translates it into a probability distribution corresponding to the initial random variable $\tilde{x}$. Now imagine that this investor receives some 'good news' about the future of the company that issued the risky stock. Given an unchanged degree of optimism on the part of the investor, the good news is reflected in the fact that the best outcomes from holding the asset become more probable and the worst outcomes become less probable. This idea is formalised by saying that $\tilde{x}$ is transformed into $\tilde{y}$ where, for all t,

$$\text{Prob}\{\tilde{x} < t\} > \text{Prob}\{\tilde{y} < t\}$$

which necessarily implies:

$$\text{Prob}\{\tilde{x} > t\} < \text{Prob}\{\tilde{y} > t\}$$

The reader will, of course, recognise the notion of first-order stochastic dominance of $\tilde{y}$ over $\tilde{x}$ that was presented in Part One.

Before proceeding with the comparative statics analysis, we would like to point out that the same kind of change could occur without new information but simply because the individual becomes more optimistic about the future of the firm whose stock is under consideration for purchase. The exogenous changes considered in this section can come from new information, from changes in the attitude of the investor or from a combination of the two.

To begin the comparative statics analysis simply, while taking advantage of the analysis of the previous case, we assume that the improvement in $\tilde{x}$ is accomplished by a uniform shift of its density to the right. Specifically, $\tilde{x}$, initially characterised by $\mu + \tilde{\varepsilon}$, becomes $\tilde{x}' = \mu' + \tilde{\varepsilon}$ where $\mu' > \mu$. To take advantage of this particular structure, we write the initial problem as follows:

$$\text{Max}_a E[U(w_0(1 + i) + a(\mu + \tilde{\varepsilon} - i))]$$

for which the first-order condition is:

$$E[U'(\tilde{w}_f)(\mu + \tilde{\varepsilon} - i)] = 0 \qquad (9.18)$$

Our object is to study the impact of a change in μ on a^*. First, intuitive reasoning suggests the nature of the results to expect. Specifically, if one carefully inspects Equation (9.18) and the definition of $EU(\tilde{w}_f)$ that precedes it, it becomes clear that an increase in μ has an effect that is quite similar to that of a decrease in i. Note, however, that the change in μ will not have the identical effect of a change in i. Specifically, as it appears in the definition of $\tilde{w}_f$, μ affects final wealth only because it enters multiplicatively in combination with a, whereas i influences $\tilde{w}_f$ in combination with a and w_0 (with opposite signs).

This difference allows us to use profitably the concept of partial risk aversion described above, to study the impact of a change in μ. Specifically, using a now well-known technique, differentiate the left-hand side of Equation (9.18) to write:

$$\text{sgn}\,\frac{\mathrm{d}a^*}{\mathrm{d}\mu} = \text{sgn}(E[U'(\tilde{w}_f) + U''(\tilde{w}_f)(\mu + \tilde{\varepsilon} - i)a^*]) \qquad (9.19)$$

If, following Fishburn and Porter (1976), we highlight $U'(\tilde{w}_f)$ in the expected value, then we can write:

$$\text{sgn}\,\frac{\mathrm{d}a^*}{\mathrm{d}\mu} = \text{sgn}\left(EU'(\tilde{w}_f)\left[1 + \frac{U''(\tilde{w}_f)}{U'(\tilde{w}_f)}(\mu + \tilde{\varepsilon} - i)a^*\right]\right) \qquad (9.19\text{a})$$

The coefficient of absolute risk aversion (with the opposite sign) evaluated at $\tilde{w}_f$ appears in Equation (9.19a) and is multiplied by a sum of money, $(\mu + \tilde{\varepsilon} - i)a^*$, that is different from $\tilde{w}_f$. The coefficient of partial risk aversion also appears and, if it is always less than one, $\mathrm{d}a^*/\mathrm{d}\mu$ will be positive. Theorem 9.2 can thus be stated.

Theorem 9.2 If partial risk aversion is everywhere less than (greater than) 1, then $\mathrm{d}a^*/\mathrm{d}\mu$ is positive (negative).

Since many people expect that an increase in μ will increase a^*, this result seems to suggest that partial risk aversion is probably less than 1.

To give a less technical explanation of the analysis, we proceed to the graphical representation of the results and distinguish between the substitution effect and the wealth effect. As usual, curves μ, i and $\mu\rho$ in Figure 9.8 describe the initial situation with the solution a^*. If μ increases to μ', the horizontal line shifts upward in parallel fashion. If the marginal cost of risk remained the same then the new curve $\mu'\rho'$ would be achieved by shifting the curve $\mu\rho$

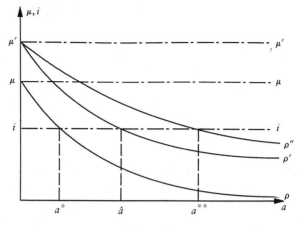

Figure 9.8

upward by a constant amount ($\mu' - \mu$). Since of course the horizontal line i is unchanged, the new equilibrium would be at $\hat{a}$, which is necessarily larger than a^*.

However this considers only one of the two effects. Since μ exceeds i, a^* is positive and the increase in μ induces an implicit increase in the wealth of the investor. From this it follows that if the absolute risk aversion decreases with wealth, then the marginal cost of risk is reduced. Thus one obtains the curve $\mu\rho''$, which describes the marginal benefit of additional investment in a and lies everywhere above $\mu\rho'$. This effect reinforces the other effect and so if A_a is decreasing in w then da^*/dw is positive when the individual initially holds a positive quantity of the risky asset.

Hence, graphical analysis is very similar in its appearance and conclusions to the graphical analysis developed for the study of the effect of change in i.

Having acquired some intuition by studying a special case, we now consider the general case in which the distribution of $\tilde{x}$ is transformed into $\tilde{y}$ with $\tilde{y} >_1 \tilde{x}$. This assumption implies, as we saw in Chapter 7, that $\mu_y > \mu_x$ but, in contrast to the case just considered, we do not require that the shift of $f(x)$ towards the right to generate $g(x)$, be uniform.

To clarify the technical steps that are to follow, we note from the start that, for all positive values of a, the change from $\tilde{x}$ to $\tilde{y}$ necessarily increases[11] $E(U)$ due to the definition of first-order stochastic dominance itself. In Figure 9.9(a) and (b) the initial curve, denoted $E[U(\tilde{x})]$ for brevity, is concave in a (see the second-order condition of Equation (9.6a)) and its maximum is attained at a^*. The change from $\tilde{x}$ to $\tilde{y}$ maintains the concavity of $E[U(\tilde{y})]$ and, as mentioned above, places $E[U(\tilde{y})]$ above $E[U(\tilde{x})]$ for all a.

However, on comparing parts (a) and (b) of Figure 9.9, one sees immediately that there are two possible cases. In the first, the change from

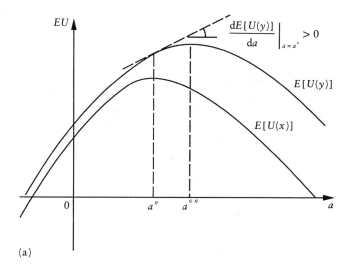

(a)

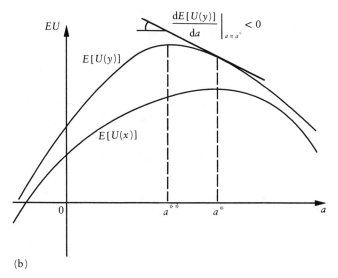

(b)

Figure 9.9

$E[U(\tilde{x})]$ to $E[U(\tilde{y})]$ implies that the new optimal value of a^* (a^{**}) exceeds the old (Figure 9.9(a)). In contrast, it can be that $a^{**} < a^*$ as in Figure 9.9(b).[12]

Examining Figure 9.9 furnishes an infallible test to establish which case is relevant: it suffices to evaluate the slope of $E[U(\tilde{y})]$ with respect to a at point a^* which is optimal for $E[U(\tilde{x})]$. If this slope is positive, as in Figure 9.9(a), then the concavity of $E(U)$ automatically implies that the optimum for $E[U(\tilde{y})]$ is attained after a^* and that $a^{**} > a^*$.

Conversely, if at point a^* that is optimal for $E[U(\tilde{x})]$, the slope of $E[U(\tilde{y})]$ is negative, the concavity of function $E(U)$ automatically implies that a^{**} is less than a^*, as can be seen in Figure 9.9(b). Our strategy for the proof will be based on this observation: we will calculate $dE[U(\tilde{y})]/da$ and evaluate it at the particular point $a = a^*$. Then we will ask about the sign of the resulting expression. Each time the sign can be declared to be positive or negative, it will be possible to compare a^* and a^{**} unambiguously.

Since the analysis is a bit delicate, we will develop it in some detail. The initial problem and its first-order condition are written as Equation (9.10). However, for the purposes of the proof, we will express $E(U)$ explicitly for a continuous distribution $\tilde{x}$:

$$\text{Max} \int_m^n U[w_0(1 + i) + a(x - i)]f(x) \, dx$$

where m and n are, respectively, the smallest and largest possible values of $\tilde{x}$ and $\tilde{y}$ (with $\tilde{y} >_1 \tilde{x}$). The first-order condition takes the form:

$$\int_m^n U'(w_f)(x - i)f(x) \, dx = 0 \tag{9.20}$$

where $w_f \equiv w_0(1 + i) + a^*(x - i)$ with a^* representing the solution to Equation (9.20).

To avoid all confusion and to facilitate a comparison with what follows, we rewrite Equation (9.20) in a more detailed manner:

$$\int_m^n U'(w_0(1 + i) + a^*(s - i))(s - i)f(s) \, ds = 0 \tag{9.20a}$$

where s plays the role of x – because the density function that is used is f – and will shortly play the role of y.

If the individual is now confronted with $\tilde{y}$ where $\tilde{y} >_1 \tilde{x}$, $E[U(\tilde{y})]$ is written as

$$E[U(\tilde{y})] = \int_m^n U[w_0(1 + i) + a(s - i)]g(s) \, ds$$

where g is the density function of $\tilde{y}$ and s plays the role of y.

Deriving $dE[U(\tilde{y})]/da$ and evaluating it at $a = a^*$ yields:

$$\left. \frac{dE}{da} \right|_{a = a^*} = \int_m^n U'[w_0(1 + i) + a^*(s - i)](s - i)g(s) \, ds \tag{9.21}$$

and, of course consistent with the above discussion, the sign of this expression will determine the sign of $a^{**} - a^*$.

Since the left-hand side of Equation (9.20a) equals zero, studying the sign of Equation (9.21) is the same as examining the sign of:

$$\int_m^n U'\left[w_0(1+i) + a^*(s-i)\right](s-i)(g(s) - f(s))\,ds \qquad (9.22)$$

To determine the sign of Equation (9.22) it is necessary to integrate by parts to derive an expression with $G(s) - F(s)$, the sign of which is known from the first-order stochastic dominance relationship. This yields:

$$[U'(\cdot)(s-i)[G(s) - F(s)]]_m^n - \int_m^n \{U'(\cdot) + (s-i)U''(\cdot)a^*\}[G(s) - F(s)]\,ds$$

where $(\cdot) = [w_0(1+i) + a^*(s-i)]$.

Since $G(n) = F(n) = 1$ while $G(m) = F(m) = 0$, the first expression is zero and so the sign of Equation (9.22) equals the sign of:

$$-\int_m^n \left\{U'(\cdot)\left[1 + (s-i)\frac{U''(\cdot)}{U'(\cdot)}a^*\right]\right\}[G(s) - F(s)]\,ds \qquad (9.22a)$$

Since $G(s) - F(s) \leqslant 0$ and U' is positive, the integral in Equation (9.22a) is negative when the bracketed expression is positive and this, in turn, occurs when partial risk aversion is less than 1. Specifically, for $s < i$, there is no problem as to the sign of the bracketed expression: it is necessarily positive for all risk-averse decision-makers. In contrast, if $s > i$, its sign can be either positive or negative unless partial risk aversion:

$$A_p = -(s-i)a^* \frac{U''(\cdot)}{U'(\cdot)}$$

is restricted to be less than 1.

It thus turns out that, despite the generalisation of the exogenous shock considered (> 1 instead of $\mu_y = \mu_x +$ constant), one can assert a theorem that is of the same nature as Theorem 9.2, that is:

Theorem 9.3 For $a^* > 0$, if partial risk aversion is everywhere less than one, an improvement in the distribution of $\tilde{x}$ that is unanimously preferred by decision-makers exhibiting $U' > 0$ induces an increase in the demand for the risky asset.

Thus we find once again an argument in favour of imposing an upper bound of 1 on the coefficient of partial risk aversion. Specifically, this yields, in the general case of an improved distribution in the sense of first-order stochastic dominance, a result that is comparable to that obtained in the special case of an increase in μ, other things being equal.

It is interesting to note, with Fishburn and Porter, that if one rejects all assumptions on U except $U' > 0$ and $U'' < 0$ then there is still a way to obtain intuitive comparative statics results if one is prepared to place restrictions on

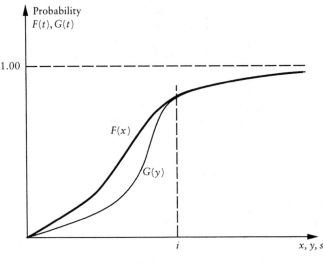

Figure 9.10

the probability distributions.[13] Specifically, if each time that s is larger than i, $G(s) = F(s)$, then the sign of Equation (9.22a) will be unambiguously negative. The ambiguity when $s > i$ comes from the bracketed expression, but if it is systematically multiplied by zero $[G(s) = F(s)]$ then this ambiguity does not affect the integral because, for $s < i$, the bracketed expression is uniformly positive and thus the sign of the integral is perfectly clear. To require that, for all $s > i$, $G(s) = F(s)$, means that no change in the distribution of the risky return takes place above i (above i, G and F coincide) while all favourable changes (compatible with $>_1$) take place for realisations of the return that are less than i. An example of a change from $\tilde{x}$ to $\tilde{y}$ that will induce an increase in a^* for all risk-averse individuals is given in Figure 9.10. All the improvement occurs at values of x that are less than the threshold represented by i. Above i the two curves coincide so that if $t \geqslant i$:

$$\text{Prob}\{\tilde{x} > t\} = \text{Prob}\{\tilde{y} > t\}$$

For changes of the type illustrated in Figure 9.10, no restrictions on U (except $U' > 0$ and $U'' < 0$) are required to predict that the investor will invest more in the risky asset. When G differs from F to the right of i, the same conclusion cannot be reached without the help of a restriction on the level of partial risk aversion (Theorem 9.3).

9.4 An increase in risk with constant expected value

Now suppose that the distribution of $\tilde{x}$ becomes riskier while maintaining the same expected value. Intuition suggests that such a change should reduce a^* for a risk-averse individual. Once again, intuition is a bit too optimistic and will be misled by the subtleties of the theory of choice under uncertainty. We will see that the overly general notion of an increase in risk (presented in Chapter 5) must be restricted in order to obtain the expected results in every case.

For the convenience of the reader, we repeat the central result of Chapter 5 with a notation that is slightly modified for our present purposes. If two distribution functions $F(s)$ and $G(s)$ exhibit the same expected values, and if G is riskier than F in the sense defined in Chapter 5 then, for all concave functions $h(s)$,

$$\int_{-\infty}^{+\infty} h(s)f(s)\,ds > \int_{-\infty}^{+\infty} h(s)g(s)\,ds \tag{9.23}$$

or, equivalently,

$$\int_{-\infty}^{+\infty} h(s)[g(s)-f(s)]\,ds < 0 \tag{9.23a}$$

This mathematical result has a very interesting economic interpretation when h represents a utility function because one can then say that, for a risk-averse individual, welfare given F (that is, $E(U)$) is higher than welfare given G when the change from F to G entails an increase in risk with constant mean.

Returning to the problem at hand, consider the first-order condition given F, that is,

$$\int_{m}^{n} U'\,[w_0(1+i) + a^*(s-i)]\,(s-i)f(s)\,ds = 0 \tag{9.24}$$

Given G, the derivative of expected utility with respect to a evaluated at a^*, is:

$$dE(U)/da\,|_{a=a^*} = \int_{m}^{n} U'\,[w_0(1+i) + a^*(s-i)](s-i)g(s)\,ds \tag{9.24a}$$

If this expression can be shown to be negative then, by the usual reasoning, it will follow that a^{**} – the optimal solution given G – is less than a^*.

Since the integral in Equation (9.24) is zero, showing that the integral in Equation (9.24a) is negative is equivalent to showing that:

$$\int_{m}^{n} U'\,[w_0(1+i) + a^*(s-i)]\,(s-i)\,[g(s)-f(s)]\,ds < 0 \tag{9.25}$$

Comparison of Equations (9.25) and (9.23a) immediately yields the key to the solution. If it can be shown that $U'(\cdot)(s-i)$ (which plays the role of $h(s)$) is concave in s, it will follow that a^{**} is less than a^*.

To establish whether $U'(\cdot)(s - i)$ is concave, it is sufficient to check its second derivative:

$$\partial^2 [U'(s - i)]/\partial s^2 = 2U''a + a^2(s - i)U''' \qquad (9.26)$$

It is clear from Equation (9.26) that the sign of U'' ($U'' < 0$) is insufficient to determine the sign of $\partial^2 [U'(s - i)]/\partial s^2$ and is thus insufficient to predict the reaction of a risk-averse decision-maker to an increase in risk. So we arrive at one of the most controversial conclusions (in our opinion) of the modern theory of risk: if only the assumption $U'' < 0$ is imposed, and if any increase in risk with constant mean is allowed, there remain so many degrees of freedom in the formulation of the problem that it is impossible to derive a general conclusion concerning the behaviour of a rational decision-maker. It follows that if one wishes to derive results that are consistent with intuition, it is necessary to impose more restrictions on the nature of the problem. These restrictions include:

(a) restrictions on the form of U in addition to the assumptions that it is increasing and concave;
(b) restrictions on the definition of increased risk.

In the following pages we will present a brief overview of these two approaches.

9.4.1 Restrictions on the form of utility

We have already seen in the preceding comparative statics exercises that some intuitively plausible results could be obtained by assuming that partial risk aversion is everywhere less than 1.

It is not too surprising that we find the same condition here, but since the problem is more complicated, we must complement it by another condition in order to derive a convincing comparative statics result. We begin by stating the result (Theorem 9.4) which we then prove.

Theorem 9.4 For $a^* > 0$, if partial risk aversion is everywhere increasing in s and less than one, an increase in the risk associated with $\tilde{x}$ (with $E(\tilde{x})$ constant) reduces the demand for the risky asset.

In the present framework, partial risk aversion can be defined by the formula:

$$A_p = -(s - i)a^* U''(w_f)/U'(w_f)$$

and its derivative with respect to s is:

$$\partial A_p/\partial s = -a^* \frac{U''}{U'} - (s - i)a^{*2} \left\{ \frac{U'U''' - (U'')^2}{(U')^2} \right\}$$

or, after obvious simplification,

$$\partial A_p/\partial s = \frac{1}{U'}\ [-a^*U''(1 + A_p) - (s - i)a^{*2}U''']$$

Since $1/U'$ is necessarily positive, it follows that $\partial A_p/\partial s > 0$ implies a positive sign for the bracketed expression. Furthermore, if A_p is less than 1, the positive value of a^* combined with the negative sign of U'' implies that

$$0 < -a^*U''(1 + A_p) - (s - i)a^{*2}U''' < -2a^*U'' - (s - i)a^{*2}U'''$$

from which it follows, from multiplying by -1, that

$$2a^*U'' + (s - i)a^{*2}U''' < 0 \qquad (9.27)$$

Since the left-hand side of Equation (9.27) equals the expression obtained in Equation (9.26), it is clear that, if the conditions of Theorem 9.4 are satisfied, $U'(s - i)$ is concave in s. So when the random variable becomes riskier while exhibiting the same expected value, a^* decreases.

This comparative statics result lends support to Hypothesis 4.2, sometimes attributed to Arrow (1970), which restricts the behaviour of relative risk aversion (a special case of partial risk aversion) as wealth increases. Specifically, for $a^* > 0$, an increase in s implies an increase in final wealth, and thus Hypothesis 4.2 coincides with one of the conditions that is used to generate the very intuitive comparative statics result given by Theorem 9.4. However, the conditions of Theorem 9.4 also require that A_p be less than 1. Thus, although A_p must be an increasing function of w (or of s), it must nevertheless remain less than 1. This result is not consistent with numerous empirical studies which, surprisingly, have produced estimates of relative risk aversion of 2 or 3.

9.4.2 Restriction of the notion of an increase in risk

The discussion in Section 9.4.1 highlights the very general nature of the notion of increasing risk and of the necessity of narrowing its scope. The approach employed in Section 9.4.1 is by far the most common in literature. It does not restrict the definition of increasing risk but it compensates for this by imposing stronger assumptions than risk aversion on the utility function. In recent years, a potentially interesting competing approach has been developing. With this approach, minimal assumptions are made on U ($U' > 0$ and $U'' < 0$) but the notion of increased risk is more narrowly defined. A representative article along these lines is by J. Meyer and M. Ormiston (1985). These two authors define a special case of increasing risk that is not unintuitive and that automatically yields the expected comparative statics result for all risk-averse decision-makers.

To begin, assume, as we have done before, that the distribution of $\tilde{x}, f(x)$, takes on values between a minimum m and a maximum n. The special case of increasing risk is defined by the removal of density from anywhere between m and n, and its transfer outside or to the boundaries of this interval. It follows that some outcomes outside of the interval $[m, n]$ that were impossible under random variable $\tilde{x}$ become possible under random variable $\tilde{y}$. In addition, none of the outcomes of $\tilde{x}$ between its bounds m and n exhibit an increase in density function. In other words, an outcome in $[m, n]$ is never more likely under $\tilde{y}$ than under $\tilde{x}$. We see once again, in this special case of an increase in risk, the intuition underlying the notion of a transfer of weight as described in Chapter 5 . There, we removed weight from somewhere in the density of $\tilde{x}$ and shifted it to the left and right of the interval from which it was subtracted. The same kind of operation is undertaken in the case of Meyer and Ormiston (MO) but it is required further that the weight be transferred sufficiently far to the left and right, namely, to the boundaries of the initial distribution or beyond.[14]

To formalise this, assume that $\tilde{x}$ is defined on the interval $[m, n]$ so that:

$$\int_m^n f(s)\, \mathrm{d}s = 1$$

and

$$\int_m^n sf(s)\, \mathrm{d}s = E(\tilde{x}) = \mu$$

where s represents x (here) or y, as appropriate.

If a weight $t(s) \geqslant 0$ is removed from $f(s)$ over the interval $[m, n]$, and if it is transferred to the outside of the interval in such a way as to maintain the same expected value, a new random variable $\tilde{y}$ is defined, characterised by:

$$\int_{m'}^{n'} t(s)\, \mathrm{d}s = 0 \quad \text{where } m' \leqslant m \text{ and } n' \geqslant n; \qquad \text{(a)}$$

$$\int_{m'}^{n'} st(s)\, \mathrm{d}s = 0 \qquad \text{(b)}$$

$$t(s) \geqslant 0 \qquad \text{on the intervals } [m', m] \text{ and } [n, n']; \quad \text{(c)}$$

$$t(s) \leqslant 0 \qquad \text{on the interval } [m, n]. \qquad \text{(d)}$$
$$\text{(9.28)}$$

Conditions (a) and (b) in Equation (9.28) guarantee respectively that the new random variable[15] $\tilde{y}$ is indeed a density function and has the same expected value as $\tilde{x}$. They coincide perfectly with the definition of Rothschild and Stiglitz (RS). The two other conditions define the particular approach of Meyer and Ormiston: they imply that the integral condition of RS holds but the integral condition of RS does not require such strict assumptions as (c) and (d).

An example of increasing risk in the sense of MO was presented in Figure 5.5(a) and (b).

It is possible to show without too much difficulty that if $\tilde{x}$ is subjected to a Meyer–Ormiston increase in risk then all risk-averse individuals who initially choose a positive and finite level of a^* will reduce their investments in the risky asset. To see this, reconsider the first-order condition expressed in Equation (9.20a). If $f(s)$ is transformed into $g(s)$, then the derivative of $E(U)$ given $g(s)$ evaluated at a^* is:

$$dE(U)/da\,|_{a=a^*} = \int_{m'}^{m} U'(\cdot)(s-i)g(s)\,ds$$

$$+ \int_{m}^{n} U'(\cdot)(s-i)g(s)\,ds + \int_{n}^{n'} U'(\cdot)(s-i)g(s)\,ds \quad (9.29)$$

If Equation (9.29) can be shown to be negative, It will necessarily follow that the optimal value of a will be smaller under $g(s)$ than under $f(s)$.

By subtracting the optimisation condition given $f(s)$ (namely, Equation (9.20a)), from Equation (9.29) and using the definition of $t(s)$ it can be shown that:

$$dE(U)/da\,|_{a=a^*} = K = \int_{m'}^{m} U'(\cdot)(s-i)t(s)\,ds + \int_{m}^{n} U'(\cdot)(s-i)t(s)\,ds$$

$$+ \int_{n}^{n'} U'(\cdot)(s-i)t(s)\,ds \quad (9.29a)$$

Thus it is necessary to show that Equation (9.29a) is negative in order to generate the desired comparative statics result.[16]

Given that i is necessarily in the interval $[m, n]$ – because otherwise there would not have been a finite solution for a^* initially – it is obvious that the first integral in Equation (9.29a) is negative because it is the sum of the products of three terms, two of which are always positive (U' and $t(s)$) and one of which is always negative ($s - i$). By similar reasoning, it follows that the third integral is necessarily positive. The sign of the middle integral is ambiguous because it sums products that are sometimes positive (when $s < i$) and sometimes negative (when $s > i$).

The method of proof consists of first dividing the middle integral into two pieces of unambiguous sign. Then an expression which is larger than K is shown to be negative, implying that K is negative as well.

Rewrite K as follows:

$$\int_{m'}^{m} U'(\cdot)(s-i)t(s)\,ds + \int_{m}^{i} U'(\cdot)(s-i)t(s)\,ds$$

$$+ \int_{i}^{n} U'(\cdot)(s-i)t(s)\,ds + \int_{n}^{n'} U'(\cdot)(s-i)t(s)\,ds$$

Given that, by assumption, a^* is positive, risk aversion implies that U' is decreasing in s. It follows that U' evaluated at $s = m$ is greater than (is less than) U' evaluated at $s > m$ ($s < m$). So, since similar reasoning applies at $s = n$, one can write:

$$K' = U'\left[w_0(1 + i) + a^*(m - i)\right]\left[\int_{m'}^{m}(s - i)t(s)\,ds + \int_{m}^{i}(s - i)t(s)\,ds\right]$$

$$+ U'\left[w_0(1 + i) + a^*(n - i)\right]\left[\int_{i}^{n}(s - i)t(s)\,ds + \int_{n}^{n'}(s - i)t(s)\,ds\right] > K$$

$$(9.30)$$

The proof that K' is negative is a little long but not difficult. It is contained in Appendix 7.

Since K' is negative, K is also negative, and thus an increase in risk that satisfies the conditions of MO in addition to those of RS induces a reduction in risky activities.

These remarks complete our study of the demand for a risky asset and its comparative statics analysis. The detailed examination that we have undertaken for this case will facilitate the analysis that follows. However, we have already observed a general tendency: although they seem very intuitive, the notions of risk aversion and increasing risk are too general to allow unambiguous comparative statics predictions. We emphasise that this result is similar to results in microeconomic theory and particularly in consumer theory under certainty. In that field, the assumption that utility is increasing in consumption and the assumption that the budget constraint is linear are inadequate to establish that the demand for a good is decreasing in the good's price, even though such a conclusion seems intuitive. Of course, in risk theory we impose not only the assumption that U' is positive but also the assumption that U'' is negative. Nevertheless, since the problem is more complex under uncertainty, the additional restriction is insufficient to guarantee unambiguous comparative statics results.

Exercises

9.1 Returning to the general problem stated at the beginning of Section 9.2.3 (p. 122) consider the following special case: the utility function is logarithmic

$$U = \ln W_f$$

and the lottery $\tilde{x}$ is binary with:

x_1	p	$(x_i < i < x_2)$
x_2	$1 - p$	

Its expectation is denoted μ.

Questions
(a) Express the expected utility for this problem.
(b) Write the optimality condition and solve explicitly for a^* (after short manipulations you will obtain a linear equation in a^*).
(c) By looking at the signs of the numerator and denominator of a^*, examine under which condition a^* is positive and show that it satisfies the property that

$$a^*(\mu - i) \geqslant 0$$

(d) Express da^*/dW_0 and show that it is positive for $a^* > 0$. Relate the positive sign of da^*/dW_0 to the property of the absolute risk aversion function that characterises a logarithmic utility function.
(e) If x_1 decreases (to $x'_1 < x_1$) and if x_2 increases (to $x'_2 > x_2$) in such a way that μ is constant, show that you face a strong increase in risk and that a^* necessarily decreases (when a^* is initially positive).
(f) Instead of considering a strong increase in risk as in (e) imagine now that *ceteris paribus* the probability of x_1 falls (so that the probability of x_2 increases). What will happen to a^*? Relate your result to our discussion of first-order stochastic dominance (Section 9.3.3).

9.2 Let a risky asset $\tilde{x}$ have a distribution of returns such that low returns are highly likely while very high returns are possible but with a small probability. Such a situation may (but need not) be modelled, e.g. by the exponential density function

$$f(x) = \lambda e^{-\lambda x} \qquad x \geqslant 0, \lambda > 0$$

the shape of which is depicted in Figure 9.11.
An individual with a negative exponential utility function $(-e^{-\gamma W_f})$ can divide their initial wealth W_0 between a safe asset with return i and a risky asset of return $\tilde{x}$. Determine the optimal risky investment a^*.

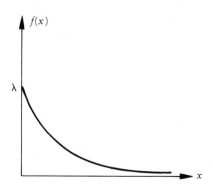

Figure 9.11

Once you have expressed a right answer, compute da^*/dW_0 and interpret the result with reference to the behaviour of the absolute risk aversion coefficient for a negative exponential utility. Show also that an increase in risk aversion (that is in γ) reduces the demand for the risky asset. Finally, from the optimal value of a^*, show that a^* is positive (negative) whenever $E(\tilde{x})$ in greater (smaller) than i.

Hints:

1. Remember that

$$\int_0^\alpha \lambda e^{-\lambda x} e^{-tx} dx = \frac{\lambda}{\lambda + t}$$

   (this is the moment generating function for an exponential density).

2.

$$E(\tilde{x}) = \frac{1}{\lambda}$$

   for the exponential density.

9.3 Suppose that the risk-free rate is $i = 0.05$ and that the initial and final distributions of returns of the risky asset are, respectively,

x	$p(x)$	y	$p(y)$
0.02	0.33	0.02	0.25
0.05	0.33	0.05	0.25
0.10	0.33	0.10	0.50

Questions
(a) Show that such a shift in the distribution of returns has no effect on the optimal portfolio of any risk-averse decision-maker.
(b) More generally, show that if $\tilde{y}$ is $\tilde{x}$ with probability q and i with probability $(1 - q)$, $\forall q \in [0, 1]$ the change in the distribution of returns from $\tilde{x}$ to $\tilde{y}$ has no effect on the optimal portfolio.
(c) Find the value of q that was used to construct lottery $\tilde{y}$ from lottery $\tilde{x}$.

Notes

1. In spite of this difference, as will become clear, the concepts from Part One are very useful in Part Two.
2. The reader can verify that, when $k = 0$, the solutions correspond to those in Section 9.2.1. This is not surprising – indeed it is comforting – because $k = 0$ implies risk neutrality and thus the implicit adoption of the expected value criterion.

3. This confirms our previous assertion that risk aversion does not imply the rejection of all risks.

4. If a were negative, the covariance would be positive because the increase in x would reduce w_f and increase U'.

5. The fact that it is a cost of risk can be established by intuitive reasoning. To understand that $\mathrm{cov}(U', \tilde{x})/E(U')$ is a marginal and not an average cost, note the presence of a marginal utility and the fact that this formula results from the derivative of $E(U)$ with respect to a. A formal proof is found in the excellent article by D. Baron (1970).

6. Indeed, this result can be formally proved: it is sufficient that U'' be negative. The proof is somewhat difficult and is presented in detail in Appendix 5. The reader might also be satisfied by an intuitive justification: since Equations (9.6) and (9.9) are only different ways to present the same first-order condition, the second-order condition should be satisfied under the same circumstances, namely, $U'' < 0$.

7. Indeed, for the problem under uncertainty to have a finite solution in a, $\tilde{x}$ cannot take values that are systematically larger or systematically smaller than i. For example, if the lowest possible value of x were greater than i, even a riskophobe would go infinitely into debt to purchase the risky asset. In a sense, in this case the risk of loss from the risky investment disappears and the solution $(a^* = +\infty)$ is entirely determined by the fact that the risky return must exceed the risk-free return.

8. These properties do not imply that $U'(w_f)(x - i)$ is an increasing function in x. An example of a function that exhibits these properties but which is not everywhere increasing in x is illustrated in Figure 9.5.

9. Stated in this way the result seems obvious. However its proof, which is in Appendix 6, requires a few technical steps, albeit simple ones.

10. The sign of $\mathrm{d}m/\mathrm{d}i$ is necessarily the opposite of the sign of $\mathrm{d}a/\mathrm{d}i$ because, due to the budget constraint with w_0 constant, an increase in a can only be achieved with a decrease in m.

11. Since $\tilde{y} >_1 \tilde{x}$, $a(\tilde{y} - i) >_1 a(\tilde{x} - i)$ as long as a is positive, and adding a constant $[w_0(1 + i)]$ to each side does not change the stochastic dominance relationship. It follows that $E[U(\tilde{w}_f)]$ given $\tilde{y}$, is greater than $E[U(\tilde{w}_f)]$ given $\tilde{x}$.

12. It is not impossible that $a^{**} = a^*$ either. We leave to the reader the task of graphically illustrating this case.

13. This reflects the inevitable trade-off between the restrictions on U and those on F that one must accept to generate intuitively plausible comparative statics results. A large majority of the literature examines restrictions on U. More recently, attention has been paid to the alternative restrictions on F. See Meyer and Ormiston (1985), Eeckhoudt and Hansen (1980) and Black and Bulkley (1989).

14. The definition of Meyer and Ormiston should not be confused with the very original definition proposed by Sandmo (1971) and nicely called a 'stretching' of the density. For an analysis of the relationship between the two notions see Meyer and Ormiston (1989).

15. The density of $\tilde{y}$, $g(s) = g(y)$, is defined simply by $g(s) = f(s) + t(s)$. It follows, for example, that $g(s) \leqslant f(s)$ on $[m, n]$. Furthermore, on $[m', m]$ and $[n, n']$, $g(s) = t(s)$.

16. For what it's worth, we point out that the proof given here is not found in MO because they consider the case where the argument of U, that is, w_f, is strictly concave in the decision variable.

References

Arrow K, (1970), *Essays in the Theory of Risk-Bearing*, North-Holland, Amsterdam and London.

Baron D. (1970), Price uncertainty, utility and industry equilibrium in pure competition, *International Economic Review*, vol. 11, 463–480.

Black J. and G. Bulkley (1989), A ratio criterion for signing the effect of an increase in uncertainty, *International Economic Review*, vol. 30, 119–130.

Eeckhoudt L. and P. Hansen (1980), Minimum and maximum prices, uncertainty and the theory of the competitive firm, *American Economic Review*, vol. 70, 1064–1068.

Fishburn P.C. and B. Porter (1976), Optimal portfolios with one safe and one risky asset: effects of changes in rate of return and risk, *Management Science*, vol. 22, 1064–1073.

Meyer J. and M. Ormiston (1985), Strong increases in risk and their comparative statics, *International Economic Review*, vol. 26, 425–437.

Meyer J. and M. Ormiston (1989), Deterministic transformation of random variables and the comparative statics of risk, *Journal of Risk and Uncertainty*, vol. 2, 179–188.

Sandmo A. (1971), On the theory of the competitive firm under price uncertainty, *American Economic Review*, vol. 61, 65–73.

10 The demand for insurance

10.1 Types of contracts studied and basic notation

An insurance contract is fundamentally a contract for 'transferring risk', and it is important to understand its basic forms.[1] Initially, an individual or a firm faces a risk and wishes to be covered against it without, however, giving up the source of the uncertainty. In the problem of optimal risky asset holdings examined in Chapter 9, the decision-maker could be covered by liquidating the risky assets held or by choosing not to acquire risky assets. In the insurance problem studied here, the source of the risk (generally a physical asset: building, automobile, machine) remains the property of the decision-maker, who attempts to protect against the financial consequences of possible damages by putting an insurance contract into place. To begin, assume that the decision-maker holds two sources of income: a 'risk-free' element denoted w_0 and a risky element worth L. The risk studied here is the risk of physical damage (fire, accident) that could destroy all or part of the value of L.[2] The level of damage from the potential disaster is denoted $\tilde{x}L$ where $\tilde{x}$ is a random variable defined on $[0, 1]$, with density function $f(x)$, and representing the fraction of L that is damaged. For protection, the decision-maker enters into an insurance contract that essentially specifies two things.

1. The amount of indemnity I and its relation to the level of damage suffered. Although this relation can take on many very diverse legal forms covered in numerous clauses of the contract, its mathematical formulation is simple and will be written as:

$$I = I(xL) = I(X)$$

where X is the absolute value of the damage and where function I has the following properties:

(a) If $X = 0$, $I = 0$ because the absence of damage rules out the payment of an indemnity.
(b) dI/dX is non-negative because the indemnity cannot be lower when the damage is higher. Combining this restriction with the previous one implies, of course, that $I \geqslant 0$.

(c) dI/dX cannot exceed 1 because otherwise the insured would benefit from an increase in the damage from the disaster. Since $I(0) = 0$, the fact that dI/dX never exceeds 1 guarantees that $I \leqslant X$.

2. In exchange for its obligation, the company demands payment of a premium P, the value of which is independent of the realisation of $\tilde{x}$. P is based on the expected value of the indemnity which, at the time the contract is signed, is random. To the extent that time passes between the signing of the contract and the payment of the indemnity, $I(\tilde{x}L)$ must be interpreted as the present value of the indemnity, that is, as the present value of a future random flow.

The expected value of $I(\tilde{x}L)$, called the 'actuarial content' of the policy (or its pure premium or its actuarial value) is measured by:

$$E(I(\tilde{x})) = \int_0^1 I(xL)f(x)\,dx$$

if the company has the same information as the insured as to the risks. This symmetry of information is manifested by the company's use of the same density function for $\tilde{x}$ ($f(x)$) as the insured uses.[3] Once the actuarial content is evaluated, the premium P is given by:

$$P = (1 + \lambda)E(I(\tilde{x}L))$$

where it is assumed that the various charges (sales charges, management fees, remuneration for services, etc.) are expressed as a rate, λ, per monetary unit of actuarial content. When λ equals zero, it is said that the premium is actuarial.

Although the problem described above is naturally interpretable in the context of insurance, it turns out that its solution – though technically possible – is difficult. It requires using mathematical tools that are beyond the scope of this text, because the decision variable is a function (I). For this reason, we will restrict attention in this text to two special cases of the general problem which are widely observed in the world of insurance. These two special cases consist of restricting the function $I(x)$ to be of a particular form. In the first case, which gives rise to the co-insurance contract, we assume:

$$I = a\tilde{x}L$$

where a is a number chosen by the insured subject to the constraint that $0 \leqslant a \leqslant 1$. In this contract, the indemnity is proportional to the loss.

If $a = 0$ then, whatever the extent of the damage, the indemnity is zero. This is the case of no coverage, which is sometimes called the total retention of risk. In contrast, at the other extreme, if $a = 1$ then the indemnity covers exactly the amount of the damage and thus the insured faces no risk (or at least, no more financial risk) because of succeeding in transferring all of it to the insurance company. It is intuitive that a risk-averse individual has a tendency to prefer this outcome and, of course, if the premium were independent of a then all risk-averse decision-makers would choose $a = 1$. Unfortunately for them, this is not the case[4]: to achieve lower risk they will have to pay a higher price and choose a larger a. This trade-off in the context of co-insurance is dealt with in Sections 10.2 and 10.3.

Once the elements of co-insurance (which is a 'linear' contract because I is linear in x) are well understood, we can turn our attention for the first time in Part Two to globally non-linear (but piece-wise linear) contracts. A contract with a deductible, denoted d, implies that I has the following form:

$$I(xL) = 0 \qquad \text{if } xL \leqslant d$$

$$I(xL) = xL - d \qquad \text{if } xL > d$$

which is shown graphically in Figure 10.1. There is no payment from the insurer if the loss is less than the deductible. Once the loss exceeds the deductible, the insurer reimburses the difference and the insured suffers a net loss equal to the deductible.

Note that function I satisfies all the conditions mentioned above and that it is piece-wise linear: it is horizontal between 0 and d and has a 45° slope between d and L.

The higher line, $I = xL$, reflects the maximum coverage attainable. The true coverage $(I(xL))$ is below the maximum possible and, the higher d is, the further $I(x)$ lies away from $I = xL$. Specifically, an increase in d implies worse

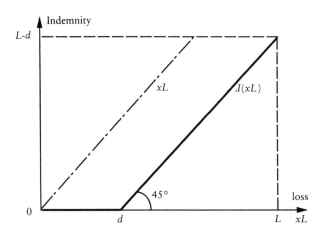

Figure 10.1

coverage for the insured. There are two extreme cases which are directly comparable to the extreme cases mentioned in the case of co-insurance:

(a) $d = 0$ implies full insurance for the insured because the damage is completely reimbursed (the actual curve coincides with the maximal coverage). $d = 0$ is thus equivalent to $a = 1$ in the case of co-insurance;

(b) $d = L$ corresponds to the complete absence of insurance because every level of x corresponds to an indemnity of zero. $d = L$ is equivalent to $a = 0$ in the co-insurance contract.

Although an increase in d increases the level of risk retained by the individual (and thus displeases the riskophobe), it also contributes to a decrease in the premium (which makes any decision-maker better off). Thus, for d, as for a, one must consider the trade-off between these two contradictory effects. This is examined in detail in Section 10.4. Before treating an example in Section 10.6, we compare the two contracts in terms of welfare for the insured in Section 10.5.

10.2 The co-insurance contract (the case of a single risk)

If the decision-maker has access to only this kind of contract, and chooses not to accept it ($a = 0$) then the expected utility is:

$$E[U(\tilde{w}_f)] = \int_0^1 U(w_0 + L - xL)f(x)\, dx$$

In contrast, if some insurance coverage is acquired this expression becomes:

$$E[U(\tilde{w}_f)] = \int_0^1 U(w_0 + L - xL + axL - (1 + \lambda)a\mu L)f(x)\, dx$$

where, on the one hand, the indemnity (axL) is added to final wealth and, on the other, the premium ($P = (1 + \lambda)a\mu L$) is deducted.

To determine the optimal amount of a, consider the associated first- and second-order conditions:

$$dE[U(w_f)]/da = \int_0^1 U'[w_f(x)]L(x - (1 + \lambda)\mu)f(x)\, dx = 0$$

$$(10.1)$$

and

$$d^2E/da^2 = \int_0^1 U''[w_f(x)]L^2(x - (1 + \lambda)\mu)^2 f(x)\, dx < 0 \quad (10.2)$$

with $w_f(x) = [w_0 + L - xL + axL - (1 + \lambda)a\mu L]$.

The second-order condition is automatically satisfied for a risk-averse decision-maker.

Before proceeding to the interpretation of these results and to their comparative statics analysis, we emphasise one simple point which is very important, not only for theoretical analysis but also for understanding the principles of management. Often, in large companies, insurance decisions (and their complement, decisions concerning retention of risk) are made by one or several people who do not participate in investment choices within the firm. It is thus possible that an organisation will adopt a very conservative attitude in some areas (for example, insurance) while the finance or marketing departments take extremely risky positions. The illogic and danger of this segmentation are clear if one compares Equation (10.1) – slightly modified – with Equation (9.6), the optimality condition for holding a risky asset. Specifically, rewrite Equation (10.1) as:

$$\int_0^1 U'[w_0 + L - (1 + \lambda)\mu L - (1 - a)L(x - (1 + \lambda)\mu)](x - (1 + \lambda)\mu)f(x)\,dx = 0$$

$$(10.3)$$

and note that the argument of U' has:

(a) a non-random term $w_0 + L - (1 + \lambda)\mu L$, interpretable as the certain wealth associated with full coverage;
(b) a random term $L(x - (1 + \lambda)\mu)$ multiplied by a decision variable $(1 - a)$. In this context $(1 - a)$ reflects the fraction of the risk retained by the insured.

The argument of U' in Equation (9.6) has the same structure as in Equation (10.3) because, due to Equation (9.4), w_f is composed of a non-random term $[w_0(1 + i)]$ and a random variable $(x - i)$ multiplied by a decision variable a representing the amount invested in the risky asset.

In addition, in Equation (9.6) as well as in Equation (10.3), U' is multiplied by a random variable that can take on positive and negative values. For Equation (9.6) this random variable is $(\tilde{x} - i)$ and for Equation (10.3) it is $L(\tilde{x} - (1 + \lambda)\mu)$.

It is thus clear that there exists a great similarity between the problems of investment in a risky asset and insurance. This fact is amply confirmed by the following considerations. As is very often the case for general equilibrium reasons (see CAPM, Chapter 15) the expected return from a risky asset exceeds the risk-free return i and thus an increase in the holdings of the risky asset (a) has two effects: on the one hand the expected value of final wealth $E(w_f) = w_0(1 + i) + a(\mu - i)$ increases, while on the other the risk faced by the individual grows. In the insurance problem, if the premium includes a positive loading factor then an increase in coverage (a) also has two effects: on the one hand, the expected value of final wealth $E(w_f) = w_0 + L(1 - \mu) - \lambda a\mu L$

diminishes while, on the other, the risk faced by the insured decreases. Furthermore, at a technical level, note that in both cases w_f is a linear function of a.

It is thus clear that the two decisions (holding risky assets and buying insurance) exhibit a (linear) trade-off between return and risk: the acceptance (or refusal) of a higher risk is compensated (paid for) by a higher (lower) expected wealth.

Finally, we point out that, if the insurance decisions were expressed in terms of the retention of risk $(1 - a)$ rather than coverage (a), the retention of risk would be exactly identical to a risky investment: an increase in the amount of risk retained increases the expected value of final wealth.

This analogy between investment and insurance not only suggests insights into management and organisation as noted above, it will also permit an easy comparative statics analysis of the properties reflected in Equation (10.1) since they must be similar to the comparative statics properties already established for Equation (9.6).

Before proceeding to the comparative statics exercises, we note that Equation (10.1) as well as Equation (9.6) lends itself to a simple transformation that makes clear the elements of marginal cost and marginal benefit. Specifically, using the definition of covariance, Equation (10.1) can be rewritten as:

$$\text{cov}(U', \tilde{x})/E(U') = \lambda\mu \tag{10.4}$$

The right-hand side is easy to interpret: it represents the cost, in terms of expected final wealth, of an increase in a per franc invested in the property subjected to the risk. Specifically,

$$dE(w_f)/da = -\lambda\mu L$$

which corresponds to a 'total cost' of $\lambda\mu L$ and thus $\lambda\mu$ corresponds to a cost per franc invested in L.

The left-hand side of Equation (10.4) is positive because, in the context of insurance, $\text{cov}(U', \tilde{x})$ is positive. Specifically, with $\tilde{x}$ representing a loss, an increase in its realisation makes the individual poorer if $a < 1$ and increases marginal utility[5] $(U'' < 0)$; thus x and U' move in the same direction. This positive term measures the marginal benefit per unit of L of better coverage, and it is easy to show that it is decreasing if $U'' < 0$ Specifically, with a little algebra, one obtains:

$$\frac{d\text{cov}(U', \tilde{x})}{da} = \frac{E[U''(\tilde{x} - (1 + \lambda)\mu)^2]}{\{E[U']\}^2}$$

which is indeed negative if the decision-maker is risk averse. This means in practice – consistent with intuition – that the marginal benefit of coverage is greater when the initial coverage is lower.

The first-order condition expressed as in Equation (10.4) has a simple graphical representation. In Figure 10.2, $\lambda\mu$ is a horizontal line with respect to a while the marginal benefit curve is everywhere decreasing. The latter attains a value of zero at $a = 1$. This is not an accident: when $a = 1$ all risk is eliminated and an increase in a, were it permitted, would not provide any marginal benefit. Formally, when $a = 1$ final wealth is certain $(=w_0 + L - (1 + \lambda)\mu L)$ and thus U' is constant, which implies that its covariance with x is zero.

Thanks to Figure 10.2, we can very easily prove a well-known result from the economic theory of insurance. It is stated as follows:

Theorem 10.1 if $\lambda > 0$ then $a^* < 1$ while $\lambda = 0$ implies $a^* = 1$.

This result says that if the premium is actuarially fair ($\lambda = 0$), a riskophobe insures 100 per cent of the risk. Specifically, the insurance has zero marginal cost (in terms of its impact on $E(w_f)$) but it carries the benefit of a reduction in risk. This leads to an extreme choice, namely, $a^* = 1$. We already obtained this result at the end of Chapter 7.

In contrast, if the proposed contract has a positive loading factor ($\lambda > 0$), the potential insured will not purchase full coverage: some degree of risk retention maximises welfare.

Technically, the result just mentioned is obvious: since marginal benefit is everywhere decreasing and is zero at $a = 1$, the optimal value of a – determined by the intersection of marginal benefit and marginal cost – necessarily lies to the left of $a = 1$ if $\lambda\mu$ does not coincide with the horizontal axis, that is, if λ is strictly positive.

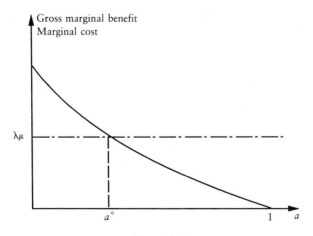

Figure 10.2

It follows that all comparative statics analysis can be accomplished by studying the effect of an exogenous shock first on each of the curves and then on their intersection. We begin this exercise by studying the effect of a change in w_0. This effect is the simplest to analyse because w_0 does not affect the horizontal line $\lambda\mu$.

10.2.1 The effect of a change in w_0

The effect of a change in w_0 on the optimal level of co-insurance is transmitted by the impact of w_0 on absolute risk aversion. If the increase in w_0 causes a fall in absolute risk aversion then the decision-maker perceives a lower marginal benefit of coverage since risk is feared less. The marginal benefit curve thus shifts to the left while maintaining its horizontal intercept at $a^* = 1$ (the horizontal intercept is independent of w_0). This situation is represented in Figure 10.3.

Since the change in w_0 does not affect $\lambda\mu$, the comparative statics result is completely due to the shift of marginal benefit curve. If A_a is decreasing the marginal benefit of coverage decreases when w_0 increases, and this is reflected in a downward shift of the corresponding curve (see the vertical arrows). The new point of intersection between the new curve and the horizontal line $\lambda\mu$ must lie to the left of the initial point and thus $a^{**} < a^*$.

Of course these results that have been obtained graphically, can be generated algebraically. The interested reader can attempt this using as a guide the reasoning developed in Chapter 9 for the study of the sign of $\mathrm{d}a^*/\mathrm{d}w_0$ when a^* is interpreted as the holdings of a risky asset. Here a^* represents a rate of insurance coverage and, as we have already suggested, one can repeat

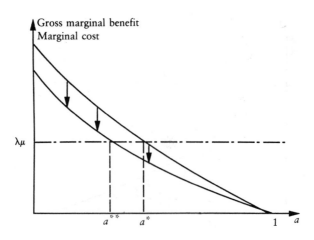

Figure 10.3

– with signs reversed – all of the analysis that is pertinent to the problem of holding risky assets.

10.2.2 The effect of a change in λ

A priori, there is a tendency to believe that an increase in the loading factor should, all other things being equal, lead to a greater retention of risk and a reduced demand for the transfer of risk via the insurance market. An examination of this problem reveals that things are really less simple than it seems and that indeed there are two opposing effects. These can be well presented

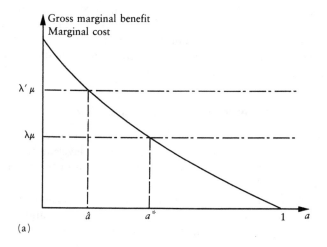

(a)

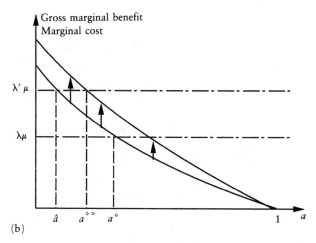

(b)

Figure 10.4

graphically so it is not necessary to resort to mathematical tools.[6] When λ increases, the horizontal line in Figure 10.2 shifts upward (see Figure 10.4(a)). If this were the only effect then a^* would necessarily decrease from a^* to $\hat{a}$. This is the most intuitive effect. It may be called the substitution effect: the increase in λ induces the insured to substitute the retention of risk for the transfer of risk. Meanwhile a more subtle effect, illustrated in Figure 10.4(b), works against the first effect and can indeed reverse it. For the insured (with $a^* > 0$), the increase in the loading factor is the same as a decrease in wealth. If the insured exhibits decreasing absolute risk aversion in wealth (Hypothesis 4.1) the 'fear' of risk increases and the marginal benefit of coverage increases at every level of a.

This effect, called the wealth effect, increases a given Hypothesis 4.1 and thus the net result is ambiguous. Figure 10.4(b) illustrates a situation where, on net, the increase in λ induces a reduction in a^* to a^{**}. However, if absolute risk aversion were rapidly decreasing in w_f, it is easy to imagine a situation where a^{**} would exceed a^*. Insurance would then be a 'Giffen good', that is, a good whose demand increases when its price rises.

10.2.3 A change to a more dangerous distribution

Initially risk is represented by a random variable with expected value μ. The premium depends on the loading factor and on the level of coverage chosen by the decision-maker: $P = (1 + \lambda)a\mu L$. The insurer and the insured initially have the same information.

Suppose now that, for some reason, known only to the insured, the risk $\tilde{x}$ deteriorates, that is, the risk becomes represented by a random variable $\tilde{y}$ where $\tilde{y} >_1 \tilde{x}$. In Chapter 6, the notion of first-order stochastic dominance implied a positive change in the sense that $\tilde{y} >_1 \tilde{x}$ implied $E[U(\tilde{y})] > E[U(\tilde{x})]$ for all individuals with $U' > 0$, because $\tilde{x}$ and $\tilde{y}$ corresponded to favourable events (levels of wealth). Here $\tilde{x}$ is a level of loss (an unfavourable random variable), so that relationship $\tilde{y} >_1 \tilde{x}$ represents a deterioration of expected wealth. Thus actuaries would refer to $\tilde{y}$ as being more dangerous. This interpretation is illustrated in Figure 10.5.

As required by the relationship $\tilde{y} >_1 \tilde{x}$, $G(t) \leqslant F(t)$ for all t in the interval $[0, 1]$. In the present context, this means that with $\tilde{y}$ the probability of realising a loss smaller than t is less than with $\tilde{x}$. In other words, the probability of a large loss is always greater with $\tilde{y}$ than with $\tilde{x}$ (or at least equal) and this means that $\tilde{y}$ exhibits a higher level of danger.

Of course, $\tilde{y} >_1 \tilde{x}$ implies $E(\tilde{y}) > E(\tilde{x})$. If the insurance company could observe the increased risk it would raise the premium. Taking into account the adjustment of the premium would complicate the analysis and thus we will assume that – no doubt because of inadequate information – the company does not change its prices. This assumption is not unrealistic in the short term, because adjusting the premium upwards or downwards can take time.

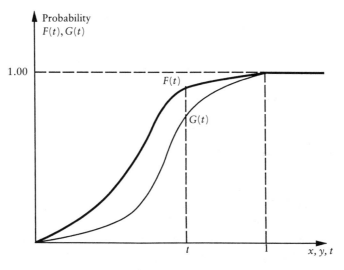

Figure 10.5

The question that we pose can be summarised as follows: if an insured risk deteriorates and the premium does not change, in which direction will the holder of the policy change a^*? Intuition suggests that a^* will increase,[7] but a detailed analysis of the question shows that this is not necessarily so.

As usual, we begin with the first-order condition under $\tilde{x}$ written in the following form:

$$\int_0^1 U'(\cdot)(s - (1 + \lambda)\mu)f(s) \, ds = 0 \qquad (10.5)$$

When the risk deteriorates, it is the sign of:

$$dE(U)/da \mid_{a=a^\circ} = \int_0^1 U'(\cdot)(s - (1 + \lambda)\mu)g(s) \, ds \qquad (10.5a)$$

that determines whether a^* increases or decreases. We emphasise the fact that we retain the value of $\mu = E(\tilde{x})$ even though $E(\tilde{y}) > E(\tilde{x})$: this follows from our assumption that the company does not react to the change in risk.

To obtain $a^{**} > a^*$, it must be shown under what conditions the expression in Equation (10.5a) is positive. Theorem 10.2 furnishes some conditions of a familiar type.

Theorem 10.2 If partial risk aversion is less than one, a deterioration in a risk insured at a constant premium induces an increase in the demand for insurance.

To prove the theorem it is sufficient to subtract Equation (10.5) from Equation (10.5a). This does not change the sign and it yields:

$$\int_0^1 U'(\cdot)[s - (1 + \lambda)\mu][g(s) - f(s)]\, ds \qquad (10.6)$$

Next integrate by parts using:

$$dv = [g(s) - f(s)]\, ds$$

to show, after some straightforward simplifications, that Equation (10.6) can be equivalently written as:

$$-\int_0^1 U'(\cdot)\left[1 - (1 - a^*)L(s - (1 + \lambda)\mu)\frac{U''}{U'}\right][G(s) - F(s)]\, ds$$

Since, by assumption $[G(s) - F(s)]$ is negative, if the expression in brackets is positive for all s then it follows that a^* will increase. Noting that $(1 - a^*)L$ is a sum of money corresponding to the amount of risk retention, one can rewrite the bracketed expression in terms of partial risk aversion. Then by following the procedure employed in Chapter 9 one can easily prove Theorem 10.2.

10.3 The co-insurance contract (with multiple risks)

In the preceding sections we assumed the decision-maker faced a single risk and would insure against it. However, in reality, for firms as well as for individuals, the insurance decision is not made independently: it is made together with a multitude of other decisions that place the economic agent in risky situations for which there is often no insurance available. This means that the sum of non-insurable risks that the decision-maker faces (fluctuations in the value of stocks, in long-term interest rates, strikes, product life, etc.) may be far greater than the value of insurable risks. It is thus important to examine how these exogenous risks affect the coverage of the insurable risk.

Surprisingly, there are very few articles dedicated to this question, no doubt because it is technically more complicated. Indeed, we will not cover it in detail here but we should at least point out its existence and describe a first attempt at its solution.

To state the problem, we recall the definition of final wealth in the framework of a single insurable risk:

$$\tilde{w}_f = w_0 + L(1 - \tilde{x}) + aL(\tilde{x} - (1 + \lambda)\mu) \qquad (10.7)$$

There is clearly a single source of risk, represented by $\tilde{x}$, which induces an optimal level of coverage denoted a^*.

The simplest way to introduce multiple risks is to assume that initial wealth itself is uncertain and that at the end of the period its contribution to final wealth is:

$$w_0(1 + \rho + \tilde{\varepsilon}) \tag{10.8}$$

where $\rho + \tilde{\varepsilon}$ is the random rate of appreciation (or depreciation) that applies to the set of assets other than L and where, by assumption, $E(\tilde{\varepsilon}) = 0$ so that ρ represents the expected return to the decision-maker's other activities.

Under these conditions final wealth becomes:

$$\tilde{w}_f = w_0(1 + \rho + \tilde{\varepsilon}) + L(1 - \tilde{x}) + aL(\tilde{x} - (1 + \lambda)\mu) \tag{10.9}$$

and the two sources of risk affecting the level of final wealth are clearly exhibited. The question then is how the presence of $\tilde{\varepsilon}$ affects the optimal value of a.

This question is not a simple one, notably because it requires us to consider an element that has been mentioned very little until now: the degree of dependence between the risks. At first sight one is inclined to think that $\tilde{x}$ (for example, a well-specified risk of fire destroying a building or a machine) is independent of $\tilde{\varepsilon}$, which represents a set of very diverse risks due, for example, to the effects of international or industrial economic conditions on the activities of the firm. This assumption is often satisfactory, but it is not always valid. For example, if economic and financial conditions are particularly favourable for a firm (reflected in a large positive realisation of $\tilde{\varepsilon}$), it is very likely that the firm will increase the rate of production and thus augment the risk of various accidents (fire, machine breakdown, work-related accidents). This case suggests – and exhibits – a positive dependence between $\tilde{\varepsilon}$ and $\tilde{x}$ so the risks will have a tendency to reinforce each other. In contrast, one might argue that if the firm is in difficulty (reflected in a negative realisation of $\tilde{\varepsilon}$), it will try to economise on costs of prevention and security, and will thus make the distribution of $\tilde{x}$ more dangerous. This latter interpretation suggests, contrary to the former, a negative dependence. Taking into account the potential dependence between the two random variables further complicates the analysis, which is already difficult for the case of independence.

To begin with, imagine that $\tilde{\varepsilon}$ and $\tilde{x}$ are independent. The problem then consists of choosing a value of a to maximise:

$$E[U(\tilde{w}_f)] = \int_x \int_\varepsilon U[w_0(1 + \rho + \varepsilon) + L(1 - x)$$
$$+ aL(x - (1 + \lambda)\mu) \, dG(\varepsilon) \, dF(x) \tag{10.10}$$

where the double integral reflects the presence of two random variables that are independent, because their joint distribution – say $h(\varepsilon,x)$ – equals the product of the marginal densities $g(\varepsilon)$ and $f(x)$.

The first-order condition associated with Equation (10.10) yields the optimal value of a, denoted $\hat{a}$, which we can compare with the optimal value when there is a single risk, a^*.

Intuitively it seems that, when faced with two independent risks, a risk-averse decision-maker will choose better coverage against the insurable risk. In some sense, the purchase of better coverage for the insurable risk should provide indirect partial protection against the non-insurable risk. Careful analysis of the question shows once again that intuition is not completely valid and that its justification rests on assumptions that are stricter than simple risk aversion.

Indeed, one must appeal to the notion of prudence to make progress. We do this in detail in Appendix 8 for the case of independence. Here, we will simply present an example – using quadratic utility – to highlight the role of prudence (a characteristic of U) and the role of dependence or independence between the random variables (a characteristic of the risks) in the demand for insurance. We choose the quadratic utility function because its simplicity allows an explicit solution for the optimal values of a. Furthermore, as we indicated in Chapter 6, this utility function exhibits everywhere a zero (and thus constant) degree of prudence. We will see that this hypothesis leads to counter-intuitive results for the case of independent risks, which justifies – *a contrario* – the different assumptions made in the more general framework developed in Appendix 8. Finally, as we will see, because it allows explicit solutions for the case of dependent risks, quadratic utility makes possible some simple and pertinent remarks about these otherwise analytically complex situations.

We thus employ the utility function

$$U = w_f - \beta w_f^2 \qquad \text{with} \beta > 0 \text{ and } 1 - 2\beta w_f > 0$$

In the case of a single risk, w_f is written as in Equation (10.7), so that

$$E(\tilde{w}_f) = w_0 + L(1 - \mu) - a\lambda\mu L \tag{10.11}$$

and

$$\text{Var}(\tilde{w}_f) = \sigma^2(\tilde{w}_f) = (1 - a)^2 L^2 \sigma^2(\tilde{x}) \tag{10.12}$$

Since, for quadratic utility,

$$E[U(\tilde{w}_f)] = E(\tilde{w}_f) - \beta E(\tilde{w}_f^2)$$
$$= E(\tilde{w}_f) - \beta[E(\tilde{w}_f)^2 + \sigma^2 \tilde{w}_f)] \tag{10.13}$$

one obtains:

$$dE[U(\tilde{w}_f)]/da = -\lambda\mu L - 2\beta[w_0 + L(1 - \mu) - \lambda\mu a]$$
$$\times (-\lambda\mu L) + 2\beta L^2 \sigma^2(\tilde{x})(1 - a) = 0 \tag{10.14}$$

and, after some manipulation,

$$a^* = \frac{-\mu\lambda[1 - 2\beta(w_0 + L(1 - \mu))] + 2\beta L\sigma^2(\tilde{x})}{2\beta L(\sigma^2(\tilde{x}) + \mu^2\lambda^2)} \qquad (10.15)$$

Expression (10.15) deserves careful consideration because it is the first time that we have encountered an explicit solution for insurance demand. We offer a few brief comments:

1. The second-order condition derived from Equation (10.14) indicates that the extreme point is a maximum. Specifically:

    $$d^2 E[U(\tilde{w}_f)]/da^2 = -2\beta\lambda^2\mu^2\mu^2 - 2\beta L^2\sigma^2(\tilde{x})$$

    is negative if β is positive.
2. If $\lambda = 0$ (actuarial premium) then it is optimal to choose $a^* = 1$, consistent with the general principle stated in Section 10.2. Similarly, if λ, is strictly positive, a^* must be less than 1. Note in addition that if λ, is sufficiently large relative to $\sigma^2(\tilde{x})$, a^* could very well be negative. The economic interpretation of this result is simple: the price of insurance can become so high that the decision-maker decides to sell insurance rather than buy it.
3. If $\beta = 0$ (risk neutrality) then a^* approaches $-\infty$ for $\lambda > 0$. Specifically, a risk-neutral individual is attracted by the positive expected return resulting from the sale (and not the purchase) of insurance and pays no attention to the risk generated by the transaction.
4. If $\sigma^2(\tilde{x})$ increases – *ceteris paribus* – a^* increases, as is perfectly intuitive.
5. Unfortunately – and this is the weakness of quadratic utility – a^* is an increasing function of w_0 because, for quadratic utility, absolute risk aversion increases with wealth. This contradicts our intuition and the notion that an increase in wealth induces a firm to become its own insurer.

We now study the impact of a risk attached to w_0 and independent of $\tilde{x}$. Final wealth is thus defined as in Equation (10.9) where, in order to make the comparison as direct as possible, we assume that $\rho = 0$. Under these conditions, $E(\tilde{w}_f)$ has exactly the same form as Equation (10.11). Only the expression for $\sigma^2(\tilde{w}_f)$ is modified, becoming:

$$\sigma^2(\tilde{w}_f) = (1 - a)^2 L^2\sigma^2(\tilde{x}) + w_0^2\sigma^2(\tilde{\varepsilon}) \qquad (10.16)$$

Since, between Equations (10.12) and (10.16), the variance increases by a constant, its derivative with respect to a does not change. Thus, although adding 'noise' to w_0 reduces the welfare of the risk-averse agent (because $\sigma^2(\tilde{w}_f)$ is higher), the optimality condition is unchanged. It follows that the optimal value of a is unaffected by the presence of a second independent risk.

This result is not a strength but a weakness of the quadratic model, because one would expect that $\hat{a}$ (the solution given multiple independent risks – see above) exceeds a^*. The absence of a difference between $\hat{a}$ and a^* is an artifact of constant prudence, which always equals zero with quadratic utility. This point is developed in detail, as mentioned above, in Appendix 8.

Although quadratic utility is not very convincing for the case of independence, it is useful in giving an idea of the role of covariance between risks. Suppose specifically that the covariance between $\tilde{x}$ and $\tilde{\varepsilon}$ (which we denote $\text{cov}(\tilde{x}, \tilde{\varepsilon})$) is non-zero. This relationship between the two random variables does not affect $E(\tilde{w}_f)$ but does affect $\sigma^2(\tilde{w}_f)$ substantially. Specifically, using well-known results about the calculation of variance, one obtains from Equation (10.9) with $\rho = 0$:

$$\sigma^2(\tilde{w}_f) = (1 - a)^2 L^2 \sigma^2(\tilde{x}) + w_0 \sigma^2(\tilde{\varepsilon}) - 2(1 - a)Lw_0 \text{cov}(\tilde{x}, \tilde{\varepsilon})$$

$$(10.17)$$

A comparison of Equations (10.16) and (10.17) reveals several interesting facts. In the first place, if the covariance between $\tilde{x}$ and $\tilde{\varepsilon}$ is positive, the variance of $\tilde{w}_f$ is reduced. This is logical because in some sense the deterioration in the risk of loss (increase in $\tilde{x}$) is on average compensated by a better performance of the returns from the insured's other assets. Conversely, a negative covariance augments $\sigma^2(\tilde{w}_f)$ (unless $a = 1$) because bad (good) realisations of $\tilde{x}$ and bad (good) realisations of $\tilde{\varepsilon}$ tend to go together, which accentuates the variability of $\tilde{w}_f$. Substituting Equation (10.17) into (10.13) and recalculating the derivative of $E[U(\tilde{w}_f)]$ with respect to a yields:

$$dE[U(\tilde{w}_f)]/da = -\lambda\mu L - 2\beta[w_0 + L(1 - \mu) - \lambda\mu La](-\lambda\mu L)$$
$$+ 2\beta L^2 \sigma^2(\tilde{x})(1 - a) - 2\beta Lw_0 \, \text{cov}(\tilde{x}, \tilde{\varepsilon}) = 0$$

The solution in a (denoted $\hat{a}$) is:

$$\hat{a} = \frac{-\mu\lambda[1 - 2\beta(w_0 + L(1 - \mu))] + 2\beta L\sigma^2(\tilde{x}) - 2\beta w_0 \, \text{cov}(\tilde{x}, \tilde{\varepsilon})}{2\beta L(\sigma^2(\tilde{x}) + \mu^2\lambda^2)}$$

$$= a^* - \frac{w_0 \, \text{cov}(\tilde{x}, \tilde{\varepsilon})}{L(\sigma^2(\tilde{x}) + \mu^2\lambda^2)} \qquad (10.18)$$

Of course Equation (10.18) generalises Equation (10.15) which, recall, also yields the value of $\hat{a}$: specifically, if $\text{cov}(\tilde{x}, \tilde{\varepsilon}) = 0$ then $\hat{a} = a^*$. In contrast, a positive covariance reduces the desired level of coverage. This is not surprising: thanks to the positive covariance between the risk of loss $\tilde{x}$ and the other risk, the decision-maker automatically and without cost, benefits from a reduction in the total risk[8] as represented, in the case of quadratic utility functions, by the variance of $\tilde{w}_f$ (cf. Equation (10.17)). This obviously reduces the need to go to the insurance market for coverage against the insurable risk. Conversely, a negative covariance increases $\hat{a}$: the additional variability of $\tilde{w}_f$ generated by negative covariance, induces the insured to purchase better coverage against the insurable risk in order to control, as much as is economically desirable, the total risk.

Thus we come to the end of our first and brief excursion into situations of multiple risks. We will return to these questions in another context in Part Three. Furthermore, the reader who is especially interested in this subject is invited to read Appendix 8, which illustrates the role of the concept of positive (and not necessarily constant) prudence in the study of this subject which, in our view, has a promising future.

10.4 The deductible

Having considered the demand for insurance when the contract takes the form of proportional co-insurance, we now consider the same demand when the contract has a deductible clause d, that is, when the indemnity function is of the form:

$$I(x,d) = \max(0, xL - d) \tag{10.19}$$

The insurance premium is tied to the level of the chosen deductible by the following pricing formula:

$$P(d) = (1 + \lambda) \int_0^1 I(x,d)f(x)\,dx = (1 + \lambda) \int_{d/L}^1 (xL - d)f(x)\,dx$$

$$\tag{10.20}$$

As before, the premium is proportional to the actuarial value of the policy or, in other words, to the expected liability of the insurer. The parameter λ represents the loading factor. It is useful to observe that the pricing formula, Equation (10.20) can be integrated by parts to obtain the following equivalent formula:

$$P(d) = (1 + \lambda)[(L - d) - L \int_{d/L}^1 F(x)\,dx] \tag{10.20a}$$

It is interesting to calculate the derivative of the premium with respect to the chosen deductible. One obtains:

$$P'(d) = (1 + \lambda)\left[-1 + L\frac{1}{L}F\left(\frac{d}{L}\right)\right]$$

$$= -(1 + \lambda)(1 - F(d/L)) \tag{10.21}$$

where $1 - F(d/L)$ is the probability that the loss will be greater than the deductible. This term appears because the loss must be greater than the deductible before an increase in the deductible will reduce the liability of the insurer.

It is clear that the premium is a decreasing function of the deductible, since its derivative is unambiguously negative. A risk-averse individual thus faces a dilemma that we must resolve: on the one hand there is the desire to be well covered against risk by choosing a small deductible, but on the other wishes to limit the cost of insurance, an objective that is attained by choosing a high deductible. It is thus clear that there is a trade-off between the reduction of risk and the preservation of expected final wealth, just as in the case of co-insurance. We note that here the premium is a non-linear function of the insured's decision variable, unlike the previous case.[9] This will not, of course, simplify the problem. Indeed, the problem of insurance demand with a deductible is very different from the problem of demand for a risky asset. This is due, on the one hand, to the non-linearity of the reimbursement function, and on the other to the non-linearity of price.

With such an insurance contract, final wealth takes the following form:

$$w_f(x) = w_0 + L - xL + \max(0, xL - d) - P(d) \qquad (10.22)$$

and expected utility is:

$$E[U(\tilde{w}_f)] = \int_0^1 U[w_f(x)]f(x)\,dx$$

Note that the minimum wealth is realised when the loss exceeds the deductible, in which case final wealth equals:

$$w_f^{\min} = w_0 + L - d - P(d) \qquad (10.23)$$

To derive the optimal deductible, differentiate the insured's expected utility with respect to the decision variable[10]:

$$dE[U(\tilde{w}_f)]/dd = -P'(d)\int_0^1 U'(w_f)f(x)\,dx + \int_0^1 U'(w_f)\frac{\partial I}{\partial d}f(x)\,dx$$

$$= -P'(d)\int_0^1 U'(w_f)f(x)\,dx + \int_{d/L}^1 U'(w_f)(-1)f(x)\,dx$$

$$= (1 + \lambda)[1 - F(d/L)]E[U'(\tilde{w}_f)] - U'(w_f^{\min})[1 - F(d/L)]$$

$$(10.24)$$

The second equality is obtained by observing that the indemnity is independent of the deductible when $xL < d$. The third equality is due to Equation (10.21) and the fact that w_f is equal to $w_f^{\min}$ when $xL > d$. The first term of Equation (10.24) corresponds to the gain in expected utility resulting from the reduction in the premium of $(1 + \lambda)(1 - F)$ which is achieved when the deductible is increased by one unit. The second term represents the loss of expected utility due to the increase in the deductible. Specifically, this increase directly induces an equivalent decrease in $w_f^{\min}$, which will be realised with probability $[1 - F(d/L)]$. Thus there is a 'premium effect' and a 'coverage effect'.

At the optimal deductible, d^*, dEU/dd must equal zero. In accordance with the above discussion, this is equivalent to requiring that the marginal gain due to a decrease in the premium equal the marginal loss due to a reduction in coverage. In other words, it must be that:

$$H = (1 + \lambda)E[U'(\tilde{w}_f)] - U'(w_f^{min}) = 0 \qquad (10.25)$$

or, equivalently, that:

$$(1 + \lambda)E[U'(\tilde{w}_f)] = U'(w_f^{min}) \qquad (10.26)$$

The second-order condition[11] is not studied here. Note, however, that in contrast to the previous problem, risk aversion is not a sufficient condition for the second-order condition to be satisfied. There are two reasons for this. The first comes from the fact that the indemnity function I is non-linear in the deductible. Furthermore, the premium is non-linear. These two facts can make the objective function convex despite the concavity of the utility function. Maximising a convex objective function, with its 'corner solutions', is not a simple matter. It can be the case, therefore, that the solution given by Equation (10.25) minimises expected utility! Nevertheless, we assume in what follows that the individual is sufficiently risk averse that the problem is globally concave.[12]

We now return to the study of Equation (10.26). First note that, since $w_f(x)$ is greater than w_f^{min} for all x, it follows that $U'[w_f(x)]$ must be less than $U'(w_f^{min})$. Thus $EU'(\tilde{w}_f)$ is less than $U'(w_f^{min})$. Yet if the loading factor λ is zero, the necessary condition for a maximum implies that $EU'(\tilde{w}_f)$ equals $U'(w_f^{min})$. This is only possible if $w_f(x) = w_f^{min}$ for all x. Consequently, it must be that coverage is complete in this case, that is, that $d^* = 0$. Conversely, when the loading factor is positive ($\lambda > 0$), it must be that $EU'(\tilde{w}_f) < U'(w_f^{min})$ if Equation (10.26) holds, implying that $w_f(x)$ is strictly greater than w_f^{min} for some values of x. This is only possible if $d^* > 0$. These results are combined in the following theorem. This theorem is virtually equivalent to Theorem 10.1 on co-insurance.

Theorem 10.3 If $\lambda > 0$ then $d^* > 0$ while if $\lambda = 0$ then $d^* = 0$.

We can illustrate this result by considering a binary risk and using the graphical method presented in Chapter 7. Assume that x takes on the value 0 with probability p and 1 with probability $1 - p$. The insurance premium in this case is calculated in the following way:

$$P(d) = (1 + \lambda)(1 - p)(L - d)$$

Here the premium is a linear function of d. Wealth in the good state (without a loss) is thus:

$$w_{f_g}(d) = w_0 + L - P(d)$$

and wealth in the bad state (with a loss of L), w_f^{min}, is:

$$w_{f_b}(d) = w_0 + L - d - P(d)$$

In Figure 10.6, where final wealth in the good state is measured on the horizontal axis and final wealth in the bad state is measured on the vertical axis, the lack of any insurance $(d = L)$ is represented by the point $(w_0 + L, w_0)$. The introduction of a possibility of insurance allows the insured to choose from among a set of possible contracts graphically represented by the locus of points $(w_{f_g}(d), w_{f_b}(d))$. Since final wealth is a linear function of d, this locus of points is a line segment in Figure 10.6. One end of the segment corresponds to a lack of insurance with $d = L$. The other end corresponds to full insurance $d = 0$ and thus lies on the $45°$ line:

$$w_{f_g}(0) = w_{f_b}(0) = w_0 + L - (1 + \lambda)(1 - p)L$$

It is important to note that the absolute value of the slope of the line segment equals:

$$\frac{1 - (1 + \lambda)(1 - p)}{(1 + \lambda)(1 - p)} = \frac{p}{1 - p} - \frac{\lambda}{(1 + \lambda)(1 - p)}$$

which is less than $p/(1 - p)$ if λ is positive. A point on the interior of the segment corresponds to a partial insurance contract with $0 < d < L$. The rational decision-maker chooses the point on the segment that maximises the expected utility, that is, the point on the segment that lies on the highest indifference curve. At this point, d^*, the slope of the segment must be equal to the slope of the indifference curve. Recalling that the slope of the

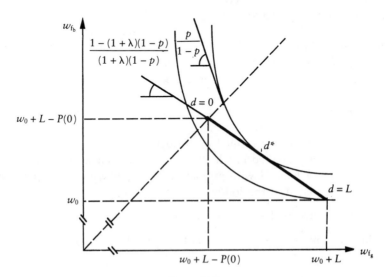

Figure 10.6

indifference curve corresponds to the marginal rate of substitution between consumption in the two states, and using formula (7.4), we write the necessary condition for a maximum as:

$$\frac{p}{1-p} - \frac{\lambda}{(1+\lambda)(1-p)} = \text{MRS}_{bg} = \frac{pU'(w_{f_g})}{(1-p)U'(w_{f_b})} \qquad (10.27)$$

When the loading factor λ is zero, the left-hand side equals $p/(1-p)$. Now we know that MRS equals $p/(1-p)$ along the 45° line. Condition (10.27) thus requires $d^* = 0$.

In contrast, when λ is positive, the left-hand side is smaller than $p/(1-p)$. Since we know that MRS decreases along an indifference curve (due to the convexity of the indifference curves) and that it equals $p/(1-p)$ along the 45° line, Condition (10.27) can only be satisfied below that line, that is, at a point where d^* is positive. This confirms the content of Theorem 10.3, if that is still necessary.

It is also clear graphically that over-insurance ($d < 0$) is never optimal. In contrast, it is possible that no insurance ($d = L$) is optimal. In this case one obtains a corner solution (see Figure 10.7). Specifically, in this case the individual would like to sell insurance, because the optimal indemnity $I(L) = L - d^*$ is negative.[13] Selling insurance is rational for slightly risk-averse individuals who are attracted by the remuneration paid for this service.

The reader can also verify that Condition (10.27) is equivalent to the first-order condition, Equation (10.26). Specifically, Equation (10.27) can be rewritten as follows:

$$(1-p)(1+\lambda)[pU'(w_{f_g}) + (1-p)U'(w_{f_b})] = (1-p)U'(w_{f_b})$$

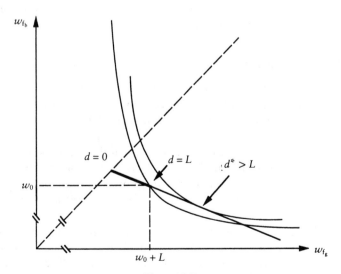

Figure 10.7

Dividing by $(1 - p)$, one obtains Equation (10.26). It is interesting to estimate the optimal deductible d^*. Consider the case of the power utility function introduced in Chapter 4: $U(w) = \text{sgn}(\beta)w^\beta$. Remember that this case corresponds to constant relative risk aversion with $A_r = 1 - \beta$. Using Equation (10.27) with this specification yields:

$$p - \frac{\lambda}{1 + \lambda} = p(w_{f_g}/w_{f_b})^{\beta - 1} \tag{10.28}$$

or, equivalently,

$$d^*/w_{f_g} = 1 - \left[1 - \frac{\lambda}{(1 + \lambda)p}\right]^{1/A_r} \tag{10.29}$$

since $w_{f_b} = w_{f_g} - d^*$. Equation (10.29) determines the optimal deductible of an agent with constant relative risk aversion A_r as a function of the characteristics of risk (p) and the cost of insurance (λ). It is generally believed that relative risk aversion is close to 1 (logarithmic utility). In this case, *it must be that the deductible, expressed as a fraction of the final wealth without loss, is equal to* $\lambda/p(1 + \lambda)$. We illustrate this with the following example: if the loading factor is 22 per cent of the actuarial value, an individual with unitary relative risk aversion facing a loss with a probability of 10 per cent should choose a deductible that corresponds to approximately 22 per cent of his wealth.

Even though the case of binary risks is special, its pedagogical qualities have led us to analyse its basic characteristics. It only illustrates the general case for arbitrary risks. To follow the pattern of the previous sections, we should now embark on some comparative statics analysis. To avoid being repetitive in the presentation of comparative statics techniques under uncertainty, we limit ourselves to what is essential in the analysis.

10.4.1 Effect of a change in w₀

To understand the effect of an increase in wealth on the optimal deductible, one can, as a first approximation, consider the special case represented by Equation (10.29), with binary risk and constant relative risk aversion. In this case the deductible is proportional to the wealth $w_{f_b} = w_0 - L - P$. It is thus increasing in w_0. Using the same techniques as in the previous sections, it can be shown that this is only true because A_a is decreasing in this special case ($A_r = wA_a$ is constant). Indeed, it can be shown that *an increase in initial wealth implies a reduction in the demand for insurance when absolute risk aversion is decreasing.*

In the limit, the individual becomes their own insurer when sufficient reserves have been established for protection against the risk of loss. This kind of behaviour is observed in many situations in practice. When one buys a new car on credit, extended coverage is generally purchased. Later, as the loan is repaid (an increase in net wealth), insurance coverage is reduced by an increase (up to L in the limit) in the deductible.[14] The same kind of behaviour is observed for growing firms, when they decide either to create a captive or to set up a retention fund. This provides yet another argument in favour of Hypothesis 4.1.

10.4.2 Effect of a change in λ

Now consider an increase in the price of insurance, that is, in λ. As before, there is a wealth effect and a substitution effect. An increase in the cost of insurance reduces the wealth of the insured and induces a positive or negative reaction, depending on the derivative of A_a (wealth effect). In contrast, the insured wishes to substitute some retention of risk for some insurance when the market price increases (substitution/price effect). When absolute risk aversion is constant, the wealth effect is non-existent and only the price effect matters. In this case, the increase in the price of insurance reduces demand. In contrast, when absolute risk aversion decreases, the wealth effect moves in the opposite manner to the price effect and the total effect is ambiguous.

10.4.3 The change to a riskier distribution

Few general results have been derived concerning the effect of an increase in risk on the optimal deductible. This is, of course, due to the non-linearity of the indemnity function, which rules out the use of the usual techniques. Two simple results can nevertheless be established:

1. Consider an increase in risk solely due to changes in the distribution of losses above the level of the deductible. In other words, consider a transformation of F into G such that $G(t) = F(t)$ for all t less than d^* and such that the two distributions have the same expected value. An example of such an increase in risk is presented in Figure 10.8.

    Note that in this case the insurer would not change the premium, even if the increase in the risk that is being insured were observed. The reason for this is that the actuarial value of the policy – upon which the calculation of the premium is based – is unchanged. The reader can verify this by using the pricing formula, Equation (10.20a) while remembering that, since the mean is unchanged,

$$\int_0^1 F(t) \, \mathrm{d}t = \int_0^1 G(t) \, \mathrm{d}t$$

which implies that:

$$\int_{d^*/L}^1 F(t) \, \mathrm{d}t = \int_{d^*/L}^1 G(t) \, \mathrm{d}t \tag{10.30}$$

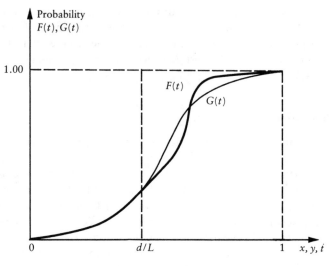

Figure 10.8

because $F(t) = G(t)$ for all t less than d^*. This result is due to the fact that – given a pricing formula such as Equation (10.30) – the insurer does not charge a risk premium for the risk that is assumed.

It thus follows that the distribution of final wealth of the insured is unaffected by the increase in risk. On the one hand, the same premium continues to be paid, and on the other, the distribution of the risk that is continually held is unchanged. Specifically, the insured has transferred the increased risk to the insurer at no cost. Thus, the insured does not care about the increase in risk considered here.

Theorem 10.4 Increases in risk at a constant mean that affect only losses which are greater than the deductible d^* affect neither the optimal deductible nor the premium.

2. Alternatively, consider an increase in risk that affects only the distribution of losses that are less than the deductible d^*, that is, $F(t) = G(t)$ for all t greater than d^*. Such an increase in risk is drawn in Figure 10.9. Clearly, this will not affect the premium paid because the risk transferred to the insurer is unaffected. In contrast, the structure of the risk retained by the insured is upset. This situation is thus exactly the opposite of the situation studied above. Here, the change from F to G entails a riskier distribution of w_f.

The key to the solution to this problem is found in the analysis of the first-order condition, Equation (10.25) which we reproduce here for the convenience of the reader.

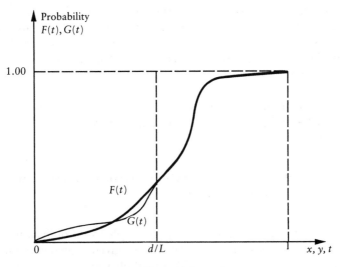

Figure 10.9

$$H = (1 + \lambda)E[U'(\tilde{w}_f)] - U'(w_f^{\min}) = 0$$

At constant d^* – and thus a constant premium – the change from distribution F to distribution G affects only $E[U'(\tilde{w}_f)]$ in this equation. The reader surely anticipates the appearance of the prudence concept, which measures the impact of an increase in risk on expected marginal utility. Indeed, if the insured is prudent ($U''' > 0$), then the increase in the riskiness of $\tilde{w}_f$ implies an increase in $E[U'(\tilde{w}_f)]$. Thus H, which is zero at d^* before the increase in risk, becomes positive. Since H is a decreasing function of the deductible (from the second-order condition), a higher d than d^* is necessary to re-establish $H = 0$. We thus have the following result.

Theorem 10.5 If the insured is prudent, an increase in risk over losses that are less than the deductible d^* will induce an increase in the optimal deductible.

This result may seem paradoxical: here is an increase in risk that reduces the demand for insurance. It is nevertheless explainable in the following way: an insured who faces an increase in risk can adopt one of two strategies. Either coverage can be increased by reducing the level of the deductible, or reserves can be increased to better prepare for the realisation of the risky outcome. The second strategy is accomplished by cutting back on insurance demand, that is, by choosing a larger deductible. This is the typical strategy of a *prudent* individual, and constitutes precautionary savings. The existence of this insurance strategy (the retention of risk) explains why an increase in risk can reduce the demand for coverage. Note that for quadratic utility functions (with zero prudence), the demand for insurance is not affected by this kind of increase in risk.

One can naturally consider increases in risk that combine the results of Theorems 10.4 and 10.5 to obtain more general results.

10.5 The superiority of deductible insurance over co-insurance

Having reviewed the two principle forms of insurance policies, the following is a legitimate question to ask: given a predetermined pricing system, which form of insurance will riskophobes prefer? Depending on their attitudes toward risk and the properties of those attitudes, will some choose co-insurance, others deductible insurance, others a combination of the two, and others a still more sophisticated contract? This is the question that we study in this section. Whereas before the form of the contract was imposed by the insurer, we now allow the insured to freely choose.

Very generally, an insurance contract is described by two 'objects': the premium to be paid, P, and the indemnity function $I(xL)$. Of course, the insurance premium depends on the indemnity function. We have assumed until now that the insurer tied the premium only to the actuarial value of the policy, that is, to the expected indemnity. Up until now we have assumed a linear relationship – with a proportional loading factor – between the premium and the actuarial value, but now we assume more generally that

$$P = f(EI) \tag{10.31}$$

where EI designates the actuarial value of the policy and f is an increasing function in its argument. We note that this assumption, although more general than the linear assumption, is not exempt from criticism. For example, as we know, it implies that the insurer does not include a risk premium in the price schedule since only the average liability (EI) is considered when evaluating the risk. This price schedule thus implicitly assumes that the insurer is risk neutral.[15] To guarantee a positive expected profit on each contract, it must be that $f(EI)$ is greater than EI, which implies a positive loading factor.

Now suppose that the insured can freely choose, from among all the possible and imaginable indemnity functions, the one that maximises expected utility. Briefly, the insurer presents a pricing formula that guarantees a positive expected profit regardless of the insured's choice, and then lets the client choose a contract. There are, however, two constraints on this choice. These two constraints were presented at the beginning of this chapter:

(a) on the one hand, the indemnity cannot be greater than the loss because otherwise the insured would abandon all attempts at prevention or, worse still, would actually help to bring about a loss[16];

(b) on the other hand, the indemnity cannot be negative.[17]

Several kind of indemnity functions are represented in Figure 10.10. The reader will recognise the deductible and co-insurance contracts, and also the contract combining the deductible and co-insurance contracts. There also exist on the market contracts with a 'disappearing deductible': below the deductible no indemnity is paid; above the deductible the entire loss is covered. This type of clause is found in some maritime contracts. Another example is the indemnity with a ceiling which, as its name implies, imposes an upper bound on the indemnity. Finally, one can imagine all kinds of other 'custom-made' indemnity functions $I(xL)$ that satisfy the condition $0 < I(xL) < xL$.

We could proceed by writing down the expected utility maximisation problem of the insured who must choose the form of the contract. This has been done by several authors of whom the first was Kenneth Arrow, Nobel laureate in economics. The problem is complicated because the 'decision variable' is a *function*. The solution to this problem thus requires mathematical techniques from the calculus of variations or optimal control theory. We do not follow this path because our colleague Harris Schlesinger[18] has recently demonstrated a very elegant way to use the notions of stochastic

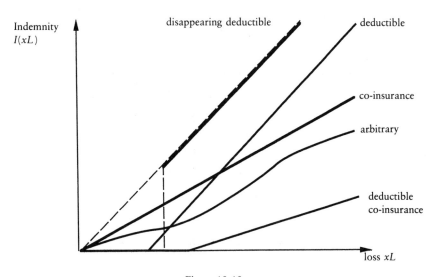

Figure 10.10

dominance to prove the central result simply. This result is presented in Theorem 10.6, due to Arrow (1970).

Theorem 10.6 If an insurance company is willing to offer insurance contracts with premiums that depend only on the actuarial value of the corresponding contract, then the contract chosen by a risk-averse individual takes the form of a contract with a deductible.

To prove this theorem, we will show that, regardless of the level of the premium chosen by the insured, the deductible contract is preferred over all other forms of contract with the same premium. More specifically, we will prove that all contracts other than the deductible contract imply greater risk in terms of final wealth than does the deductible contract costing the same price. This thus implies that all risk-averse individuals choose the deductible contract.

We begin by choosing some level for the premium P and defining the random variable $\tilde{y}$ as the final wealth after loss but before indemnity. Thus:

$$y = w_0 + L - xL - P$$

Of course, this variable is only meaningful if the indemnification is not instantaneous. In Figure 10.11, the cumulative distribution function of $\tilde{y}$ is represented with support in the interval $[w_0 - P, w_0 + L - P]$. This distribution function is denoted $H(y)$.

The derivation of $\tilde{w}_f$ from $\tilde{y}$ for a particular indemnity function represents an application of first-order stochastic dominance. Specifically,

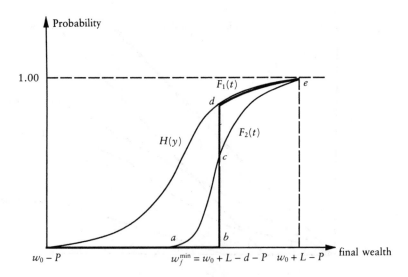

Figure 10.11

define final wealth $\tilde{w}_f$ as the sum of wealth before indemnification and the indemnification itself which is constrained to be positive or zero: $w_f = y + I(xL)$. This implies that $\tilde{w}_f >_1 \tilde{y}$, exactly as for the change from $\tilde{x}$ to $\tilde{z}$ in Chapter 6: one adds to a random variable something that is always positive. Thus, the distribution function of final wealth, denoted F, is always 'below' H, regardless of the indemnity function considered. The requirement that I be positive plays a crucial role in this result.

In Figure 10.11, we have drawn the distribution function of final wealth F_1 with a contract containing a deductible d and for which the premium is P. With such a contract, there is no indemnity for losses between 0 and d. Thus, F_1 corresponds to H, the distribution function without indemnity, on the interval of final wealth $[w_0 + L - d - P, w_0 + L - P]$. In contrast, the probability of having final wealth less than $w_f^{min} = w_0 + L - d - P$ is zero: $F_1(w_f) = 0$ for all $w_f < w_f^{min}$ All the weight to the left of w_f^{min} is transferred to w_f^{min} with a deductible contract. It can be verified that F_1 (first-order) stochastically dominates H: F_1 is 'below' H.

We now show that, relative to F_1, any other contract costing the same premium entails an increase in risk at a constant mean in terms of final wealth. Specifically, any other distribution function, F_2 for example, must always lie between 0 (by definition of a distribution) and H (by stochastic dominance). This implies that F_2 is necessarily greater than F_1 (= 0) to the left of w_f^{min} and that F_2 is necessarily less than F_1 (=H) to the right of w_f^{min}.

Furthermore, since the premiums are equal, the expected indemnities are also, because the premium depends only on the expected indemnity, by assumption. Thus, expected wealth is the same for both contracts. Graphically, this implies that the area abc equals the area cde. It is thus clear that F_2 constitutes what is called an increase in risk relative to F_1. Riskophobes that choose a contract with premium P thus opt for F_1 and its associated deductible contract rather than any other contract with premium P. Since this reasoning applies to any other premium, Theorem 10.6 follows.

Note that we have not attempted in this proof to determine the optimal premium or the optimal deductible. For this, the reader is referred to the analysis carried out in the preceding section. The preference for deductible contracts is independent of the intensity of the insured's risk aversion. One can thus employ the notion of increased risk to derive this result for all riskophobes. In contrast, the optimal deductible depends on the insured's degree of risk aversion. Thus it is impossible to use the notion of increased risk to determine d^*.

We have thus just proved the superiority of deductible contracts over all other types, and notably over co-insurance contracts. The deductible form allows the insured to best manage the transfer of risk. This transfer is costly because the insurer imposes a loading factor. This implies a reduction in the expected value of final wealth. However, it also reduces its variability. The deductible allows the maximum reduction in risk for a given reduction in expected value.

To reinforce the intuition for this very important result, consider a discrete risk where x can take the values $x_1, x_2, ..., x_n$ with probabilities $p_1 = p_2 = ... = p_n = 1/n$. In the absence of insurance, the variance of final wealth is:

$$V(\tilde{w}_f) = L^2 \left[\sum_{j=1}^{n} p_j x_j^2 - \left(\sum_{j=1}^{n} p_j x_j \right)^2 \right]$$

Suppose that the insured decides to insure against one of the states of nature, but only one. Let this state be state i, without loss of generality.[19] One franc of indemnity in this state requires the payment of a premium equal to $(1 + \lambda)p_i$ in the case of a proportional loading factor. Since the expected indemnity is only p_i, it follows that there is a loss in expected final wealth equal to $(1 + \lambda)p_i = \lambda p_i = \lambda/n$. This is the marginal cost of coverage in State i. However, the corresponding reduction in variance is:

$$\frac{\partial V(\tilde{w}_f)}{\partial I(x_i)} = \frac{\partial V(\tilde{w}_f)}{\partial x_i}$$

$$= L^2 \left[2p_i x_i - 2p_i \sum_{j=1}^{n} p_j x_j \right]$$

$$= \frac{2L^2}{n} [x_i - \mu]$$

The first equality comes from the fact that an increase in the indemnity in state i is strictly equivalent, in terms of the reduction in variance, to an equal reduction in the amount of the loss. We conclude that the marginal cost in terms of the lost expected final wealth $\tilde{w}_f$ is independent of x_i while the marginal benefit in terms of the reduction of the variance of $\tilde{w}_f$ is an increasing function of the loss x_i. It is thus obvious that if the insured can choose the state of the world i in which the indemnity of 1 F must be paid, state i will be chosen that corresponds to the highest marginal benefit, that is, the state in which the loss is greatest. Insurance will be refused against those states where the marginal cost of coverage λ/n is greater than the marginal benefit, that is, those states where the loss is small. This illustrates the logic of the deductible.

We can use the same reasoning sequentially for a second franc, and then a third, etc., each time asking where the additional franc ought to be spent. It then becomes clear that the insured will 'knock the top off' the largest losses by choosing the states where the retained loss is greatest. This is precisely the principle underlying the deductible contract. The underlying idea is that the cost of insurance depends linearly on the indemnity, while its benefit is a quadratic function of indemnity.

Exercises

10.1 Show that the standard portfolio problem and the co-insurance problem can both be rewritten as:

$$\text{Max } E[U(x_0 + \alpha \tilde{x})]$$
$$\text{\small a}$$

where α is the demand for the risky asset or the retention rate of the policy-holder, whereas $\tilde{x}$ is the excess return of the risky asset or the full-insurance premium minus the loss.[20] In the light of this relationship, show how to derive the results presented in Chapter 9. In particular show that Theorem 10.1 is the co-insurance equivalent to the fact that the demand for the risky asset is positive iff the expected return is larger than the risk-free rate.

10.2 Consider the standard co-insurance problem presented in Section 10.2 for the specific case of a power utility function $U(W = \text{sgn}(\beta), w^\beta, \beta \leqslant 1$. Show that the optimal retention rate, i.e. one minus the co-insurance rate, is proportional to the initial wealth net of the full insurance premium.

10.3 Show that the optimal rate of coverage is not necessarily positive. Give a counter-example. Can you provide an intuitive argument for this?

10.4 Prove that an increase in risk aversion reduces the optimal deductible.

10.5 Suppose that the insurance tariff is defined by:

$$P = 0 \qquad\qquad \text{if } a = 0$$
$$P = P_0 + (1 + \lambda)a\mu L \qquad \text{for } a > 0$$

instead of

$$P = (1 + \lambda)a\mu L \qquad \text{for } a \geqslant 0$$

P_0 can be interpreted as an entry fee to the insurance market to cover overhead costs.

Questions
(a) Show that an increase in P_0 reduces the demand for insurance under decreasing absolute risk aversion when a is initially strictly positive.
(b) Using an example with a specific utility function (e.g. a logarithmic one) and a specific density function (e.g. a binary one) show that there exists a value of the loss of P_0 such that the individual is indifferent between not insuring or buying the optimal value a^*.

Notes

1. As the discussion makes clear, the notion of transferring risk should not be confused with that of suppressing risk.

2. Like practically all assets, L is also subject to a financial risk of appreciation or depreciation of its value. This risk is not studied in this chapter because taking multiple sources of risk into account poses some delicate problems. See, however, Section 10.3.

3. When the insured and the insurer do not have the same information, the problem becomes very difficult. This is currently very much discussed in the literature on 'asymmetric information' (see Chapter 16).

4. Specifically if $I = a\tilde{x}L$ then $P = (1 + \lambda)a\mu L$, where $\mu = E(\tilde{x})$ and where P is linearly increasing in a.

5. If $a = 1$ (complete coverage) then $dw_f/dx = 0$ and at that point and that point alone $\text{cov}(U', \tilde{x}) = 0$, which means that the gross marginal benefit of a is zero.

6. The interested reader should eventually consult the article by Briys *et al.* (1989).

7. This assumption is common in the literature on signalling theory. There it is generally assumed that an insured who demands higher coverage implicitly reveals to the insurer that the situation has become more dangerous.

8. N. Doherty and H. Schlesinger (1983) call this phenomenon 'homemade insurance'.

9. However, when risk is binary (x takes on the values 0 or 1), $F(d/L)$ is constant on $[0, 1]$ and equals the probability that the loss will be avoided. In this case, $P(d)$ is proportional to d. Specifically, with a binary risk, there is no fundamental difference between the co-insurance contract and the deductible contract, since all that matters is the amount of reimbursement in the case of loss.

10. To write $\partial I/\partial d$ is an abuse of notation because I is not differentiable in d when $xL = d$. Nevertheless, this purely technical problem is solved by separating the integral EU into two parts for $x < d/L$ and $x > d/L$.

11. For an analysis of the second-order condition, see the article by H. Schlesinger (1981).

12. One could also restrict the type of risk considered. For example, it is easily shown that the second-order condition is satisfied with binary risks, as is apparent in Figure 10.6.

13. Note, however, that the model is inadequate for the analysis of negative indemnities. Specifically, since $\lambda I(xL)$ represents the administrative cost of the contract and the payment for insurance services, to have negative coverage would imply negative costs and payments for the insurer, which is unacceptable. A more reasonable

specification would consist of considering costs of the type $\lambda \, | \, I(xL) \, |$. The corner solution – which is typical with non-differentiable objective functions such as the 'absolute value' function – with $I(L) = L - d^* = 0$ is then more reasonable.

14. A different interpretation of this phenomenon is that, as the value of the insured good falls over time, one reduces the insurance coverage as a result. Even so, it seems that the coverage expressed as a percentage of the value of the good decreases over time.

15. Other pricing formulas that take the insurer's risk aversion into account and that consider other forms of the insurers' management cost function have been studied in the literature. Briefly, a contract that combines a deductible and co-insurance is optimal when the insurer is risk averse and/or the insurer faces convex management costs. If one assumes a fixed cost per loss, the optimal indemnity function is discontinuous at zero. A summary of this literature is presented in Gollier (1991).

16. Actually, it can be shown that this constraint is never binding. The insured does not wish to over-insure because that would create a new and costly risk.

17. This prevents the insured from becoming an insurer. One can ask about the appropriateness of imposing such a constraint in this model. This question is complex and cannot be broached in the context of this book. The reader should know, however, that the results of the model are hardly changed if this constraint is relaxed.

18. We refer here to an article written jointly with C. Gollier: Gollier and Schlesinger (1994).

19. We point out that we have here a contingent claim tied to state i. In the jargon of economists, a general insurance contract is nothing more than a 'basket' of contingent claims.

20. In the co-insurance problem, x_0 stands for $W_0 + L$ from which one has to deduct the full insurance premium.

References

Arrow K. (1970), *Essays in the Theory of Risk-Bearing*, North-Holland, Amsterdam and London.

Briys E., G. Dionne and L. Eeckhoudt (1989), More on insurance as a Giffen good, *Journal of Risk and Uncertainty*, vol. 2, 415–420.

Doherty N. and H. Schlesinger (1983), Optimal insurance in incomplete markets, *Journal of Political Economy*, vol. 91, 1045–1054.

Gollier C. (1991), The economic theory of risk exchanges: a review, in *Contributions to Insurance Economics*, G. Dionne (ed.), Kluwer Academic Press, Boston.

Gollier C. and H. Schlesinger (1994), Second-best insurance contract design in an incomplete market, *Scandinavian Journal of Economics*, forthcoming.

Schlesinger H. (1981), The optimal level of deductibility in insurance. *Journal of Risk and Insurance*, vol. 48, 465–481.

11 : The production decision under uncertainty

11.1 An overview of subjects discussed

While there exist many parallels between the demand for risky assets and the choice of insurance coverage (in the framework of co-insurance), the production decision under uncertainty is somewhat of an 'odd man out' relative to the other problems. Of course, it still has many points in common with them which will be highlighted. Nevertheless, because of the great diversity of questions that are encountered, the analysis of the production decision has some unique aspects as well.

For example, in production theory it is natural to distinguish between two sources of uncertainty that, as we will see briefly below, are not mutually exclusive.

The first source of uncertainty is tied to the *technology* or the climate, or more generally to the process of production. In this context we distinguish:

(a) planned production, denoted a, for which the costs are immediately and irrevocably incurred;
(b) actual production, which will differ from a for many reasons (strikes, climate, breakdowns, etc.) and which possibly (but not necessarily) will entail additional costs or sometimes even reduce costs if the realisation of the random outcome is favourable.

The relationship between actual production ($\tilde{a}$) and planned production (a) can take different forms. For example, the risk may be additive and then

$$\tilde{a} = a + \tilde{\varepsilon} \tag{11.1}$$

with $E(\tilde{\varepsilon}) = 0$ by assumption. This assumption, which considerably simplifies the analysis (see below), is not very realistic because, applied to agriculture, it means that a drought has the same absolute effect on the part-time gardener as on the large agricultural corporation in terms of the difference between the planned and actual levels of production.

It must thus be conceded that a multiplicative model is generally preferable, that is,

$$\tilde{a} = a(1 + \tilde{\varepsilon}) \tag{11.2}$$

with $E(\tilde{\varepsilon}) = 0$. Here it is assumed that the exogenous shock affects actual production proportionally to the size of the firm's project. Of course, even though we will not delve into the subject, one can imagine that additive and multiplicative uncertainty can coexist within the same firm.

Once a choice has been made between the additive and multiplicative models to characterise the technological risk, the subject is still not exhausted. We have so far mentioned the impact of randomness on the level of production. Even though this aspect is undoubtedly the most important, the effect of the difference between the plan and the realisation on the costs of production should also be specified. To highlight this aspect, consider as an example a farmer who plans to produce an output a and who, to this end, has incurred the expense of seeds, fertiliser and labour denoted $c(a)$ with, of course, $c'(a) > 0$ (that is, positive marginal cost). When, at the end of the process, the harvest comes, other costs must be incurred. Some depend on a and, to the extent that they could be planned (for example, the rental of farm equipment), they should logically be incorporated (and discounted if necessary) in $c(a)$.

In contrast, other costs are random and depend on the realisation of the random variable $\tilde{\varepsilon}$. Thus, if the harvest surpasses 'expectations' ($\tilde{\varepsilon} \geqslant 0$) then more labour must be employed. This induces an additional cost that depends on the level of $\tilde{\varepsilon}$ and is denoted $d(\varepsilon)$ with $d'(\varepsilon) > 0$. Conversely, if the harvest is abnormally poor ($\varepsilon \leqslant 0$) then two effects will play a role: some savings are possibly realised on planned costs but, on the contrary, the producer might also face unexpected costs, for example, to remove the failed crop. Since a detailed examination of these questions would take us too far afield, we introduce them in this chapter only as a (presumably) useful starting point for further study.[1]

Having considered the first source of uncertainty, we now turn to the second, which is best known and depends on the uncertainties generated by markets. In this category, and limiting discussion to the case of perfect competition, one can consider the uncertainty surrounding input and output prices or the uncertainty surrounding demand at a fixed price. If one considers market structures that are more complicated than perfect competition, then these two forms of uncertainty can be combined (see, for example the articles by Leland (1972) and Baron (1971).

In this chapter we restrict attention to the case of perfect competition and we do not consider uncertain input prices. Thus the cost functions are assumed to be perfectly known *ex ante*. We specifically study two problems.

1. *Uncertain output prices*, which practically always correspond to situations where there exists a delay in production. At the moment of beginning production, the entrepreneur knows with certainty the costs that must be incurred and the production that will result. However, what is unknown is the output price at which the product can be sold

and thus this price is represented in the problem by a random variable, denoted $\tilde{p}$, for which the density function, $f(p)$, represents the expectations of the producer as to the present value of this future price.

2. *Uncertain demand* faced by a distributor for a product whose price is previously fixed but for which the purchase order must be sent before the level of demand is revealed. This problem is well known in the operations research literature as the 'newsboy problem' which, surprisingly, has been little studied in the economic literature dedicated to risk theory.[2]

Before reviewing the different themes mentioned so far, we point out that this chapter will give us the opportunity to broach (more exactly, to brush over) two important subjects: the role of futures markets and the value of flexibility (or of information).

We begin our analysis with market uncertainty because it has received the most attention in pure economics. Next we move to technological uncertainty, which has been studied more in the agricultural economics journals. We never mix the two sources of uncertainty even though this case is both interesting and realistic because good (bad) harvests often accompany mediocre (profitable) prices. Unfortunately, the subject of multiple sources of risk is too recent to be systematically studied in an introductory textbook.

Before the reader broaches the technical aspects of the chapter, we recall attention to the fact that, in the interest of conciseness, we will not repeat here the proofs that have been done, *mutatis mutandis*, in different contexts in the previous two chapters. It is thus important that the reader have a good grasp of these proofs in order to understand the more technical aspects of the present chapter.

11.2 Market uncertainty: basic elements

11.2.1 Output price uncertainty under perfect competition

Under perfect competition, the producer knows that everything that is produced can be sold and, since there is no technological uncertainty, the decision variable, a, represents planned production as well as actual production and the volume of sales. The costs associated with this activity are divided into total variable costs ($c(a)$ with $c'(a) > 0$) and fixed costs B so that the total cost is $c(a) + B$. Total revenue is random because the output price (or more precisely its present value) is not known with certainty. Given the assumption of perfect competition, the density of $\tilde{p}$, $f(p)$, is not affected by a; it represents the producer–seller's 'beliefs' about the future.

Given these assumptions, the producer's final wealth is:

$$\tilde{w}_f = w_0 + \tilde{\pi} = w_0 + \tilde{p}a - c(a) - B \tag{11.3}$$

where $\tilde{\pi} = \tilde{p}a - c(a) - B$ is the period's profit from the production activity. In the context of a firm, w_0 measures the initial wealth of the owner, that is, the value of assets minus the value of liability owed to third parties. Our presentation in Equation (11.1) implicitly imposes the (heroic) assumption that none of the assets or liabilities is subject to changes in value during the current period unless – by some extraordinary chance – the changes exactly cancel each other out. We thus essentially only allow for risk in the production activity itself; we do this because it is technically difficult to take multiple risks into account (see, for example, Section 10.3).

If, as we have always assumed, the decision-maker's objective is to maximise the expected utility[3] of final wealth and that the level of production a must be chosen without knowing the price at which it can be sold, the optimal value of a is obtained by solving:

$$\frac{dE[U(\tilde{w}_f)]}{da} = E[U'(\cdot)(\tilde{p} - c'(a))] = 0 \tag{11.4}$$

The structure of this equation is exactly parallel to those encountered in the study of asset demand, Equation (9.6), and in the study of the choice of co-insurance, Equation (10.1). The only difference is due to the nature of $c'(a)$ which here plays the role of i (in Equation (9.6) or the role of $(1 + \lambda)\mu$ in Equation (10.1): whereas these last two terms represented constants, $c'(a)$ can be variable in a because we have not required *a priori* that marginal cost be constant. This difference plays an important role in the analysis of some questions (see Section 11.3) but it does not affect significantly study of the comparative statics properties of Equation (11.4). To convince the reader of this we make two rather brief comments to show that the methods developed previously apply without difficulty to the problem of production under price uncertainty.

1. Using the properties of covariance, it is possible to rewrite Equation (11.4) to show that at the optimum:

$$E(\tilde{p}) = c'(a) - \frac{\text{cov}(U', \tilde{p})}{E(U')} \tag{11.5}$$

The left-hand side Equation (11.5) is the gross marginal benefit (or marginal revenue) of an increase in production and the right-hand side is its marginal cost. The marginal cost has two terms. The first, $c'(a)$, is well known in microeconomic theory: it is the physical marginal cost associated with an increase in a. The second term is a bit more subtle. Its denominator is clearly positive and for a risk-averse decision-maker it is easy to show that $\text{cov}(U', \tilde{p})$ is negative. Specifically, if the realisation of $\tilde{p}$ is higher, all other things equal, w_f is larger and U' is smaller: there is thus a negative correlation between U' and p in the case of risk aversion. This implies that the right-hand side contains, in addition to $c'(a)$, a 'psychological' marginal cost of increasing a that is due to the coexistence of risk aversion and uncertainty surrounding $\tilde{p}$. By increasing a, the producer increases the risk that is taken. The covariance term represents the loss of expected utility due to this increase in risk.

The sum of these two marginal costs constitutes the total marginal cost which, at the optimum, must equal the marginal benefit $E(\tilde{p})$. This analysis is illustrated in Figure 11.1 where $E(\tilde{p})$ is a horizontal line that is independent of the decision-maker's production choice because of the assumption of perfect competition. If marginal physical cost is increasing, a curve like $c'(a)$ is obtained. In the case of risk neutrality, this marginal cost alone would be pertinent[4] and the optimum would be at the intersection of $E(\tilde{p})$ and $c'(a)$ that is, at $\hat{a}$. The result would be the same if the uncertain price were replaced by a certain price equal to $E(\tilde{p})$.

The presence of both uncertainty surrounding $\tilde{p}$ and risk aversion leads us to add to $c'(a)$ a psychological marginal cost measured by $-\text{cov}(U', \tilde{p})/E(U')$. This has been shown to be positive. In the same way, it can be shown to be increasing in a. This generates a higher marginal cost curve that leads to an optimal value of a, a^*, that is clearly less than $\hat{a}$. This graph (and the algebraic analysis upon which it is founded) confirms what one would expect: the riskiness of the output price reduces the level of production that is chosen by a risk-averse decision-maker.

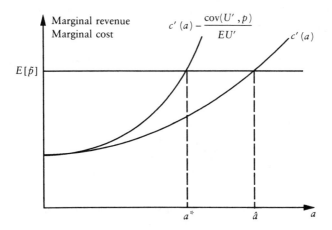

Figure 11.1

Once again we encounter analysis, reasoning and conclusions that were presented in the other two problems. This confirms that there is much similarity between all these decisions even though, at first glance, they seem very different. The point is again reinforced by the comparative statics exercise that follows.

2. Under certainty with perfect competition, the level of fixed costs does not affect the production choice (except the decision to leave the market when B is too large). This result – which does not fail to confuse many managers – does not generalise to the case of an uncertain output price. To prove this it is first shown that the second-order condition for a maximum is satisfied. Specifically, when U'' is negative and when physical marginal costs are non-decreasing,

$$\frac{d^2E}{da^2} = E[U''(\tilde{p} - c'(a))^2 - c''(a)U']$$

is necessarily negative. Under these conditions,

$$\text{sgn} \frac{da^*}{dB} = \text{sgn} \frac{\partial H}{\partial B}$$

where H stands for the left-hand side of the first-order condition in Equation (11.4). Now

$$\frac{\partial H}{\partial B} = -E[U''(\tilde{p} - c'(a))] \tag{11.5a}$$

and the sign of this expression is generally ambiguous because $\tilde{p} - c'(a)$ can be either negative or positive. However, an appeal to Hypothesis 4.1 allows $\partial H/\partial B$ to be signed. The result is stated in the form of Theorem 11.1 and it is proven by a technique that is nearly the same as the one adopted in Chapter 9 to establish conditions under which a risky asset is a normal good.

Theorem 11.1 If absolute risk aversion is decreasing in wealth, an increase in fixed costs reduces the optimal level of production.

To prove this, we use as before the everywhere positive function $\beta(w_f) = -U''(w_f)/U'(w_f)$ which, by assumption, is decreasing in w_f. Using this function, Equation (11.5) can be rewritten as:

$$\frac{\partial H}{\partial B} = E[\beta(w_f)U'(w_f)(\tilde{p} - c'(a))] \tag{11.6}$$

If the function $\beta(w_f)$ were constant, it could be passed through the expected value operator and only the first-order condition, which is zero at the optimum, would remain within the expectation. In contrast, when $\beta(w_f)$ is decreasing in w_f, small values of $\tilde{p}$ reduce w_f and increase $\beta(w_f)$ according to Hypothesis 4.1. Thus, in Equation (11.6) the negative terms $(p < c'(a))$ have a relatively larger weight than if $\beta(w_f)$ were constant. Since the opposite occurs for $\tilde{p} > c'(a)$, it is obvious that if β is decreasing in w_f then $\partial H/\partial B$, and thus $\partial a^*/\partial B$, are negative.

This proof requires no new techniques: we have briefly presented it essentially to convince the reader of the unity that exists between all these decisions under uncertainty that exhibit a single risk and a single decision variable.

What is happening intuitively? When B increases, initial wealth falls and thus, by virtue of Hypothesis 4.1, the risk aversion of the decision-maker increases. Therefore the willingness to engage in risky activities is reduced, which implies a decrease in the level of production.

The interested reader may, as an exercise, verify that under Hypothesis 4.1 an increase in fixed costs induces an increase in the marginal psychological cost associated with an increase in a. To do this, calculate the derivative of $\operatorname{cov}(U', \tilde{p})/E(U')$ with respect to B and use an approach similar to that adopted in Appendix 5.

Of course many other comparative statics results can be derived in the present context. However, since they duplicate the results obtained in Chapters 9 and 10, we do not mention them here.

11.2.2 Demand uncertainty (at a fixed output price)

We turn now to a problem that has received enormous attention in operations research and has stirred practically no interest in risk theory. We will only present it and mention the difficulties that arise, hoping that this brief exposition will motivate subsequent research.

Let there be a producer for whom the final output price is determined exogenously. This might result from governmental regulation of prices (as in European agriculture, for example) or it might reflect the situation of a distributor *vis-à-vis* a producer who imposes the retail price.[5] This fixed price is denoted p and it exceeds the per unit cost (assumed constant and denoted c) of acquisition or production of the merchandise ($p > c$).

The source of the uncertainty comes from the fact that the order (or the production) must be made before the level of demand is known. Demand is thus random at the time that the decision is made and is denoted $\tilde{d}$. There are two cases.

1. If $d > a$ then the producer sells a and realises a profit π defined by

$$\pi = pa - ca - c_0(d - a) - B \qquad \text{for } d > a \qquad (11.7)$$

where constant c_0 represents the per unit cost of unsatisfied demand.

One may imagine that this is a penalty that results from not satisfying demand. This penalty may be imposed by regulation or it may represent the present monetary value to the firm of lost customer loyalty on the part of unsatisfied clients.

2. Conversely, if $d < a$ then the firm finds itself with an unsold inventory of $a - d$. Each unsold unit might create revenue (for example, the producer might take back the unsold product at a predetermined price) or cost (for example, the disposal of unsold merchandise). In any case, the per unit value of the unsold inventory is denoted p_0 where the sign of p_0 may be positive or negative. If p_0 is positive then common sense suggests that $p_0 < p$ because otherwise the distributor would have an incentive to generate unsold inventory!

When $d < a$, π is:

$$\pi = pd - ca + p_0(a - d) - B \qquad \text{for } d < a \qquad (11.8)$$

$$= (p - p_0)d - (c - p_0)a - B \qquad (11.8a)$$

In the intermediate case where $d = a$, note that Equations (11.7) and (11.8) lead to the same level of profit, namely,

$$\pi = (p - c)a - B$$

Rewriting Equations (11.7) and (11.8) in a standard form yields:

$$\pi = (p_0 - c)a + (p - p_0)d - B \qquad \text{if } d \leqslant a$$
$$\pi = (p - c + c_0)a - c_0 d - B \qquad \text{if } d \geqslant a \qquad (11.9)$$

Given that the parameters are treated as constants, it is obvious that a finite solution for a can only be obtained if $(p - c + c_0)$ and $(p_0 - c)$ are of opposite sign. It is assumed of course that $p - c + c_0$ is positive and $p_0 - c$ is negative.

In the presentation of the operations research problem it is assumed that the investor maximises expected profit:

$$\text{Max } E(\tilde{\pi}) = \int_0^a [(p_0 - c)a + (p - p_0)d] \ dF(d)$$

$$+ \int_a^\infty [(p - c + c_0)a - c_0 d] \ dF(d)$$

where $F(d)$ is the cumulative distribution function for $\tilde{d}$, which is assumed to be known by the decision-maker.

Calculating $dE(\tilde{\pi})/da$ and setting the result equal to zero yields:

$$\frac{F(a)}{1 - F(a)} = \frac{p - c + c_0}{c - p_0} \qquad (11.10)$$

The right-hand side of Equation (11.10) contains the certain parameters of the problem while the left-hand side reflects the characteristics of the distribution of d evaluated at a. Note that the left-hand side is a monotone increasing function of a (because $dF(a)/da = f(a) \geqslant 0$) and thus if p and c_0 increase and/or if c and p_0 decrease, the optimal value of a increases as is consistent with intuition. Note also that if F is replaced by G which first-order stochastic dominates it – this corresponds to an increase in demand – then for all a:

$$\frac{G(a)}{1 - G(a)} < \frac{F(a)}{1 - F(a)}$$

Given that the right-hand side of Equation (11.10) is constant, the optimal solution will be greater under G than under F. Thus, to re-establish Equation (11.10) after an increase in random demand (in the sense of first-order stochastic dominance), the purchase order must be made larger.

The operations research approach is very attractive if it is assumed that lottery d will be played a large number of times with independent draws from one period to the next. In this case the expected value criterion is perfectly defensible. However, if the distributor must choose the order size and if there is dependence[6] over time in the levels of d, it is easy to believe that a decision is not based solely on the expected return and that the degree of risk aversion is relevant. To capture this new aspect, we employ an increasing and concave utility function in w_f with $\tilde{w}_f = w_0 + \tilde{\pi}$, where $\tilde{\pi}$ is defined as in Equation (11.9). Under these conditions the problem is:

$$\text{Max} \int_0^a U(\cdot)\, dF(d) + \int_a^{+\infty} U(\cdot)\, dF(d)$$

where $U(\cdot) = U(w_f)$, and its first-order condition becomes:

$$\frac{\int_0^a U'(\cdot)\, dF(d)}{\int_a^{+\infty} U'(\cdot)\, dF(d)} = \frac{p - c + c_0}{c - p_0}$$

Although it can be interesting, the study of this first-order condition – new until now – has certain subtle aspects. The reason is found in the particular relationship between w_f and the random variable d in this problem. In all the previously considered cases the relationship between the pay-off w_f and the random variable was either everywhere non-increasing or everywhere non-decreasing. In most cases it was linearly increasing or linearly decreasing, and when it was not globally linear (for example, in the case of the deductible) the derivative of w_f with respect to the random variable never changed sign.[7] Here, by contrast, if c_0 is negative then final wealth is first increasing in d for $d \leqslant a$ and then decreasing thereafter as can be observed in Figure 11.2, where d_M denotes the largest possible value of d. It is this rather peculiar

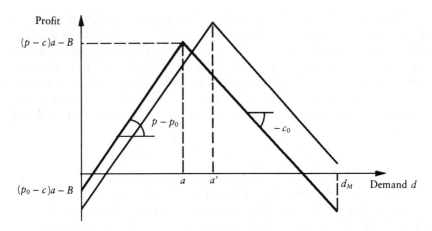

Figure 11.2

relationship between w_f and d that creates the special features of the analysis. As can be seen in Figure 11.2, an increase in a (from a to $a' > a$) shifts the entire profit function toward the right, making some intervals of a less favourable and others more favourable.

Finally, note that in the special case where $c_0 = 0$, the relationship between profit and demand has the familiar properties of final wealth with deductible insurance illustrated in Figure 11.3. In the even more special case where $c_0 = p_0 = 0$, the reader will not be surprised to learn that the first-order condition for a^* is absolutely similar to the one obtained for the optimal

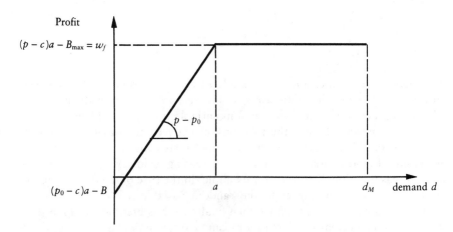

Figure 11.3

deductible (Equation (10.26)). Specifically, one can derive from the first-order condition written above that:

$$\frac{c}{p} E[U'(w_f)] = [1 - F(a)] U'(w_f^{max})$$

where w_f^{max} is the maximal final wealth of the decision-maker obtained when demand exceeds the inventory purchased. The reader can use the techniques presented in Section 10.4 to analyse this case.

We now conclude our analysis by examining two very different subjects which nevertheless have similar content.

11.3 Two extensions: value of flexibility (or of information) and the role of futures markets

11.3.1 The value of flexibility (or of information)

To introduce this subject, it is best to begin with an example of the 'newsboy problem', under the assumption of risk neutrality, and to introduce the notions of flexibility and information. Let the parameters be assigned the following values:

$$p = 25 \qquad c = 15 \qquad c_0 = 4 \qquad \text{and} \qquad p_0 = 1$$

Furthermore, d is uniformly distributed between $d = 0$ and $d = 100$. An application of Equation (11.10) yields:

$$\frac{a/100}{1 - (a/100)} = \frac{14}{14} = 1$$

so $a^* = 50$ and, as a result, after a few calculations we have:

$$E(\tilde{\pi}) = 150$$

If now we allow the distributor the possibility of ordering the newspapers just after demand is revealed,[8] it is clear that $a = d$ will be ordered for any level of revealed demand, because this maximises profit. For each possible value of d, under these conditions a profit is realised that is equal to $(p - c)d = 10d$. So when this situation is evaluated using the expected value criterion, where there is perfect flexibility (and/or information),

$$E(\tilde{\pi}) = \int_0^{100} \frac{1}{100} (10d)d(d) = \left[\frac{1}{100} 5d^2\right]_0^{100} = 500$$

is obtained which represents a significant increase in expected profit (from 150 to 500) and suggests that the value of the information (or flexibility) is 350. Thus, ignoring any question concerning the interest rate, the timing of the order (before or after the value of d is known) can play a very important role in the evaluation of an opportunity. The spectacular increase in $E(\tilde{\pi})$ can be explained as follows: when a is chosen *ex ante* (before the value of d is revealed), it is determined partly as a function of the value of certain parameters and partly as a function of expected demand $E(\tilde{d})$. This implies that a can be different from the realisation of d. When d takes on extreme values, this can result in either large losses (d close to zero) or large forgone profits (d close to d_M). These two uncomfortable situations are completely avoided if technology is flexible and/or if information is perfect because in this case a, chosen *ex post*, can 'stick to' d.

Having suggested the notions of flexibility and information in the context of the 'newsboy problem', we consider them in the context of a decision-maker facing an uncertain $\tilde{p}$. It follows rather clearly from the definition of the problem and its first-order condition (Equation 11.4) that a is chosen before $\tilde{p}$ is known. If p were known when a is chosen, the producer's problem would be, for each p,

$$\text{Max}_a \; U(w_0 + pa - c(a) - B) \tag{11.11}$$

which has the same solution for a as the classical question under certainty,

$$\text{Max}_a pa - c(a) \tag{11.11a}$$

because U is a monotonically increasing function, and because w_0 and B are constants that do not influence the optimal decision under certainty.

If $\tilde{p}$ is revealed before a is chosen or if the technology allows a to be determined when the realisation of $\tilde{p}$ is known (instantaneous production), the optimisation rule for each p is:

$$p = c'(a) \tag{11.12}$$

which allows us to write – using the notion of an implicit function – the short-term supply equation, that is, $a(p) = c'^{-1}(p)$. In this case the expected utility evaluated before p is known and a is adjusted, is:

$$E[U(\tilde{w}_f)] = \int_0^{-\infty} U(w_0 + pa(p) - c[a(p)] - B)f(p) \, dp$$

Of course, since $a(p)$ maximises profit for each realisation of p, it is obvious that for all p:

$$pa(p) - c[a(p)] \geqslant pa^* - c(a^*)$$

where a^* is the optimum corresponding to the decision made under price uncertainty. It follows that:

$$\int_0^{+\infty} U(w_0 + pa(p) - c[a(p)] - B)f(p) \, dp$$

$$> \int_0^{+\infty} U(w_0 + pa^* - c(a^*) - B)f(p) \, dp$$

One can then ask what sum of money I can be subtracted from the situation with flexibility or perfect information to achieve the same welfare as in the situation without flexibility (information). I is called the value of the information or the value of perfect flexibility. Given the inequality derived above, it is clear that the value of information is always positive. Formally, I is the solution to:

$$\int_0^{+\infty} U(w_0 + pa(p) - c[a(p)] - B - I)f(p)\, \mathrm{d}p$$

$$= \int_0^{+\infty} U(w_0 + pa^* - c(a^*) - B)f(p)\, \mathrm{d}p \quad (11.13)$$

It is easily verified that, when the decision-maker is risk neutral, the value of the information is equal to the difference in expected profit with or without information. This is the maximum amount that an individual is prepared to pay in order to obtain complete information. With a little more effort and some sometimes rather cumbersome notation, the value of imperfect information can be defined. It rests on the statistical notion of a partition. We will not give a formal definition here but will simply suggest the idea in the context of the 'newsboy' example.

Assume that, before placing an order, the vendor receives some vague but trustworthy information of the type: 'demand will be strong $(d > 50)$' or conversely, 'demand will be weak $(d \leqslant 50)$'. This is a situation intermediate between the absence of information (see Section 11.2) and perfect information previously mentioned.

To evaluate this imperfect but trustworthy information,[9] we first examine the optimal strategy to be adopted after receiving either possible message. If the decision-maker receives the information '$d > 50$' then the distribution of d remains uniform but is restricted to the interval $[50, 100]$ so that $f(d) = 1/50$ on this interval.

As a result, $F(d) = (d - 50)/50$ for $50 \leqslant d \leqslant 100$ and Equation (11.10) implies that at the optimum:

$$\frac{(a - 50)/50}{1 - (a - 50)/50} = \frac{14}{14} = 1$$

from which it follows that the optimal value of a, denoted a^+ is 75.

In the same way, it can be shown that given the message '$d \leqslant 50$' it is optimal to order $a^- = 25$.

The variables a^+ and a^- indicate that the optimal order is conditional on the possible information: 'strong demand' ('+') or 'weak demand' (−).

Once the optimal values of a have been obtained it is easy to calculate the conditional expected profits given the messages. A little arithmetic reveals that:

$$E(\tilde{\pi}/a^+)] = \frac{1}{50} \int_{50}^{75} [(-14)75 + 24d] \, d(d)$$

$$+ \frac{1}{50} \int_{75}^{100} [(14)75 - 4d] \, d(d)$$

$$= 575$$

$$E[\tilde{\pi}/a^-)] = \frac{1}{50} \int_{0}^{25} [(-14)25 + 24d] \, d(d)$$

$$+ \frac{1}{50} \int_{25}^{50} [(14)25 - 4d] \, d(d)$$

$$= 75$$

To evaluate the situation before the imperfect information is received, note that there is one chance out of two of learning that the event '$d > 50$' will materialise and yield the result 575 and there is one chance out of two of learning that '$d \leqslant 50$' will prevail and yield a profit of 75. The expected value of the result with this imperfect information is thus:

$$\frac{1}{2} \, 575 + \frac{1}{2} \, 75 = 325$$

In summary, the hierarchy follows that in Table 11.1.

When there is risk neutrality, these values also represent expected utility. This example illustrates a perfectly general result: the value of perfect information $(500 - 150)$ clearly exceeds the value of imperfect information $(325 - 150)$. Furthermore, some information – albeit imperfect – is better than no information at all.

All of the concepts developed as examples in the context of the newsboy problem generalise, with the help of additional notation, to the case of continuous uncertainty surrounding the output price. We do not broach this subject here because the most important insight has already been established with the simple case.

Table 11.1

	E(Result)
• without information	+150
• imperfect information	+325
• perfect information	+500

Before moving to another subject, we point out that the concept of the value of information (or flexibility) has been the object of comparative statics studies. There the relationships between value of information and exogenous parameters such as the individual's wealth, risk aversion, and the riskiness of the lottery are examined. For an excellent survey of this fascinating but some-what difficult literature see Hilton (1981) or, more recently, M. Willinger (1989).

11.3.2 The existence and the role of futures markets

The study of flexibility (and information) showed how costly it is for a producer to have to fix the level of activities (a) before knowing the outcome of the random variable resulting from the market ($\tilde{p}$ or $\tilde{d}$). To protect against this 'delayed uncertainty'[10] the producer is willing to make some monetary investments either for the adoption of a more costly but more adaptable technology or for more research to obtain pertinent information. However, there has long been, for some kinds of production, a socially less costly alter-native for containing the risk surrounding $\tilde{p}$: the writing of futures contracts[11] at a price that is fixed and known before a is chosen. Specifically, at the beginning of the period the individual knows the price, p_t, for delivery of one unit of merchandise to the futures market at the end of the period. There are also some expectations about what the spot price will be at the end of the period, that is, about what we have been calling $\tilde{p}$. The producer bases two decisions on these two elements: on the one hand the level of production a is chosen and on the other there is the choice how much to sell on the futures market,[12] a_t. The profit at the end of the period is denoted:

$$\tilde{\pi} = \tilde{p}(a - a_t) + p_t a_t - c(a) - B \tag{11.14}$$

where $(a - a_t)$ necessarily represents the total quantity sold on the spot market if one assumes that the producer's horizon stops at the end of the period, as will be the case, for example, if the good is not stored for later periods. Note that if a_t is negative, then the quantity sold on the spot market exceeds the current production.

In order to maximise welfare, the producer must choose the values of a and a_t to solve:

$$\text{Max } E[U(\tilde{w}_f)] = \int_0^\infty U(w_0 + p(a - a_t) + p_t a_t - c(a) - B)f(p)\, \mathrm{d}p$$

The first-order conditions for this problem are:

$$\frac{\partial E[U]}{\partial a} = \int_0^\infty U'(\cdot)[p - c'(a)]f(p)\, \mathrm{d}p = 0 \tag{11.15}$$

$$\frac{\partial E[U]}{\partial a_t} = \int_0^\infty U'(\cdot)(-p + p_t)f(p)\, \mathrm{d}p = 0 \tag{11.15a}$$

From Equation (11.15a) it follows that:

$$p_t E(U') = E(U' \tilde{p})$$ (11.16)

and if this result is substituted into Equation (11.15) then that optimality condition becomes:

$$p_t E(U') = c'(a) E(U')$$ (11.17)

or, since. $E(U')$ is strictly positive,

$$p_t = c'(a)$$ (11.17a)

This equation contains an interesting result that belongs to the family of 'separation theorems'. Actually Equation (11.17a) says that the decision of how much to produce is made independently (separately) from the decision of how much to sell on the futures market (a_t) and that, furthermore, the only pertinent indicator for the choice of a is the (certain) unit price prevailing today in the futures market. In some sense, the existence of a futures market allows the risk-averse producer to make a production decision without worrying about the uncertainty surrounding $\tilde{p}$, the spot price. The only pertinent guide for choosing a is the futures market price; uncertainty and risk aversion do not enter until it is time to choose a_t. The choice of a_t is influenced by the uncertainty surrounding $\tilde{p}$ and by the decision-maker's degree of risk aversion. Specifically, using algebraic methods that are now familiar to us, Equation (11.15a) or its analogue Equation (11.16) can be written as:

$$p_t = E(\tilde{p}) + \frac{\text{cov}(U', \tilde{p})}{E(U')}$$ (11.18)

where $E(\tilde{p})$ is the expected price on the spot market.

Once the optimal value of a, denoted a^*, is fixed as a function of the value of $p_t[a^* = c'^{-1}(p_t)]$, the total and marginal utility depend on the choice of a_t. At the optimum, a_t^*, must satisfy Equation (11.18). This furnishes some interesting insights into the value of a_t^* when the decision-maker is risk averse. There are two cases.

1. If $E(\tilde{p}) > p_t$, Equation (11.18) can only be satisfied if $\text{cov}(U', \tilde{p})$ is negative. Given that U' is a decreasing function of wealth, $\text{cov}(U', \tilde{p})$ is negative if and only if an increase in p induces an increase in w_f and thus a fall in U'. Now for $\Delta p > 0$ to induce an increase in wealth (and profit), according to Equation (11.14) it must be that:

$$a^* - a_t^* > 0$$

from which it follows that $a_t^* < a^*$. This result is quite logical: since $E(\tilde{p})$ exceeds p_t, a positive expected return is associated with trades on the spot market; each unit shifted from the futures market to the spot market has a net expected return equal to $[E(\tilde{p}) - p_t]/p_t$, which is positive by assumption. On the other hand, the risk increases as a_t^* is reduced and equilibrium is achieved at some point $a_t^* < a^*$.

Specifically, if $a_t = a^*$, the decision-maker bears no risk but the return is mediocre. In some sense the situation where $a_t = a^*$ 'simulates' a situation with complete insurance because all risk is eliminated at the price of a very low expected return. By reducing a_t below a^*, one can increase the expected return by accepting some risk.

2. Conversely, if $E(\tilde{p}) < p_t$ then $\text{cov}(U', \tilde{p})$ must be positive. This can only occur if an increase in p reduces wealth and increases the marginal utility U'. For an increase in p to negatively affect wealth (and thus profit) it must be that:

$$a^* - a_t^* < 0$$

that is, that $a^* < a_t^* < 0$. Once again intuition is clear. The firm chooses a^* as a function of only p_t and thus if it chooses $a_t = a^*$ it bears no risk. However, since it expects that on average $\tilde{p}$ will be less than p_t, it sees a possibility of selling in the futures market more than it produces. It can thus receive an attractive price (p_t) in the futures market and hope to purchase the amount necessary to honour its commitment, $a_t - a^*$, at a lower price in the spot market. By doing this it bears a risk, but this is compensated for by an increase in the expected return due to the net expected gain from the futures sale.[13] Some would say that the firm 'speculates' that there will be a drop in price.

In summary, a^* is chosen independently of $\tilde{p}$ and only by comparing p_t with the marginal physical cost of production. Then the firm considers the futures market and chooses the level of a_t^* relative to a^* on the basis of a comparison between p_t, $E(\tilde{p})$ and the risk incurred by the choice.

Before listing some simple comparative statics results, we point out that the futures market increases the welfare of the producer. Specifically, in the absence of a futures market, $a_t = 0$ and we encounter exactly the problem at the beginning of this chapter. To see this, it suffices to substitute $a_t = 0$ into Equation (11.14) and note that this equation is transformed into the definition of $\tilde{\pi}$ that follows Equation (11.3). When the futures market is opened, the firm always has the option of maintaining the same production and ignoring the futures market. If it changes its plans it is because it is advantageous to do so, because – in our jargon – its 'expected utility' increases. One could derive the highest entry fee a decision-maker is prepared to pay in order to have access to the futures market in the same way that one can ask how much investment is available for flexibility or information. The futures market is thus a supplementary tool of risk management that can be used along with the others. We also note that if a_t^* is positive and less than a^* (which occurs when

$p_t < E(\tilde{p})$); then the futures market provides a form of insurance because, relative to $a_t = a^*$, there is a reduction in risk and a loss of expected return.

This shows once again, as if it were necessary, the common properties of all the subjects considered in Part Two.

Many comparative statics exercises are possible. We illustrate one here and leave the others as exercises for the reader.

What would happen if, all other things equal, the level of fixed costs, B, increased? Recall that in the absence of a futures market this exogenous shock would reduce the production of a risk-averse decision-maker who, among other things, satisfies Hypothesis 4.1.

Because of the futures markets, the impact of a change in B on a^* is *zero*. Specifically, since at the optimum $p_t = c'(a^*)$, and since this condition depends in no way on B, it follows that $\mathrm{d}a^*/\mathrm{d}B = 0$ regardless of the properties of risk aversion relative to wealth. The effect of B is only reflected in a_t^*. Under Hypothesis 4.1 the reduction in wealth caused by the increase in B increases risk aversion and induces actions that control total risk. Thus, in the present case a_t^* increases.

To see this, it suffices to differentiate the left-hand side of Equation (11.15a) with respect to B to write:

$$\frac{\partial}{\partial B}\left[\frac{\partial E(U)}{\partial a_t}\right] = \int_0^{+\infty} -U''(\cdot)(-p + p_t)f(p)\,\mathrm{d}p$$

With a little algebra it can be shown that this expression is negative given Hypothesis 4.1 and thus that $\mathrm{d}a_t^*/\mathrm{d}B < 0$.

With the help of techniques that were previously applied in other circumstances, one can also examine the effect of an increase in p_t, of an increase in $E(\tilde{p})$ or, more generally, of an improvement (in the sense of first-order stochastic dominance) in the distribution of $\tilde{p}$.

11.4 Technological uncertainty

We now return to the case of technological uncertainty already mentioned at the beginning of Chapter 11. We can accomplish this quickly thanks to the tools acquired in the previous sections because technological uncertainty has many points in common with market uncertainty. We distinguish, as previously stated, between the cases of additive and multiplicative technological uncertainty.

11.4.1 Additive uncertainty

If the firm faces perfect competition and if there is no market uncertainty, additive technological risk leads to the following definition of final wealth:

$$\tilde{w}_f = w_0 + p(a + \tilde{\varepsilon}) - c(a) - B$$

where the actual quantity produced and sold on the market satisfies definition (11.1).

The choice of a^* is guided by:

$$\text{Max} \int_{-\infty}^{+\infty} U[w_0 + p(a + \tilde{\varepsilon}) - c(a) - B]f(\varepsilon)\,\mathrm{d}\varepsilon$$

where $E(\tilde{\varepsilon}) = 0$. The first derivative and the first-order condition are written as:

$$\frac{\mathrm{d}E}{\mathrm{d}a} = \int_{-\infty}^{+\infty} U'(\cdot)[p - c'(a)]f(\varepsilon)\,\mathrm{d}\varepsilon = 0$$

Given that neither p nor $c'(a)$ is random, the term $[p - c'(a)]$ can be passed through the integration sign and thus the first-order condition becomes

$$p - c'(a) = 0 \qquad\qquad (11.19)$$

In other words, the decision-maker chooses the same level of production as under certainty: *additive* technological uncertainty does not affect the optimal decision even though it, of course, reduces the welfare of a risk-averse decision-maker. This is a nice application of the principles of marginal analysis. Specifically, given its additive character, the level of uncertainty is not influenced *at the margin* by a change in a and thus at the optimum it has no effect. In other words, additive uncertainty behaves as does a fixed cost under certainty: it reduces total welfare but it does not change the optimality conditions.

Of course, the comparative statics analysis is exactly like it is under certainty because – as we have often seen – this analysis is based on first-order conditions. Since they are identical under certainty and *additive* uncertainty, they yield the same conclusions. Thus, a change in w_0 or in the risk associated with $\tilde{\varepsilon}$ does not affect the optimal value of a^*.

11.4.2 Multiplicative uncertainty

In this case, $\tilde{w}_f$ becomes:

$$\tilde{w}_f = w_0 + p[a(1 + \varepsilon)] - c(a) - B$$
$$= w_0 + pa + \tilde{\varepsilon}pa - c(a) - B \qquad\qquad (11.20)$$

Indeed, we encounter exactly the same situation as for market uncertainty. Specifically if, given market uncertainty, $\tilde{p}$ is replaced by $p + \tilde{\varepsilon}$ where $\tilde{\varepsilon} = \tilde{p} - p$, then w_f is written as:

$$\tilde{w}_f = w_0 + (p(1 + \tilde{\varepsilon}))a - c(a) - B \qquad\qquad (11.21)$$

and of course Equations (11.20) and (11.21) have exactly the same structure. It is thus unnecessary to redo the analysis: multiplicative technological uncertainty perfectly 'simulates' market uncertainty surrounding the output price.

To finish this chapter and at the same time this part, we make three remarks. The first two are more technical while the third is more 'philosophical'.

In the first place, note that one can mathematically express the relationship, which has occasionally been mentioned, between the three problems treated in Part Two. Specifically, all choice problems with a single decision variable and a single source of risk can be written in the form:

$$\text{Max}_a \; E[U(Z(a,\tilde{\theta}))]$$

where Z symbolises final wealth as a function of the decision variable a and a random variable $\tilde{\theta}$. The three problems analysed correspond to three different assumptions on the nature of the function Z. Z was linear in a and in $\tilde{\theta}$ in the asset choice and co-insurance problems. It was piece-wise linear in $\tilde{\theta}$ in the deductible problem, and it was non-linear in a in the deductible problem and in the production under price uncertainty problem.

Technically, we also point out that we have separately considered market uncertainty and technological uncertainty. In reality these often go together. Consider, for example, the agricultural sector: one source of uncertainty is the climate. If it is favourable for a producer in a region then the actual production generally surpasses what was initially planned. Furthermore, since a favourable climate for one is favourable for all (there is a positive covariance between $\tilde{\varepsilon}_i$ and $\tilde{\varepsilon}_j$, the technological random variables of i and j), there is a surplus of actual production in the entire region. If this region represents a large part of the supply of the product, one must expect a fall in the market price of the product. Of course the opposite occurs in the case of an unfavourable climate, and thus there is a negative stochastic dependence between market uncertainty and technological uncertainty. The question of relationships between individual decisions, random variables and prices is discussed in Part Three.

The third, more fundamental, remark regards the expected utility criterion itself. The careful reader has no doubt noticed that all through Part Two we have referred to the 'decision-maker', to the 'insured' and to the 'producer' and we have avoided the terms 'firm' or 'company'.

This choice is justified by the following fact: in finance theory it is argued that, in a company whose stock trades on a stock exchange, the managers should focus on expected final wealth and ignore the concepts of risk aversion.

In Part Three, we will make room for this kind of argument. However, for the benefit of readers who choose to end here the path they have travelled with us, it is perhaps good to summarise succinctly the argument from finance theory. It is based on a simple and attractive idea: profit and capital gains will be shared among the stockholders who, thanks to an adequate diversification of their investments, are able to reduce their risks in a completely efficient way. It is thus unnecessary at the level of each firm to worry about risk and it is better to maximise the expected final wealth. This will be distributed among all the stockholders who will themselves take the trouble of eliminating risk to the extent they desire. This argument from finance theory is a consequence of the 'capital asset pricing model' (CAPM) for the evaluation of assets traded on an exchange (see Part Three).

It is precisely to avoid this formidable objection from finance theory that we have referred not to firms but to individual producers (such as farmers or artisans) who do not have access to a stock exchange to finance their activities. For them, risk – which is not ultimately distributed among a multitude of stockholders – is an important parameter and the expected utility criterion is much more reasonable in this context.

If these few lines have pricked and provoked the intellectual curiosity of the reader, then resolutely turn to Part Three. No doubt there will be satisfaction, at least in part.

Exercises

11.1 The owner of a privately held firm has a logarithmic utility function and an initial wealth of 100. A single output is produced the marginal cost of which is constant and equal to 5 ($c'(a) = 5$) up to the maximum capacity of production that is reached at $a = 20$.[14] The fixed costs B amount to 2.
The only source of uncertainty is the price per unit of output that will be obtained on a competitive market. If market conditions are bad (probability 0.5) the unit price will amount to 3 but if they are good the unit price will reach 9.

Questions
(a) Write the expected utility of the producer and compute the optimal level of production. Show that an increase in the fixed cost (from 2 to 3) will reduce optimal output. Relate this result to Theorem 11.1
(b) What would output level be if a certain output price equal to 6 were guaranteed? Why does the output level increase?
(c) Compare the level of output found in Question (a) to the one that would obtain if the producer had the following price expectation: the lowest price is equal to 4 (probability $= 0.5$) and the highest one equal to 8. Justify intuitively why output is increased.
(d) Assume now that thanks to a new and more flexible production design, the producer can start production after the output price is known. How much will be produced when $p = 3$ and how much when $p = 9$? Compute the expected utility reached under this new system and compare it with the one obtained in Question (a). Then express the monetary value of flexibility.

11.2 Return to the initial data of Exercise 11.1 and assume now that the producer has access to a forward market on which a futures price prevails (p_t) equal to 7.

Questions
(a) Show that, as an application of the 'separation theorem' described after Equation (11.17a), the optimal output level will correspond to the maximal capacity ($a^* = 20$).
(b) Compute then a_1^* and explain why a_1^* exceeds a^* (you will need to compare p_1 with $E(\tilde{p})$).
(c) Solve Questions (a) and (b) again assuming now that $p_t = 6$.

11.3 A farm faces two sources of risk:

(a) the output price is random ($\tilde{p}$)
(b) the amount of fixed cost – that fluctuates with the price of land – is also random and denoted $\tilde{B}$.

The marginal cost is constant and there is no capacity limit.

Questions
(a) Write the expression for the expectation of final wealth and its variance (allowing for a possible correlation between $\tilde{p}$ and $\tilde{B}$).
(b) If the producer has a quadratic utility function, solve for the optimal a. Compare it with optimal a^* if $\tilde{B}$ were certain and equal to $E(\tilde{B})$ which you denote B.

Hint: Refer abundantly to our discussion in Section 10.3.

11.4 A farmer who lives in a competitive environment faces the following cost function:

$$c(a) = a + 0.1 a^2$$

The initial wealth amounts to 1000 and fixed costs are equal to 100. The utility function is the negative exponential function: $-e^{-\gamma W_f}$

Questions
(a) How much will this farmer produce if he is sure to obtain a unit price of 11?
(b) What happens to optimal output if there is now an uncertain output price characterised by a normal density with expected price equal to 11 and a standard deviation of 2. You should not only give the numerical solution but also express the first-order condition, especially if you want to solve Question (d).

(c) What happens to optimal output under certainty and under uncertainty when fixed costs increase. While the answer is the same in each case, they have a very different justification. Make them explicit.

(d) By comparing your first-order condition in (b) with Equation (11.5) express the marginal cost of risk for the farmer. Compare your result for the production problem with the one obtained for the portfolio problem of Chapter 9 (Figure 9.4) and represent graphically the solution to Question (b).

(e) What happens to optimal output when σ_p increases? Justify your answer with the help both of algebra and of a figure where you represent the marginal cost of risk.

11.5 The purpose of the present exercise is to illustrate the notions of information and flexibility. As a by-product we will also present some introductory remarks on additional topics not covered in this book.

Return to the example of the risk-neutral newsboy analysed in Section 11.2.2. Adopt the same numerical values for the coefficients p, c, c_0 and p_0. However, instead of considering a uniform density of demand with $E[\tilde{d}] = 50$, assume an exponential density $\lambda e^{-\lambda d}$ with $\lambda = 0.02$ so that $E[\tilde{d}]$ remains equal to 50. (Check this point by computing $0.02 \int_0^{+\infty} d e^{-.02 d} d(d)$.) If you draw this density you will notice that it makes extreme results more likely than under uniform density.

Questions

(a) Show that the optimal order is lower than 50 (compute its exact value).

Remark: As a careful reader you might be puzzled by this outcome. You know that under risk neutrality a decision-maker cares only about the expected outcome of the lottery (this fact was stated many times in various forms throughout Parts One and Two). In this exercise this is apparently no longer true. The reason is that in the newsboy problem the pay-off is *not* linear in the random variable (see again Figure 9.3). Hence the non-linearity of the pay-off in the random variable coupled with a linear utility function has the same effect as a linear pay-off coupled with a non-linear utility. To be quite general, the statement made in Parts One and Two should read: 'With linear utility (i.e. risk neutrality) and a pay-off *linear in* the random outcome, only the expected value of the lottery matters.[15]

(b) Express the expected profit of the newsboy.

(c) Compare the expected profit if the newsboy were to receive perfect information on $\tilde{d}$ or were able to order the newspapers once d is known. Derive from a comparison between b and c the value of perfect information.

(d) What is the probability that the newsboy will be given the information '$\tilde{d} \leqslant 50$'? Express in each case the density of $\tilde{d}$ conditional on the information received and the corresponding optimal order. Show that the value of partial information is lower than that of perfect information.

(e) Instead of the very crude partial information described in (d) consider now finer information consisting of the following three messages:

   (i) $\tilde{d}$ will be lower than 25
  (ii) $\tilde{d}$ will be between 25 and 50
 (iii) $\tilde{d}$ will exceed 50.

Show that the value of this 'less partial' information is greater than that found in (d) and lower than the value of perfect information. (This illustrates the notion of a 'finer partition' in statistics.)

Notes

1. For the interested reader we mention the excellent article of Turnovsky (1973). We should also note that the accounting literature on the 'cost–volume–profit' relationship sometimes makes reference to these questions.
2. For some exceptions see the bibliography of Dionne–Pellerin (1988).
3. See the end of the chapter for some remarks about this objective in the context of a firm's decisions.
4. Specifically, under risk neutrality, U' is constant and thus $\operatorname{cov}(U', \tilde{p}) = 0$ due to a fundamental property of covariance.
5. The operations research literature calls this question the 'newsboy problem'.
6. The most extreme case is where the first observed demand is systematically repeated over the entire time horizon.
7. This was the case, for example, in the theory of production where $dw_f/dp > 0$ at every point even though dw_f/da changes sign.
8. This can happen in two ways: either a technological innovation allows instantaneous delivery of newspapers to distributors or the distributor receives some privileged and perfect information about the level of demand before placing the order.
9. It is trustworthy in the following sense: if the informer announces $d > 50$ then the decision-maker assumes without a doubt that d will actually exceed 50.
10. This expression seems to be due to Drèze and Modigliani (1972) who propose it in a savings model. The uncertainty is said to be 'delayed' because it resolved after the decision is made.

11. In some sense this is a substitute not only for flexibility and information but also for the transfer of risk by insurance. Specifically, since the risk considered is speculative, there does not exist an insurance market to protect the decision-makers.

12. $a_t < 0$ means that the producer is a buyer on the futures market.

13. If $p_t = E(\tilde{p})$, it is easy to see that $a_t^* = a^*$. Specifically, at $a_t^* = a^*$, the producer bears no risk and is not tempted to bear any because the expected profit associated with such a course is zero.

14. This means that it is impossible to produce more than 20 units of a.

15. Apparently, W. Oi (1961) is the first author to have stressed this point.

References

Baron D. (1971), Demand uncertainty in imperfect competition, *International Economic Review*, vol. 12, 196–208.

Dionne G. and M. Pellerin (1988), Investissement en incertitude: extension du problème de la taille optimale d'une usine, in *Incertain et Information*, G. Dionne (ed.), Economica et Vermette, Montreal, 256–281.

Drèze J. and F. Modigliani (1972), Consumption decisions under uncertainty, *Journal of Economic Theory*, vol. 5, 308–335.

Hilton R. (1981), Determinants of information value, *Management Science*, vol. 27, 57–64.

Leland H. (1972), Theory of the firm facing uncertain demand, *American Economic Review*, vol. 62, 278–291.

Oi W. (1961), The desirability of price instability under perfect competition, *Econometrica*, vol. 29, 58–64.

Turnovsky S. (1973), Production flexibility, price uncertainty and the behavior of the competitive firm, *International Economic Review*, vol. 14, 395–413.

Willinger M. (1989), Risk aversion and the value of information, *Journal of Risk and Insurance*, vol. 56, 320–328.

PART Three
Markets for uncertainty

12 General description of the problems treated

In Part Two we attempted to determine the supplies and demands of economic agents in an uncertain world. For a given price, the agents choose their demands and supplies to maximise their expected utility. Thus, a capital owner chooses the demand for a risky asset given the random return, which itself depends on the purchase price because it is the discounted sum of flows divided by the purchase price. More simply, the insurance demand is determined given the price of insurance, that is, its price schedule. Finally, the producer fixes supply given a random output price.

This is the classical approach in economic theory, but it is still incomplete because the price of transferring risk is assumed to be known. Yet, given competition, the prices themselves are the consequences of individual actions. For completeness, we must now consider how these prices are established.

Anyone with a minimal knowledge of economic theory knows the importance of this question. It is the fundamental problem of determining the economic value of things. In the present context, it goes much further than simple knowledge of the 'equilibrium price' of 'goods' that we are considering here, that is, the risks. For, given a knowledge of the equilibrium prices, we are also able to determine the final allocation of these risks. Who bears the economic risk of the possibility of an earthquake in California or the loss of a space shuttle? Who bears the large risks of our modern economies, the stock-market crashes, the oil shocks, changes in interest rates and, alas, risks of war?

It is not an exaggeration to say that the possibility of transferring risks from one group of individuals to another has been an important vehicle for economic growth of the last two hundred years. Henry Ford said that the true builders of the skyscrapers in New York were the insurers. Without them, undoubtedly, few people would have imagined such projects, given their inherent risks. This example can be multiplied for each time that the risk of an undertaking would be excessive if the entrepreneur had to bear all of it. It suffices to see the part played in our economies by the insurance sector and, even more, by the financial sector in general, the stock exchange in particular being the centre *par excellence* of the transfer of risks.

It is one thing to determine who ends up bearing the system's risks in equilibrium; it is another to determine how risk *should* be shared in the same system. This is the difference between the study of the real (the positive approach) and the study of the ideal (the normative approach). In this third part, we begin by answering the second question. Specifically, in Chapter 13, we define the notion of efficient risk-sharing without any reference to 'markets' and we characterise such allocations of risk.

In Chapters 14 and 15 that follow, we attempt to determine whether the market system that is ours is capable of efficiently distributing risks. We assume in both cases that markets are perfectly competitive and that prices equilibrate supplies and demands. We are thus interested in the properties of the equilibrium price of risks and their consequences in terms of the equilibrium allocation. The difference between Chapters 14 and 15 comes from the market structure considered. In Chapter 14 we assume that there exists a market for each contingent claim, as defined in Chapter 7. In Chapter 15, we drop this assumption and assume that only markets for financial assets exist (stock markets).

There are two broad types of models currently in existence. The first, called the complete markets model, was initially proposed by Arrow (1953) and Debreu (1959) in the 1950s. The second came a little later and is called the capital asset pricing model (CAPM). Their two principle authors, Markowitz (1952) and Sharpe (1963), were awarded the Nobel prize in economics in 1990 for this contribution.

In Chapter 16, we study a difficult problem from the economic theory of uncertainty. In previous chapters, we assumed that everyone has the same information: the insurer knew perfectly the risk that had just been underwritten; the purchaser of a used car had the same information as the seller about the quality of the engine; no one in the stock market had inside information. All these assumptions are obviously unrealistic and they are therefore abandoned in Chapter 16. That chapter chronologically follows the preceding chapters since these problems have only been broached by researchers from the beginning of the 1970s, with an explosion in the number of publications in the decade that followed. These models are generically called models of asymmetric information and, more specifically in the context of insurance, models of adverse selection.

References

Arrow K. (1953), *Le rôle des valeurs boursiere pour la répartition la meilleure des risques*, Éditions du CNRS, Paris.

Debreu G. (1959), *Theory of Value*, Wiley, New York.

Markowitz H. (1952), Portfolio selection, *Journal of Finance*, vol. 6, 77–91.

Sharpe W. (1963), A simplified model for portfolio analysis, *Management Science*, vol. 9, 277–293.

13 Efficient risk-sharing

Many mechanisms exist today which permit the transfer of risk from one economic agent to another. The markets that organise these mechanisms are insurance markets and financial markets. But there also exist private means for achieving transfers of risks: interest rate swaps and mortgage loans are two examples. Do these transfers of risk improve welfare in an economy, or is it instead a 'zero sum game', a machine to make profit to the detriment of the transferers, without widespread benefit for society? To the great relief of insurers, insurance agents and stockbrokers, we show here that the transfer of risk is a *potential* source of large improvements in economic efficiency and social welfare.

In Chapter 13, we prove that there exists a way of reallocating risks that makes everyone better off. The reader is warned that the derivation of this efficient reallocation is done outside of any 'market' context. To simplify the presentation, we assume that *there exists a benevolent and omnipotent planner who has the ability and the authority to reallocate risks in society*. We will help this planner by giving simple rules that allow an efficient allocation of the risks to be imposed. This approach is thus purely normative.

Of course, such a planner does not really exist so society is left to itself to reallocate individual risks as well as it can. Will it be able to achieve a reallocation of risks where all the potential gains from risk-sharing are exploited? This is the question that will be studied in Chapters 14 and 15, in which markets where risks are traded are introduced. Here, therefore, we only make brief reference to a market system that allows the risk reallocation that would be imposed by the social planner. Although our presentation in this chapter seems very close to the context of a planned economy, this is only for pedagogical reasons, with the goal of establishing the characteristics of an efficient outcome. Clearly, we must keep separate the discussion of what is desirable and the question of how to achieve it. Chapters 14 and 15 establish that a market economy allocates risks as well as an economy controlled by an omnipotent social planner, and indeed certainly better given the incentives that exist in a competitive system.

To simplify, we will consider an economy without production, that is, an exchange economy, in order to concentrate on the problem that interests us here. Production is introduced in subsequent chapters, without any change in the analysis presented in this chapter. Our economy is composed of n individuals; the number n could be very large. Each individual is characterised by two things: their utility function, which describes their attitude toward risk, and the initial relative endowment of the single consumption good that exists in this economy. The utility function of individual i is denoted $U_i(w_f)$, with $U_i' > 0$ and $U_i'' < 0$.

The risk comes from the fact that the initial endowments are random. To define the random variable, we use notation from Chapter 7, that is, the notation of the state of the world. Assume that there exist a finite[1] number of states of the world indexed by the letter s which can take on the values $1, 2, ..., S$. The number of possible states, S, can be arbitrarily large. We further assume that everyone has the same expectations as to the state of the world that will be realised. In other words, there is a unique probability distribution $\{p_1, p_2, ..., p_S\}$ in the population that gives the perceived probability of each state being realised.

Individual i's initial endowment is represented by the random variable $w_{0i}(\tilde{s})$. The randomness that affects the final wealth of the individuals can come from a large number of sources: risks of accident for the owners of physical goods, technological risks for entrepreneurs, risks of illness for workers, etc. We exclude from this list anything that we have called market risk because it is endogenous in this kind of model (see Chapters 14 and 15). Recall that there are no prices here because all exchanges are imposed by the planner.

The economy's resources in a particular state are simply the sum of the initial endowments in that state, since there is no production. This aggregate wealth in state s is denoted $w_0(s)$ and corresponds to:

$$w_0(\tilde{s}) = \sum_{i=1}^{n} w_{0i}(\tilde{s}) \tag{13.1}$$

We know that there exists an aggregate risk in the economy, or a social risk, if w_0 is not constant across states.

A risk allocation is defined by n functions $w_{f_i}(s)$, $i = 1, 2, ..., n$, representing the final wealth of the n individuals in each of the S states. A risk allocation is said to be feasible if the sum of the individuals' final wealth equals the aggregate wealth w_0 in each state:

$$\sum_{i=1}^{n} w_{f_i}(s) = w_0(s) \tag{13.2}$$

This means that the planner can never distribute, in any state, more than is available after appropriating all of the resources. There follows a definition of an efficient division or allocation of risks.

Definition A risk-sharing arrangement $\{w_{f_1}(s), \ldots, w_{f_n}(s)\}$ is Pareto efficient if and only if:

(a) it is feasible;
(b) there exists no other feasible allocation that generates an increase in the expected utility of an individual without reducing the expected utility of at least one other individual.

It is no doubt necessary to justify such a definition. Among all the allocations of risk that the planner can choose, there exist a large number for which one can find a way to redistribute the random wealth and increase the welfare of everyone. It is thus reasonable to think of these allocations as being inefficient because the population would unanimously agree to such a redistribution: a planner who proposed a Pareto-inefficient outcome would have serious problems retaining their position! It is difficult to see why anyone would not put into effect an allocation that is better for everyone.

It is important to grasp that this definition is made *ex ante*, that is, before the state of the world is known. It is because the situation is evaluated before the risk is resolved that an individual's expected utility of final wealth is used to measure welfare. It is a question of sharing the *random variable*. Ex post, or after the resolution of the risk as to the state of the world, it is possible that some individuals have lower welfare – as measured by $U[w_{f_i}(s)]$, the current utility – than they would have had in autarchy ($U[w_{0i}(s)]$). *Ex post*, the wonderful unanimity for a Pareto-improving redistribution (that is, one which increases everyone's expected utility) no longer exists.

We would also like to reconsider the feasibility constraint (13.2). In each state, what is distributed corresponds to what is available in that state. In other words, there is no way to transfer wealth from one state of the world to another, as an insurer does by collecting premiums in the good states and paying indemnities in the bad. As noted above, there is no extra-terrestrial insurer nor does the planner have any personal wealth that can be used to play that role.

Another assumption that is implicitly contained in constraint (13.2) is that there are no transaction costs, since the sum that is finally received is exactly equal to the sum initially available. Not a single 'crumb' disappears when the pie $w_0(s)$ is divided *ex post*. There is no loss due to the exchange, or in other words, there is no loss due to the increase in entropy. This, of course, constitutes only an approximation to reality.[2] Alas, to our knowledge there do not yet exist models that introduce transaction costs into this type of analysis.

In the case where $n = 2$, the problem can be represented graphically, as in Figure 13.1. On the X and Y axes, the expected utilities of Individuals 1 and 2, respectively, are measured. A risk allocation is then represented by a point

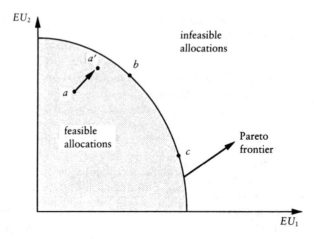

Figure 13.1

in the graph, showing the expected utility of each individual under the allocation. The first task is to find the locus of points corresponding to the feasible allocations. It can be shown that this corresponds to an area whose boundary is a decreasing concave curve, due to the risk aversion of the agents. This curve is called the Pareto frontier because it corresponds to the locus of Pareto-efficient allocations. Specifically, with an allocation represented by the point a, it is possible to find another feasible allocation a' that increases the utility of both agents, but such a possibility does not exist for points b or c on the curve that separates the feasible allocations from the infeasible allocations.

As shown in Figure 13.1, there exist a large number of efficient allocations like b or c. This indeterminacy is resolved in Chapter 14 by analysing the allocation obtained by competitive contingent claims markets. The important question is then, whether this allocation lies on the efficient frontier, or whether it lies on the interior of the feasible, but inefficient, zone.

13.1 The Borch condition and the Edgeworth box

In this section we study the basic condition that must be satisfied by a Pareto-efficient allocation. We begin by showing that to each efficient allocation there corresponds a list of positive real numbers $\lambda_1, \lambda_2, ..., \lambda_n$ such that the efficient allocation maximises the function F defined by:

$$F = \sum_{i=1}^{n} \lambda_i EU_i(w_{f_i}(\tilde{s}))$$

$$= \sum_{i=1}^{n} \lambda_i \left[\sum_{s=1}^{S} p_s U_i(w_{f_i}(s)) \right] \tag{13.3}$$

subject to the constraint that $\{w_{f_1}(s), \ldots, w_{f_n}(s)\}$ be feasible. Specifically, we take the feasible allocation that maximises Equation (13.3). If there existed another feasible allocation which, compared with this optimal solution, increased the expected utility of some individuals without reducing the expected utility of the others, it is clear that this new allocation would imply an increase in F, since the weights λ_i are strictly positive, and thus the optimal allocation would not be optimal. Therefore, such a feasible allocation cannot exist, so the optimal solution of the maximisation problem is certainly Pareto efficient. Conversely, it can be shown that each efficient allocation is the solution to a maximisation of F with appropriately chosen weights.

This result can be illustrated by Figure 13.2. For a pair $\{\lambda_1, \lambda_2\}$, the locus of allocations that generate the same value of F, say F_1, is a line with slope $-\lambda_1/\lambda_2 < 0$. By shifting the line to the right and parallel to itself, one obtains a higher value of F, $F_2 > F_1$. The search for a feasible solution that maximises F is thus equivalent to choosing a point in the feasible zone that is on the highest iso-F line possible. It is clear that such a point lies on the Pareto frontier, that is, it corresponds to an efficient allocation of risks.

It is clear that the choice of weights is tied to the distribution problem. A larger λ_1 relative to λ_2 corresponds to a steeper slope for the iso-F lines and a maximising solution to problem (13.3) that generates higher expected utility for Individual 1 and lower expected utility for Individual 2. It is up to the planner to choose a particular point on the Pareto frontier, or equivalently, the values of λ_1 and λ_2. The choice of weights is not studied here: the problem of the fairness of an allocation is not directly related to the question of economic efficiency.

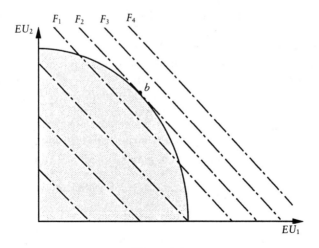

Figure 13.2

To characterise the efficient solutions, it therefore suffices to select the strictly positive weights $\{\lambda_1, \ldots, \lambda_n\}$ arbitrarily and to solve the problem of maximising F subject to the constraint (13.2). Using μ_s to denote the Lagrange multiplier of constraint (13.2) in state s, one can derive the following first-order condition:

$$\lambda_i p_s U_i' [w_{f_i}(s)] = \mu_s \qquad \text{for all } s \text{ and all } i \qquad (13.4)$$

This condition can be rewritten without the multiplier by dividing Equation (13.4) by the equivalent condition for $w_{f_j}(s)$. This yields:

$$p_s U_i' [w_{f_i}(s)] = \frac{\lambda_j}{\lambda_i} p_s U_j' [w_{f_j}(s)] \qquad \text{for all } s, i \text{ and } j \quad (13.5)$$

More specifically still, if one wishes to remove the weights λ, it suffices to divide Equation (13.5) by the equivalent condition for t. This yields:

$$\frac{p_s U_i' [w_{f_i}(s)]}{p_t U_i' [w_{f_i}(t)]} = \frac{p_s U_j' [w_{f_j}(s)]}{p_t U_j' [w_{f_j}(t)]} \qquad \text{for all } s, t, i \text{ and } j \quad (13.6)$$

The ratios of marginal utility in two different states of the world thus appear. Appealing to Chapter 7, we know that this corresponds to the marginal rate of substitution between consumption in state s and consumption in state t. Therefore Equation (13.6) can be rewritten as:

$$\text{MRS}_{st}^i = \text{MRS}_{st}^j \qquad \text{for all } s, t, i \text{ and } j \qquad (13.7)$$

where the left-hand side (or right-hand side) is the marginal rate of substitution for Agent i (or Agent j) for contingent claims s and t. This condition says that *if a risk allocation is Pareto efficient then it must be that the marginal rates of substitution between consumption in state* s *and consumption in state* t *are the same for all individuals in the population.*

This condition is called the Borch (1962) condition, after the name of the Norwegian actuary–economist who played a big role in the development of the economics of risk and insurance.[3]

In the rest of this section, we present a non-technical proof of the Borch condition, using a purely graphical method. Assume that the economy is composed of two individuals and that there exist only two possible states. We can then employ the graphical method presented in Chapter 7.

Reconsider the example of the two citrus farmers. Individual $i = 1$ farms in a greenhouse while Individual $i = 2$ farms in a field. Individual 2's production depends on the weather, which may be good ($s = g$) or bad ($s = b$). To fix ideas, assume that:

$$(w_{01}(g), w_{01}(b)) = (900, 900)$$
$$(w_{02}(g), w_{02}(b)) = (1000, 500)$$

The initial endowments and the utility functions, as represented by the indifference curves, appear in Figure 13.3(a) and (b) for Agents 1 and 2,

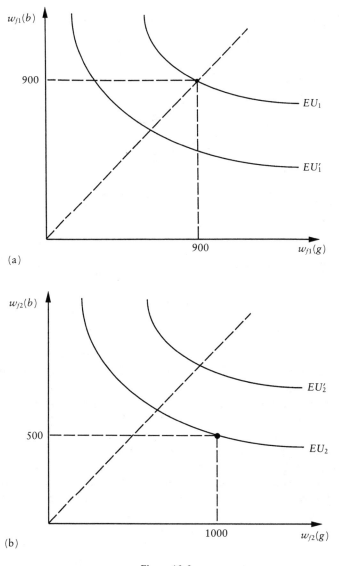

Figure 13.3

respectively. The two graphs are combined by rotating Figure 13.3(b) 180°
and imposing it on Figure 13.3(a) so that the two points representing the initial
endowment coincide.

The resulting graph, Figure 13.4, is called the Edgeworth box. The initial
endowment corresponds to point w. The contingent wealth of Individual 1
in each state is measured from origin 1 while the contingent wealth of

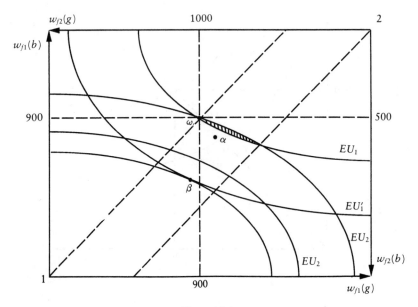

Figure 13.4

Individual 2 in each state is measured from origin 2. The set of allocations corresponding to zero risk for Individual 1 (or 2) is represented by the 45° line from origin 1 (or 2).

First note that the dimensions of the box are equal to aggregate wealth in each state: 1900 (length) for the state $s = g$ and only 1400 (height) for the state $s = b$. Also note that a point in the box represents a particular feasible allocation. Point α, for example – corresponding to individual final contingent wealth of $(w_{01}(g), w_{01}(b)) = (1000, 800)$ and $(w_{02}(g), w_{02}(b)) = (900, 600)$ – is clearly feasible. Since the box is not square, there is social risk in this economy. This implies that there exists no allocation in which the individuals bear no risk: the two 45° lines do not cross.

We now show that the point w of initial endowments (autarky) is inefficient. The set of feasible allocations that generate an increase in expected utility for Individual 1 is represented graphically by the area that lies above EU_1. Similarly, the set of allocations that generate an increase in expected utility for Individual 2 is represented by the area that lies below EU_2.

The intersection of the two areas is non-empty and is represented by the shaded area. A point in this intersection is an allocation that, *ex ante*, increases the welfare of both individuals at once. Point w is thus not Pareto efficient. We have just shown that the economic agents have an incentive to negotiate a risk-sharing arrangement: there is potentially a mutually beneficial exchange.

For an allocation of risk to be efficient, it must be that the intersection of the areas corresponding to an increase in expected utility of each individual is empty. It is easy to see that this implies that the indifference curves are tangential at an efficient point. The allocation β, for example, is Pareto efficient: there is no other allocation that increases the expected utility of both individuals simultaneously.

Recall that the slope of an indifference curve is the marginal rate of substitution. The tangency condition is thus equivalent to the equalisation of the marginal rates of substitution, that is, the Borch condition.

Figure 13.5 shows the set of allocations that satisfy this tangency condition. This is the 'contract curve' containing all the efficient risk allocations. Point ω is not contained in it.

The validity of the Borch condition can also be illustrated with a simple numerical example. Suppose that the marginal rates of substitution were different, for example, $MRS_{st}^1 = 1$ and $MRS_{st}^2 = 2$. Remember the definition of the marginal rate of substitution: it is the smallest amount that must be paid in state s to compensate the loss of a franc in state t. This means that Individual 1, who has unitary MRS, is indifferent between the initial risk and another risk whereby a franc in state t is given up for a franc in state s. The expected utility would not change. Suppose that the planner forces this exchange with Agent 2, who has MRS equal to 2. Agent 2 thus receives a franc in state t and gives up a franc in state s. This is certainly a feasible exchange.

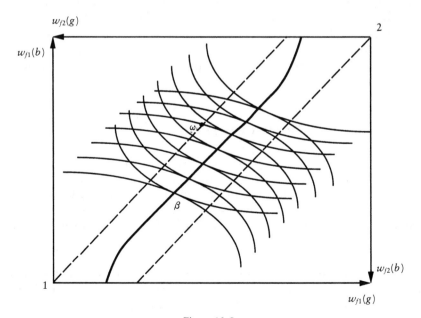

Figure 13.5

Now, to compensate the loss of a franc in state s, Agent 2 must receive at least 0.5 francs in state t. However, the described exchange gives one franc in that state. The expected utility is thus higher. While the welfare of 1 is unchanged by this feasible exchange, the planner succeeds in increasing the welfare of Agent 2: thus the initial allocation could not have been Pareto efficient. This reasoning applies whenever the marginal rates of substitution are different, so the Borch condition is necessary for Pareto efficiency.

It is easy to show that when the economic agents are risk averse, the second-order condition of the planner's problem is immediately satisfied.[4] The Borch condition is thus necessary and sufficient for a feasible allocation to be Pareto efficient. In the rest of this chapter, we study the properties derived from this condition. Specifically, this condition does not immediately furnish much information for the planner who must organise exchanges to achieve efficiency. Fortunately, the properties that we will derive from it will greatly simplify their life. They are two in number and they completely describe an efficient allocation. They must be sequentially applied, beginning with the mutuality principle. As we shall see, this principle allows the elimination of all diversifiable risks. Then a rule is proposed for the sharing of non-diversifiable risk, if there is any. These two rules are complementary.

A remark is necessary at this stage of the presentation. The equalisation of the marginal rates of substitution is a classical condition for Pareto efficiency under certainty. It is encountered here, interpreted under uncertainty, where the goods exchanged are not classical physical goods, but contingent claims. The only peculiarity of the analysis under uncertainty comes from the additive form of the consumer's objective function (expected utility). We will make full use of this peculiarity in the following two sections. This will allow a much simpler characterisation of the efficient allocations under uncertainty than can be achieved under certainty, where one can go little further than the equalisation of the marginal rates of substitution.

13.2 The mutuality principle

To completely characterise the allocation of risks, the analytical form of the functions $w_{f_i}(s)$ must be derived. Since the initial endowments are random, a state of the world can be defined by the endowments of each agent in that state, $s = (w_{01}, \ldots, w_{0i}, \ldots, w_{0n})$. A particular allocation can thus be characterised by a set of n functions of n variables each:

$$w_{f_i}(w_{01}, \ldots, w_{0i}, \ldots, w_{0n}) \tag{13.8}$$

The final wealth of each individual is a function of their own initial endowment in that state as well as of the initial endowments of the other individuals who make up the society. This is a way of saying that the risks of each are partially borne by the others through the exchange of risk. This is the classical situation of a mutual where the contribution (or the premium) of each member depends on the losses suffered by all. Definition (13.8) is the most general imaginable. One could, for example, imagine a solution where Individual i retains 15 per cent of their own risk, accepts 10 per cent of Agent j's risk, and accepts 5 per cent of Agent k's risk. One would then have:

$$\frac{\partial w_{f_i}}{\partial w_{0i}} = 0.15$$

$$\frac{\partial w_{f_i}}{\partial w_{0j}} = 0.10 \qquad\qquad (13.9)$$

$$\frac{\partial w_{f_i}}{\partial w_{0k}} = 0.05$$

Anecdotally, this is typically what occurs at Lloyd's of London, truly a market for insurance contracts. The members of this society are called 'names'. Each name is free to underwrite, or participate in, the risks borne by other names. This is done by indicating for each risk underwritten by Lloyd's, how much is borne by each name. The system is rather complex and it is difficult to see who is bearing what risk. We will show in this section that efficient risk allocations satisfy a very special property, called the mutuality principle. The sharing of risk is then much easier to characterise.

Theorem 13.1 (Mutuality principle). A Pareto-efficient risk allocation has the property that each individual's final wealth depends only on the aggregate wealth of the economy in the realised state:

$$w_{f_i}(s) = W_{f_i}[w_0(s)] \qquad\qquad (13.10)$$

Proof The proof of Theorem 13.1 is relatively simple. It suffices to show that if there exist two states, s and t, that exhibit the same aggregate wealth $[w_0(s) = w_0(t)]$, then the final wealth of each agent must be the same in the two states ($w_{f_i}(s) = w_{f_i}(t)$ for all i). If we succeed in establishing this property of efficient allocations, then we will have shown that:

$$w_{f_i}(w_{01}, \ldots, w_{0n}) = w_{f_i}(w'_{01}, \ldots, w'_{0n})$$

$$\text{if } \sum_{j=1}^{n} w_{0j} = \sum_{j=1}^{n} w'_{0j}$$

This is another way of saying that each agent's final wealth depends only on aggregate initial wealth.

Assume, contrary to fact, that $w_0(s) = w_0(t)$, but that there exists an agent i such that $w_{f_i}(s)$ is greater than $w_{f_i}(t)$. The Borch condition (13.6) and risk aversion then imply that $w_{f_j}(s)$ is greater than $w_{f_j}(t)$ for all j. Aggregate final wealth is thus higher in state s than in state t.

Now the feasibility condition (13.2) stipulates that aggregate final wealth always equals aggregate initial wealth. By assumption, aggregate initial wealth is the same in both states. We have thus obtained a contradiction: $w_{f_i}(s)$ cannot be larger than $w_{f_i}(t)$. Similarly, it can be shown that $w_{f_i}(s)$ cannot be less than $w_{f_i}(t)$. Thus, when aggregate wealth is the same in two states, each individual's final wealth must also be the same in the two states. This implies that feasible allocations of final wealth that satisfy the Borch condition can only depend on aggregate wealth in the corresponding state. Q.E.D.

A graphical proof of the mutuality principle is based on the fact that the contract curve depicted in Figure 13.5 depends only on the shape of the indifference curves and the *size* of the Edgeworth box representing $w_0(g)$ and $w_0(b)$. It is independent of the position of the initial endowment point within the box.

Whereas, from definition (13.8), function w_{f_i} is a function of n variables in a given state of the world, function W_{f_i} is a function of a single variable, which will, of course, greatly simplify the analysis. Thus, an efficient allocation of risks entails the following procedure: in each state, the planner begins by collecting the aggregate net wealth of the economic agents, that is, $w_0(s)$. Then, without considering the contribution of each individual in this state, these resources are distributed according to a previously established allocation rule. In this way, the final wealth of each individual depends on the initial wealth of all individuals only through the total initial wealth. Of course, rather than consider a complete transfer of $w_{0i}(s)$ to a common pool followed by the transfer of each $w_{f_i}(s)$ from the pool, the planner can simply effect transfers equal to $w_{f_i}(s) - w_{0i}(s)$ for each i.

This type of risk-sharing is encountered in the Israeli kibbutzim, for example: each individual contributes the fruits of their labour into a common pot, whether it be a salary from outside work or the product of labour inside the organisation. This example is undoubtedly the simplest form of applying the mutuality principle. The term 'principle of mutuality' refers, of course, to a kind of organisation that is known in the real world (without a planner): the mutual.[5] Many applications of the mutuality principle are encountered in economic life, whether in financial markets, labour markets, credit markets or insurance markets. The case of financial markets is analysed in more detail in Chapter 15.

Note that a system like the one represented by Equation (13.9) cannot be Pareto efficient because the final wealth of Agent i depends on the distribution of the aggregate loss across agents. To satisfy the mutuality principle, it is necessary that each agent i accept an identical share of the risks borne by the others. Specifically, the mutuality principle implies that the share of Agent j's risk that is borne by Agent i satisfies:

$$\frac{\partial w_{f_i}}{\partial w_{0_j}} = \frac{\partial W_{f_i}}{\partial w_0} \frac{\partial w_0}{\partial w_{0j}} = \frac{\partial W_{f_i}}{\partial w_0} 1 = \frac{\partial W_{f_i}}{\partial w_0}$$

which is independent of j. In other words,

$$\frac{\partial w_{f_i}}{\partial w_{0j}} = \frac{\partial w_{f_i}}{\partial w_{0k}} \qquad \text{for all } i, j \text{ and } k \qquad (13.11)$$

Note that by taking $j = i$, one sees that individual i does not bear a greater share of their own risk than of others' risks. Thus all risks are completely turned over to the pool. It is important to observe that the share of each individual in the collective risk is unknown at this stage. This question is considered in the next section.

The intuition behind the mutuality principle is simple: it is a question of *disseminating* – or *diversifying* – the individual risks as much as possible. To illustrate, consider an economy composed of two agents each with the same attitude towards risk and who have identically distributed initial wealth. Assume the variance of each individual's wealth is σ^2 and their covariance is σ_{12}. Consider the following risk-sharing arrangement: the planner, conscious of the mutuality principle, decides that in each state the initial endowments will be collected and redistributed equally[6] between the two agents. Therefore, each agent bears 50 per cent of their own risk, but also 50 per cent of the other agent's risk. If the variance is used as an index of risk, the quantity of risk borne by each individual is, by symmetry,

$$\begin{aligned} \text{Var}[\tilde{w}_{f_i}] &= \text{Var}[0.5\tilde{w}_{01} + 0.5\tilde{w}_{02}] \\ &= (0.5)^2\sigma^2 + (0.5)^2\sigma^2 + 2(0.5)(0.5)\sigma_{12} \\ &= 0.5[\sigma^2 + \sigma_{12}] \end{aligned} \qquad (13.12)$$

When choosing an equitable risk-sharing arrangement, the planner succeeds in reducing (as much as possible) the risks borne by each agent. Specifically, we know that the covariance, σ_{12}, is always smaller than the variance[7], σ^2. This implies that:

$$\begin{aligned} 0.5[\sigma^2 + \sigma_{12}] = \text{Var}[\tilde{w}_{f_1}] = \text{Var}[\tilde{w}_{f_2}] &< \text{Var}[\tilde{w}_{01}] \\ &= \text{Var}[\tilde{w}_{02}] = \sigma^2 \end{aligned}$$

The exchange of risk permits the risk borne by each of the two individuals to be reduced costlessly. The aggregate gain from the exchange corresponds to:

$$\begin{aligned} \{\text{Var}[\tilde{w}_{01}] + \text{Var}[\tilde{w}_{02}]\} - \{\text{Var}[\tilde{w}_{f_1}] + \text{Var}[\tilde{w}_{f_2}]\} \\ = \sigma^2 - \sigma_{12} = \sigma^2[1 - \rho] > 0 \quad (13.13) \end{aligned}$$

where $\rho = \sigma_{12}/\sigma^2$ is the correlation coefficient between the initial individual risks. The gain from an equitable risk-sharing arrangement that satisfies the mutuality principle depends on these parameters. The gain is largest when the two risks are perfectly negatively correlated ($\rho = -1$). In that case, what one agent gains the other loses, and the individual risks can be completely eliminated by diversification. This is the case that was studied in Chapter 7, where there is no social risk: the individual risks are socially diversifiable. The creation of a mutual then clearly improves the economic system composed of riskophobes.

In contrast, the gain is zero when the risks are perfectly positively correlated ($\rho = 1$). When one agent gains some amount, the other does the same: diversification offers no social benefit. A mutual has no *raison d'être* in this case. An example of a situation where individual risks are strongly correlated is the risk of an earthquake in San Francisco. For this type of risk, the inhabitants of this city cannot form a purely regional mutual. There would be virtually no gain.[8]

The most classic case is when the risks are independent. In this case, ρ is zero and the optimal strategy succeeds in dividing the variance of the individual risks in half by diversification. More generally, in an economy composed of n identical[9] individuals facing identical and independently distributed risks (i.i.d) with variance σ^2, the creation of a mutual where the risks are equally distributed generates an allocation such that:

$$V[\tilde{w}_{f_i}] = V[(\tilde{w}_{01} + \ldots + \tilde{w}_{0n})/n] = n\sigma^2/n^2 = \sigma^2/n \qquad (13.14)$$

In other words, the variance of each individual's risk is divided by n. This is the law of large numbers. When the size of the population approaches infinity, the risk borne by each individual approaches zero and the risks are completely diversified in the individual portfolios. This is only possible if the risks are independent – or weakly dependent – and if their number is sufficiently large.

Figure 13.6 shows the density functions $f_n(t)$ of final wealth for $n = 1$, 2 and 3, when the initial wealths are independent and uniformly distributed on $[0, 1]$. This implies that $\sigma^2 = 1/12$. When $n = 2$, it can be verified that, for all

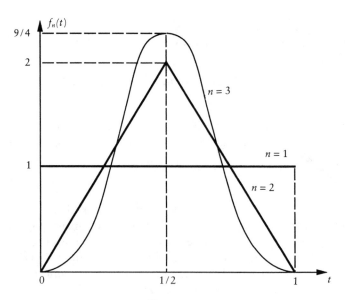

Figure 13.6

$t < 0.5$, the distribution function of $\tilde{w}_{fi} = (\tilde{w}_{01} + \tilde{w}_{02})/2$ takes the following form:

$$F_2(t) = \int_0^{2t} \int_0^{2t - w_{01}} 1 dw_{01} \, dw_{02} = 2t^2$$

It follows that:

$$f_2(t) = F_2'(t) = 4t$$

The symmetric line is obtained for $0.5 < t < 1$. It is then easily verified that the variance of $\tilde{w}_{f_i}$ equals $1/24 = \sigma^2/2$, as is predicted by Formula (13.14). It is shown in Figure 13.6 that the change from f_1 to f_2 entails a reduction in risk at constant mean: weight is transferred from the extremes toward the centre. Diversification is preferred by all riskophobes. The same kind of reasoning can be applied to the change[10] from $n = 2$ to $n = 3$, where even more weight is concentrated towards the centre of the distribution. The larger n becomes, the more the distribution of final wealth approximates a 'bell-shaped' normal distribution (central limit theorem). In the limit, using the law of large numbers, the density function collapses on the point $t = 0.5$.

In general, a social risk – or non-diversifiable risk – exists either because the size of the mutual is too small or because the risks are correlated. Then there is the question of how to divide this risk among the different members of the pool. This is a question of characterising the functions $W_{f_i}(w_0)$, since we know that efficient allocations of risk must take this form. This question is broached in the following section. This is the logical next step after the mutuality principle, that eliminates the diversifiable risk, but leaves open the question of how to share the residual risk surrounding w_0.

13.3 Sharing non-diversifiable risk

Comparing the contingent marginal utility of the individuals $i = 1, 2, \ldots, n$ and using the mutuality principle of Equation (13.10), the Borch condition, Equation (13.5) can be rewritten as follows:

$$U_i'[W_{f_i}(w_0)] = \frac{\lambda_1}{\lambda_i} U_1'[W_{f_1}(w_0)] \qquad \text{for all } w_0 \text{ and } i \quad (13.15)$$

Recall here that w_0 is the aggregate initial wealth of the individuals. Differentiate this condition with respect to w_0:

$$U_i''(W_{f_i}) W_{f_i}'(w_0) = \frac{\lambda_1}{\lambda_i} U_1''(W_{f_1}) W_{f_1}'(w_0)$$

Dividing the last equality by the previous equality, one obtains:

$$-\frac{U_i''(W_{f_i})}{U_i'(W_{f_i})} W_{f_i}'(w_0) = -\frac{U_1''(W_{f_1})}{U_1'(W_{f_1})} W_{f_1}'(w_0)$$

or, equivalently,

$$W_{f_i}'(w_0) = \frac{A_{a_1}(W_{f_1})}{A_{a_i}(W_{f_i})} W_{f_1}'(w_0) \quad \text{for all } i = 2, ..., n \qquad (13.16)$$

where $A_{a_i}(W_{f_i})$ is the coefficient of absolute risk aversion, evaluated at W_{f_i}, of the ith member of the mutual. Equation (13.16) indicates that the sensitivity of an individual's final wealth to variations in the wealth of the pool should be inversely proportional to their absolute risk aversion, or directly proportional to their risk tolerance expressed as:

$$T_{a_i}(W_{f_i}) = [A_{a_i}(W_{f_i})]^{-1} = -\frac{U_i'(W_{f_i})}{U_i''(W_{f_i})} \qquad (13.17)$$

To characterise the sensitivity of W_{f_i} directly as a function of w_0, recall the feasibility condition $\Sigma_{i=1}^{n} W_{f_i}(w_0) = w_0$. This necessarily implies that

$$\sum_{i=1}^{n} W_{f_i}'(w_0) = 1 \qquad (13.18)$$

The combination of conditions (13.16) and (13.18) yields the efficient rule of non-diversifiable risk-sharing. Specifically, it must be that:

$$1 = \sum_{i=1}^{n} W_{f_i}'(w_0) = \sum_{i=1}^{n} W_{f_1}'(w_0) \frac{A_{a_1}(W_{f_1})}{A_{a_i}(W_{f_i})}$$

$$= A_{a_1}(W_{f_1}) W_{f_1}'(w_0) \sum_{i=1}^{n} A_{a_i}^{-1}(W_{f_i})$$

A simple manipulation of the terms in this last equality yields:

$$W_{f_1}'(w_0) = \frac{[A_{a_1}(W_{f_1})]^{-1}}{\sum_{k=1}^{n} [A_{a_i}(W_{f_i})]^{-1}} \qquad (13.19)$$

By symmetry, and using the definition of risk tolerance, one finally obtains:

$$W_{f_i}'(w_0) = \frac{T_{a_i}(W_{f_i})}{\sum_{k=1}^{n} T_{a_k}(W_{f_k})} \quad \text{for all } i = 1, 2, ..., n \qquad (13.20)$$

Here it is clear why using the concept of risk tolerance is preferable to using its inverse, the concept of risk aversion.

Theorem 13.2 A Pareto-efficient risk allocation has the property that the sensitivity of an individual's final wealth to the wealth of the pool equals the absolute risk tolerance of this individual expressed as a percentage of the sum of the absolute risk tolerances of the group. In other words, an increase in w_0 should be shared in the pool proportionally to the absolute risk tolerance of each member.

Note that this condition is independent of the weights λ_i that determine a particular Pareto-efficient allocation. Does this mean there exists only one solution to the problem? No, because condition (13.20) is a system of n ordinary differential equations for which the n unknowns are the functions $W_{f_i}(w_0)$. Now, to solve this system, n arbitrary initial conditions $W_{f_i}(0)$ are needed. There thus exist an infinity of feasible allocations that satisfy condition (13.20).

Note also that the rule presented in this theorem is independent of the probability of each state. In other words, the Pareto-efficient rule of risk-sharing does not depend on the characteristics of the individual risks nor, thus, on those of the non-diversifiable risk. There is thus no need for a comparative statics analysis of the impact of an increased risk on the efficient allocation. There is no effect.

A simple special case is where there is one individual in the group, say individual $j = 1$, who is risk neutral. In this case, T_{a_1} approaches infinity as does the denominator of Equation (13.20). It follows that for all i different from 1, $W'_{f_i}(w_0)$ is zero. In contrast, for $i = 1$, Equation (13.20) is of the type $\lim_{t \to \infty} t/(c + t)$, which means that $W'_{f_1} = 1$. The solutions of the system of differential equations are thus of the form:

$$W_{f_1}(w_0) = W_{f_1}(0) + w_0$$
$$W_{f_i}(w_0) = W_{f_i}(0) \qquad \text{for } i = 2, ..., n$$

In summary, if there is a risk-neutral individual in the pool, it is Pareto efficient for them to bear all of the non-diversifiable risk, leaving the riskophobes 100 per cent covered. Note again that the $W_{f_i} = W_{f_i}(0)$ are indeterminate. One solution is for the planner to transfer all the variability of wealth from the riskophobes to Individual 1, leaving each riskophobe, for example, with what they would have received, on average, in autarky $[W_{f_i}(0) = E(\tilde{w}_{0_i})]$. But this is only one example of an efficient risk allocation. The planner could also decide to remunerate agent $i = 1$ for 'insurance service' by paying a risk premium from the endowments of the riskophobes $[W_{f_i}(0) < E(\tilde{w}_{0_i})]$.

It can also be verified that when an individual is infinitely risk averse ($T_a = 0$), the planner must make sure that this person takes no part in the allocation of social risk. In all the other cases, $W'_{f_i}(w_0)$ lies between 0 and 1. In general, the solutions of the system Equation (13.20) are non-linear in w_0 because the right-hand side of the equation is a function of w_0. A typical solution is drawn in Figure 13.7. In that case, Individual 1's absolute risk aversion (or tolerance) decreases (or increases) more quickly than that of the

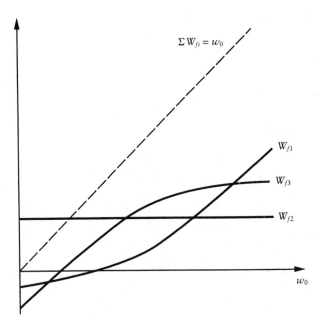

Figure 13.7

others, implying that W'_{f_1} is increasing in w_0. Individual $i = 2$ is very risk averse. This implies that they will bear a small part of the social risk (W'_{f_2} is small, indeed zero).

There exist four special cases for which efficient risk-sharing arrangements are represented by linear rules of the form:

$$W_{f_i}(w_0) = a_i + b_i w_0 \tag{13.21}$$

with

$$\sum_{i=1}^{n} a_i = 0$$

and

$$\sum_{i=1}^{n} b_i = 1$$

in order to satisfy the feasibility condition.

1. We already know one case: it is the one where there is a risk-neutral member of the pool.
2. In the second special case, all the members have negative exponential utility functions. This implies constant absolute risk aversion and hence constant absolute risk tolerance. Here, the right-hand side of Equation

(13.20) is constant. Since $W'_{f_i}(w_0)$ is constant, $W_{f_i}(w_0)$ is linear. In the case where the absolute risk aversions are not only constant but also identical, the right-hand side of Equation (13.20) equals $1/n$: all the members bear an equal share of the social risk. The a_i are arbitrary here: they constitute *ex ante* monetary transfers that are arbitrarily imposed by the planner.

3. A more subtle case is where the relative risk aversions are constant and identical $A_{r_i}(W_{f_i}) = A_r$. Then:

$$W'_{f_i}(w_0) = \frac{[A_{a_i}(W_{f_i})]^{-1}}{\sum\limits_{k=1}^{n} [A_{a_k}(W_{f_k})]^{-1}}$$

$$= \frac{W_{f_i}(A_{r_i})^{-1}}{\sum\limits_{k=1}^{n} W_{f_k}(A_{r_k})^{-1}}$$

$$= \frac{(A_r)^{-1} W_{f_i}}{(A_r)^{-1} \sum\limits_{k=1}^{n} W_{f_k}}$$

$$= \frac{W_{f_i}}{w_0}$$

The solution to this differential equation is $W_{f_i}(w_0) = b_i w_0$, meaning that Agent i's relative share of income from the pool (W_{f_i}/w_0) is a constant (b_i).

Here all the a_i are zero in the formula (13.21) and the b_i are arbitrary. This solution is particularly attractive because of the simplicity of its organisation: it suffices to announce the share (in per cent) of the pie that each member will receive *ex post*. This type of solution is illustrated in Figure 13.8. *The division of the risk into percentage shares is optimal when relative risk aversions are constant and identical.*

4. Finally, it can be shown that optimal risk-sharing also takes a linear form with quadratic utility functions: $U_i(w_{f_i}) = w_{f_i} - \beta_i w_{f_i}^2$. Here the system (13.20) becomes:

$$W'_{f_i}(w_0) = \frac{T_{a_i}(W_{f_i})}{\sum\limits_{k=1}^{n} T_{a_k}(W_{f_k})} = \frac{(2\beta_i)^{-1} - W_{f_i}}{\sum\limits_{k=1}^{n} (2\beta_k)^{-1} - W_{f_k}}$$

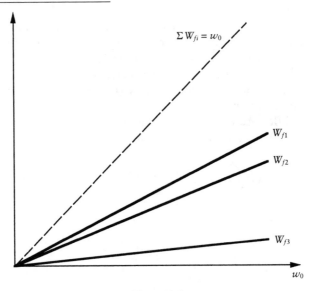

Figure 13.8

It is easily verified that the solutions of this system are of the type, Equation (13.21) with:

$$a_i = \frac{1}{2\beta_i} - b_i \sum_{k=1}^{n} \frac{1}{2\beta_k}$$

To conclude the discussion of the linearity of risk-sharing rules, it can be said that only some forms of hyperbolic absolute risk aversion utility functions (see Section 4.3.5) induce linear rules. Linear rules are the simplest to put into practice and are most often observed (with deductibles).

Thus, although the mutuality principle stated that all risks should be aggregated, the optimal rule for sharing this aggregate risk (non-diversifiable risk) is not necessarily the egalitarian rule $1/n$. Indeed, this is only the rule when all the individuals have the same attitudes towards risk. One can ask why at the optimum certain members must accept a larger share of the common risk. The intuition underlying the answer to this question reflects the trade-off for the planner between wanting to reduce the risk of all members and wanting to make the relatively less risk-averse members bear a relatively large part of the non-diversifiable risk.

To confirm this intuition, consider once again the case of $n = 2$. Maximising a weighted sum of expected utility, as was done in Equation (13.3), is the same as maximising the weighted sum of the certainty equivalents of final wealth. Since there are no transactions costs, this problem is the same as that of minimising the sum of the risk premiums. The chosen distribution of expected wealth reflects the value of the weights λ_i and is thus arbitrary. Keep in mind that the problem studied in this chapter is the same as the problem of *finding a risk-sharing arrangement that minimises the (non-weighted) sum of the individual risk premiums*. In the framework of an economy with small risks, the planner can, on the one hand, use the Arrow–Pratt approximation formula, Equation (3.16) and, on the other, use a linear rule as a good approximation for an efficient allocation. Variable b represents Individual 1's share of the risk surrounding w_0, with variance σ^2. In this notation the variance of W_{f1} (or W_{f2}) equals $b^2\sigma^2$ (or $(1-b)^2\sigma^2$). Problem (13.3) can thus be rewritten in the following way:

$$\min v(b) = \frac{b^2\sigma^2}{2T_{a_1}} + \frac{(1-b)^2\sigma^2}{2T_{a_2}} \tag{13.22}$$

where T_{a_1} and T_{a_2} are evaluated at the average expected wealth. The first-order condition for this problem corresponds to:

$$\frac{b^*}{T_{a_1}} - \frac{(1-b^*)}{T_{a_2}} = 0$$

The second-order condition is automatically satisfied if $A_{a_1} + A_{a_2}$ is positive. After multiplying by T_{a_1} and T_{a_2}, one obtains:

$$b^* = \frac{T_{a_1}}{T_{a_1} + T_{a_2}} \tag{13.23}$$

To minimise the sum of the individual risk premiums, each member must accept a risk that is proportional to their absolute risk tolerance. This is the result already presented in Theorem 13.2. It is clear that the sum of the individual variances is not minimised, but rather a sum that is weighted by the absolute aversions. It is only when the absolute risk aversions are identical that Equation (13.22) is equivalent to the minimisation of the variances of w_{f_i}, giving the equal division $b^* = 1/n$ which allows maximum gain from the dissemination of the non-diversifiable risk.

To conclude, define the following parameter:

$$T_a(w_0) = \sum_{k=1}^{n} T_{a_k}[W_{f_k}(w_0)] \tag{13.24}$$

T_a is the sum of the individual absolute risk tolerances in the pool. It is interesting to observe, in the context of this example, that at the optimum $v(b^*)$ equals:

$$v(b^*) = \frac{(T_{a_1}/T_a)^2\sigma^2}{2T_{a_1}} + \frac{(T_{a_2}/T_a)^2\sigma^2}{2T_{a_2}} \tag{13.25}$$

$$= \frac{\sigma^2}{2T_{a_2}}[T_{a_1} + T_{a_2}]$$

$$= \frac{\sigma^2}{2T_a}$$

To evaluate a risk, the *group* calculates the variance of the risk and divides by twice the parameter T_a. Recall that the premium of a (small) risk for an *individual* equals the ratio of the variance to two times their absolute risk tolerance. Analogously, Equation (13.25) suggests that T_a, the sum of the individuals' tolerances, can be thought of as the *group*'s absolute risk tolerance.

We formalise this in the general case by defining an *ex post* welfare index for the group as the weighted sum of individual utilities:

$$V(w_0) = \sum_{i=1}^{n} \lambda_i U_i [W_{f_i}(w_0)] \tag{13.26}$$

In the formulation of the problem given in Equation (13.3), we defined the objective function F as the expected value of V, which is consistent with the approach taken here: we maximise an *ex ante* index of social welfare defined as the expected value of the *ex post* index of social welfare. Calculating the derivative of V given a Pareto-efficient solution yields:

$$V'(w_0) = \sum_{i=1}^{n} \lambda_i U_i'[W_{f_i}(w_0)] W_{f_i}'(w_0)$$

$$= \lambda_1 U_1' [W_{f_1}(w_0)] \sum_{i=1}^{n} W_{f_i}'(w_0)$$

$$= \lambda_1 U_1' [W_{f_1}(w_0)]$$

The second equality is obtained by using Equation (13.15) and the third by using Equation (13.18). From this, the second derivative of V is immediately obtainable:

$$V''(w_0) = \lambda_1 U_1'' [W_{f_1}(w_0)] W_{f_1}'(w_0)$$

If the index of absolute risk tolerance for the group is defined by:

$$T_a(w_0) = - \frac{V'(w_0)}{V''(w_0)}$$

it follows that:

$$T_a(w_0) = - \frac{\lambda_1 U_1' [W_{f_1}(w_0)]}{\lambda_1 U_1''(W_{f_1}(w_0)) W_{f_1}'(w_0)}$$

$$= - \frac{U_1'(W_{f_1})/U_1''(W_{f_1})}{T_{a_1} \Big/ \sum_{k=1}^{n} T_{ak}(w_0)} = \sum_{k=1}^{n} T_{ak}(w_0)$$

which corresponds to definition (13.24). It is important to remember that this result is only obtainable given an efficient allocation of risks within the group.

Theorem 13.3 The absolute risk tolerance of an efficient pool of risk-averse individuals equals the sum of the individuals' absolute risk tolerances. In the same way, the absolute risk aversion of a pool equals the inverse of the sum of the individuals' absolute risk tolerances.[11]

It turns out that one can use all of the technology presented in Part Two of this book to discuss the choices of a group rather than of an individual, using V as a 'utility' function. Specifically, this clearly fits into the framework of maximising the expected value of a function that is concave in final wealth w_0. For example, a group is willing to acquire a risk if its bid price is less than its expected value plus the risk premium measured with the function V (Equation (13.25) for a small risk). The group makes risky investment decisions and insurance decisions by using function V as a utility function. The rules are exactly identical to those derived in Part Two.

Since T_a is much larger than the risk tolerance of each member taken individually, one would expect that the optimal decisions of the group would be much riskier than those that would be observed if the decisions were decentralised without the possibility of reallocation within the group. Consequently, a group of individuals has possibilities of risk retention that are much greater. This is partly due to the opportunities for diversification within the group and partly due to the transfer of risk towards the least risk-averse members (or the richest members, if absolute risk aversion is decreasing, as required by Hypothesis 4.1). This is why one always looks for organisations to undertake risky activities. This is why there are joint stock companies and co-insurance arrangements between insurance companies to bear the risks associated with projects such as the launching of a rocket or a satellite. Without this diminution of risk aversion in an economy, thanks to the creation of risk pools, many risky projects would not have been undertaken and we would undoubtedly not have known the economic expansion that we have observed over the last two centuries. This comment presupposes that our economies have succeeded in organising efficient risk allocations, despite the absence of a planner.

The problem of collective decisions under uncertainty is thus central in economic analysis. Many other microeconomic applications can be analysed in this way. There is, for example, the problem of an investment company (or club) that must make decisions in the name of a group of stockholders. There is also the analysis of a life insurance company that must choose an investment portfolio, the profits of which are redistributed to the policy-holders as dividends. The same kind of analysis applies in the study of the debt management decisions of a government, a quintessential collective decision. Finally, even the decisions of a head of household must be analysed in this light, taking as the objective not the expected utility of the head of household but the expected value of V. (The choice of the weights for the father, mother and each of the children in this function is (un)fortunately left to the discretion of families, which suggests the prediction that there will be occasional broken dishes!)

Quantitatively, it suffices to reuse the results derived for the individual's decision, replacing U by V and using Theorem 13.3. Remember, however, that this is only valid if there is efficient risk-sharing within the group.

Finally, and to conclude this chapter, we emphasise one of the central assumptions of the model, that is, the absence of social loss due to the exchange or absence of transactions costs. To lift the veil from problems connected to this heroic assumption would take too much time. However, we would like to answer a piercing question that perhaps the reader has in mind: we have just shown that, in at least four cases, co-insurance – that is, linear risk-sharing – is Pareto efficient. Co-insurance is thus unanimously preferred to an arrangement exhibiting a deductible.

Yet, we proved exactly the opposite in Section 10.5. The inconsistency disappears when one understands that the insurance premium reflects the management costs of the contract with a risk-neutral insurer (the insurance premium contains no risk premium).[12] We thus showed, in the section in question, that the best risk-sharing arrangement, when costs are linear and the insurer risk neutral, is a contract with a deductible.

It could be shown here that the best risk-sharing arrangement when costs are linear and the insurer risk-averse, is a contract that combines co-insurance and a deductible, with a rate of co-insurance corresponding to $T_{a_1}/(T_{a_1} + T_{a_2})$. We have elsewhere given the reason for the optimality of the deductible (cost reduction). In this chapter we have presented the intuition for co-insurance (risk-sharing).

Exercises

13.1 Show that the optimality condition (13.6) and (13.7) can be arrived at by maximising the expected utility of one individual (i) subject to the constraints that the other individual (j) reaches a pre-assigned level of expected utility and that the reallocation of the risks is feasible. Interpret the Lagrange multipliers associated with the constraint on j's level of expected utility in terms of the paretian frontier of Figure 13.1.

13.2 Prove first graphically (for two states of the world) and then mathematically (for N states) that, in the absence of social risk, all Pareto-efficient allocations of risk lie along the certainty line when the agents have identical beliefs (each state of the world is attached a single probability by all members of the community). Show that in the absence of social risk, the certainty line is no longer Pareto efficient when beliefs are different.

13.3 An exchange economy is made of two individuals with a logarithmic utility function. There are two equally likely states of the world yielding the following initial random wealths:

$$\text{prob}(b) = \tfrac{1}{2}: \qquad W_{01}(b) = 1 \qquad W_{02}(b) = 3$$
$$\text{prob}(g) = \tfrac{1}{2}: \qquad W_{01}(g) = 3 \qquad W_{02}(g) = 3$$

Questions
(a) Compute first the covariance (σ_{12}) between the initial wealth levels and then the covariance between each individual risk and the aggregate risk.
(b) Show that all Pareto-efficient risk-sharing arrangements should satisfy:

$$\frac{W_{f1}(g)}{W_{f1}(b)} = \frac{W_{f2}(g)}{W_{f2}(b)} = \frac{6}{4}$$

As a result show that any reshuffling of initial wealth that does not modify aggregate wealth in each state has no impact on the optimal risk-sharing rule.
(c) Imagine that Individual 1 insists on having $W_{f1}(b) = 2$. What is the corresponding Pareto-efficient arrangement? Which argument would Individual 2 use to refuse such a solution? What is, in fact, the maximal value of $W_{f1}(b)$ that Individual 2 might tolerate?
(d) Show graphically that the Pareto-efficient arrangements lie along the line joining the origins of the Edgeworth's diagram.
(e) Returning to the condition obtained in *b*, show that the linear sharing rule:

$$W_{f1} = b_1 W_0$$

satisfies the condition expressed in (b). Relate that result to a property of the relative risk-aversion coefficient for a logarithmic utility function.

13.4 Return to the data of Exercise 13.3 but consider now that the two individuals have negative exponential utility function, more precisely:

$$U_1 = -e^{-\gamma_1 W_{f1}} \text{ and } U_2 = -e^{-\gamma_2 W_{f2}}$$

Questions
(a) Show that along the contract curve:

$$W_{f1}(g) - W_{f1}(b) = \frac{\gamma_2}{\gamma_1 + \gamma_2} \, 2$$

where $2 = W_0(g) - W_0(b)$

(b) Since $W_{fi}(g) - W_{fi}(b)$ is the change in final wealth for member i after the risk-sharing arrangement and since $W_0(g) - W_0(b)$ is the change in collective wealth, show that you recover, in this example, the result presented in Equation (13.20).

(c) Notice the similarity between the solution to this exercise and the one already obtained for Exercise 2.3 (especially Question (b)).

13.5 In this chapter we assumed that there is an agreed-upon probability distribution for the occurrence of the possible states of the world. Suppose, on the contrary, that there is no agreement about the distribution of probabilities. Show that the mutuality principle does not hold in that case.

13.6 Consider an economy with two individuals. Initial wealths are i.i.d. with $\tilde{w}_{0i} \sim N(\mu, \sigma^2)$. Suppose also that $U_i(w) = -e^{-w}$.

Questions

(a) Describe the efficient risk-sharing which is such that $E\tilde{w}_{fi} = \mu$, i.e. the 'fair' efficient risk-sharing.

(b) Suppose that a rule initially prohibits risk-sharing. How much money is each individual ready to pay to eliminate the rule in order to attain the fair efficient risk allocation?
Hint: Use the fact that the Arrow–Pratt approximation is exact in this case.

(c) Suppose that the initial rule is that individual $i = 1$ bears 75 per cent of the aggregate risk and individual $i = 2$ bears the remainder. Calculate the trade surplus generated by changing the rule to the efficient '50–50' sharing rule.

13.7 Consider an economy with two individuals $i = 1, 2$. Each individual is endowed with a sure initial wealth and with an exponential utility function $U_i(w) = -\exp(-A_{ai}w)$. There exist two independent risky assets $j = 1, 2$ and a risk-free asset. Returns $\tilde{x}_1$ and $\tilde{x}_2$ of the risky assets are normal i.i.d. with $\sigma^2 = 1$. The expected excess return is 1. Individual $i = 1$ may only buy risky asset $j = 1$, whereas individual $j = 2$ may only buy risky asset $j = 2$.

Questions

(a) Show that the demand for the risky asset $j = i$ by individual i is $a_i^* = (A_{ai})^{-1}$, in autarky.
Hint: Use the property that $EU_i = -\exp(-A_{ai}\mu + 0.5 A_{ai}^2\sigma^2))$.

(b) Suppose alternatively that individuals $i = 1$ and $i = 2$ are allowed to freely share their revenues.
Show that, as a result, this will double the demand for both assets.

Notes

1. The assumption that the number of states of the world is finite is used only to simplify the presentation. The results generalise immediately with a continuous random variable.
2. In a market economy, insurers must cover the costs of administering the contracts and so must the financial intermediaries. These efforts expended to transfer risks constitute a dead weight loss for the economy because they could have been used to produce consumption goods. Think again about the size of these sectors in our economies.
3. For an evaluation of the contribution of K. Borch to the theory of risk-sharing, see J. Lemaire (1990) and C. Gollier (1991).
4. The Hessian matrix is a diagonal matrix whose diagonal elements are of the form $\lambda_{ifs}U_i''[w_{fi}(s)] < 0$. This matrix is clearly negative definite.
5. This is how mutuals operate: each member receives a guarantee of protection against loss, but the premium to be paid – and thus final wealth – depends on the results of the group, that is, on the aggregate loss suffered by the members.
6. The planner could at this stage consider a different distribution rule than '50–50'. This problem is considered in the next section. There we show that, for individuals with the same attitude toward risk, the 50–50 rule is optimal for sharing non-diversifiable risk, that is, it minimises the variance.
7. Recall that the correlation coefficient – which here is the ratio of the covariance to the variance – is between -1 and 1.
8. Except with the goal of creating a financial reserve in case of a big earthquake. This would be a strategy of precautionary saving, which has nothing to do with what we are studying here in this atemporal model.
9. The case where individuals have different attitudes towards risk is studied in Section 13.3. The optimal distribution of risks is then not necessarily symmetric, as is assumed here.
10. One has: $f_3(t) = 27t^2/2$ for $t < 1/3$ and $f_3(t) = (27t^2/2) - [9(3t - 1)^2/2]$ for $1/3 < t < 1/2$. For $t > 1/2$, the function is symmetric around $t = 1/2$.
11. It can thus be said that the absolute risk aversion of a group of size n equals n times the *harmonic* mean of the individuals' absolute risk aversions.
12. To show the equivalence between the two problems, consider a division between two individuals. The insured and the insurer are respectively represented by the letters $i = 1$ and $i = 2$. Assuming that the payment of an indemnity I generates a cost λI borne by the insurer, the problem of efficient risk-sharing is written in the following manner:

$$\max \ \lambda_1 E[U_1(\tilde{w}_{f_1})] + \lambda_2 E[U_2(w_{02} + P - (1 + \lambda)I(x))]$$

If the insurer is risk neutral, one can define $U(w) = w$. The above problem is then equivalent to:

$$\max \lambda_1 E[U_1(\tilde{w}_{f_1})] + \lambda_2[P - (1 + \lambda)EI(x)]$$

Using the Lagrange method, this problem is itself equivalent to the problem of maximising the expected utility of the insured subject to the constraint that the premium paid be proportional to the actuarial value of the policy, that is, the problem studied in Chapter 10.

References

Borch K. (1962), Equilibrium in a reinsurance market, *Econometrica*, vol. 30, 424–444.

Gollier C. (1991), The economic theory of risk exchanges: a review, in *Contributions to Insurance Economics*, G. Dionne (ed.), Kluwer Academic Press, Boston.

Lemaire J. (1990), Borch's theorem: a historical survey of applications, in *Risk, Information and Insurance*, H. Loubergé (ed.), Kluwer Academic Press, Boston, and Association de Genève.

14

The complete markets model

In Chapter 13, we discussed the way to redistribute risks in an economy to achieve 'the best possible' allocation. This discussion was done without any reference to market structure, thanks to the intervention of a planner. But as we write this, we do not know what is to become of this kind of planned economy.

It is thus important to consider how to construct a system of markets in which economic agents may act freely while achieving a Pareto-efficient risk allocation. This is the goal of the present chapter and Chapter 15. We begin with the help of a model in which there exist enough (risky) assets to achieve any risk allocation by buying and selling only these assets. This is the complete markets model. In Chapter 15, we make an alternative assumption that brings us to the famous model for evaluating financial risks. We observe that, in both cases, when individuals act to maximise their expected utility and when there is perfect competition, the resulting allocation is Pareto efficient. Also, in both cases one can express the equilibrium prices and the resulting outcomes in terms of the firms' investment strategies.

14.1 Markets for contingent claims and arbitrage

We take up again the model from Chapter 13: there are S states of the world with probabilities $p_1, ..., p_S$. To begin, there is no production because we do not introduce firms until Section 14.2.4. There are n individuals indexed by $i = 1, ..., n$. All agents maximise their expected utility, with $U_i(w_{f_i})$ representing the concave utility function of Agent i. The initial endowment is random and is denoted by $w_{0i}(\tilde{s})$. There are no transactions costs.

14.1.1 The basic assumption

Remember the notion of a pure asset, that is a contingent claim, introduced in Chapter 7. In an economy with L physical goods, a contingent claim corresponds to one of these goods delivered in a particular state and only in that state. There are thus LS contingent claims in such an economy. More specifically, in an economy with a single physical good ('money') a pure asset denoted s corresponds to the promise to deliver one physical unit of this good in state s, and only in state s. Thus there can be, at most, S different pure assets in this economy. The complete markets assumption is stated as follows.

> **Assumption 14.1** *Ex ante*, there exist as many different pure assets in the economy as there are realisable states of nature.

Denote the price of the contingent claim s in the corresponding market by Π_s. Assumption 14.1 means that each individual can purchase or sell this pure asset at price Π_s before observing the realisation of the state of the world. This has important implications for the consumption plans $w_{f_i}(\tilde{s})$ that the agents can adopt given the risks.

For example, consider the case of an individual facing a constant endowment w_{0i} in every state, except in state s where a loss L is suffered, implying a lower wealth equal to $w_{0i} - L$. The existence of the market for the contingent claim s allows this risk to be covered by purchasing L units of the relevant pure asset at a total price of $\Pi_s L$. To finance this purchase, P units of each pure asset could be sold with:

$$\sum_{t=1}^{S} P\Pi_t = L\Pi_s \tag{14.1}$$

from which it follows that

$$P = L\Pi_s \Big/ \sum_{t=1}^{S} \Pi_t \tag{14.2}$$

If this trade is made, the agent enjoys complete insurance guaranteeing final wealth of $w_{0i} - P$. Of course, nothing says that this is the consumer's optimal strategy. We will return to this problem later. Note that P can be interpreted as the insurance premium paid to fully cover the risk in question. An insurer who wished to sell this insurance contract would not ask for an insurance premium greater than P. Otherwise, the consumer would prefer to construct their own coverage by participating in the contingent markets and following the strategy presented above.

The numerator of P in Equation (14.2) is the price of the pure asset corresponding to state s; its denominator is the price of guaranteed delivery of one unit regardless of the state of the world. This is the price of the 'sure' good. In what follows, we choose this certain good as numeraire by assigning it a unitary price:

$$\sum_{s=1}^{S} \Pi_s = 1 \tag{14.3}$$

The price of delivery of 1 F with certainty costs 1 F. This means that the interest rate is zero. The introduction of a positive interest rate would not cause any problems. We prefer to opt for a simpler notation, by using Equation (14.3).

We have just formalised the notion of an insurance contract as a 'basket' of contingent claims. One can imagine different baskets, representing different kinds of contracts, such as contracts with co-insurance or deductibles.

This model is thus very rich in possibilities. It is indeed the richest that one can imagine, because it allows all possible risk allocations in the economy. It also allows a simple representation of the assets that are traded in practice. We have just seen the case of the insurance contract. Another example is a common stock. A common stock is a contingent promise of a dividend and a capital gain. This can be formally represented by a random variable $q_j(\tilde{s})$, where j indexes the particular financial asset. The value $q_j(s)$ is defined as the sum of the dividend and the capital gain of asset j in state s. An asset for which the value of q is independent of the state is a risk-free asset.

We will thus represent an asset with a vector $(\mathbf{q}_j(1), \mathbf{q}_j(2), ..., \mathbf{q}_j(S))$. A risk-free asset is thus described by a vector $(\mathbf{q}, \mathbf{q}, ..., \mathbf{q})$, and its price equals $\mathbf{q}$ because it corresponds to $\mathbf{q}$ units of the monetary numeraire. The pure asset s corresponds to a vector composed only of zeros except for a 1 in the sth position: $(0, 0, ..., 0, 1, 0, ..., 0)$. It follows once again that a real asset, such as an insurance contract, is a basket of pure assets. Indeed, in this model, there is no difference between a financial asset and an insurance contract. The financial asset j is a basket containing $q_j(1)$ units of pure asset $s = 1$, $q_j(2)$ units of pure asset $s = 2$, and so on.

14.1.2 The arbitrage argument

The arbitrage argument underlies all of modern financial theory. Based on this reasoning, one can, for example, calculate the equilibrium price of a financial asset from the equilibrium prices of the pure assets. If P_j is the equilibrium price of financial asset j, it must necessarily satisfy:

$$P_j = \sum_{s=1}^{S} q_j(s)\Pi_s \tag{14.4}$$

The right-hand side of this condition is the value of the basket of pure assets that corresponds to the financial asset j. Condition (14.4) follows from a simple arbitrage argument, as does the equilibrium price of an insurance contract. Suppose that P_j were larger than the right-hand side of (14.4). Then one could make a riskless profit by duplicating the financial asset j – that is, by creating the basket of pure assets $[q_j(1), ..., q_j(S)]$ – and selling it on the market as asset j. The cost of this strategy equals the right-hand side of Equation (14.4) while the resulting revenue equals P_j, which is larger. A positive profit is thus achieved without risk, since the portfolio thus created is immediately resold. Any individual, risk averse or risk loving, would adopt this strategy, implying that this situation is inconsistent with (competitive) equilibrium. Conversely, when the price of the financial asset is less than the price of the corresponding basket of pure assets, everyone would wish to buy the financial asset and sell the basket of pure assets.

This may all seem relatively abstract, since contingent claims and pure assets are rarely observed. Whoever heard of the possibility of buying a promise of payment of an indemnity in the case of scholastic failure, as would be desirable from the point of view of a risk-averse student? Who would be willing to insure us against poor sales of this book? Where might I find an asset that would guarantee a given income conditional on the collapse of the world economic system along with the injury of my favourite cyclist just as he is about to win the world championship? Obviously there do not exist contingent markets for the majority of possible events such as these, individual or collective. Fortunately, we will now suggest another approach, which is a bit more convincing. The reader who wishes to get to the essential material on first reading may, however, set this approach aside and skip directly to Section 14.2, accepting Assumption 14.1 as representing the real world.

14.1.3 An equivalent assumption

Assume there exist J financial assets characterised by the vectors $[q_j(s)]$. These could be traded assets (stocks, treasury securities, futures, options, etc.), insurance contracts, horse race wagers or any other form of conditional promises for which markets are observed. There are thus J markets where the different financial assets are traded. We ask whether it is possible to construct portfolios of these financial assets so as to duplicate the contingent payments of the pure assets. Consider an example with three states of the world and three financial assets defined by the following contingent payments:

$$
\begin{aligned}
&\text{asset } j = 1: \ q_1 = (1,1,1)\\
&\text{asset } j = 2: \ q_2 = (0,1,0)\\
&\text{asset } j = 3: \ q_3 = (0,3,-1)
\end{aligned}
\tag{14.5}
$$

Asset 1 is riskless. Assets 2 and 3 can be interpreted as common stocks.

A portfolio is defined by the amount of each of the real assets in the portfolio. Thus the vector $a = (1,1,0)$ represents the portfolio containing one unit of Assets 1 and 2 and no units of Asset 3. The owner of such a portfolio receives 1 F in state 1, paid by Asset 1. Similarly, in state 2, the owner of this portfolio receives an income of 2 F, 1 F from Asset 1 and the other franc from Asset 2. In short, this portfolio provides a contingent income of $1q_1 + 1q_2 + 0q_3 = (1,2,1)$. A portfolio can contain a negative quantity of some assets. In that case the owner is said to be 'short' some assets. The owner of a portfolio $a = (-2,0,0)$ must pay 2 F whatever the state of the world.

It is easy to verify that the pure asset $s = 1$ is duplicated by the portfolio $q_1 = (1, -4, 1)$. Specifically, the random income from such a portfolio equals $q_1 - 4q_2 + q_3 = (1,0,0)$. In this way one can artificially construct the pure asset $s = 1$. An individual who wished to obtain 1 F only in state $s = 1$ could simply acquire this portfolio. In the same way, the pure asset $s = 2$ is duplicated by the portfolio $a_2 = (0, 1, 0)$ because the financial asset $j = 2$ is precisely this pure asset. Finally, the pure asset $s = 3$ corresponds to the portfolio $a_3 = (0, 3, -1)$. In summary, the pure assets can be duplicated by the following portfolios:

$$\text{pure asset } s = 1: \text{portfolio } a_1 = (1, -4, 1)$$
$$\text{pure asset } s = 2: \text{portfolio } a_2 = (0, 1, 0) \qquad (14.6)$$
$$\text{pure asset } s = 3: \text{portfolio } a_3 = (0, 3, -1)$$

The reader can now easily verify that the set of portfolios (14.6), viewed as a 3×3 matrix, is none other than the inverse of the 3×3 matrix of the contingent payments from the real assets. This is natural because this matrix characterises the transformation from the basis of financial assets to the basis of pure assets, where each of these form a basis for the space of consumption plans $[w_f(s = 1), w_f(s = 2), w_f(s = 3)]$. This means that one can construct any consumption plan (expressed as a vector in R^3) either from a portfolio of pure assets or from a portfolio of financial assets. The transformation matrix is the matrix (14.6). Thus, the consumption plan under which one consumes 1 unit in state 1, 6 units in state 2, and nothing in state 3, can be obtained either from a portfolio of pure assets $1 = (1, 6, 0)$ or from a portfolio of real assets $(1, 2, 1)$. It can be verified that the vector $(1, 2, 1)$ is the product of the matrix (14.6) and the vector a. We will not pursue this brief informal presentation any further. It is straightforward for those who have a minimal knowledge of linear algebra.

Nevertheless, an extremely important question is whether it is always possible to move between pure assets and real assets. The answer is negative. Take, for example, an economy composed of only the three following financial assets:

$$\text{asset } j = 1: q_1 = (1, 1, 1)$$
$$\text{asset } j = 2: q_2 = (0, 1, 0) \qquad (14.7)$$
$$\text{asset } j = 3: q_3 = (1, 0, 1)$$

This set of financial assets is insufficient to generate all consumption plans. For example, the reader will search in vain for a portfolio that will generate the consumption plan $(1, 0, 0)$. More generally, it is only possible to generate the consumption plans under which the same amount is consumed in states 1 and 3, because each of the three assets offers the same dividends in these two states. Consequently, these three assets do not form a basis for R^3: the asset $j = 1$ is a linear combination (here, a sum) of the other two. Equivalently, matrix (14.7) is not invertible, in contrast to matrix (14.5).

In summary, the complete contingent markets model is only equivalent to a system of financial markets if there exists a subset of financial assets that forms a basis for R^S. In that case, and only in that case, all the results obtained with the complete contingent markets model have analogous results in a model where only classical financial markets exist. These results are derived by using a pure arbitrage rule. Thus, an assumption that is equivalent to Assumption 14.1 is the following.

Assumption 14.1a There exists a subset of financial assets that form a basis for R^S. In other words, any consumption plan can be generated by a portfolio of financial assets.

Note that this has as corollary that there exist at least as many financial assets as states of the world: $J \geqslant S$.

In what follows, we refer to pure assets rather than real assets. We know how to go from one to the other. For example, having derived the prices Π_s of the pure assets, one can calculate the equilibrium prices of the real financial assets (and of insurance contracts) by using (14.4) to rule out arbitrage. One can also derive the demand for financial assets from the demand for pure assets by using the matrix for transforming the basis.

14.2 Competitive equilibrium and the welfare theorem

Here we impose Assumption 14.1. We will construct a model of markets that will allow us to calculate the individual demands for pure assets as well as their prices in 'equilibrium'. More specifically, we will consider a model of perfect competition: each agent takes the price structure as given and determines the optimal demand for each asset as a function of these prices.

In a market economy, each agent i chooses the demand for pure assets to maximise the expected utility subject to a budget constraint. Financial markets open before the state of the world is realised. This allows risks to be traded. Each agent participates in these markets *ex ante* and buys and sells according to need. Recall that the purchases and sales are exchanges of contingent promises of delivery. The budget constraint is expressed as follows: the cost of the pure assets purchased must equal the total income available at the time of the trades (*ex ante*) plus the revenue generated by the sales of other pure assets. More simply, the value of the net demand for pure assets must equal the available income:

$$\sum_{s=1}^{S} \Pi_s [w_{f_i}(s) - w_{0i}(s)] = R_i \tag{14.8}$$

where R_i denotes agent i's available income at the time of the trades (*ex ante*). Specifically, $w_{f_i}(s) - w_{0i}(s)$ is the net demand for the pure asset s by Agent i. If $w_{f_i}(s) - w_{0i}(s)$ is negative, then the agent supplies asset s. The term $\Pi_s [w_{f_i}(s) - w_{0i}(s)]$ thus equals the economic value of the demand for asset s by agent i. The left-hand side of Equation (14.8) represents the net value of Agent i's demand, which must equal the available income *ex ante*. We assume in what follows, that R_i is zero. This is consistent with the model from Chapter 13 where the only available income was *ex post* income. Thus consumer i's problem is to choose a consumption plan $[w_{f_i}(1), ..., w_{f_i}(S)]$ to maximise:

$$E[U_i(\tilde{w}_{f_i})] = \sum_{s=1}^{S} p_s U_i[w_{f_i}(s)] \qquad (14.9)$$

subject to the constraint that

$$\sum_{s=1}^{S} \Pi_s [w_{f_i}(s) - w_{0i}(s)] = 0 \qquad (14.10)$$

In this problem, the prices Π_s are treated as constants. This results from the assumption that there are a large number of agents participating in each of these markets. Each agent has a negligible effect on the markets and has no power to negotiate prices. The consumer's problem is illustrated in Figure 14.1 for an economy with two states of the world, $s = g$ and $s = b$. The budget line has a slope equal to Π_g/Π_b (in absolute value): this is the additional quantity of the pure asset $s = b$ that can be acquired by selling a unit of the pure asset $s = g$. Note also that the budget line passes through the point that represents the initial endowment, because the individual can always choose not to trade.

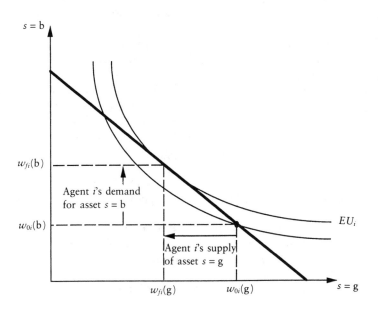

Figure 14.1

Each agent solves their own maximisation problem and goes to the pure asset markets to carry out the purchases and sales dictated by the solution. An equilibrium condition for the markets is that everyone is able to carry out their desired consumption plan:

$$\sum_{i=1}^{n} [w_{f_i}(s) - w_{0i}(s)] = 0 \qquad \text{for all } s = 1, ..., S \qquad (14.11)$$

This condition equates supply and demand in each market. If the aggregate net demand is positive (or negative) in the market for the pure asset s, then there is excess demand (or supply) in this market and some net buyers (or sellers) will be unable to carry out their trading plan. This cannot be an equilibrium because prices would react to this rationing. If aggregate wealth in state s is defined as:

$$w_0(s) = \sum_{i=1}^{n} w_{0i}(s)$$

then Equation (14.11) can be written as:

$$\sum_{i=1}^{n} w_{f_i}(s) = w_0(s) \qquad \text{for all } s = 1, ..., S \qquad (14.11a)$$

The total amount consumed in state s equals the available resources in that state. This is the feasibility condition (13.2) introduced in Chapter 13. A competitive solution thus describes a feasible allocation of the economy's resources.

This describes the model of perfectly competitive financial markets in an exchange model with complete markets. In summary, a system of prices $\{\Pi_s \mid s = 1, ..., S\}$ and an allocation $\{w_{f_i}(s) \mid i = 1, ..., n; \ s = 1, ..., S\}$ describe a competitive allocation if and only if, first, $\{w_{f_i}(s) \mid s = 1, ..., S\}$ solves problem (14.9) given prices Π_s and, second, supply equals demand in each market. This definition is very similar to a model of perfectly competitive physical goods markets without uncertainty. The only notable difference is due to the additive form of the objective function.

14.2.1 Properties of the competitive equilibrium

We begin by solving Agent i's expected utility maximisation problem. We use the Greek letter ξ_i as the Lagrange multiplier corresponding to the budget constraint (14.10). The first-order condition for $w_{f_i}(s)$ is written as follows:

$$p_s U_i'[w_{f_i}(s)] = \xi_i \Pi_s \qquad \text{for all } s = 1, ..., S \text{ and } i = 1, ..., n$$

$$(14.12)$$

The second-order condition requires

$$p_s U_i'' [w_{f_i}(s)] \leqslant 0 \tag{14.13}$$

which is automatically satisfied if risk aversion is assumed. The combination of conditions (14.10), (14.11a), and (14.12) completely describes a competitive solution. This set of equations is a system of $nS + S + n$ equations in $nS + S + n$ unknowns: the nS final levels of consumption $w_{f_i}(s)$, the S prices Π_s and the n Lagrange multipliers ξ_i. Crossing our fingers, we hope there is a solution. By analogy to the model with certainty, we know that there exists an infinity of solutions,[1] which allows us to add a normalisation condition (14.3) to force uniqueness of the solution.

In Figure 14.1, we have also illustrated Agent i's optimal solution. This optimal solution $[w_{f_i}(g), w_{f_i}(b)]$ is classically represented by a point of tangency between the budget line and the indifference curve that passes through the point. The reader will be spared the classical comparative statics analysis – an equal change in $w_{0i}(g)$ and $w_{0i}(b)$ (pure wealth effect), a change in price, etc. – because it is similar, if not identical, to the analysis under certainty. Our goal is, remember, to derive the equilibrium prices and allocation of risks in the economy.

In general, competitive equilibrium prices depend on the individuals' utility functions and the distribution of initial endowments, as well as on the probability distribution of the states. The simplest case to study is undoubtedly the case where there is a risk-neutral individual. Assume, without further loss of generality, that $U_1'(w) = 1$ for all w. Condition (14.12) then implies that the equilibrium price of a pure asset is proportional to the probability that the corresponding state occurs:

$$\Pi_s = p_s / \xi_1$$

Since we have normalised prices so that their sum equals 1, it must be that:

$$1 = \sum_{s=1}^{S} \Pi_s = \sum_{s=1}^{S} p_s / \xi_1 = 1 / \xi_1$$

implying that $\xi_1 = 1$, and thus that

$$\xi_1 = p_s \tag{14.14}$$

When at least one agent in the economy is risk neutral the competitive equilibrium price of a pure asset equals the probability that the corresponding state is realised. Thus, the promise to pay an individual L francs if and only if state s is realised costs $p_s L$ francs in equilibrium. This is precisely the actuarial value of the promise. More generally, due to the non-arbitrage rule (14.4), the price of an asset equals its expected value in equilibrium:

$$P_j = \sum_{s=1}^{S} q_j(s) \Pi_s = \sum_{s=1}^{S} q_j(s) p_s = E(q_j) \tag{14.15}$$

If the price of a risky asset equals the expected value of its dividend, its expected return is zero, by definition. At this price, no riskophobe is prepared to take the risk of holding the asset. Conversely, with the prices of pure assets equal to the probabilities that the corresponding states occur, riskophobes can construct insurance contracts at the actuarial premium. We know that, in this case, riskophobes choose to insure fully against all risks, as is stated in Theorems 10.1 and 10.3. It is easily verified here that riskophobes fully cover themselves at the optimum. This is done by using condition (14.12), which can be written as follows:

$$p_s U_i'[w_{f_i}(s)] = \xi_i p_s$$

After division by p_s, it is clear that the marginal utility of every agent is independent of the states. For the riskophobes, this implies that their final wealth is certain: the randomness faced by the riskophobes is sold to the risk-neutral agents at actuarial cost. In the competitive equilibrium, the riskophobes transform their random wealth into a certain wealth with the same expected value. All the riskophobes attain greater welfare as a result of the trades. Only the risk-neutral agents have unchanged welfare, because they sell the insurance without a loading factor that would guarantee them an expected profit. This is due to the fact that the solution is a competitive one and, thus, the risk-neutral agents cannot gain an economic profit from their positions as insurance sellers.

In the general case, a competitive solution generates an increase in the welfare of all the agents in the society, as can be seen, for example, by analysing Figure 14.1. Specifically, an agent can, at worst retain the same level of welfare as in autarky by refusing to trade. Since the aim is to maximise welfare, a trade will be sought that will increase expected utility. Unfortunately for the risk-neutral agents, their indifference curves are lines that are parallel to their budget lines. As a result, movements along their budget lines do not increase their welfare.

We have just completely characterised a competitive equilibrium for a special case (with at least one risk-neutral agent). The general case is much more difficult to analyse. In Section 14.2.3 below, we present another case that is particularly attractive in terms of its results: it is the quadratic case. Before that we should present a fundamental and well-known property of competitive equilibria; we refer to their efficiency.

14.2.2 The first welfare theorem

We indicated above that in the competitive equilibrium, all risk-averse agents increase their expected utilities. Are all the potential gains from trade exhausted in equilibrium? In other words, is it still possible to find another feasible allocation that increases the expected utility of some without reducing the expected utility of others? More concisely, is the competitive equilibrium

Pareto efficient? It will be proved that one can answer this last question in the affirmative.

Theorem 14.1 Competition in complete financial markets generates a Pareto-efficient allocation of risks in the economy.
Proof To prove this result, it suffices to show that, in equilibrium, all agents have the same marginal rate substitution between consumption in any two states s and t. We know from Chapter 13 that this condition is necessary and sufficient for a feasible allocation to be Pareto efficient (Equation 13.7). Now, this condition is a direct consequence of the first-order condition, Equation (14.12). Specifically, consider this condition for an individual i in states s and t:

$$p_s U_i' [w_{f_i}(s)] = \xi_i \Pi_s$$
$$p_t U_i' [w_{f_i}(t)] = \varepsilon_i \Pi_t$$

Taking the ratio of these two equalities yields:

$$\frac{p_s U_i' [w_{f_i}(s)]}{p_s U_i' [w_{f_i}(s)]} = \frac{\Pi_s}{\Pi_t} \tag{14.16}$$

Now recall that the left-hand side of Equation (14.16) is precisely the marginal rate of substitution between consumption in state s and consumption in state t, as defined by Equation (7.4). We thus have:

$$\mathrm{MRS}_{st}^i = \frac{\Pi_s}{\Pi_t} \tag{14.17}$$

This condition is the mathematical statement of the tangency condition between the indifference curve and the budget line, as it appears in Figure 14.1. If the same steps are taken for Individual j, it can be deduced that

$$\mathrm{MRS}_{st}^j = \frac{\Pi_s}{\Pi_t} \tag{14.17a}$$

These last two conditions are combined in condition (14.17b), which follows:

$$\mathrm{MRS}_{st}^i = \mathrm{MRS}\frac{j}{st} = \frac{\Pi_s}{\Pi_t} \tag{14.17b}$$

The marginal rates of substitution are equal to each other and correspond to the ratio of the pure asset prices in the two states considered. The first part of the previous sentence implies the conclusion that the competitive equilibrium is Pareto efficient. Q.E.D.

In Figure 14.2, the competitive equilibrium for an economy with $n = S = 2$ is illustrated in an Edgeworth box. The competitive equilibrium point belongs

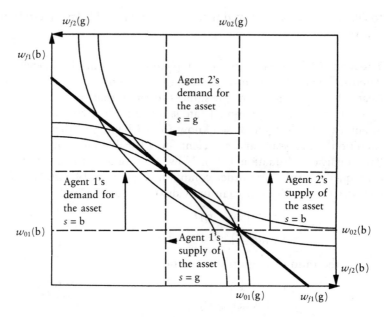

Figure 14.2

to the contract curve representing the locus of Pareto-efficient allocations. The budget line is a line through the point representing the initial endowments. The slope of this line equals Π_g/Π_b (in absolute value). At the competitive allocation, the indifference curves of the agents are tangential, meaning that the MRS values are identical. Each agent's demands and supplies for each asset in equilibrium are also shown. With this budget line, the aggregate net demand for each pure asset is zero. Knowing the slope of this line allows one to calculate the equilibrium prices, using the normalisation rule $\Pi_g + \Pi_b = 1$.

A price system that is not a competitive equilibrium price system, because it does not satisfy the equilibrium condition (14.11), is shown in Figure 14.3. If the trades are made sequentially then Individual 2 does not wish to pass point x coming from w_0. Individual 1, who wishes to trade to point y given the prevailing prices, thus finds that both demand for the pure asset $s = b$ and supply of the pure asset $s = g$ are rationed. Given competition, with a large number of agents of each type, there will be pressure for Π_b to increase and for Π_g to decrease. The slope of the budget line will decrease, closing[2] the gap between x and y that represents the level of rationing.

Finally, the problem where Agent 1 is risk neutral, so that the indifference curves are lines with the same slope as the budget constraint, is illustrated in Figure 14.4. One ends up with the competitive equilibrium solution that was described previously.

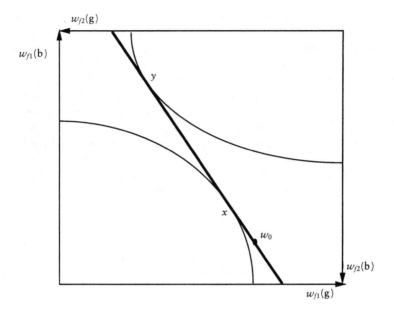

Figure 14.3

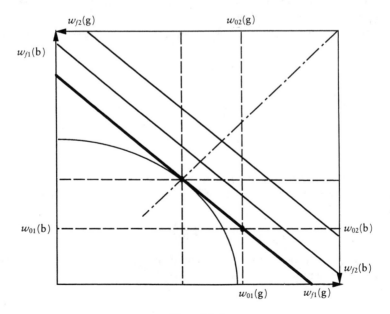

Figure 14.4

This result, called the 'first welfare theorem', has heavily influenced the economic debate, both initially in the models with certainty and later in the models with uncertainty. It allows liberal economists (in the classical sense of the term) to extol competitive markets without outside intervention. Such policies are 'for the best'. A market economy does 'as well' as a planner. The chaos of a system where each individual tries to achieve the selfish objective of personal welfare nevertheless results in an allocation that maximises collective welfare as measured by a weighted sum of individual welfare. Elementary, my dear Adam Smith, with your invisible hand altered to take uncertainty into account. Specifically, as altered by Kenneth Arrow (1953) and Gerard Debreu (1959), who were the first to extend the welfare theorems to economies with uncertainty, in the mid-1950s.

14.2.3 A special case: quadratic utility

In this section we attempt to describe, as completely as possible, the competitive equilibrium when individuals have the quadratic utility function:

$$U_i'(w_{f_i}) = 1 - 2\beta_i w_{f_i} \tag{14.18}$$

We know the limits of such an assumption (Hypothesis 4.1 is not satisfied and the level of prudence is zero, for example). Nevertheless, this example has the advantages of a simple exposition and results that are similar to those of the other classic model of finance: CAPM. So we put our scruples aside temporarily and, to compensate, in Appendix 9 we briefly present the results for negative exponential utility.

In the quadratic case, the first-order condition for the expected utility maximisation problem is:

$$p_s[1 - 2\beta_i w_{f_i}(s)] = \xi_i \Pi_s \tag{14.19}$$

or equivalently, after dividing by p_s and $2\beta_i$,

$$\frac{1}{2\beta_i} - w_{f_i}(s) = \frac{\xi_i}{2\beta_i} \frac{\Pi_s}{p_s} \qquad \text{for all } s = 1, \dots, S \text{ and } i = 1, \dots, n \tag{14.19a}$$

Taking a particular individual i, sum Equation (14.19) over all $s = 1, \dots, S$. Due to the linearity of marginal utility and the normalisation (14.3), this yields:

$$1 - 2\beta_i E(\tilde{w}_{f_i}) = \xi_i \qquad \text{for all } i = 1, \dots, n$$

Recall that the left-hand side of this equality equals $2\beta_i T_{a_i}$, where T_{a_i} is the absolute risk tolerance measured at $E(\tilde{w}_{f_i})$. It follows that:

$$\frac{\xi_i}{2\beta_i} = T_{a_i} \qquad \text{for all } i = 1, \dots, n \tag{14.20}$$

Now reconsider the first-order condition (14.19a) and sum over all $i = 1, ..., n$ for a given s. From Equation (14.20), the equilibrium condition (14.11a), and the linearity of marginal utility, this method allows us to write:

$$\sum_{i=1}^{n} \frac{1}{2\beta_i} - w_0(s) = \frac{\Pi_s}{p_s} \sum_{i=1}^{n} T_{a_i} \qquad \text{for all } s = 1, ..., S$$

Defining $T_a = \Sigma_{i=1}^{n} T_{a_i}$ and $c = \Sigma_{i=1}^{n} (1/2\beta_i)$, we can write:

$$\Pi_s = p_s T_a^{-1} [c - w_0(s)]$$

Finally, since the sum of the Π_s must equal 1, the summation of the previous equality over all s implies that:

$$1 = T_a^{-1} [c - E(\tilde{w}_0)]$$

Eliminating c from the last two equations implies:

$$\Pi_s = p_s [1 - T_a^{-1} \{w_0(s) - E(\tilde{w}_0)\}] \qquad \text{for all } s = 1, ..., S$$

$$(14.21)$$

This equation is fundamental: it describes the competitive equilibrium price of pure assets. The price is a function of two contingent variables and one parameter. The two contingent variables are the probability that the state is realised and the difference between realised aggregate wealth and mean aggregate wealth. The parameter is the economy's level of absolute risk tolerance. We consider each element in turn.

1. *The probability that the state is realised.* All other things equal, the price of a pure asset is proportional to the probability that the corresponding state is realised. In two states, s and t, that exhibit the same aggregate wealth, the price of the pure asset s is double that of the pure asset t if $p_s = 2p_t$. It can be shown that this property holds independently of the form of the utility functions. Thus it is possible to define a competitive price per probability unit: Π_s/p_s.

2. *The aggregate wealth in the state.* All other things equal, the price of a pure asset is a decreasing linear function of aggregate wealth in the corresponding state. This is a reflection of the economic phenomenon that the price of a good depends positively on its relative scarcity. If there exists a state in which aggregate wealth equals the *ex ante* mean of aggregate wealth, then the price of the corresponding pure asset equals the probability that the state is realised: its price is its actuarial value. When w_0 exceeds its *ex ante* expected value, the price of the pure asset is less than its actuarial value. Conversely, when w_0 is less than its *ex ante* expected value, the price of the pure asset is greater than its actuarial value.

3. *The level of absolute risk tolerance in the economy T_a.* The sensitivity of the price per probability unit (Π_s/p_s) to changes in the economy's

aggregate wealth equals the inverse of the absolute risk tolerance in the economy. An increase in aggregate wealth of 1 F reduces the price per probability unit of a pure asset by T_a^{-1} francs. The greater the risk tolerance of the pool is, the smaller is the dispersion of prices per probability unit around their mean of one. If there exists a risk neutral individual in the pool, the absolute risk tolerance of the pool is infinite because all risk is efficiently transferred to that individual. In that case, there is no dispersion in the prices per probability unit and $\Pi_s = p_s$ for all s. All prices are actuarial.

For completeness, it can be verified that with this system of contingent prices, the share of the aggregate risk borne by a member of the pool equals the share borne in the Pareto framework. Specifically, rewrite condition (14.19a) in the following form:

$$w_{f_i}(s) = \frac{1}{2\beta_i} - T_{a_i} \frac{\Pi_s}{p_s}$$

$$= \frac{1}{2\beta_i} - T_{a_i}[1 - T_a^{-1}\{w_0(s) - E(\tilde{w}_0)\}]$$

$$= k_i + \frac{T_{a_i}}{T_a} w_0(s) \tag{14.22}$$

Note that the final wealth of an agent depends only on the aggregate wealth in the economy, as required by the mutuality principle. Furthermore, i's share of the aggregate risk equals i's absolute tolerance expressed as a percentage of the risk tolerance of the pool. What is new here relative to Chapter 13 is that we have found a decentralised risk allocation mechanism that generates this property. Each agent, given the prices of the financial assets, accepts and indeed wishes to bear a Pareto-efficient share of the risks. In addition, the value of k_i is endogenous to the model, but its calculation is of little pedagogical interest.

Another important consequence of the structure of the equilibrium prices of pure assets comes from the ability to calculate the equilibrium prices of real financial assets. Formula (14.4), the non-profitable arbitrage condition, allows us to verify that:

$$P_j = \sum_{s=1}^{S} q_j(s)\Pi_s$$

$$= \sum_{s=1}^{S} p_s q_j(s)[1 - T_a^{-1}\{w_0(s) - E(\tilde{w}_0)\}]$$

$$= \mu_j - T_a^{-1} \sum_{s=1}^{S} p_s q_j(s)\{w_0(s) - E(\tilde{w}_0)\}$$

$$= \mu_j - \text{cov}(\tilde{q}_j, \tilde{w}_0)/T_a \tag{14.23}$$

where μ_j is the expected value of income $\tilde{q}_j$ and $\text{cov}(\tilde{q}_j, \tilde{w}_0)$ is the covariance between the income generated by the asset (dividend plus capital gain) and the aggregate income of the economy.

In equilibrium, the price of a financial asset equals the expected value of its future income minus a risk premium. The importance of this formula lies in the calculation of the equilibrium risk premium. We are already acquainted with the risk premium that allows each individual to evaluate a risk. In other words, we are already acquainted with the risk premium that allows calculation of the *use value* of a risk. In the present context, as a first approximation, it equals half the ratio of variance of the risk to the individual's risk tolerance (see the Arrow–Pratt formula). In calculating the equilibrium price of a risk, we derive its *economic value*, rather than its use value. There is thus a 'market risk premium' and a 'use risk premium'. The latter notion is specific to an individual and can thus differ from individual to individual.

The market risk premium is common to all the agents and it equals the ratio of covariance between the income generated by the asset and the aggregate income w_0 to the absolute tolerance of the efficient pool made up of all economic agents. Consequently, two elements distinguish the market risk premium from the use risk premium.

1. *Risk tolerance*. Rather than considering the individual absolute tolerance, we consider the sum represented by T_a. Because all risk is efficiently shared by members of the pool, the absolute tolerance of the market is reduced. When there exists a risk-neutral agent in the market, the risk premium of the market is zero because the tolerance of the market is infinite: all risk is 'purchased' by the risk-neutral individual. In this case, equilibrium prices are actuarial, as was said before.

2. *The level of risk*. Instead of variance, the covariance between the income from the asset and the aggregate income w_0 is taken as the measure of risk. *A priori*, it may seem paradoxical that there is no market risk premium associated with a risky asset that is not correlated with aggregate income. The reason is that the risk associated with such an asset is completely diversifiable in private portfolios which are, recall, perfectly correlated with w_0 (condition (14.22)). Since it is completely diversifiable, the risk of a portfolio is not increased when its share of this asset is augmented. In equilibrium, there can be no market risk premium for this asset ($P_j = \mu_j$) because otherwise everyone would wish to increase the holdings of this asset in their portfolio. In contrast, when there is a positive correlation between q_j and w_0, an increase in the holdings of asset j increases the risk in the agents' portfolios. To induce them to hold this asset, one must offer them a risk premium by reducing the asking price below μ_j. Finally, when the correlation between the return to asset j and w_0 is negative, an increase in the holdings of this asset in the agents'

portfolios reduces their risk. To equilibrate supply and demand, this asset's price must thus exceed μ_j, by a cost that reduces the expected return ($\mu_j/P_j < 1$), in order to offset the benefit of risk reduction from holding the asset.

We will not go much farther in the analysis of this model, because its main results reappear in similar form in Chapter 15. To conclude, we point out that this technique can also be applied for insurance pricing. An individual who wishes to sell an initial endowment $w_{0i}(\tilde{s})$ on the market can get a price equal to:

$$P_i = E\left[w_{0i}(\tilde{s})\right] - \frac{\text{cov}\left[w_{0i}(\tilde{x}), w_0(\tilde{s})\right]}{T_a} \tag{14.23a}$$

If an individual holds initial wealth that is not correlated with aggregate wealth, then this individual can sell the endowment *ex ante* for a price equal to its expected value. In this case, certain final wealth is enjoyed of $E\left[w_{0i}(\tilde{s})\right]$. To attract this consumer, an insurer must offer an actuarial premium for this full insurance contract. More generally, *formula (14.23a) represents the competitive equilibrium insurance premium of the risk* w_{0i}, for full coverage. In particular, the competitive insurance premium is actuarially unfavourable (positive loading factor) if the risk to the insurer is positively correlated with the market risk. For an interesting development of this kind of reasoning, the reader may refer to D'Arcy and Doherty (1988).

14.2.4 Investment decisions and market information

Until now, we have considered an exchange economy, that is, an economy without production and thus without firms. The introduction of a production process and of firms into the analysis is, of course, a necessary step. Since we present the elements of this problem in the framework of CAPM in Chapter 15, we limit ourselves here to the analysis of some important points regarding the investment decisions of firms under uncertainty.

This problem was already mentioned in Chapter 11 for the case of a firm owned by a single individual, so that the profit of the firm also constituted the income of the individual. We will now consider the case of a joint stock company where the profits are distributed proportionally to the number of shares held when dividends are paid. In addition, each shareholder can at any time sell shares at the market price.

A firm is completely described by the structure of share ownership and by its production function. For simplicity, we consider firms with a single factor of production: capital. The volume of production from a capital investment of size a is random and can thus be described by the function $f_j(a, s)$. This specification typically represents a technological uncertainty. Firms are created at the beginning of the period. The shareholders contribute capital

proportionally to their shares. The collected capital corresponds to an investment of size a. The investments are made before the state of the world is
known. After the state of the world is observed, production begins.

If firms sold their production *ex post*, we would be back to the models
studied in Chapter 11 with technological uncertainty and price uncertainty,
and with the additional problem of determining the objective function of a
joint stock company that does not have a single owner. To simplify, it suffices
to cast the problem in the framework presented in this chapter: the complete
markets model. *Firms, rather than sell* ex post, *sell their production* ex ante
on contingent markets.[3] Given the prices of the pure assets, the profit of firm
j choosing investment a equals:

$$\pi_j(a) = \sum_{s=1}^{S} \Pi_s f_j(a, s) - a \tag{14.24}$$

Note that in the quadratic model presented previously, this formulation is
equivalent to:

$$\pi_j(a) = E[f_j(a)] - \frac{\text{cov}[f_j(a), w_0]}{T_a} - a \tag{14.24a}$$

This profit is certain. This can be interpreted as an insurance policy for
the firm, since a contingent market is a special case of insurance markets: the
first term on the right-hand side of Equation (14.24) is the price of the insured
future revenue flow $f(a, s)$. In the absence of uncertainty regarding the profit
thus insured, there is no associated risk premium. Such a risk premium would
have had to be measured differently for each shareholder according to their
risk aversion. Thus one problem is solved: everyone's evaluation of this
project, and thus the market's evaluation as well, equals $\pi_j(a)$. An individual
who wishes to buy this firm and its profits after the investment has been
decided but before s is known would have to pay $\pi_j(a)$ under competition. In
summary, $\pi_j(a)$ is the economic value of the firm *ex ante*; it is also the use
value for all the shareholders. Each shareholder wishes to maximise $\pi_j(a)$ in
order to maximise wealth without additional risk, whatever the attitude
towards risk or the share in the ownership of the firm. *There is unanimity for
the choice of the investment* a^* *that satisfies the first-order condition of the
maximisation problem for* $\pi_j(a)$:

$$\sum_{s=1}^{S} \Pi_s \frac{\partial f_j(a^*, s)}{\partial a} = 1 \tag{14.25}$$

With complete contingent markets, all investment has a non-random market
value. To maximise the welfare of its shareholders, a firm need only maximise
the market value of its investments. By maximising the market value of the
shares held by the shareholders, the firm achieves unanimous approval for its
decisions at shareholder meetings. The shareholders thus obtain the maximum
risk-free benefit either by sharing the profit or by selling their shares.

Consequently, firms need only one piece of information to make their decisions: the equilibrium prices of the pure assets Π_s. That knowledge permits the unambiguous calculation of the unanimously desired value of a^*. The decision-maker's problem is thus greatly simplified: there is no need to know the characteristics of the shareholders. If there are no pure assets, the prices Π_s that are needed can be derived by observing the prices of assets that prevail in financial markets that satisfy Assumption 14.1a. The way to obtain these implicit prices was presented previously. One can thus summarise the firm's decision-maker's problem as follows:

(a) observation of the equilibrium prices of the financial assets P_j;
(b) calculation of the implicit prices Π_s of the pure assets;
(c) calculation of the certain profit $\pi_j(a)$;
(d) calculation of a^* that maximises the certain profit.

Once again, this model may seem very abstract: firms that sell their future production on contingent markets are rarely observed. The reason is that contingent markets are incomplete. When markets are incomplete, the move from Step a to Step b is impossible for the producer, as we will show by example in the following section. This has as a corollary that the profit of firms is random and therefore, that there is not necessarily unanimity among share-holders regarding the decisions to be made. Firms are thus concerned about risk-taking. What decision rules should be suggested to producers in this case? This question is open; different schools of thought are still wrestling with it.[4]

Here, then, is a difficult question: what happens when markets are incomplete? This question is analysed in more detail in the following section in the context of an exchange economy.

14.3 Incomplete markets: an introduction

Return to the example of the three assets (14.7) in an economy with $S = 3$. We know that this set of markets is incomplete. Assume that the competitive equilibrium prices of these assets are $P_1 = 3$, $P_2 = 1$ and $P_3 = 2$. Since the sum of the two assets $j = 2$ and $j = 3$ yields the same structure of contingent income as asset $j = 1$, it must be that $P_2 + P_3 = P_1$ to rule out profitable arbitrage. Since it is impossible to construct a portfolio with the same structure of contingent revenues as $q = (1, 0, 0)$, it is impossible to derive the value of Π_1 by observing P_1, P_2 and P_3. Individuals (as well as firms) are thus unable to solve their problem as expressed in Equation (14.9). What can they do?

Consider the extreme case where there is no possibility of transferring income from one state of the world to another, either through contingent markets or through financial markets. In this case there is no possibility of trade, either *ex ante* or *ex post*, in our model with a single good. Each agent consumes their endowment $w_0(s) = w_f(s)$. There is no possible transfer of risk in such an economy and the corresponding allocation of risks is Pareto inefficient with probability 1: neither the mutuality principle, nor the rule of sharing risks proportionally to absolute risk tolerance can be satisfied. *In a very general way, when markets are incomplete, the competitive solution is not Pareto efficient.*

Why are markets incomplete? There are many answers to this question. The simplest relies on the existence of transactions costs that are greater than the marginal benefit generated by a new contingent market. A more complicated explanation rests on the existence of asymmetric information between buyers and sellers. This point is analysed in detail in Chapter 16.

In the rest of this section, we present three methods for improving the allocation of risks in the economy: opening new markets to reduce incompleteness; constructing private agreements to mitigate the deficiencies of the markets; and finally controlling prices on spot markets.

14.3.1 Reducing market incompleteness

Undoubtedly the simplest way to reduce the inefficiency of markets due to their incompleteness is to open new markets, hoping that these will offer new opportunities for risk-sharing. The explosion of new financial products (options, for example) in the 1980s is undoubtedly consistent with this strategy: firms and individuals found new ways to manage and transfer their risks by participating in these markets.

As an example, consider an economy with two states of the world and a single financial asset with liquidation value $q(s = g) = 3$ in the good state and $q(s = b) = 1$ in the bad state. Markets are obviously incomplete in such an economy because $J < S$.

Now open a 'call' option market where the underlying asset is the one described above. A call is the right, but not the obligation, to acquire the underlying asset at a predetermined price, called the strike price. Consider a call with a strike price of 2. *Ex post*, if the good state is realised ($s = g$), the holder of the call will exercise their right. This will generate a profit of $3 - 2 = 1$, because a price of 2 must be paid (the strike price) to acquire the asset that is sold for 3. The call is said to be 'in the money' in that state. In contrast, in the bad state, the holder of the call certainly does not exercise their right because the asset would cost 2 but could only be sold for 1: the option is said to be 'out of the money'. The income from the call in the bad state is thus zero. The random income from the call is therefore $q(s = b) = 1$ in the good state and $q(s = m) = 0$ in the bad state.

Taking into consideration both the market for the underlying asset and the market for the option, one perceives that the markets are complete. Specifically, the income matrix

underlying asset: 3 1
option: 1 0

is invertible. If the price of the underlying asset is 2.5 and if the price of the call is 0.25, it can be verified that the implicit prices of the pure assets[5] are $\Pi_g = 0.25$ and $\Pi_b = 1.75$. Observing such market prices will permit economic agents to solve their maximisation problems.

14.3.2 Explicit and implicit contracts

If some contingent markets do not exist, some mutually beneficial exchanges cannot be accomplished: the competitive allocation is inefficient. In the simplest case, two risk-averse agents have final outcomes that are perfectly negatively correlated. The loss of mutual benefit due to the incompleteness of markets is evident here and it is clear that the discovery of this fact would induce the two agents to negotiate a *private* contract to share these risks. The same reasoning can be applied to a risk-neutral agent who negotiates a contract to transfer risk from an individual whose final wealth is random in an incomplete economy. In both cases, it is possible to construct a contract that increases the expected utility of both agents, who share the social benefit of the exchange. This is domain of the *theory of contracts*. Agents privately organise a Pareto-efficient risk-sharing arrangement in the form of insurance and reinsurance contracts as well as a large number of commercial contracts such as lines of credit, mortgage loans, commercial franchises, etc. The technique of interest rate swaps between firms facing flows of debt reimbursement also comes to mind.

The *theory of implicit contracts*, principally applied to labour and credit markets, is more complex. A survey of this literature has been done by S. Rosen (1985). With this approach, contracts are not explicitly written and thus are not enforceable: one cannot go to court if one party or the other breaks the implicit terms of the contract. The technique is nevertheless similar. However, the agreement must be such that each party always has the incentive to meet any implicit obligations under the agreement. This condition is called the incentive compatibility constraint This constraint leads to a Pareto-inefficient solution, because the Pareto-efficient solutions generally violate the incentive compatibility constraint. In other words, at the efficient solutions, one party or other will have an incentive to break the implicit agreement or to cheat. Deviations from Pareto efficiency are thus necessary to remove the risk that the contract will be broken.

14.3.3 Spot price rigidity

A third possibility for reducing market inefficiency would be intervention by a regulator or a planner. In the 'best' of cases, an enlightened planner (in the classical sense of the term) who is extremely ingenious, trustworthy and dictatorial, could impose a Pareto-efficient solution by transferring wealth among agents in each state. This is, by the way, the point of view of Chapter 13.

Of course, such an 'ideal' planner does not exist; for one thing, our govern-
ments are unstable and are not always enlightened nor ingenious; for another,
dictatorial planning reduces incentives and is thus inefficient and inexorably
leads to chaos. It follows that a solution of forced exchanges at set prices and
quantities does not really make any sense.

In contrast, regulating only prices makes a lot more sense. The planner,
rather than controlling all exchanges *ex post*, could decide to let agents freely
choose the quantities they wish to trade on spot markets where trades take
place *ex post*, but could fix the prices at which agents may trade goods on
these markets. While in the first system with imposed transfers the number of
variables to control equals nS (the transfers across n agents in the S states), the
second system requires control of only S variables (the spot prices). This is a
major simplification in an economy made up of several million individuals.
This system corresponds much more to the realities of our modern economies:
the state more or less controls some prices; it does not control the quantities
traded at those prices. For example, a government may more or less control
salaries but it does not control employment, which is left to the discretion of
the employers.

To fix ideas, consider a relatively simple example in which there exist only
spot markets. Consider an exchange economy with two available goods:
money and another good. Indeed, to observe the *ex post* exchanges, that is,
the spot markets, one must consider an economy that contains at least one
economic good that is traded for money. In this example, the economy is
composed of two types of agents.

1. Agents of type $i = 1$ are risk neutral and have w_{01} monetary units in
    each state of the world. In contrast, they initially have no units of the
    other good. They can nevertheless acquire some on the spot market
    (*ex post*) at a price of $P(s)$ per unit. The consumption of q units of
    this good in state s generates an increase in welfare of $sg(q)$, expressed
    in monetary units, with $g'(q) > 0$ and $g''(q) < 0$. Thus final welfare in
    state s when q is consumed corresponds to:

    $$w_{f1}(s) = w_{01} + sg(q) - P(s)q \qquad (14.26)$$

    expressed in monetary units. The utility of consumption is random.
    This randomness is captured by the random variable s, which takes on
    non-negative values.[6] Here the state of the world directly affects the
    individual's utility (state-dependent utility function), whereas before it
    only affected each individual's endowment. For example, the utility of
    an umbrella depends on the state of the world (s then measures rain-
    fall), just as does the utility of an ice cream cone or a cold beer (when
    s measures air temperature).
2. Individuals of type $i = 2$ are risk averse with a concave utility function
    $U_2(w_{f2})$. They initially have w_{02} monetary units and one unit of the

good in each state. They get no utility from consuming the good and thus want to sell it on the market.

Furthermore, there are k Type 2 individuals for each Type 1 individual. The supply of goods in each state is thus completely inelastic and equals k per Type 1 individual. In contrast, a Type 1 individual's demand depends on price P and the state s. The demand function $q^d(P,s)$ satisfies the maximisation condition for w_{f1} in each state:

$$sg'(q^d) = P(s) \tag{14.26a}$$

It is easy to show that q^d is a decreasing function of P. Specifically, differentiation of this equation with respect to P yields:

$$sg''(q^d) \frac{\partial q^d}{\partial P} = 1 \tag{14.27}$$

Since the second derivative of $g(q)$ is negative (satiation), it must be that q^d is decreasing in P. The elasticity of demand is defined as:

$$\eta^d(P,s) = \frac{P}{q^d(P,s)} \frac{\partial q^d}{\partial P} = \frac{sg'[q^d(P,s)]}{sq^d(P,s)g''[q^d(P,s)]}$$

$$= \frac{g'(q^d(P,s))}{q^d(P,s)g''[q^d(P,s)]}$$

It will be assumed in what follows that this elasticity is constant, implying that $g'(q) = \eta^d q g''(q)$ for all q. Of course η^d is negative.

We will limit ourselves to analysing a system without contingent markets, but with a spot market where the good trades for money *after* the state of the world is observed. This is indeed a different model from the one analysed for complete markets where contingent promises were traded *before* the state of the world was observed. The competitive equilibrium on each spot market is described in Figure 14.5. For each state s_i there is a demand curve $q^d(P, s_i)$ and a competitive equilibrium point represented by the intersection of the supply and demand curves.

It turns out that at the competitive equilibrium characterised by the trade $q^c(s)$ and price $P^c(s)$, all Type 2 agents sell their units of the good: $q^c(s) = k$. This is desirable in terms of resource allocation because Type 2 agents do not benefit from holding the good while Type 1 agents always derive a positive marginal utility from it. *It is said that a system of competitive spot markets generates an efficient allocation of resources*, ex post.

In contrast, the allocation of risks is inefficient *ex ante*. The equilibrium prices $P^c(s)$ are random, as is shown in Figure 14.5. More specifically, condition (14.26) implies that:

$$P^c(s) = sg'(k) = s \tag{14.28}$$

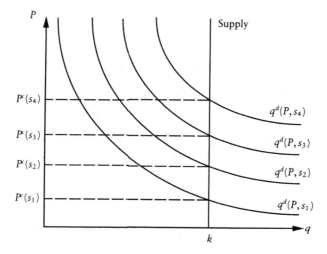

Figure 14.5

assuming, without loss of generality, that $g'(k) = 1$. Now, Type 1 agents are risk neutral; this implies that they should optimally bear all the risk. This is not the case, however, because the final wealth of Type 2 agents is random and can be written as $w_{f2}(s) = w_{02} + P^c(s) = w_{02} + s$. It is said that *a system of competitive spot markets generates a Pareto-inefficient risk allocation, ex ante*.

In such a system without contingent markets and without private contracts between Type 1 and Type 2 agents guaranteeing a fixed price, one can imagine the intervention of a planner fixing prices $P(s)$ on the spot markets and letting the agents buy and sell at this price, *ex post*. The naive solution would be to impose a constant price P_0 to fully insure the risk-averse agents against price variability. Alas, this is not a good solution. Specifically, consider a case s where the competitive price $P^c(s)$ is less than P_0, as represented in Figure 14.6. In this case, the price is 'too high' so it induces Type 1 buyer to reduce demand below k, given the weak desire there is in this state for consumption of the good. In such a situation, some Type 2 sellers would not be able to sell. The probability of finding a buyer is exactly $q^d(P_0, s)/k < 1$. The sellers would thus face a risk in state s; they would receive income equal to $w_{02} + P_0$ with probability $q^d(P_0, s)/k$ and w_{02} otherwise.

Though the planner initially wished to insure the incomes of Type 2 agents by fixing a constant price, a different kind of risk was created. Furthermore, the price rigidity created an inefficiency in the resource allocation *ex post*, because Type 1 individuals do not receive all of the good which provides them positive marginal utility in that state while some Type 2 agents hold the good even though it gives them no utility. It is thus doubtful that such a policy of price controls is the best way to guarantee the sellers' income.

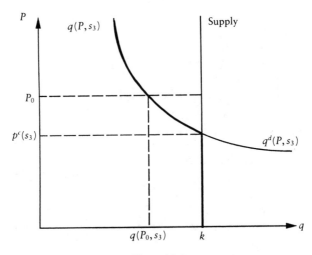

Figure 14.6

The problem of a planner who controls only prices $P(s)$ can be described as follows. As in Chapter 13, it is a matter of finding a solution in which it is impossible to increase the expected utility of one type of agent without reducing the expected utility of the other. The only difference is that the solution is a policy of controlling spot prices rather than a policy of controlling the quantities that are transferred. We know that the search for such a solution boils down to maximising a weighted sum of expected utilities, with strictly positive weights λ_i; at the solution that corresponds to the maximum of the weighted sum, it is impossible by definition to find another plan that will increase everyone's expected utility. We thus write:

$$\max \left\{ \lambda_1 E\left[w_{01} + sg\left[q(P(s), s)\right] - P(s)q(P(s), s)\right] \right.$$
$$\left. + \lambda_2 E\left[\frac{q(P(s), s)}{k} U_2(w_{02} + P(s)) + \frac{k - q(P(s), s)}{k} U_2(w_{02})\right]\right\}$$

$$(14.29)$$

The planner's decision variables are, of course, the spot prices $P(s)$. The function $q(P, s)$ represents the quantities freely exchanged on the market in state s if price P is imposed. It is easily shown that the traded quantities are equal to the minimum of supply and demand:

$$q(P, s) = \min\{q^d(P, s), k\} \qquad (14.30)$$

This function is represented by the solid line in Figure 14.6, for $s = s_3$. When P exceeds $P^c(s_3)$, Type 1 agents demand less than k and some sellers are rationed. In contrast, when P is less than $P^c(s_3)$ only k is supplied while demand exceeds k, so demanders are rationed: each demander finds only k units on the spot market (assuming the same rationing across demanders).

The second term in the planner's objective is the expected utility of the representative Type 2 agent. There are two sources of uncertainty: the first has to do with the state that will be realised; this is what the expected value operator captures. The second has to do with the risk of not being able to sell. The probability of selling a unit of the good equals $q(P(s), s)/k$ in state s, in which case there is an income of $w_{02} + P(s)$. A solution to the planner's problem, Equation (14.29), is called a 'second best solution', because there are not as many possibilities for risk-sharing as in the complete markets model.

We prove the following theorem in Appendix 10.

Theorem 14.2 A second-best solution has the property that the planner fixes two price limits, $P_{\min}$ and $P_{\max}$ with $P_{\min} < P_{\max}$. The optimal price control policy follows the following rule: if, in state s,

(a) $P^c(s)$ exceeds $P_{\max}$ then the price $P(s)$ is fixed at $P_{\max}$;
(b) $P^c(s)$ is less than $P_{\min}$ then the price $P(s)$ is fixed at $P_{\min}$;
(c) $P^c(s)$ is between $P_{\min}$ and $P_{\max}$ then the price $P(s)$ is fixed at $P^c(s)$.

Furthermore $P_{\min}$ and $P_{\max}$ satisfy the following condition:

$$- \eta^d \frac{U_2(w_{02} + P_{\min}) - U_2(w_{02})}{P_{\min}}$$

$$= U_2'(w_{02} + P_{\min}) - U_2'(w_{02} + P_{\max}) \quad (14.31)$$

In summary, the planner's optimal price policy is to impose a minimal spot price and a maximal spot price. If the competitive equilibrium price on the spot market lies in this interval, the planner does not intervene. If the spot price exceeds $P_{\max}$ then the planner caps the trading price at $P_{\max}$. Conversely, if the spot price falls below the floor $P_{\min}$, the spot price is held at $P_{\min}$. In this case, the suppliers of the good are rationed: some of the sellers do not find counterparts on the market at the controlled price. The policy is thus an extremely simple one for which it is sufficient to observe the competitive price and intervene as a function of this price and the imposed bounds. Such a price control policy is represented in Figure 14.7.

Consequently, a second-best optimum with controlled spot prices does not achieve an efficient allocation of risks because, on the one hand, the price is random even if it is contained in a more or less narrow band, and on the other hand, there exists the risk of rationing in some states. Similarly, this policy does not achieve an efficient allocation of resources in all states: when $P^c(s)$ is less than $P_{\min}$ the socially desirable transfer of the good from Type 2 to Type 1 agents is incomplete. Globally, the second-best optimum constitutes

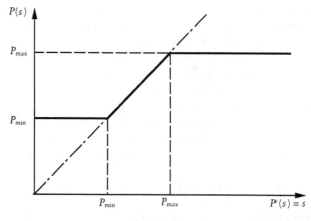

Figure 14.7

the best compromise between the objectives of efficient risk allocation *ex ante* and efficient resource allocation *ex post*.

This compromise is reflected in the relationship (14.31) which links P_{min} and P_{max}. For quadratic utility, it is shown in Appendix 10 that this formula is equivalent to the following:

$$P_{max} - P_{min} = -\eta^d T_{a2} \tag{14.32}$$

where T_{a2} is the risk tolerance of Type 2 individuals evaluated at $w_{02} + 0.5 P_{min}$. The maximum variability accepted by the planner equals the product of the demand elasticity (in absolute value) and the absolute risk tolerance of the sellers. When their risk tolerance is low, the planner emphasises insuring the risk from spot price variability by decreasing the spread. Similarly, when the demand elasticity is low, the price controls have a relatively weak effect on rationing, thus permitting the planner to reduce the spread.

From this we conclude that, when markets are incomplete, some price rigidity is Pareto superior to a system where spot prices freely fluctuate with changes in supply and demand. The intuition for this result is that when financial markets do not efficiently do their work of transferring risk, fixing market prices for goods plays a positive role in risk-sharing in the economy.

We conclude this section with the following remark: rather than interpreting the model presented here as a model of an exchange economy without production, one can consider the non-monetary good as an input in a production process that is owned by Type 1 agents. The function g is then a production function using input q and s is the random output price on foreign markets. This input can be labour or capital, loaned by Type 2 individuals who initially own it to Type 1 individuals acting as entrepreneurs.

To reduce the market uncertainty due to the price variability, attempts have often been made to fix prices outside of the rules of competition. This is true, for example, for foreign exchange, credit, agriculture and even labour markets (minimum wages, etc.) which play a central role in our modern economies. If only these external price controls are implemented, it is clear from the above discussion that risk is not necessarily reduced because another kind of uncertainty is implicitly created. Specifically, by preventing the equilibration of supply and demand, one creates random quantity rationing: the farmer does not know whether all of the production will be sold at the imposed price; the unskilled worker does not know whether a job can be found at the minimum wage; the newspaper vendor may find some unsold inventory left. Thus price rigidity does not necessarily reduce risk. What kind of risk, price risk or quantity risk, is preferred by riskophobes? Would households rather not know tomorrow's salary in exchange for secure employment, or would they choose fixed salaries with a risk of unemployment? Recent work,[7] from which we have just presented the central result, has demonstrated that an intermediate solution with a minimum price and a maximum price is optimal. Complementary mechanisms must then be established to compensate the rationed individuals: reimbursement of the vendor's unsold newspapers, unemployment insurance, purchase of surplus agricultural product by the government, etc. This analysis would carry us beyond the scope of this book.

Exercises

14.1 In an exchange economy with two risk-averse individuals homogeneity of beliefs about the likelihood of any state and no social risk, prove that $\Pi_s = p_s$ so that the value of any financial security is equal to its expected outcome. Explain intuitively why such a result holds.

14.2 Return to the data of Exercise 13.3 and assume there are now markets for contingent claims in each of the two states of the world.

Questions
(a) If the individuals have no other resource than their initial wealth endowment ($R_i = 0$) write down their demand equation for contingent claims in each state.
(b) Express the equilibrium price Π_b and Π_g and show that at this equilibrium price, one reaches a Pareto-efficient risk-sharing arrangement. Why are Π_b and Π_g different from p_b and p_g?
(c) Although you are not allowed to use Equation (14.21) directly – since it applies to quadratic utilities – show nevertheless that in accordance with that equation the sign of the difference between Π_b and p_b is linked to that of the difference between $W_0(b)$ and $E(\tilde{W}_0)$.

(d) Returning to (b) compute the equilibrium price of a partial insurance contract against the loss of 2 $(3 - 1)$ undergone by Individual 1 in state b that would 'mimic' the solution reached through the complete market of contingent claims.

(e) How much should one pay for a risky prospect giving 0.50 unit of wealth under state b and 0.75 unit of wealth under state g. Why is the price below the expected value of the prospect? Design a risky asset such that its price will exceed its expected value. Relate your discussion to Equation (14.23) by computing the covariance between the return of the risky asset and the collective risk.

14.3 Consider an economy with two agents $i = 1, 2$ and

$$u_1(w) = \sqrt{w}; \ u_2(w) = \ln w$$

There are two possible states of nature $s = 1, 2$, with $p_1 = p_2 = \frac{1}{2}$. Initial endowments are the same for both agents, with

$$W_{0i}(s = 1) = 1$$
$$W_{0i}(s = 2) = 2$$

for $i = 1, 2$.

Questions
(a) Does there exist an undiversifiable risk?
(b) Suppose that markets are complete. Determine the competitive equilibrium price and allocation of risk. Explain why agent $i = 2$ is partially insured by agent $i = 1$.
(c) Suppose that there is a change in the probability of the states, with $p_1 = 0.25$ and $p_2 = 0.75$. Examine the impact of this change on the equilibrium.

14.4 Define $\hat{\pi}_s = \pi_s/p_s$, the contingent price is state s per unit of probability. Using the first welfare theorem together with Equations (14.12) and (14.20), show that

(a) $\hat{\pi}_s$ depends upon s only through $W_0(s)$, i.e. if $\exists s, s'$ such that $w_0(s) = w_0(s')$, then $\hat{\pi}_s = \hat{\pi}_{s'}$. So, $\hat{\pi}_s = \hat{\pi}(w_0(s))$.
(b) $\hat{\pi}$ is a decreasing function of w_0.

(c) Show that $\dfrac{\partial \hat{\pi}}{\partial w_0} = -\hat{\pi} \cdot T_a$.

14.5 Consider an economy with complete contingent markets and with n individuals with constant absolute risk aversion. Show that an increase in one individual's risk aversion raises the dispersion of contingent prices.

Hint: See Equation (A9.5) in Appendix 9.
Discuss the effect of this change in price dispersion on risk-sharing.

14.6 Consider an economy with three assets and three possible states. The contingent payments are:

$$\text{asset } j = 1: q_1 = (3, 2, 1)$$
$$\text{asset } j = 2: q_2 = (0, \tfrac{1}{2}, 1)$$
$$\text{asset } j = 3: q_3 = (2, 1, 0)$$

Questions
(a) Does this economy satisfy Assumption 14.1a, i.e. are markets complete?
(b) Suppose that the prices of these assets are respectively $P_1 = 2$, $P_2 = 1$ and $P_3 = 1$. Are they arbitrage-free?
(c) Suppose that $P_1 = 2$, $P_2 = \tfrac{1}{2}$ and $P_3 = 1$. Derive the competitive price of a fourth asset that has contingent payments $q_4 = (6, 5, 4)$. Can you do the same with the fifth asset $q_5 = (1, 0, 0)$, i.e. the call on Asset 1 with exercise price 2?

14.7 Consider an economy with $S = 3$, and $\pi_1 = \tfrac{2}{4}$, $\pi_2 = \tfrac{1}{4}$, $\pi_3 = \tfrac{1}{4}$. A firm has an investment project requiring 2 units of capital. It would generate a contingent total revenue net of non-capital costs represented by $(3, 4, 2)$. The firm has no money on its own to finance the project by itself. Two strategies are considered:

1. The firm issues new bonds. The price of a bond $(1, 1, 1)$ is $\tfrac{2}{4} + \tfrac{1}{4} + \tfrac{1}{4} = 1$. So by issuing two bonds it gets enough money to finance the project. The profit is thus $(1, 2, 0)$.
2. The firm issues a right to a share α of profits, i.e. it issues an equity. The price that the firm gets for issuing this right $(3\alpha, 4\alpha, 2\alpha)$ is $\tfrac{2}{4}(3\alpha) + \tfrac{1}{4}(4\alpha) + \tfrac{1}{4}(2\alpha) = 3\alpha$. To get enough money to finance its investment, the firm must issue a right to $\alpha = \tfrac{2}{3}$ of future profits. The owner of the firms still retains a net profit represented by the vector $(1, \tfrac{4}{3}, \tfrac{2}{3})$.

Questions
(a) Show that the owner of the firm is indifferent between the two strategies.
(b) More generally, show that the owner of the firm is indifferent among all mixtures of strategies (1) and (2), independent of the contingent prices π_s. This is the essence of the famous Modigliani–Miller theorem (Modigliani and Miller 1958).

Notes

1. A discussion of this problem can be found in most microeconomic textbooks that contain a section on general equilibrium. Specifically, the reader should refer to Walras' law.
2. This tendency to close the gap is not guaranteed. To understand this, study the stability problems of competitive equilibria under certainty.
3. It can be shown that it is always more advantageous to sell on contingent markets rather than spot markets. Indeed, when contingent markets are complete the spot markets disappear because no one uses them.
4. For a survey of the literature on this question, one can read the excellent article by Jacques Drèze (1982).
5. Asset prices are not normalised as in Equation (14.3) because the prices of the real assets were previously fixed.
6. This is called state dependent utility. For example, suppose the good is an ice cream or an umbrella. Then the utility from consuming the good depends on weather conditions represented by the variable s.
7. The interested reader should refer to the articles by Gollier (1992) and Drèze–Gollier (1993).

References

Arrow K. (1953), Le rôle des valeurs boursières pour la répartition la meilleure des risques, Editions du CNRS, Paris.

D'Arcy S.P. and N. Doherty (1988). *The Financial Theory of Pricing Property-Liability Insurance Contract*, Heubner Foundation Monograph 15, R. D. Irwin, Homewood.

Debreu G. (1959), *Theory of Value*, Cowles Foundation Monograph 17, Yale University Press, New Haven.

Drèze J.H. (1982), Decision criteria for business firms, in *Current Developments in the Interface: Economics, Econometrics, Mathematics*. M. Hazewinkel and A. H. G. Rinnooy and Kan (eds.), D. Reidel Publishing Company, Dordrecht, 27–53. Reproduced in J. H. Drèze (1987), *Essays on economic decision under uncertainty*, Chapter 15, Cambridge University Press, Cambridge.

Drèze J.H. and C. Gollier (1993), *Risk sharing on the labour market and second-best wage rigidities, European Economic Review*, vol. 37, 1457–1482.

Gollier C. (1992), *On the efficiency of credit rationing*, Groupe HEC, Paris, manuscript.

Modigliani F. and M. Miller (1958), The cost of capital, co-operation finance and the theory of investment, *American Economic Review*, vol. 48, 261–297.

Rosen S. (1985), Implicit contracts: a survey, *The Journal of Economic Literature*, vol. 23, 613–628.

15 The capital asset pricing model

Chapter 13 and 14 would be sufficient in and of themselves if they did not rest on the controversial assumption of complete markets. In this chapter, we relax this assumption while retaining the same goals: to determine how markets evaluate and distribute risks. Alas, obtaining these practical results cannot be done without cost in terms of alternative assumptions.

The basic assumption here is that economic agents use the mean variance criterion to derive their optimal strategies. This criterion for making portfolio choices leads to a model developed by Markowitz at the beginning of the 1950s which is an extension of the one suggested for a single risky asset in Chapter 9. Based on the results obtained in this framework, the capital asset pricing model (CAPM), which can be derived from it, is then proposed. This model can be interpreted as an alternative to the complete markets model. Furthermore, for good measure, the two bodies of theory – complete markets and CAPM – were separately crowned by the Nobel prize: with Arrow and Debreu on one side and Markowitz and Sharpe on the other.

It seems that the CAPM theory is largely favoured by financiers, while economists prefer to build on the complete markets model. CAPM has the advantage of being much more operational than its competitor. Conversely, the complete markets approach fits ideally into the set of theories from microeconomics and general equilibrium, as we showed in Chapter 14. We will nevertheless show here that the two theories exhibit results that are fundamentally very close to each other.

15.1 Portfolio risk and the efficient frontier

Following Markowitz (1952), in this chapter we take an approach that is slightly different as to the sources of risk than the one adopted in Chapters 13 and 14. Previously, we basically considered an exchange economy, although we did suggest how to introduce production into the model. The risks came from the random initial endowments of the agents. Here we assume instead that the initial endowments are certain. All the risks come from the existence of a productive sector with random profitability. These risks are ultimately borne by individuals through their portfolios containing assets from this sector. The reason for the difference in the sources of risk comes from the desire to analyse stock markets in particular, whereas we previously emphasised the general character of the complete markets approach.

Stock markets are places where entrepreneurial risks are transferred from firms to individuals. Our experience as teachers induces us to remind the reader that 'firms' are never anything other than associations of individuals. A firm does not suffer from bearing risk; it is the members of the association who, by ultimately bearing the risk, face the consequences. Fundamentally, there are two types of members in the company: the employees and the stockholders. In the CAPM model, it is assumed that only stockholders bear the entrepreneurial risk.[1] The question is thus to determine how the company's risks are divided between financial market investors and how markets set the prices of the financial assets that are traded.

15.1.1 The model

The economy is composed of n capital holders and J firms. Traditionally, the capital holders are indexed by the letter $i, i = 1, \dots, n$, while the firms are indexed by the letter $j, j = 1, \dots, J$. The firms are held by stockholders, through a system of joint stock ownership. Let a_{ij} be the share of wealth that Individual i invests in Firm j. To each firm there corresponds an asset that it puts on the market in order to finance itself.

In this static economy, the agents begin by trading assets on stock markets. Then the pledge is turned over to the firms which, after production and sales, generate profits that are distributed to stockholders in proportion to the number of shares that they hold at the time of distribution. Finally, the capital holders harvest the fruit of their investments, consuming their income. Thus the world ends.

The individuals' investment choices are, of course, determined by their expectations about the return to these investments. Since investments are generally risky, these expectations must be defined *ex ante* by describing the joint distribution function of the dividends paid by the J firms. This is, by the way, what we previously did by defining the revenue $q_j(s)$ generated by firm j in each state of the world s and stipulating the probability of each state's occurrence. The flow could also be defined in terms of the rate of return, by defining the return of asset j in state s by:

$$r_j(s) = \frac{q_j(s)}{P_j} \tag{15.1}$$

where P_j is the current bid price of asset j. In what follows, we will use the notion of rate of return instead of the notion of the dividend, remembering, when it is convenient, how one can be transformed into the other given price P_j.

There is no doubt that a complete characterisation of the joint distribution function of the returns is an extremely complex task and that it is beyond the mental (or informational) capabilities of the investors, because J and S are astronomical. To simplify the characterisation of expectations and to build an attractive model, we make the following assumption:

Assumption 15.1 Economic agents use the mean variance criterion to make their decisions when faced with uncertainty.

If this is the case, then the expected returns can be characterised by two distinct elements:

1. *The expected return of the assets.* The expected return of asset j is $\mu_j = E[(\tilde{r}_j)]$. The column vector μ, of which the transpose is:

$$\mu' = (\mu_1, \mu_2, \ldots, \mu_J) \tag{15.2}$$

summarises the various expected returns.

2. *The variance–covariance matrix of the returns.* The variance of asset j's return is written as $\sigma_{jj} = \mathrm{Var}(\tilde{r}_j) = E[(\tilde{r}_j - \mu_j)^2]$. In parallel fashion, the covariance between the returns of asset j and asset k is written as: $\sigma_{jk} = \mathrm{cov}(r_j, r_k) = E[(r_j - \mu_j)(r_k - \mu_k)]$. Of course, $\sigma_{jk} = \sigma_{kj}$. The information on the J variances and the $J(J-1)/2$ covariances is summarised in the following matrix:

$$\Sigma = \begin{pmatrix} \sigma_{11} & \sigma_{12} & \cdots & \sigma_{1J} \\ \sigma_{21} & \sigma_{22} & \cdots & \sigma_{2J} \\ \vdots & \vdots & \ddots & \vdots \\ \sigma_{J1} & \sigma_{J2} & \cdots & \sigma_{JJ} \end{pmatrix} \tag{15.3}$$

Σ is a symmetric square matrix ($\sigma_{ij} = \sigma_{ji}$) called the variance–covariance matrix. We will assume that this matrix is invertible. This assumption corresponds to the idea that one stock is not a linear combination of the others.[2]

Note that we have explicitly departed from the 'states of the world' formulation of uncertainty, even though the formulation presented here can be explicitly derived from it. Indeed, the objective is to construct an alternative to the model presented in Chapter 14.

All moments of the joint distribution function of stock returns that are higher than second order are assumed to be superfluous for determining optimal portfolios. This obviously reduces the amount of information that must be known before the model can be analysed. This assumption can be justified in two different ways. The simplest is to assume that all economic agents have quadratic utility. Specifically, we know that, in this case, expected utility is a function of only the first two moments of final wealth: the mean and the variance (see Section 4.3.1).

Another way is to assume that the distribution of returns is a multivariate normal distribution, that is, that

$$\tilde{r}' = (\tilde{r}_1, \tilde{r}_2, ..., \tilde{r}_n) \sim N(\mu', \Sigma) \tag{15.4}$$

Indeed, it follows then that the final wealth of each capital holder is also normally distributed[3] given that it is a linear combination of the firms' returns:

$$\tilde{w}_{fi} = w_{0i} \sum_{j=1}^{J} a_{ij}\tilde{r}_j \tag{15.5}$$

The normality of $\tilde{w}_{f_i}$ implies that its distribution can be completely characterised by its mean and its variance. This also implies that an individual's expected utility can be parameterised by the mean and the variance of $\tilde{w}_{f_i}$:

$$E[U_i(\tilde{w}_{f_i})] = f_i(E[\tilde{w}_{f_i}], \text{Var}[\tilde{w}_{f_i}]) \tag{15.6}$$

In this case, the expected utility criterion and the mean variance criterion are equivalent, with a bijection between the functions U_i and f_i. For example, when the utility function is of the negative exponential type, we showed in Chapter 9 that the expected utility of final wealth is given by:

$$
\begin{aligned}
E[U_i(\tilde{w}_{f_i})] &= f_i(E[\tilde{w}_{f_i}], \text{Var}[\tilde{w}_{f_i}]) \\
&= -\exp[-A_{a_i}E[\tilde{w}_{f_i}] + 0.5 A_{a_i}^2 \text{Var}[\tilde{w}_{f_i}]] \\
&= g_i(E[\tilde{w}_{f_i}] - 0.5 A_{a_i}\text{Var}[\tilde{w}_{f_i}])
\end{aligned} \tag{15.7}
$$

with $g'(\cdot) > 0$.

These two assumptions – quadratic utility and the normality of returns – support Assumption 15.1. Given the problems associated with the quadratic case, the normality hypothesis is probably preferable. Many random variables are normally distributed in practice. If the returns to a firm are a function of the average of a large number of independent factors, then normality can be assumed as a working hypothesis because of the central limit theorem. For this reason we use Assumption 15.1a, a special case of Assumption 15.1, in what follows.

Assumption 15.1a The returns to the financial assets are multivariate normally distributed, that is, they satisfy condition (15.4).

In what follows we use the graphical representation introduced in Figure 15.1. In the graph, the variance of an asset is measured on the horizontal axis and the expected value is measured on the vertical axis. An asset is represented by a point in that space. The set of assets on the market is represented by a 'cloud' of points.

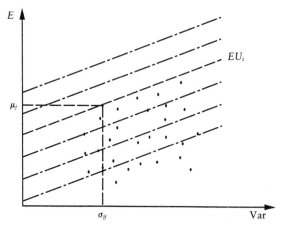

Figure 15.1

An indifference curve can also be represented in this graph. An indifference curve for Individual i is composed of a set of assets (or of portfolios) that generate the same expected utility f_i. The slope of an indifference curve corresponds to the marginal rate of substitution between the expected value and the variance. This has already been discussed in Chapter 2. Recall that when an individual is risk averse, the indifference curves are increasing. The steeper the slope is, the higher the degree of risk aversion is. Horizontal indifference curves reflect risk neutrality. In the case of negative exponential utility, condition (15.7) implies that the indifference curves are lines with slope equal to $A_a/2$. This is represented in Figure 15.1.

If the problem were simply to choose a single asset, it would suffice to draw the investor's family of indifference curves on the graph. The solution would then be to choose the asset represented by the point lying on the highest indifference curve. By this choice, the individual would achieve the optimal trade-off between risk and expected return as a function of risk aversion. On average neither the least risky asset nor the asset that is most profitable would be chosen. As can be seen very simply in the graph, higher risk aversion is associated with steeper indifference curves and the capital holder has a greater tendency to opt for a lower risk asset. Some assets in the 'interior' of the 'cloud' will never be chosen.

15.1.2 Portfolio diversification and the efficient frontier

Of course, it is rarely observed that investors 'put all their eggs in one basket'. In reality, the capital holder's problem is much more complex than the choice of a single asset to the exclusion of all others. In practice, it is a question of constructing a *portfolio* of assets with the goal of best using the opportunities to diversify that are present in the economy. To solve this problem, we must first determine how to evaluate the expected return and the risk of a portfolio. Indeed, the characteristics of a portfolio can be summarised by its expected return and its risk, given the above assumption. A portfolio can thus, in the same way as a single asset, be graphically represented by a point in Figure 15.1. Consequently, the possibility of acquiring a portfolio rather than a single asset 'simply' increases the number of points to be considered relative to the number in the problem initially posed.

Consider a particular portfolio represented by the row vector: $\mathbf{a}_i = (a_{i1}, \ldots, a_{iJ})$ with

$$\sum_{j=1}^{J} a_{ij} = 1 \tag{15.8}$$

Note that the values of the a_{ij} need not be constrained to lie between 0 and 1: the case where the capital holder is 'short' some assets is also considered. The typical case corresponds to the situation where an individual borrows the risk-free asset (if it exists) to trade for a risky asset (that is, a 'short position' is established in the risk-free asset). We calculate the properties of a portfolio a_i in terms of the mean and variance of the return. The return $\tilde{r}_p$ of this portfolio is:

$$\tilde{r}_p = \sum_{j=1}^{J} a_{ij}\tilde{r}_j = a_i\tilde{r} \tag{15.9}$$

where the term to the right is the inner product of a row vector and a column vector. Consequently, the expected return equals:

$$E[\tilde{r}_p] = E\left[\sum_{j=1}^{J} a_{ij}\tilde{r}_j\right] = \sum_{j=1}^{J} a_{ij}\mu_j = a_i\mu \tag{15.10}$$

The expected return of a portfolio is the average of the returns of the assets that comprise it, weighted by the share of each asset in the group. Calculating the variance of the portfolio's return is less simple. The reader who has some knowledge of multivariate statistics can directly verify that:

$$\text{Var}[\tilde{r}_p] = \text{var}[a_i\tilde{r}]$$

$$= \sum_{j=1}^{J} \sum_{k=1}^{J} a_{ij}a_{ik}\sigma_{jk}$$

$$= a_i\Sigma a_i' \tag{15.11}$$

where a_i' is the transpose of a_i, that is, the corresponding column vector.

Alternatively, one can remember that the variance of a sum of random variables equals the sum of the variances plus twice the sum of the covariances:

$$\text{Var}[\tilde{r}_p] = \text{Var}\left[\sum_{j=1}^{J} a_{ij}\tilde{r}_j\right]$$

$$= \sum_{j=1}^{J} \text{Var}[a_{ij}\tilde{r}_j] + 2\sum_{j=1}^{J}\sum_{k>j}^{J} \text{cov}[a_{ij}\tilde{r}_j, a_{ik}\tilde{r}_k]$$

$$= \sum_{j=1}^{J} a_{ij}^2\sigma_{jj} + 2\sum_{j=1}^{J}\sum_{k>j}^{J} a_{ij}a_{ik}\sigma_{jk} \qquad (15.12)$$

Conditions (15.11) and (15.12) are equivalent; one is the matrix transcription of the other.

Conditions (15.10) and (15.12) allow the representation of any portfolio a_i as a point in mean variance space. If all points corresponding to portfolios were represented in this space, the result would be the set of points that can be constructed from the J financial assets traded on the market. Such an area has been drawn in Figure 15.2.

An immediate property of this area is that it contains the set of financial assets, each represented by a single point. Indeed, a portfolio containing a single asset can always be constructed $(a_i = (0, ..., 1, ..., 0))$. On the other hand, will this zone contain the entire space? If this were the case, it would mean that it is possible to acquire a portfolio with unbounded expected return for a given risk. This is, of course, impossible, as we will show in the following example.

To show how Equations (15.10) and (15.12) can be used to construct the zone that represents the different feasible portfolios, we analyse a special case

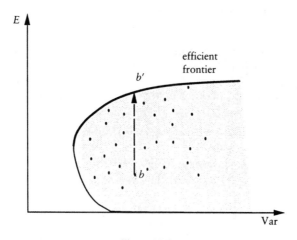

Figure 15.2

with two assets ($J = 2$) that have the same variance $\sigma_{11} = \sigma_{22}$ and covariance $\sigma_{12} = \rho\sigma_{11}$, where ρ is the correlation coefficient of the returns and thus lies between -1 and $+1$. These two assets are represented in Figure 15.3, with $\mu_1 < \mu_2$,

Here a portfolio is a pair of real numbers (a_{i1}, a_{i2}) satisfying condition (15.8). We thus have one degree of freedom in the portfolio choice when $J = 2$. We analyse the choice of a_{i1} and impose $a_{i2} = 1 - a_{i1}$. From Equation (15.10) the expected return of the portfolio in question is:

$$E[\tilde{r}_p(a_{i1})] = a_{i1}\mu_1 + (1 - a_{i1})\mu_2 \tag{15.13}$$

Similarly, from (15.12) it can be deduced that the variance of the portfolio's return equals:

$$\begin{aligned}\text{Var}[\tilde{r}_p(a_{i1})] &= a_{i1}^2\sigma_{11} + (1 - a_{i1})^2\sigma_{22} + 2a_{i1}(1 - a_{i1})\sigma_{12} \\ &= \sigma_{11}[a_{i1}^2 + (1 - a_{i1})^2 + 2a_{i1}(1 - a_{i1})\rho] \end{aligned} \tag{15.14}$$

While the expected value of the return varies linearly with a_{i1}, the variance is a quadratic function of this variable. It is therefore not surprising that the locus of feasible portfolios given two available assets is a parabola like the one drawn in Figure 15.3. Equations (15.13) and (15.14) are the two parametric equations for this parabola.

For a 'standard' portfolio where a_{i1} lies between 0 and 1, observe that

$$\text{Var}[\tilde{r}_p(a_{i1})] = \sigma_{11}[a_{i1}^2 + (1 - a_{i1})^2 + 2a_{i1}(1 - a_{i1})\rho] \leqslant \sigma_{11} \tag{15.15}$$

The variance of the portfolio is smaller than the variance of the assets that comprise it: the parabola 'points' to the left. This is due to diversification,

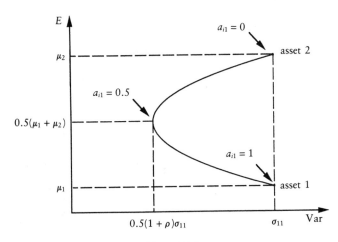

Figure 15.3

which is already well understood at this stage. The portfolio with the smallest variance is obtained by setting the derivative of $\text{Var}\,[\tilde{r}_p(a_{i1})]$ equal to zero. This yields:

$$2a_{i1} - (2(1 - a_{i1}) + 2(1 - 2a_{i1})\rho = -2(1 - 2a_{i1})(1 - \rho) = 0$$

Consequently, $a_{i1} = \tfrac{1}{2}$ and the portfolio with minimum variance[4] is the one that contains the same proportion of each asset. It has an expected return of $(\mu_1 + \mu_2)/2$ and a variance equal to:

$$\text{Var}\,[\tilde{r}_p(\tfrac{1}{2})] = \frac{1 + \rho}{2}\,\sigma_{11} \tag{15.16}$$

The benefit of diversification is greater for a smaller correlation between the two assets. When the two assets are perfectly and positively correlated ($\rho = +1$) there is no gain: $\text{Var}\,[\tilde{r}_p(a_{i1})] = \sigma_{11}$ for all values of a_{i1} and condition (15.15) is satisfied with equality. The locus of feasible portfolios is then represented by a vertical line at σ_{11}.

Conversely, if the assets are perfectly negatively correlated ($\rho = -1$), then the maximal gain is achievable, because the risk can be completely suppressed by the choice of $a_{i1} = \tfrac{1}{2}$: in that case $\text{Var}\,[\tilde{r}_p(\tfrac{1}{2})] = 0$. In the case of independent risks ($\rho = 0$), the variance can be halved: $\text{Var}\,[\tilde{r}_p(\tfrac{1}{2})] = \sigma_{11}/2$. These three cases are represented in Figure 15.4. Figure 13.6, presented in Chapter 13 in another context, is a good illustration of the advantages of diversification. There the distributions of returns t for portfolios containing 1, 2 and 3 assets with uniformly and independently distributed returns are illustrated.

In the special case where $J = 2$, we observe that the locus of portfolios that can be constructed is not an area like the one drawn in Figure 15.2, but a curve. This is due to the fact that there is only one degree of freedom (a_{i1}).

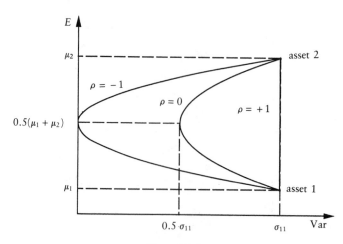

Figure 15.4

If a third asset is added to the example an area is obtained, because then there is a second degree of freedom. The simplest way to verify this is to consider a portfolio of three assets (a_{i1}, a_{i2}, a_{i3}), such as a portfolio that contains a_{i3} of the new asset and ($1 - a_{i3}$) of an artificial asset composed of Assets 1 and 2 in the proportions $a_{i1}/(a_{i1} + a_{i2})$ and $a_{i2}/(a_{i1} + a_{i2})$, respectively. This artificial asset is represented by a point on the curve in Figure 15.3, because it is nothing other than a particular portfolio containing Assets 1 and 2. In calculating the mean, variance and covariance of the new asset and the artificial asset, we find ourselves once again in the two asset case. Thus, each artificial asset corresponds to a curve representing the portfolios that can be created from this artificial asset and Asset 3. A few of these curves are illustrated in Figure 15.5. Since there exist an infinity of artificial assets, there also exist an infinity of curves which together constitute a two-dimensional area that represents the portfolios that can be constructed with three assets.

Since there exist points in the mean variance space that do not correspond to any portfolio, there must exist a boundary between the zone of portfolios that can be constructed from existing assets and the zone that no portfolio can achieve. The upper part of this border is called the *efficient portfolio frontier*, and it is drawn in Figure 15.2. A portfolio that is not found on the frontier is said to be inefficient. Thus portfolio b is inefficient because it is dominated by portfolio b' with the same risk (identical variance of the return) but a higher expected return. No rational individual, whether risk averse or risk loving, will ever choose portfolio b because portfolio b' is necessarily preferable. Portfolio b' is said to be 'efficiently diversified' because there exists no other with the same level of risk that exhibits a higher expected return.

The problem of analytically solving for the efficient frontier is important but difficult. It consists of finding the portfolio with the highest expected return

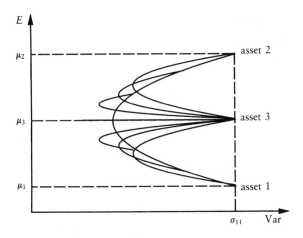

Figure 15.5

for a given risk. Solving this problem requires a computer using a method that is commonly used in operations research: quadratic programming. This problem, important in practice, is discussed in numerous articles and works on finance. We do not broach it here because it is the notion of the efficient frontier itself that we need.

It is now simple to imagine an individual's optimal portfolio given a knowledge of the efficient frontier and the investor's family of indifference curves. Figure 15.6 shows the optimal portfolios for two individuals where Individual 2 is less risk averse than Individual 1.

15.1.3 Introduction of a risk-free asset, the market line and the mutuality principle

Until now all of the assets have been assumed to be risky. Indeed, in the opposite case, if Asset i were risk-free, then the ith row of the matrix Σ would contain only zeros and Σ would not be invertible. When there exists a risk-free asset, the presentation of Figure 13.1 – where different attitudes toward risk imply different portfolio management strategies – is overturned. We assume in what follows that there exists, in addition to the J risky assets, an asset without risk whose certain return (the risk-free rate) equals r_0. A portfolio of risky assets is then represented by a vector of J elements $a_i = (a_{i1}, ..., a_{iJ})$ where the sum of the elements need not equal 1. Specifically, a share a_{i0} of individual i's wealth can be invested in the risk-free asset. It satisfies the condition:

$$a_{i0} = 1 - \sum_{j=1}^{J} a_{ij} \tag{15.17}$$

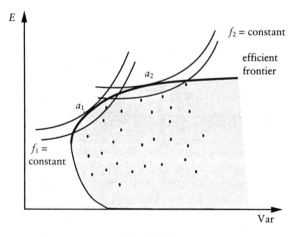

Figure 15.6

Here it is clearly seen that a_{i0} is not constrained to be positive: when a_{i0} is negative it means that Agent i borrows at the risk-free rate to invest in risky assets.

Agent i's final wealth with such a portfolio is random and is written as:

$$\tilde{w}_{fi} = w_{0i} \sum_{j=0}^{J} a_{ij}\tilde{r}_j$$

$$= w_{0i}r_0 + w_{0i} \sum_{j=1}^{J} a_{ij}(\tilde{r}_j - r_0) \tag{15.18}$$

$$= w_{0i}r_0 + w_{0i}a_i(\tilde{r} - r_0) \tag{15.18a}$$

where Equation (15.17) was used to eliminate a_{i0} and where $(\tilde{r} - r_0)$ is the column vector containing the J random variables $\tilde{r}_j - r_0$. This implies that:

$$E[\tilde{w}_{fi}] = w_{0i}r_0 + w_{0i} \sum_{j=1}^{J} a_{ij}(\mu_j - r_0) \tag{15.19}$$

and, using formula (15.11),

$$\mathrm{Var}[\tilde{w}_{f_i}] = w_{0i}^2\mathrm{Var}\left[\sum_{j=1}^{J} a_{ij}\tilde{r}_j\right]$$

$$= w_{0i}^2 \sum_{j=1}^{J} \sum_{k=1}^{J} a_{ij}a_{ik}\sigma_{jk} \tag{15.20}$$

The capital owner's problem thus corresponds to choosing a risky portfolio $(a_{i1}, ..., a_{iJ})$ that solves problem (15.21):

$$\max E[U_i(\tilde{w}_{fi})] = f_i[E(\tilde{w}_{fi}), \mathrm{Var}(\tilde{w}_{fi})] \tag{15.21}$$

The first-order condition for this problem is:

$$\frac{\partial f_i}{\partial E}\frac{\partial E}{\partial a_{ij}} + \frac{\partial f_i}{\partial \mathrm{Var}}\frac{\partial \mathrm{Var}}{\partial a_{ij}} = 0 \qquad \text{for all } j = 1, ..., J \tag{15.22}$$

Define

$$k_i = -(\partial f_i/\partial E)/2(\partial f_i/\partial \mathrm{Var}) > 0 \tag{15.23}$$

From Equations (15.19) and (15.20), the first-order condition for decision-maker i becomes:

$$0 = -2k_i w_{0i}(\mu_j - r_0) + 2w_{0i}^2 \sum_{k=1}^{J} a_{ik}\sigma_{jk}$$

$$= -k_i(\mu_j - r_0) + w_{0i} \sum_{k=1}^{J} a_{ik}\sigma_{jk} \qquad \text{for } j = 1, ..., J \tag{15.24}$$

In matrix notation this is equivalent to:

$$k_i(\mu - r_0)' = w_{0i}a_i\Sigma \qquad (15.25)$$

where $(\mu - r_0)'$ is the transpose of $(\mu - r_0)$. This is a system of J equations in the J unknowns $a_{i1}, ..., a_{iJ}$. The solution of such a system, assuming the variance–covariance matrix is invertible, is:

$$w_{0i}a_i = k_i(\mu - r_0)' \Sigma^{-1} \qquad (15.26)$$

This condition allows one to calculate Agent i's optimal portfolio from the vector μ of expected returns and the variance–covariance matrix Σ. The value of a_{i0} is obtained by subtraction, using the budget constraint (15.17). The left-hand side of (15.26) is the amount of money invested in each of the different risky assets.

Note that this result corresponds to the result obtained in Chapter 9 relative to the analysis of demand for a risky asset in the context of the mean variance criterion. Indeed, in the case where $J = 1$, $\Sigma = \sigma_{11}$ and condition (15.26) is simply

$$w_{0i}a_{i1} = k_i \frac{\mu_1 - r_0}{\sigma_{11}}$$

which is condition (9.5b), the interpretation of which need not be repeated here. Observe also that when the risks are independent, all of the covariances are zero and the matrix Σ is diagonal. Its inverse is then also diagonal and the diagonal elements of Σ^{-1} are of the form σ_{jj}^{-1}. In that case, condition (15.26) is written simply as:

$$w_{0i}a_{ij} = k_i \frac{\mu_j - r_0}{\sigma_{jj}} \qquad (15.27)$$

When the risks are independent, the amounts invested in each asset depend only on the characteristics of that asset (the mean and variance of the return). This is not true in general because Σ^{-1} is a mixture of the variances and the covariances of the assets.

The optimal risky portfolio a_i satisfies an important property: the structure of this portfolio is the same for all investors. In other words, the composition of the portfolio of risky assets is independent of the attitude towards risk. Define the row vector $\mathbf{b} = (b_1, ..., b_J) = \Sigma^{-1}(\mu - r_0)$. This vector represents the portfolio of risky assets rationally chosen by an individual with a unitary parameter k. Since condition (15.26) holds for all $i = 1, ..., n$, it follows after some simplification that, for any j and k,

$$\frac{a_{ij}}{a_{ik}} = \frac{b_j}{b_k} \qquad \text{for all } i = 1, ..., n \qquad (15.28)$$

The left-hand side of this equality is the ratio of asset j to asset k in Agent i's optimal portfolio. This ratio is independent of i. Thus, all investors opt for the same relative composition in their portfolios of risky assets, independently of their attitudes towards risk as characterised by k_i. From condition (15.26) it follows immediately that the only difference between the agents' investment decisions is in terms of size: agents with higher values of k_i will invest more in risky assets and less in the risk-free asset.

The intuition for this result is illustrated in Figure 15.7 where the efficient risky portfolio frontier and the risk-free asset are drawn. The risk-free asset corresponds to a point on the vertical axis. For a reason that will soon become apparent, we changed the measure of risk on the horizontal axis: we used the standard deviation of the portfolio return rather than its variance.[5] Consider the portfolio of risky assets P with a return of $\tilde{r}_p$ exhibiting an expected value of μ_p and a standard deviation of σ_p. The return $\tilde{r}$ of a portfolio investing α per cent in the risk-free asset and $(1 - \alpha)$ per cent in the risky portfolio P equals $\alpha r_0 + (1 - \alpha)\tilde{r}_p$, with $0 < \alpha < 1$. It follows that

$$E(\tilde{r}) = \alpha r_0 + (1 - \alpha)\mu_p$$
$$\sigma(\tilde{r}) = [(1 - \alpha)^2\sigma_p^2]^{1/2} = (1 - \alpha)\sigma_p$$

Consequently, the expected return and standard deviation of the return vary linearly in α. By varying α, one obtains a line passing through the risk-free asset and the risky portfolio, P. This is why we use the standard deviation as a measure of risk.

The best portfolio for Investor i among all the portfolios constructed from portfolio P of risky assets is portfolio c. This is the point of tangency between the 'feasibility line' $r_0 P$ and the highest possible indifference curve.

It is immediately clear, however, that portfolio c – optimal with respect to the line $r_0 P$ – is not the best portfolio that Agent i can construct from the

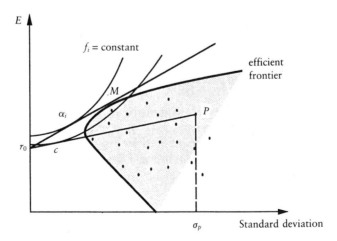

Figure 15.7

risky assets and the risk-free asset. Specifically, by choosing the risky portfolio M, one can generate the point of tangency α_ι by mixing this portfolio with the risk-free asset. It can be seen graphically that this is the optimal portfolio – the one that solves problem (15.21) – for Agent i.

The same reasoning can be applied to all agents, as shown in Figure 15.8. They all opt for the risky portfolio M, independently of the shapes of their indifference curves. The only difference is in the amount invested in the risk-free asset. Agent 1 rationally chooses α_1 between 0 and 1 whereas Agent 2, who is less risk averse, chooses $\alpha_2 = 0$. Finally, Agent 3, who is scarcely risk averse at all, opts for $\alpha_3 < 0$. All of these optimal portfolios lie on what is called the 'market line'. Portfolio M is called the 'market portfolio' whose return $\tilde{r}_M$ has an expected value of μ_M and a standard deviation of σ_M

In summary, the introduction of a risk-free asset implies the existence of a unique optimal portfolio of risky assets. To achieve the optimum it is thus sufficient that a mutual fund acquire all of the risky assets on the market and that shares of the fund be sold to the public. Then the only decision left for an investor is to determine what fractions of the fortune to invest in the risk-free asset and the mutual fund.

This is nothing other than the mutuality principle mentioned earlier. Here it is applied to the stock market. By combining all the risky assets in a single mutual fund portfolio, all diversifiable risks are eliminated and only the global risk tied to the market itself is retained. Thus the notion of diversification developed in Chapter 13 reappears here, and is summarised in Theorem 15.1.

Theorem 15.1 In the mean variance model, all agents opt for the same portfolio of risky assets, consistent with the mutuality principle.

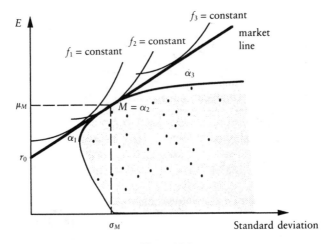

Figure 15.8

15.2 The CAPM approach

In the previous section, the distribution of returns was assumed to be known. Since returns and prices are related by (15.1), this is equivalent to saying that we took prices as given and derived the demand function for assets. We will now consider the determination of the equilibrium prices of financial assets. We consider in particular a situation of perfect competition where prices equilibrate supply and demand for each asset. We will follow the well-known presentation of W. Sharpe (1963) and J. Mossin (1973).

15.2.1 Competitive equilibrium asset prices

We already know the properties of demand summarised in condition (15.26). As to supply, we will assume that it is exogenous. If S_j represents the stock market capitalisation of asset j, the equilibrium condition is:

$$\sum_{i=1}^{n} w_{0i} a_{ij} = S_j \qquad \text{for all } j = 1, \ldots, J \tag{15.29}$$

The left-hand side of this equality is the aggregate demand for asset j. The right-hand side is the supply of this asset. In this case, the return to the market portfolio is simply:

$$\tilde{r}_M = \frac{\sum_{j=1}^{J} \tilde{r}_j S_j}{\sum_{j=1}^{J} S_j} = \sum_{j=1}^{J} \tilde{r}_j S_j \tag{15.30}$$

where total market capitalisation is normalised at 1.

One can then easily derive the market value formula by summing the investors' first-order conditions (15.24) over i:

$$(\mu_j - r_0) \sum_{i=1}^{n} k_i = \sum_{i=1}^{n} w_{0i} \sum_{k=1}^{J} a_{ik} \sigma_{jk} \qquad \text{for all } j = 1, \ldots, J$$

Define $T = \Sigma_{i=1}^{n} k_i$ and manipulate the right-hand side to obtain:

$$\mu_j - r_0 = T^{-1} \sum_{k=1}^{J} \sigma_{jk} \sum_{i=1}^{n} w_{0i} a_{ik}$$

Using the equilibrium condition (15.29), the previous expression reduces to

$$\mu_j = r_0 + T^{-1} \sum_{k=1}^{J} \sigma_{jk} S_k \tag{15.31}$$

or, using vector notation with $S = (S_1, \ldots, S_J)$,

$$(\mu - r_0)' = T^{-1} S \Sigma \tag{15.31a}$$

Returning to condition (15.31), it can be said that:

$$\mu_j = r_0 + T^{-1} \sum_{k=1}^{J} S_k \, \text{cov}(\tilde{r}_j, \tilde{r}_k)$$

$$= r_0 + T^{-1} \text{cov}\left(\tilde{r}_j, \sum_{k=1}^{J} \tilde{r}_k S_k\right)$$

$$= r_0 + T^{-1} \text{cov}(\tilde{r}_j, \tilde{r}_M) \tag{15.32}$$

In equilibrium, the expected return of a risky asset equals the risk-free return plus a risk premium that depends on parameter T and on the covariance between the return of the asset in question and the market return. The risk premium coefficient T can be obtained by summing condition (15.32) over all j. Since the sum of the μ_j weighted by the S_j is equal to the expected market return and since the weighted sum of the covariance equals $\text{cov}(\tilde{r}_M, \tilde{r}_M) = \sigma_M^2$, it follows that:

$$T^{-1} = (\mu_M - r_0)/\sigma_M^2 \tag{15.33}$$

This parameter is observable on the market and, using Equation (15.32), it is interpretable as the risk premium per unit of risk. The unit of risk is the covariance with the market risk. Combining formulas (15.32) and (15.33) leads to the fundamental evaluation equation of CAPM:

$$\mu_j = r_0 + (\mu_M - r_0) \frac{\text{cov}(\tilde{r}_j, \tilde{r}_M)}{\sigma_M^2} = r_0 + (\mu_M - r_0)\beta_j \tag{15.34}$$

The coefficient β_j is defined as the ratio of the covariance between Asset j's return and the market return to the variance of the market return. It is clear that this is a fundamental parameter for valuing an asset. An asset that is perfectly correlated with market risk has a 'beta' of one and generates an expected return of μ_M in equilibrium.

Many empirical studies have attempted to measure the 'betas' of financial assets. To measure an asset's beta with the goal of uncovering its equilibrium price, it suffices to carry out a linear regression of its return on the market return, using observations from a period that is assumed to be representative of future risk:

$$r_{jt} = a_j + b_j r_{Mt} + \varepsilon_j \tag{15.35}$$

It is known that the least squares estimator of b_j is precisely:

$$\beta_j = \text{cov}(\tilde{r}_j, \tilde{r}_M)/\sigma_M^2$$

The CAPM value formula is presented in terms of the expected return in equilibrium. It may be preferable to present the formula directly in terms of the equilibrium price, using Equation (15.1). Thus:

$$\frac{E\,[\tilde{q}_j]}{P_j} = r_0 + T^{-1}\mathrm{cov}(\tilde{q}_j/P_j, \tilde{r}_M)$$

or, after manipulating to isolate P_j,

$$P_j = \frac{1}{r_0}\,[E(\tilde{q}_j) - T^{-1}\mathrm{cov}(\tilde{q}_j, \tilde{r}_M)] \tag{15.36}$$

In equilibrium, the price of an asset equals the expected present value of future dividends minus a risk premium. We have already encountered precisely the same formula in the context of the complete markets model with quadratic utility (Equation (14.23)). There we gave the intuition for the notion of covariance with the market as a measure of an asset's risk. When an asset exhibits a weak correlation with the market, the asset's risk is more easily diversifiable in the portfolio. The risk that an investor really bears by acquiring such an asset is limited so the pay is not high for assuming this risk in equilibrium (the risk premium is small). At best, for a riskophobe, the correlation is negative and including such an asset in the market portfolio reduces the portfolio's total risk (*cf.* Figure 15.4 with $\rho = -1$). Riskophobes are thus prepared to acquire this asset even for an actuarially unfavourable price. This explains why the equilibrium risk premium is positive (in terms of the price) for risks that are negatively correlated with the market risk.

We now derive the allocation of risk in the economy. Using Equation (15.18a) one obtains:

$$
\begin{aligned}
\tilde{w}_{fi} &= w_{0i}r_0 + w_{0i}a_i(\tilde{r} - r_0)\\
&= w_{i0}r_0 + k_i(\mu - r_0)'\,\Sigma^{-1}(\tilde{r} - r_0)\\
&= w_{i0}r_0 + k_iT^{-1}S\Sigma\Sigma^{-1}(\tilde{r} - r_0)\\
&= B_i + k_iT^{-1}\sum_{j=1}^{J} S_j\tilde{r}_j \tag{15.37}\\
&= B_i + \frac{k_i}{\displaystyle\sum_{j=1}^{n} k_j}\,\tilde{r}_M
\end{aligned}
$$

The second equality is from condition (15.26). The third is due to the evaluation formula (15.31a). The fifth uses the definition of T and $\tilde{r}_M$ (Condition (15.30)). As stated in Theorem 15.1, final income depends only on the aggregate return $\tilde{r}_M$: this is the mutuality principle. Note that the functional relationship between the two variables is linear.

A related question is that of determining whether the allocation of social risk, or of market risk, among economic agents is efficient. We consider a special case by assuming that the utility functions are negative exponentials. In this case, Condition (15.7) applies and the partial derivatives of f_i imply that $k_i = (A_{ai})^{-1} = T_{ai}$, Individual i's absolute risk tolerance. Consequently, Equation (15.37) becomes:

$$\tilde{w}_{f_i} = B_i + \frac{T_{a_i}}{T_a} \tilde{r}_M \qquad (15.38)$$

where $T_a = T = \Sigma_{i=1}^{n} k_i$ equals the sum of individual absolute risk tolerances. The share of non-diversifiable risk that an individual bears in equilibrium equals the absolute risk tolerance expressed as a percentage of absolute risk tolerance in the economy. This implies, as we know, that the risk-sharing arrangement is Pareto efficient. This result is not surprising since we know that Pareto-efficient allocations are linear in the case of negative exponential utility. A company that sells stock offers a linear allocation of risk to its stockholders: the benefits are divided in proportion to the shares of stock held.

It is thus clear that this system of risk-sharing through stock ownership can efficiently organise the allocation of risks in an economy where Pareto efficiency implies linearity. This holds in the exponential case, but also in the case of quadratic utility as well as in the case of 'power' utilities with the same relative risk tolerance for everyone (*cf*. Section 13.3). In contrast, for every other case, a system of transferring risk by stock ownership cannot achieve an efficient risk allocation. It can only manage a linear approximation (Equation (15.35)) to a Pareto-efficient solution. This conclusion is summarised in Theorem 15.2.

Theorem 15.2 In the mean variance model, the allocation of non-diversifiable risk is only efficient if Pareto-efficient rules are linear.

15.2.2 Comments

The CAPM approach has generated a lot of theoretical and empirical research since its invention. Presenting these extensions and analyses is largely beyond the scope of this book. The potential applications are the same as those presented in Chapter 14. One may, for example, be interested in the investment policies of a corporation. By observing the price of risk $T^{-1} = (\mu_M - r_0)/\sigma_M^2$ on the market, a company's management can determine the investment that maximises the value P_j of the firm, given a knowledge of the parameters $E(\tilde{q}_j)$ and $\text{cov}(\tilde{q}_j, \tilde{r}_M)$ of the income $\tilde{q}_j$ generated by the project. Specifically, it is sufficient to calculate the market's evaluation of each project by using the rule in Equation (15.36). Other applications are related to strategies for selling assets and evaluating the cost of debt.

Similarly, one might be interested in the way an insurance company calculates the premium associated with a risk. Specifically, recall that an insurance contract is simply a particular kind of financial asset. The same technology can thus be applied. In particular, one can use the concept of the beta of a risk: an individual who faces a risk of *losses* that are positively correlated with the market return can enjoy an actuarially favourable premium, in a world without transactions costs. Empirically, this is the case with the risk of a 'machine breakdown', a risk that is naturally higher in booms (high r_M) due to the intensive utilisation of the machines. One should expect relatively favourable premiums for insurance against this kind of risk. In contrast, 'unemployment risk' is strongly negatively correlated with market risk. One should thus expect a high price for unemployment insurance products. Indeed, there exist few private contracts against this risk; it is generally managed by the state.

To conclude, we remind the reader of the numerous assumptions underlying the model, some of which limit the generality of the results.

1. Returns have a jointly normal probability distribution. This is only true as a first approximation because the tails that are actually observed are thicker than is the case for normal distributions. This assumption implies that the characteristics of an asset can be summarised by the mean and variance of its return.
2. All agents have the same expectations concerning asset returns. This is certainly not true: specialists and financial analysts possess better information. Some even have inside information. These problems are analysed in Chapter 16.
3. Financial markets are competitive: agents take prices as given. This is only an approximation to reality because some agents, such as 'market makers', have a non-negligible impact on transactions that allows them to affect prices. A new strand of analysis called 'micro-foundations of financial markets' attempts to round out the few theoretical elements available on this question. This is also briefly considered in Chapter 16.
4. There exists a risk-free asset on the market. This assumption is also an approximation to reality. Its violation implies the loss of the mutuality result, as can be seen in Figure 15.6.
5. The absence of transactions costs. This is certainly an important criticism of the model. When there are transactions costs, individual portfolios are not necessarily efficient (on the efficient frontier) because the cost of adjustment may exceed its benefit.
6. There is no state: there are no market regulations or income taxes. Taxation introduces inefficient distortions, just as in the models under certainty. However, it should be noted that taxation also provides a form of risk-sharing among individuals: proportional income taxes act as a co-insurance contract between capital holders and the state.

7. Asset supply is inelastic. This is inconsistent with the strategies that firms are observed to adopt with regard to raising capital on stock markets.

8. All risks can be traded on markets. If an individual cannot sell the risks that are specific to themselves (such as a risk affecting human capital), it is easy to verify that a portfolio will be sought that is negatively correlated with this kind of non-financial income in order to create some 'homemade insurance'. Under these conditions, individuals choose different portfolios, thus violating the mutuality principle. Appendix 8 shows that the existence of a non-transferable risk induces prudent agents to exhibit greater risk aversion, thus reducing their demand for risky assets.

This concludes the presentation of the mean variance model, the results of which have been shown to be close to those obtained in the context of complete markets. In both cases, we have shown how risks can be traded in an economy and at what price. By doing so, we have been able to show how to derive the market value of risks from individual evaluations.

Exercises

15.1 Consider an economy with risky assets (and no risk-free asset). Expected returns are respectively $\mu_1 = 1$, $\mu_2 = 2$, $\mu_3 = 2$. The variance–covariance matrix is:

$$\Sigma = \begin{pmatrix} 1 & 1 & 1 \\ 1 & 4 & 0 \\ 1 & 0 & 2 \end{pmatrix}$$

Questions

(a) Show that a portfolio that contains the same proportion of Assets 2 and 3 is not efficient.

Hint: Show that an increase in a_3 that is compensated by a reduction in a_2 does not change the expected return of the portfolio, but reduces the variance of its return.

(b) Consider the following programme:

$$\min_{a = (a_1, a_2, a_3)} \quad a \Sigma a'$$

subject to:

$$a_1\mu_1 + a_2\mu_2 + a_3\mu_3 = E$$
$$a_1 + a_2 + a_3 = 1$$

for some prespecified E. Prove that the solution of this programme is an efficient portfolio. Using this method, find the efficient portfolio whose expected return is $E = 1.5$.

15.2 Consider an economy with the three risky assets described in Exercise 15.1 and with a risk-free asset whose return is $r_0 = \frac{1}{2}$.

Questions
(a) Determine the optimal composition of the risky portfolio.
(b) Determine the optimal portfolio of an individual with utility
   $U_i(w) = -\exp(-w)$.
(c) Determine the equation of the market line.

15.3 Suppose that one may not borrow at the risk-free rate to invest in a risky asset (no short-sale constraint). Show that the set of portfolios that are optimally selected by a risk-averse investor is represented in Figure 15.7 by segment $r_0 - M$ followed by part of the efficient risky portfolio frontier to the right of M.

Notes

1. Rare are the attempts to integrate CAPM technology with the problems of employees who indisputably bear a part of the entrepreneurial risk. One successful attempt is found in the work of J. Drèze (1989) as well as in his (1990) article.
2. The matrix would not be invertible if a stock i were a linear combination of other assets. In that case, the ith row of the variance–covariance matrix would be a linear combination of other rows, meaning that the matrix is not invertible.
3. A linear combination of normally distributed random variables is itself a normally distributed random variable.
4. It can be verified that it is indeed a minimum because the second derivative of $\text{Var}[\tilde{r}_p(a_{i1})]$ is positive.
5. The general shape of the efficient frontier remains similar to the one drawn in the mean variance graph. Actually, we have simply 'compressed' the horizontal axis.

References

Drèze J.H. (1989), *Labour Management, Contracts and Capital Markets, A General Equilibrium Approach*, Blackwell, Oxford.

Drèze, J.H. (1990), The role of securities and labor contracts in the optimal allocation of risk bearing, in *Risk, Information and Insurance*, H. Loubergé (ed.), Kluwer Academic Press, Boston, and Association de Genève, 41–65.

Markowitz H. (1952), Portfolio selection, *Journal of Finance*, vol. 6, 77–91.

Mossin J. (1973), *Theory of Financial Markets*, Prentice Hall, Englewood Cliffs.

Sharpe W. (1963), A simplified model for portfolio analysis, *Management Science*, vol. 9, 227–293.

16 Uncertainty and asymmetric information

All through Chapters 14 and 15, we have implicitly assumed that all economic agents have the same information about the set of economic and financial variables, and that they all rationally deduce the same expectations concerning future revenues. Information and expectations were *symmetric*. This is an idealisation of reality because information is costly, and it is more costly for some than for others, given the heterogeneity of access to the information network in the economy. Consequently, information is intrinsically asymmetrically distributed across the population.

To illustrate this observation, we note that a lot of ink has been devoted to 'insider trading' cases in the press, in the courts, and in economics and finance journals. In this example of asymmetric information, an agent who is better informed than the others tries to benefit from this advantage to 'beat' the market by purchasing stock (in the case of an expected price increase) or by selling stock (in the case of an expected fall in price). We will ask what happens to equilibrium prices in such a situation where expectations are heterogeneous.

In addition, we should ask how an informed agent can avoid being noticed by the market when engaging in a large transaction on the stock exchange. Won't 'uninformed agents', observing transactions at suspicious levels, react by engaging in similar transactions, and thus make the price move in the direction that is compatible with the private information of the 'informed agent'? In that case, it would follow that the equilibrium price of a stock instantaneously aggregates all significant private information that is available to the agents. Each investor would then only need to observe the current price to infer the information available to the others. This is the hypothesis known in finance as the 'informationally efficient markets' hypothesis.

Information is just as clearly asymmetrically distributed in insurance markets. It is generally believed that the insured have better knowledge about the risk that they transfer than do the insurers. In other words, in a population exhibiting 'good' risks and 'bad' risks, the insurer has only an imperfect knowledge of the distribution of indemnities that will have to be paid to a particular individual. Thus it is not possible to calculate an individual actuarial value or, as a result, a premium based on the intrinsic risk facing the insured. How should the insurer price these contracts? By choosing a non-discriminatory pricing rule that will implicitly penalise the good risks, will these now be driven away and be left only with the bad risks? Then will there be no obligation to revise the pricing rule to survive? How can wheat be distinguished from the chaff and, consequently, the good risks from bad?

The analysis of this kind of problem is admittedly complex and has generated a large number of publications. An entire book could not cover all this material. The goal of this chapter is to present some important aspects of this analysis relative to the problems of evaluating and sharing risks in an economy. The reader wishing to delve more deeply into these questions can, for example, refer to the excellent survey by Dionne and Doherty (1991). We begin by studying a goods market where some agents do not know the good's quality and we show the negative impact of such asymmetric information on the equilibrium. In the second section, a model of insurance markets is presented where the insurers do not know the quality of each individual risk that they accept. Finally, in the last section, a case of 'insider trading' on a stock market is studied.

16.1 Asymmetric information on the goods market

To analyse the impact of asymmetric information on the competitive equilibrium of a good, G. A. Akerlof (1970) proposed a simple example. It shows how, when some participants in a market are better informed than others, there may be no trades in equilibrium: the market disappears for lack of combatants! This is obviously a handicap for a decentralised system; it will never be able to organise an efficient allocation of resources.

This idea can be applied to most economic goods, whether they be products, services or financial assets. Akerlof presents the case of the used car market. The seller is perfectly informed as to the quality of the car, while the potential buyer has only a very vague idea. In equilibrium, no potential seller can find a buyer, specifically due to this problem of information.

16.1.1 Competitive equilibrium with complete information

To simplify, Akerlof considers an economy composed of two groups of risk-neutral individuals with two goods: money and a consumption good (used cars). Group 1 contains n individuals endowed with a non-random monetary sum, w_{01}, and a unit of the consumption good. The quality of the good initially held by Individual i in this group equals q_i. It is assumed that the welfare of a representative individual from Group 1, who at the end of the period has monetary wealth of w_{f1} and a good of quality q, is given by:

$$U_1(w_{f1}, q) = w_{f1} + q \tag{16.1}$$

Group 2 is composed of n risk-neutral individuals who have certain wealth of w_{02} but none of the good. The utility of a Type 2 individual who ends up holding monetary wealth of w_{f2} and one unit of the good of quality q is:

$$U_2(w_{f2}, q) = w_{f2} + \frac{3}{2} q \qquad (16.2)$$

It is clear that the marginal utility of consuming the good is larger for type 2 individuals – for whom it equals $3/2$ – than for Type 1 individuals – for whom it equals 1. From the point of view of efficient resource allocation, it is thus desirable to transfer the good from Group 1 to Group 2. It is assumed here that the marginal utility of a second unit of the good is zero for both groups.

Assume that the quality of the good held by Type 1 individuals is heterogeneous in such a way that q is uniformly distributed on the quality interval $[0, 2]$. Therefore, the proportion of goods with quality less than a given value a equals $a/2$. The average quality of goods in the population thus equals 1.

We begin by assuming that, despite this heterogeneity, all the participants have perfect and symmetric information about the quality of goods traded. In this context, the competitive equilibrium price for a good of quality q (observable) equals $p(q) = 1.5q - \varepsilon$ and the set of consumption goods is efficiently allocated to Group 2 in the competitive equilibrium with perfect information. Specifically, at this price, the Type 1 individual who owns a good of quality q sells it because it is possible to gain a positive increase in utility of $p(q) - q = (1.5q - \varepsilon) - q = q/2 - \varepsilon$. Conversely, at this price, Group 2 wishes to acquire the good with observed quality of q, because it receives a positive increase in utility of $1.5q - p(q) = 1.5q - (1.5q - \varepsilon)$. As ε approaches zero, supply and demand are equilibrated on each market $q \in [0, 2]$, that is, for any quality, all the sellers (or buyers) of this quality succeed in selling (or buying) what they wish at the prevailing price. This competitive allocation of resources is, as is well known, ideal in the sense of Pareto efficiency.

16.1.2 Competitive equilibrium with asymmetric information

Now assume that the individuals in Group 2 are unable to determine the quality of the goods put up for sale. This could be because, for example, the cost of acquiring information is prohibitively high. Nevertheless, assume that each one knows the distribution of quality in the population. While the Type 2 individuals are unable to observe the quality of a unit of the good, each Type 1 individual, in contrast, knows perfectly the quality of the good that is initially owned. There is thus (maximal) asymmetric information.

Since the buyers are unable to distinguish goods by quality, there can only be one price in the markets. Let p be the price of the consumption good.

Individuals compare the asking price with the utility of the good in consumption. A type 1 individual with a good of quality q less than the price p will want to sell the good, thus gaining a surplus of $p - q > 0$. In contrast, a Type 1 individual with a good of quality q greater than p will not put this good up for sale. Overall, the proportion of Type 1 individuals who wish to sell equals the proportion of goods with quality less than p, that is, $p/2$. If $p = 0$, nobody wishes to sell and there is no supply. Conversely, if $p = 2$ then everyone in Group 1 wishes to sell and the proportion of sellers in the group equals 1 so that supply is maximised and equals n.

An important point to notice is that the average quality of goods put on sale is $p/2$ when the market price is p.

The Type 2 agents are in a difficult situation. Acquiring a unit of the good at price p entails a risk, given the uncertainty as to the quality of the acquired good. How can this uncertainty be characterised? It would be absurd to characterise it by the uniform distribution on $[0, 2]$ that represents the distribution of quality in Group 1. After all, the analysis of supply that we just carried out can also be carried out by these individuals, who will logically deduce that the qualities *supplied* are uniformly distributed on $[0, p]$ while the average quality of marketed goods equals $p/2$. In a sense, the price reveals information to potential buyers about the quality of the supply even if there remains some uncertainty as to the quality of each individual good marketed by the sellers.

Recall that the individuals are risk neutral. It follows that the purchase of a unit of the good at price p by a Type 2 individual generates an increase in utility *ex ante* – that is, before the quality of the good is known – equal to $3/2$ of the expected quality minus the purchase price of the unit. Thus, Type 2 individuals only wish to acquire a unit of the good if the price is less than 150 per cent of the expected quality:

$$\text{Demand} = n \Leftrightarrow p < 1.5E(q) \tag{16.3}$$

$$\text{Demand} = 0 \Leftrightarrow p > 1.5E(q) \tag{16.3a}$$

However, we have just shown that individuals logically deduce the average quality of the marketed goods from the price and that the average quality equals half the price. It follows that 150 per cent of the expected quality equals $150/2 = 75$ per cent of the price. This logical reasoning by the individuals allows the characterisation, Equation (16.3), to be replaced by:

$$\text{Demand} = n \Leftrightarrow p < 0.75p \tag{16.4}$$

$$\text{Demand} = 0 \Leftrightarrow p > 0.75p \tag{16.4a}$$

Clearly, it is condition $p > 0.75p$ that systematically holds and thus demand is always zero: the average quality of the goods put up for sale is insufficient compared with the price. This is true for any price. It can always be shown that Group 1's demand for the good will be zero. There is thus always excess supply on the market. This forces the market price to fall, but it also forces the average quality of the marketed goods to fall. The only equilibrium point exhibits a zero price, where supply and demand are both zero. *In equilibrium there are no trades.* This is a catastrophic situation in terms of resource allocation! Asymmetric information has destroyed the Pareto efficiency of a competitive system for allocating resources.

Introducing risk aversion makes the situation even worse: riskophobes want to acquire the good only if its price is less than its expected quality *minus* a risk premium (*à la* Arrow–Pratt for small risks regarding quality). In other words, risk aversion further reduces demand relative to the already excessive supply.

What is the source of the problem? It is clear that the problem arises because good quality flees the market: only goods of mediocre quality are put up for sale. The owners of high quality goods choose a strategy of retaining and consuming their goods: there is 'adverse selection', implying that the average quality of the products on the market is less than the average quality of goods in the economy. This is what is called the 'lemons principle'.

The willingness to sell represents, for uninformed agents, a *signal* of a low quality good (a 'lemon'). They use this informative signal to deduce a conditional expectation: the expected quality is 1 for a random good, but the expected quality of a good, conditional on that good being offered for sale, is only $p/2 < 1$. The offer of sale signals that quality is less than p.

This explains why a new car loses 20–30 per cent of its value on leaving the dealer's lot: after driving a few miles, its happy owner gains some asymmetric information. When it is put up for sale, this implicitly signals to the potential buyer that this car has a hidden problem: for an uninformed agent, its expected quality is reduced far below the average quality of a new car coming directly from the dealer. In the case of Akerlof's 'extreme' numerical example, the price of this car falls to zero when it leaves the dealer.

An owner of a good used car of course attempts to announce its true quality to potential buyers in order to get a good price. But such an announcement cannot be taken seriously: it is not credible because an owner of a bad used car also has an incentive to announce that it is the 'best on the market', a claim that cannot be verified before the purchase. In this sense, the owners of low quality goods impose a negative externality on the welfare of owners of high quality goods. As with Gresham's law for money, bad quality chases out good quality.

Other applications of this model are found in credit and labour markets. There also is strong asymmetry of information: entrepreneurs seeking a loan know the quality (profitability) of their projects relatively better than do their bankers. An individual seeking employment has better information about the quality (productivity) of their labour. It is clear that these information problems represent a grave shortcoming of the mechanism for allocating resource in a competitive economy with asymmetric information.

Fortunately, most agents have the ability to 'signal' their quality through different mechanisms: a limited warranty for a length of time chosen by the seller to signal confidence in the product; a prestigious diploma for an individual looking for employment; a well-constructed investment plan by the manager of an industrial project, etc. Above all, the establishment of a climate of mutual trust between a buyer and a seller through a long-term relationship also reduces the asymmetry of information. Whereas, in Akerlof's model, there exists only one signal – to sell or not to sell – the introduction of other kinds of signals reduces inefficiency by allowing the transmission of credible information by the informed party.

In the following section, we present the same kind of analysis applied to the problem of adverse selection in insurance markets.

16.2 Asymmetric information on insurance markets

Here the asymmetric information is with respect to the individual probability of loss that each insured knows, but which is unobservable by the insurer. Adverse selection arises as high-risk individuals attempt to pass for low-risk individuals. The signal is the quantity of insurance chosen by the insured (the level of the deductible). In equilibrium, we will show that the allocation of risk is inefficient and that the bad risks impose a negative externality on the good risks.

16.2.1 The insurance model with complete information

We consider an economy with two types of insured individuals. They have the same initial wealth w_0 and the same utility function U, but face a heterogeneous risk of loss. All risks are binary and the amount of the loss is L if disaster strikes. The only characteristic that distinguishes the insured individuals is the probability of no loss, here considered to be an intrinsic characteristic of a person over which there is no control. Group H, the high-risk group, avoids loss with probability p_h, whereas Group L, the low-risk group, avoids loss with probability $p_1 > p_h$.

We consider in addition a perfectly competitive insurance market, without transactions costs and with risk-neutral insurers. This necessarily implies that expected equilibrium profits on a contract are zero.

If the insurers were in a position to observe the probabilities of loss, they would offer a different price schedule for each risk group. These price schedules would be actuarially fair given the assumptions made above. In this case, we know that the insured, facing actuarial premiums, would choose full coverage. This is an application of Theorems 10.1 and 10.3 to both groups.

The graphical representation of this result is shown in Figure 16.1. Final wealth in the good state without loss is measured along the horizontal axis while wealth in the bad state is measured along the vertical axis. Without insurance, the consumption plan of an arbitrary individual is described by point 1. An actuarially neutral insurance contract does not change expected

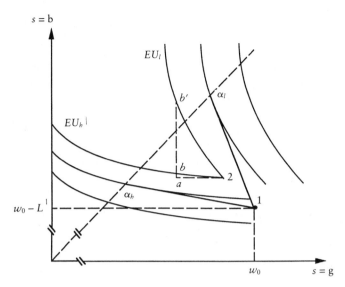

Figure 16.1

final wealth. Now we know that the locus of points representing the same expected final wealth is a line with slope $-p/(1-p)$ where p is the probability of avoiding loss (p_l or p_h). For low-risk individuals, it is the line $1\alpha_l$. It has a steeper slope than the corresponding line for high-risk individuals $1\alpha_h$ (see Chapter 7).

The preferences of the high-risk group are represented by a family of indifference curves like EU_h which represents the set of points yielding a constant expected utility. The preferences of the low-risk group are represented by indifference curves like EU_l. The slope of one of these curves at a particular point $[w(s=g), w(s=b)]$ for an individual who avoids loss with probability p equals:

$$- \mathrm{MRS}\,[w(g), w(b)] = -\frac{pU'\,[w(g)]}{(1-p)U'\,[w(b)]} \tag{16.5}$$

as was proven in Chapter 7 (Equation (7.4)). The absolute value of this slope is an increasing function of the probability of no loss. *This implies that, at every point the absolute value of the slope of the indifference curve of Group H is smaller than that of Group L, even though both groups exhibit the same utility function.*

An intuitive way to confirm the differences in the slopes of the respective indifference curves is to compare the effect of decreased wealth in the good state on the welfare of each group. A loss of wealth equal to the distance $2a$ in the good state is more painful for good risks than for bad risks, because good risks have a greater chance of finding themselves in the good state *ex post.* To compensate this loss in the good state, the wealth in the bad state must be increased more for good risks than for bad risks. The minimal compensation necessary for good risks is represented by the vertical difference *ab'*, which is greater than the distance *ab* necessary to compensate the bad risks. This implies that the slope of the good risks' indifference curves is steeper. This will play a crucial role in what follows.

Given complete information, each group faces its own pricing schedule and chooses the contract on the corresponding line that lies on the highest indifference curve. We know that the solution to this problem is point α_h for the high-risk individuals and point α_l for the low-risk individuals (*cf.* Figure 7.2). These two points lie on the 45 per cent line because they correspond to full insurance coverage.

Of course, the high risks pay a higher premium in equilibrium (α_h is closer to the origin than α_l). Thus it must be the case that insurers can unambiguously observe the quality of the risks in order to be able to impose a surcharge on the high-risk individuals.

16.2.2 The insurance model with asymmetric information

Suppose, however, that insurers are unable to directly observe the quality of the risks. In this case the solution in Figure 16.1 is untenable because all the bad risks will seek to pass themselves off as good risks in order to reduce their premiums. Since the insurers cannot directly discriminate between good and bad risks, they must offer the same contracts to the two groups of potential clients. Rothschild and Stiglitz (1976) consider an equilibrium consisting of a set of offered contracts such that:

(a) the companies' profits are zero in equilibrium;
(b) there exists no other set of contracts that would generate positive profits, given the contracts already offered in equilibrium.

All of this is based on the assumption that each insured individual chooses the offered contract that maximises the expected utility given the characteristics of the risk. The idea is that if profits are positive then new companies will enter the market and cut prices, driving profits to zero. On the other hand, if Condition (b) is violated, some companies seeking positive profits will offer alternative contracts.

A priori, the simplest solution would be to offer actuarial prices based on the average probability of avoiding loss in the population, assuming that each insurer faces a representative sample of the population. Since insurers know the proportion of good risks λ in the population, they calculate the mean probability of no loss as:

$$p_m = \lambda p_l + (1 - \lambda)p_h \qquad (16.6)$$

with $p_h < p_m < p_l$. In Figure 16.2, the set of actuarially neutral contracts

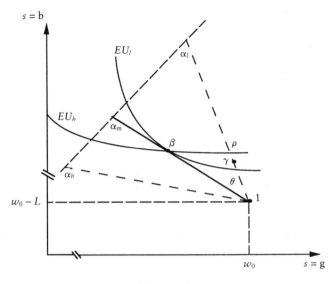

Figure 16.2

based on the mean probability of avoiding loss is a line $1\alpha_m$ of slope $p_m/(1 - p_m)$ in absolute value, lying between lines $1\alpha_h$ and $1\alpha_l$. If the sample of demand faced by an insurer is representative of the population, the expected profit is zero.

Now consider the optimal choices of individuals who are offered such contracts. For high-risk individuals, prices based on the average probability of no loss are actuarially favourable. Since the implicit loading factor in the premiums is negative, they will want to fully cover their risks by choosing the contract α_m.[1] In contrast, the price schedule is actuarially unfavourable for the good risks. Since the implicit loading factor in the premiums is positive, from Theorems 10.1 and 10.3, the good risks choose a partial insurance contract. Let this be contract β in Figure 16.2; it is optimal along line $1\alpha_m$.

Can the solution (α_m, β) – that is, where the bad risks choose α_m and the good risks choose β – be an equilibrium in the sense of Rothschild and Stiglitz? The answer to this question is obviously negative: by choosing the full insurance contract α_m the bad risks automatically signal that they are actually bad risks, because no good risk opts for this contract. Now the insurers lose on these contracts (compensated by the profits on contracts β), because they are based on too favourable a probability of avoiding loss for this group. Consequently, expected profit-maximising insurers will reject all customers who request full insurance coverage.

However, the bad risks will quickly find a solution to this problem: since their best choice α_m reveals their poor quality, they will hide by using the same strategy as the good risks, that is, by choosing contract β. That is the best they can do without being 'found out'. In summary, if the insurers offer a price schedule that is actuarially fair on average, then the bad risks will seek to pass themselves off as good risks by choosing the same contract as the good risks.

Can the solution (β, β) be an equilibrium in the sense of Rothschild and Stiglitz? We will show that this is not possible. Suppose that a new company offered contract γ on the line $1\alpha_l$, below EU_h but above EU_l. We know that this is possible because of the slopes of the two groups' indifference curves. Contract γ offers less coverage than contract β (less net wealth in the bad state) but at a lower premium (greater net wealth in the good state). In this case, the good risks will leave their old insurer to choose the new contract, because γ promises greater expected utility (γ lies above EU_l).

In contrast, for the bad risks, the reduction in the premium is insufficient to compensate for the loss of coverage, given the relatively high probability that this coverage will benefit them. They thus prefer to retain contract β. Will the new company generate a non-negative expected profit? Since γ lies on the line $1\alpha_l$, the expected profit is zero, conditional on the fact that only good risks will choose γ. It suffices to demand a slightly higher premium than the one for contract γ in order to generate a positive expected profit while retaining only the good risks. To accomplish this, the company can offer a contract γ' in the area $\beta\rho\theta$. Consequently, there exists a counter-offer γ' that generates a positive profit for the company that makes it, which violates Condition (b) of Rothschild and Stiglitz. We have just shown that, in the equilibrium proposed by Rothschild and Stiglitz, there cannot be a unique contract. The next theorem follows from this.

Theorem 16.1 With asymmetric information in insurance markets, there exists no equilibrium in the sense of Rothschild and Stiglitz with average actuarial pricing. If an equilibrium exists, each type of insured agent necessarily chooses a different contract ('separating equilibrium').

The nature of the separating equilibrium is illustrated in Figure 16.3. Consider an insurance market where the only two contracts offered are contracts α_h and δ. Thus there is a full coverage contract with a high premium (based on p_h) and a partial coverage contract with a low premium (based on p_l). It is immediately clear that, facing these options, the high-risk agents will choose α_h and the low-risk agents will choose δ. The reason for the different behaviour is that the high-risk agents perceive that the reduction in the premium associated with δ is insufficient to compensate for the loss of coverage under this contract, given the high probability of loss that they face. In contrast, the low-risk agents perceive that the premium for α_h is excessive relative to the gain from full coverage, given their low probability of loss. The partial character of the contract δ is constructed in such a way that the bad

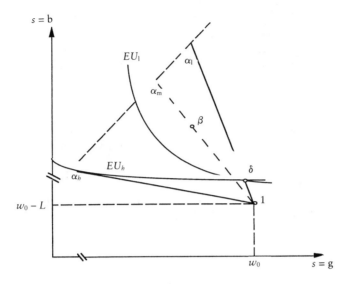

Figure 16.3

risks prefer α_h, that is, δ lies slightly below EU_h. In the limit, δ lies on the intersection of $1\alpha_l$ and EU_h.

Since the choices differ, each insured agent credibly reveals their quality by choosing contract α_h or δ. The signal of good quality from the good risks is credible because the bad risks have no incentive to mimic the good risks by choosing δ. The premiums can thus be calculated actuarially based on each group's true probability of loss. It follows that under this solution (α_h, δ), expected profits are zero for the insurance companies, consistent with property (a) of the equilibrium that we are studying here.

Does this imply that the solution (α_h, δ) is a Rothschild–Stiglitz equilibrium, that is, an equilibrium that is robust to any profitable counter-offer? It turns out that this depends on the proportion λ of good risks in the population. If λ is relatively close to 1, p_m is relatively close to p_l and the mean actuarial pricing line $1\alpha_l$ has a steep slope, as represented in Figure 16.3. In this case, consider the counter-offer β. With three contracts being offered on the market, both types of agents will opt for the new contract β, giving up their former contracts, because β lies above EU_l and EU_h. The company that offers β will thus achieve a zero-expected profit, conditional on the fact that it attracts the entire population, as is the case. By positioning itself a little to the left of β, it will continue to attract the entire population and will enjoy a positive profit. The solution (α_h, δ) is thus not a stable competitive equilibrium in this case. But we know that solution (β, β) is not a stable competitive equilibrium either. Thus, we have here a fundamental instability of the solutions under asymmetric information, because there is no Rothschild–Stiglitz equilibrium.

In contrast, if the proportion of good risks is smaller, Figure 16.4 is obtained. Here δ is preferred to β by the good risks and this counter-offer cannot be profitable if it attracts only the bad risks. In this case, Rothschild and Stiglitz (1976) have shown that the solution (α_h, δ) is an equilibrium.

Theorem 16.2 With asymmetric information, there exists a critical proportion λ_0 of low-risk individuals in the population such that:

(a) if $\lambda > \lambda_0$ then there is no equilibrium in the sense of Rothschild and Stiglitz;

(b) if $\lambda < \lambda_0$ then there exists a separating equilibrium in the sense of Rothschild and Stiglitz (α_h, δ).

When $\lambda < \lambda_0$ the stable separating competitive equilibrium implies that the bad risks impose a negative externality on the good risks in the sense that the latter are unable to acquire full coverage. Since the transfer of risk is only partial and the insurers are risk neutral, it follows that asymmetric information induces a Pareto-inefficient equilibrium in terms of risk allocation. When risk aversion is weak, the indifference curve EU_h in Figure 16.3 approaches the line $1\alpha_h$ and δ approaches the autarky point 1, implying that the good risks can no longer insure themselves. This result is similar to the one obtained by Akerlof; trades can be reduced to nothing for the good risks given information problems.

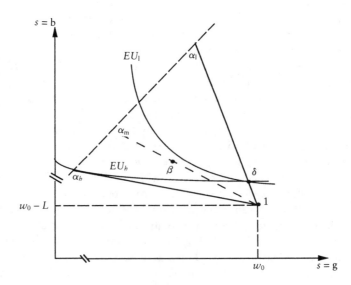

Figure 16.4

16.2.3 The reactive equilibrium of Riley–Wilson

The practitioner and the researcher in insurance certainly worry about the consequences of non-existence of a stable competitive equilibrium. Riley (1979) and Wilson (1977) have therefore sought to redefine equilibrium for insurance markets with asymmetric information. They considered 'reactive equilibria', introduced in game theory by Riley and applied to insurance by Wilson. The definition of such an equilibrium depends on the way insurance companies react when they see their clients leave them to accept counter-offers. Here, a reactive equilibrium is defined in the following way: a company that wishes to put a counter-offer on the market calculates its profitability *assuming that the other companies will abandon their unprofitable contracts following the departure of some kinds of clients.*

Thus, reconsider Figure 16.2 and solution (β, β). Looking more closely, is the counter-offer γ really profitable given the expected reaction of the injured companies? Recall that the companies that offer β are left with the bad risks after the counter-offer γ. These companies would thus suffer losses from contract β, because the premium is calculated assuming that the contract is sold to a representative sample of the population, which is no longer the case. Consistent with Wilson's definition, it will be assumed that these companies will abandon contracts β. The bad risks have nothing better than to turn to the counter-offer. This counter-offer can thus be expected to generate losses because the entire population chooses it, whereas the premium was calculated assuming that only the good risks would buy the contract. Since this counter-offer is no longer profitable given the anticipated reaction of the injured competitors, it will not be marketed. Thus (β, β) is a candidate for a reactive equilibrium, whereas it was not in the context of the Rothschild–Stiglitz equilibrium where the reactions of the other companies were ignored. The solution (β, β) is a solution where the insurers offer a unique contract with an obligatory deductible.

When a Rothschild–Stiglitz equilibrium does not exist, that is when $\lambda > \lambda_0$ (Figure 16.3), (β, β) fends off the counter-offer (α_h, δ) because nobody will choose this counter-offer. It thus turns out that (β, β) is a reactive equilibrium. In contrast, when $\lambda < \lambda_0$ (Figure 16.4), (β, β) fails to fend off the counter-offer (α_h, δ), as before. In this case, it can be shown that (α_h, δ) is a reactive equilibrium.

Theorem 16.3 There exists a critical proportion of good risks in the population such that:

(a) if $\lambda > \lambda_0$ then the unique reactive equilibrium is (β, β);
(b) if $\lambda < \lambda_0$ then the unique reactive equilibrium is (α_h, δ).

The problem of the non-existence of equilibrium in insurance markets with asymmetric information has thus been solved. For both types of equilibria, it can be said that the information problems result in Pareto-inefficient risk allocations. In each case, the bad risks impose a negative externality on the good risks.

We have discussed only one kind of problem associated with asymmetric information: the problem of adverse selection. Another large class of problems related to asymmetric information corresponds to the analysis of the 'moral hazard' problem. Whereas with adverse selection, the quality of an individual is intrinsically given, it is assumed in the context of moral hazard that this quality can be influenced by the individual's unobservable behaviour. For example, a motorist can influence the probability of an accident by driving more or less cautiously. Furthermore, the insurance itself will certainly influence the actions of the driver by reducing the amount of care, because the risk net of the insurance indemnity is reduced; indeed it is zero in the case of full coverage. If the care with which an individual drives is not observable, partial insurance coverage may be necessary in order to induce a minimal level of caution. Whereas partial insurance was useful in the adverse selection problem to induce bad risks to reveal themselves, partial insurance is useful in the moral hazard problem to induce insured individuals to reduce the level of risk. To maintain a unified presentation, we will say no more about this relatively technical subject.[2]

16.3 Asymmetric information on financial markets

In this section, we study a simple example of asymmetric information on stock markets. This example is based on an article by A. Kyle (1985), significantly simplified to bring out the essential characteristics of the problem.

The liquidation value of a financial asset is represented by a binary random variable that takes on value v_1 with probability π_v and the value $v_2 > v_1$ otherwise. Everyone knows the probability π_v of the bad state. Before the market knows the exact liquidation value, some exchanges take place on the market. Following Kyle, we assume there are three kinds of agents in the market.

1. 'Noise traders' whose aggregate demand u is a uniformly distributed random variable on $[-a, +a]$. The variables $\tilde{u}$ and $\tilde{v}$ are independently distributed. These agents base their demand on variables other than the price and expected liquidation value. They thus do not have any particular rationale and constitute random 'noise' for the market.
2. An informed risk-neutral agent who knows the liquidation price in advance. Nevertheless, the demand from the 'noise traders' is unknown at the time the agent's own demand is chosen. This demand equals x_1

when the liquidation value is v_1, and x_2 when the liquidation value is v_2. One would expect x_2 to be positive if the agent is to profit from the private information that the liquidation value exceeds the market value. In contrast, one would expect x_1 to be negative because if $v = v_1$ then the informed agent has privileged information that the market is overvaluing the asset.

3. 'Market makers' or 'specialists' who are risk neutral and who compete among themselves. They increase the liquidity of the market by taking positions opposite to those of the other two categories. They observe the aggregate demand $x + u$ and fix a price $p(x + u)$ as a function of that demand.

In summary, the 'game' takes on the form illustrated in Figure 16.5. Initially, 'nature' chooses the liquidation value v_1 (or v_2) with probability π_v (or $1 - \pi_v$). Given this value, the informed agent chooses demand x_1 or x_2. Next, the noise traders 'choose' their demand u and the specialists set a market price given the observed aggregate demand $D = x + u$. Finally, the positions are liquidated.

We begin by modelling the behaviour of the specialists. It is assumed that they use all of the available information to set the price. The only information that they have is the observation of aggregate demand $D = x + u$. It is also assumed that their experience has taught them the values of a, v_1, v_2 and π_v

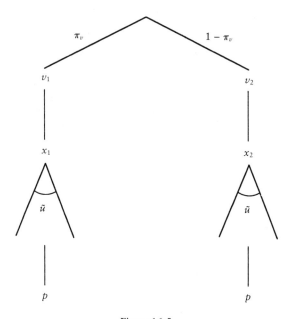

Figure 16.5

as well as the demands of the informed agent x_1 and x_2. If the specialists use Bayes' rule to calculate their expectations of $\tilde{v}$, then the result is called a Bayesian equilibrium. One might wonder how the specialists can know *a priori* the values of π_v and the conditional demands x_1 and x_2 of the informed agent. One could imagine, for example, an infinitely repeated game where, each year, the identical game is replayed. After some amount of time, the market makers would have good estimates of these variables.

Can they infer the liquidation value of the asset from the observed aggregate demand? If it were possible to observe the informed agent's demand $\tilde{x}$ instead of the aggregate demand $\tilde{x} + \tilde{u}$ then they would directly deduce the value of v, assuming that x_1 differs from x_2. This is, alas, impossible because, for example, the informed agent can hide the demand by placing orders using several intermediaries.

Nevertheless, it is sometimes possible to deduce precise information from aggregate demand. Suppose the market makers observe a demand D that is larger than $x_1 + a$. In that case, it is impossible for the liquidation value to be v_1 because the highest possible aggregate demand in the bad state is $x_1 + \max(\tilde{u}) = x_1 + a$. All the market makers will use similar reasoning if $D > x_1 + a$ is observed. Since they compete, their profit in equilibrium is zero and the price equals the liquidation value that they all correctly infer:

$$p(D) = v_2 \qquad \forall D > x_1 + a \tag{16.7}$$

Identical reasoning implies that in the Bayesian equilibrium

$$p(D) = v_1 \qquad \forall D < x_2 - a \tag{16.7a}$$

Finally, if aggregate demand between $x_2 - a$ and $x_1 + a$ is observed, then no information about the liquidation value can be deduced from this observation because a D in this interval can arise with identical probability from a demand structure $(x = x_1;\ u = D - x_1)$ or a demand structure $(x = x_2;\ u = D - x_2)$. Under such circumstances, no information is gained from the observation and the specialists' posterior probabilities on $\tilde{v}$ equal the prior probabilities: v_1 with probability π_v and v_2 with probability $(1 - \pi_v)$. Since the market makers are in perfect competition and are risk neutral, their expected profit must be zero in equilibrium. In the absence of transactions costs it follows that:

$$p(D) = \pi_v v_1 + (1 - \pi_v)v_2 = v_m \qquad \forall x_2 - a < D < x_1 + a \tag{16.7b}$$

Parameter v_m is the average liquidation value in the absence of information. To obtain these last three equations (16.7), (16.7a) and (16.7b), we have systematically – but implicitly – applied Bayes' rule.

The informed agent must determine their demand in each state. When information is received that the liquidation value is high $(v = v_2)$, then acquisition of a lot of stock (high x_2) may be desired in order to generate the maximum surplus. However, if a large market order is placed the agent may be 'found out', particularly if demand from the noise traders is high.

Specifically, if aggregate demand D exceeds $x_1 + a$ then the equilibrium price will equal the true liquidation value v_2 (Equation (16.7)) because the specialists will understand that the state must be good. Consequently, the informed agent's profit will be zero. There is thus a negative relationship between the size of the order and the probability of being caught. This implies that, at the optimum, the informed agent must trade off between the wish to buy the maximum number of shares and the wish to avoid revealing information to the market.

More cunning still is the following argument for limiting demand in the good state: by limiting x_2, the informed agent reduces the risk of being found out in the bad state. According to Condition (16.7a), a smaller value of x_2 reduces the probability that aggregate demand $x_1 + \tilde{u}$ in the bad state will fall below the critical value $x_2 - a$ that tells the market makers that the bad state has really occurred ($p = v_1$). The revelation of this information destroys the informed agent's hope for a profit because $p = v_1$; thus the informed agent does not gain from the privileged information because it has been 'signalled' to the market.

In the limiting case where $x_1 = x_2 = 0$ the specialists never obtain any information by observing aggregate demand ($-a < D < a$). The price thus always equals v_m, but the informed agent's profit is zero. Once x_2 exceeds x_1, there is a positive probability that the informed agent will be found out. The informed agent must thus accept the risk of being found out in order to be able to make a positive profit.

In contrast, the informed agent always avoids choosing demands x_1 and x_2 that differ by more than $2a$. Otherwise (that is, if $x_1 + a < x_x - a$) the informed agent's information will always be uncovered by the market-makers, because aggregate demand in the bad state ($x_1 + u < x_1 + a$) will always be less than aggregate demand in the good state ($x_2 + u > x_2 - a$). The price will then always equal the true liquidation value and the informed agent will not receive any profits.

The optimal strategy of the informed agent must therefore lie between these two extremes. To determine the optimal strategy of the informed agent, we begin by calculating the expected price in the good state. From Equation (16.7) and (16.7b) it follows that:

$$E[p \mid \text{state } 2] = E[p(x_2 + \tilde{u})]$$

$$= \int_{-a}^{a} \frac{1}{2a} p(x_2 + u) \, du$$

$$= \frac{1}{2a} \int_{-a}^{a-(x_2-x_1)} v_m \, du + \frac{1}{2a} \int_{a-(x_2-x_1)}^{a} v_2 \, du$$

$$= v_m + \frac{(v_2 - v_m)(x_2 - x_1)}{2a} \tag{16.8}$$

Specifically, if $D = x_2 + u$ is less than $x_1 + a$ then $p(x_2 + u) = v_m$ (and no information is revealed). Otherwise $p(x_2 + a) = v_2$ (and the information is revealed). It turns out that this expected price is an increasing function of the order x_2 placed by the informed agent. This is due to the fact that increasing the order increases the risk of informing the market.

Since the informed agent is risk neutral then, after having observed $v = v_2$, the demand x_2 that maximises expected profit Π_2 will be chosen:

$$\Pi_2 = x_2(v_2 - E[p \,|\, \text{state } 2]) \tag{16.9}$$

The first-order condition for this problem is:

$$0 = v_2 - E[p \,|\, x = x_2] - x_2 \frac{\partial E[p \,|\, \text{state } 2]}{\partial x_2}$$

$$= \frac{v_2 - v_m}{2a} [2a - (x_2 - x_1) - x_2]$$

or, equivalently,

$$0 = 2a - 2x_2 + x_1 \tag{16.10}$$

Similarly, the problem in the bad state is written as:

$$\max \Pi_1 = x_1(v_1 - E[p \,|\, x = x_1]) \tag{16.9a}$$

which yields a symmetric first-order condition:

$$0 = -2a - 2x_1 + x_2 \tag{16.10a}$$

Equations (16.10) and (16.10a) form a system of two equations in two unknowns for which the solution is:

$$x_1 = -\frac{2a}{3} \quad \text{and} \quad x_2 = \frac{2a}{3} \tag{16.11}$$

The optimal solution can be described in the following way: in the good state the informed agent's demand corresponds to two-thirds of the noise traders' maximal demand while in the bad state the informed agent sells an amount that corresponds to two-thirds of the noise traders' maximal supply. The specialists correctly deduce a good state with certainty whenever aggregate demand exceeds $a/3$. Similarly, they deduce a bad state when market supply exceeds the same level $a/3$. When aggregate demand lies in the interior of the interval $[-a/3, a/3]$, the specialists cannot infer anything and they set the average price v_m. Outside of this interval, prices v_1 and v_2 are observed. The informed agent's probability of being 'found out' is 66 per cent in both states.

What can one conclude from this? First, prices do not always reflect all the information available to agents so the efficient markets hypothesis does not hold. In 33 per cent of cases, the informed agent succeeds in hiding his information from the market. The acquisition of information that is unavailable to the market is thus profitable. Next, it is easier for the informed agent to conceal information when there is more noise, that is, when a is higher. It is possible to take advantage of the additional freedom to purchase more in the good state – and to sell more in the bad state – and thus enjoy higher profits on average.

More generally, we have shown how one can attempt to hide a 'signal' in order to profit from a monopoly on private information.

Exercises

16.1 Consider the numerical example presented by Akerlof and in Section 16.1, except that the distribution of quality of the good held by Type 1 individuals is $q = 1$ with probability $\frac{1}{2}$ and $q = 3$ with probability $\frac{1}{2}$.

Questions
(a) Show that there is a competitive equilibrium under asymmetric information, with $p = 3$. Explain why there is an equilibrium in this case.
(b) Is this equilibrium efficient?

16.2 Consider the model presented by Rothschild and Stiglitz and in Section 16.2. Suppose that there is a Rothschild–Stiglitz equilibrium. Due to the inefficiency of the equilibrium, the state considers the possibility of intervening in the insurance market.

Questions
(a) The first policy that is considered is to impose *compulsory* full insurance on everyone on a non-discriminatory basis (everyone pays the same premium $P = p_m L$). This is the principle underlying most social insurance systems. Discuss whether this social insurance system is Pareto-improving with respect to the Rothschild–Stiglitz equilibrium.
(b) Consider a mixed system in which everyone is covered by a compulsory insurance for 50 per cent of the loss with a non-discriminatory premium $P = \frac{1}{2} p_m L$. There exists a competitive insurance market for the risk that is not covered by compulsory insurance. Draw a graph that represents this situation. Try to determine the Rothschild–Stiglitz equilibrium if it exists.
Hint: The new graph is equivalent to Figure 16.2 except that there is a change in the position of point '1'. Is it Pareto-improving with respect to the standard Rothschild–Stiglitz equilibrium?

16.3 Consider the model presented in Section 16.3. Rather than being uniformly distributed on $[-a, a]$, suppose that the aggregate demand of noise traders is $-a$ with probability $\frac{1}{2}$ and $+a$ with probability $\frac{1}{2}$. Calculate the new equilibrium.

Notes

1. This implies a premium less than the one imposed at α_h. In this case the high-risk agents benefit from the existence of the low-risk agents. They get a 'free lunch'.
2. The interested reader is referred to Arnott (1991).

References

Akerlof G. (1970), The market for lemons: quality uncertainty and the market mechanism, *Quarterly Journal of Economics*, vol. 89, 488–500.

Arnott R. (1991), Moral hazard and competitive insurance markets, in *Contributions to Insurance Economics*, G. Dionne (ed.), Kluwer Academic Press, Boston.

Dionne G. and N. Doherty (1991), Adverse selection in insurance markets: a selective survey, in *Contributions to Insurance Economics*, G. Dionne (ed.), Kluwer Academic Press, Boston.

Kyle A.S. (1985), Continuous auctions and insider trading, *Econometrica*, vol. 53, 1335–1355.

Riley J. (1979), Informational equilibrium, *Econometrica*, vol. 47, 331–359.

Rothschild M. and J. Stiglitz (1976), Equilibrium in competitive insurance markets: an essay on the economics of imperfect information, *Quarterly Journal of Economics*, vol. 80, 629–649.

Wilson C. (1977), A model of insurance markets with incomplete information. *Journal of Economic Theory*, vol. 16, 167–207.

17 : Conclusion

Having arrived at the end of the race, the attentive reader's mind is still filled with the last formulas that have been assimilated and the realities that they reflect. Thus there is a risk of forgetting the starting point. Literary traditions, no doubt ancient, manage this risk by imposing on the authors the modest cost of drafting a conclusion with the goal of retracing the path followed and providing a general perspective.

As in all microeconomic textbooks, the study of a market is carried out in two steps: the first consists of analysing the behaviour of the participants at given prices. This is the content of consumer and producer theory: for each possible price, the supply and demand of the good to be traded are determined. Next, in a second step, the determination of these prices is analysed given the behaviour of the market participants. In a competitive context, for example, the price that results is the one that equalises supply and demand for the good. This precise structure is found in this textbook.

In order to study, in Part Three, the exchanges of risk and the prices at which these exchanges are made, we had to have 'invested' heavily in the analysis of two fundamental notions: the measurement of risk and its perception by economic agents. Such was the objective of the first part of the text, which allowed us to construct a model of decision-making under uncertainty.

Having defined in this way the framework of analysis and the goods (lotteries) to be studied in the text, we presented in Part Two several applications to individual choices under uncertainty. This is the counterpart under uncertainty of the theories of supply and demand under certainty, in the sense that the examination of these models is done assuming that the unit price – or the external elements such as the level of demand or the level of threatened loss – are exogenously given. It is in this framework that we studied portfolio, insurance and production decisions in the face of different kinds of uncertainty. Insofar as it was possible, we tried to emphasise the deep similarities that exist between these seemingly very different subjects. In this way, we indirectly gave some theoretical consistency to the practice of 'risk management', which aspires precisely to unify within a firm the approaches taken in the face of multiple and varied sources of risk.

This step where prices are exogenous is the obligatory stepping stone toward the study of price formation in markets for risk, whether they be hypothetical markets for 'contingent claims' or more realistic markets for financial assets and insurance contracts. Consistent with the results from welfare theory under certainty, we showed that under certain assumptions (for example, complete markets and symmetric information) competitive markets lead to an efficient allocation of risks among economic agents. However, as was seen in Chapter 16, the more realistic case of asymmetric information produces a less clear final judgement as to the performance of markets in terms of the efficient risk-sharing arrangement in the economy.

If we had to summarise the conclusion, we would willingly say that we have simply written a book on microeconomics dedicated to a particular good that is somewhat more difficult to grasp than the others: risk.

Appendix I

To examine the 'wealth effect' and the 'risk effect' in more detail, reconsider the case where $U = W_f^{1/2}$ with initial wealth of 10 completely invested in the risky asset $\tilde{y}$. In this case:

$$E[U(W_f)] = \tfrac{1}{2} \int_{-1}^{+1} (10 + 10y)^{1/2} \, dy = 2.9814$$

Consequently the certainty equivalent equals:

$$W_f^* = 8.8886$$

and of course, due to Equation (4.1),

$$10(1 - \pi') = W_f^* \qquad \text{so that } \pi' = 0.1110$$

Now suppose that initial wealth is increased to 14. As one might expect, the certainty equivalent increases because more wealth is preferred to less. This intuition is confirmed by the calculations that yield:

$$E[U(W_f)] = \tfrac{1}{2} \int_{-1}^{+1} (14 + 14y)^{1/2} \, dy = 3.5276$$

with a new certainty equivalent of $W_f^* = 12.4440$. Note that the increase in the certainty equivalent is accompanied by a constant π' because W_f^* increases proportionally to W_0. In the new situation π' is the solution to:

$$14(1 - \pi') = 12.444 \qquad \text{that is, } \pi' = 0.1110$$

This situation is thus one of constant relative risk aversion, as is confirmed by:

$$A_r = -W \frac{U''(W)}{U'(W)} = -W\left(\frac{-1}{2W}\right) = \frac{1}{2}$$

which is, indeed, constant.

Why does this result hold? It can be derived in two steps. Begin with $E[U(10(1 + \tilde{y}))]$. When W_0 changes from 10 to 14, *if* the individual were lucky enough to receive this increase in initial wealth with certainty then the expected utility would become $E[U(10(1 + \tilde{y}) + 4)]$ and a simple calculation shows that a utility equal to 3.6525 (which corresponds to a certainty equivalent of 13.3409) would be attained. But utility ends up at 3.5276 precisely because the additional wealth ($\Delta W = 4$) is also subjected to risk (and the individual is risk averse) so that the expression to evaluate is:

$$E[U(10(1 + \tilde{y}) + 4(1 = \tilde{y}))] = E[U(14(1 + \tilde{y}))]$$

In summary, the total effect of a change from $W_0 = 10$ to $W_0 = 14$, which increases the certainty equivalent of $W_f^* = 8.8886$ to $W_f^{'*} = 12.4440$ can be decomposed into two effects:

(a) the 'wealth effect' that would tend to increase W_f^* from 8.8886 to 13.341 if ΔW_0 were received with certainty;
(b) the 'risk effect' that lowers the certainty equivalent from 13.3444 to 12.4444 because this ΔW_0 is itself subjected to an actuarially neutral multiplicative risk and is thus less valued by a risk-averse individual.

As we have stated in the text, to say that partial risk aversion is constant is the same as saying that the risk effect lowers the certainty equivalent to the level where:

$$W_0[1 - \pi'(W_0)] = (W_0 + \Delta W_0)[1 - \pi'(W_0 + \Delta W_0)]$$

and so that

$$\pi'(W_0) = \pi'(W_0 + \Delta W_0)$$

Appendix 2

Consider an individual with utility function:

$$U = -e^{-\beta W_f}$$

who has certain initial wealth of W_0 invested at a risky rate of return $\tilde{y}$, so that:

$$\widetilde{W}_f = W_0(1 + \tilde{y})$$

We will assume that $\tilde{y}$ has a normal distribution with mean zero and standard deviation σ, denoted $N(0, \sigma)$. This random variable has support from $-\infty$ to $+\infty$ but to avoid, for all practical purposes, the realisations of $\tilde{y}$ that are less than -1 and would render W_f negative, we choose σ to be sufficiently small. For example, with $\sigma = 0.05$ the probability that $\tilde{y}$ is less than -1 is so small that it is not generally tabulated.

When evaluating the situation, the decision-maker uses the expected utility criterion and obtains:

$$E[U(W_f)] = -\int_{-\infty}^{+\infty} e^{-\beta W_0(1 + y)} f(y) \, dy \qquad (A2.1)$$

where

$$f(y) = \frac{1}{\sqrt{2\pi}} e^{-1/2(y/\sigma)^2}$$

$$= -e^{-\beta W_0} \int_{-\infty}^{+\infty} e^{-\beta W_0 y} f(y) \, dy$$

The integral on the right-hand side of this expression is a moment-generating function described in many statistics textbooks, so one may also write:

$$E[U(W_f)] = -e^{\beta W_0} e^{+\beta^2 W_0^2 \sigma^2/2}$$

$$= -e^{-\beta W_0(1 - (\beta W_0 \sigma^2/2))}$$

From Equation (4.1) it follows that:

$$-e^{-\beta[W_0(1-\pi')]} = -e^{-\beta W_0(1-(\beta W_0\sigma^2/2))}$$

and this implies

$$1 - \pi' = 1 - \frac{\beta W_0 \sigma^2}{2}$$

or, equivalently,[1]

$$\pi' = \frac{\beta W_0 \sigma^2}{2}$$

Even if σ^2 is very small, this result clearly indicates that, for sufficiently large values of W_0, π' will exceed the limiting value +1.

Note

1. It is interesting to note that in this example the true value of π' is exactly equal to the value obtained by the Pratt approximation (4.3) applied to the case of exponential U. This equality results from the normality of $\tilde{y}$ which implies that $E(U)$ is a function only of the expected value and the variance of W_f.

Appendix 3

The proof of the proposition stated in Note 1 is a little more subtle. In the first place note that:

$$L = k(U) \qquad \text{with } k' > 0 \text{ and } k'' < 0$$

implies that L'/U' is a decreasing function in W_f (or in U) because $L'/U' = k'$ and k'' is negative.

In addition, for all utility functions, $A_a = -U''/U' = -\text{d} \log U'$. It follows that[1]

$$A_a^L(W_f) > A_a^U(W_f)$$
$$-\text{d} \log L' > -\text{d} \log U'$$

or

$$\text{d} \log L' < \text{d} \log U'$$

which can also be written as:

$$\text{d} \log \left[\frac{L'}{U'}\right] < 0$$

using the properties of logarithms. Since the logarithmic function is monotone increasing, $\text{d} \log L'/U' < 0$ implies $\text{d}(L'/U') < 0$, that is, that L'/U' is a decreasing function. This corresponds to our starting point at the beginning of the proof.

Note

1. This notation represents the degree of absolute risk aversion A_a evaluated sometimes for utility function L and sometimes for U.

Appendix 4

Since, by assumption,[1] $E(\tilde{x}) = E(\tilde{y})$,

$$\int_a^b xf(x)\,\mathrm{d}x = \int_a^b yg(y)\,\mathrm{d}y \tag{A4.1}$$

Integration by parts of the form $u = x$ and $\mathrm{d}v = f(x)\,\mathrm{d}x$ yields:

$$[xF(x)]_a^b - \int_a^b F(x)\,\mathrm{d}x = [yG(y)]_a^b - \int_a^b G(y)\,\mathrm{d}y$$

Given that $F(b) = G(b) = 1$ and that $F(a) = G(a) = 0$, this expression simplifies to:

$$b - \int_a^b F(x)\,\mathrm{d}x = b - \int_a^b G(y)\,\mathrm{d}y$$

or, obviously,

$$\int_a^b F(x)\,\mathrm{d}x = \int_a^b G(y)\,\mathrm{d}y \tag{A4.2}$$

which is perfectly equivalent to Equation (5.2) because, with different notation, both Equations (5.2) and (A4.2) affirm that the areas under the distribution functions over the entire support of $\tilde{y}$ (and hence of $\tilde{x}$) are equal. As is suggested by the proof beginning at Equation (A4.1), this comes from the fact that $\tilde{x}$ and $\tilde{y}$ have the same expected value.

Note

1. To simplify the notation, we assume here that $\tilde{x}$ and $\tilde{y}$ are continuous random variables.

Appendix 5

Here we rigorously prove that the marginal cost of risk as defined in Equation (9.9) is an increasing function of a so that if U is concave then the second-order condition for a maximum is satisfied.

To achieve our objective, we must show that the expression

$$\frac{d}{da}\left[\frac{\mathrm{cov}(U',x)}{E(U')}\right]$$

is negative. The rules of differential calculus tell us that this derivative is written as:

$$\frac{E(U')\dfrac{d}{da}\mathrm{cov}(U',\tilde{x}) - \mathrm{cov}(U',\tilde{x})\dfrac{d}{da}E(U')}{\{E[U']\}^2} \tag{A5.1}$$

Now $\mathrm{cov}(U',\tilde{x}) = E[(U' - E(U'))(\tilde{x} - \mu)]$ so that:

$$\frac{d}{da}\mathrm{cov}(U',\tilde{x}) = E\{[\tilde{x} - \mu][U''(\tilde{x} - i) - E(U''(\tilde{x} - i))]\} \tag{A5.2}$$

because

$$\frac{d}{da}E(U') = E[U''(\tilde{x} - i)] \tag{A5.2a}$$

Equation (A5.2) can be simplified advantageously because $E[U''(\tilde{x} - i)]$ is a number that can be passed through the first E operator on the right-hand side. Thus:

$$\frac{d}{da}\mathrm{cov}(U',\tilde{x}) = E[U''(\tilde{x} - i)(\tilde{x} - \mu)] \tag{A5.3}$$

If Equations (A5.3) and (A5.2a) are substituted into (A5.1) it can be written as:

$$\frac{E(U')E[U''(\tilde{x} - i)(\tilde{x} - \mu)] - \mathrm{cov}(U',\tilde{x})E[U''(\tilde{x} - i)]}{[E(U')]^2} \tag{A5.4}$$

Since the denominator of (A5.4) is necessarily positive, the sign of this expression is completely determined by the sign of the numerator. Now, using Equation (9.9), the numerator can be transformed into:

$$E(U')\{E[U''(\tilde{x} - i)(\tilde{x} - \mu)] + (\mu - i)E[U''(\tilde{x} - i)]\}$$

Since,

$$E[U''(\tilde{x} - i)(\tilde{x} - \mu)] = E[U''((\tilde{x} - \mu) + (\mu - i))(\tilde{x} - \mu)]$$
$$= E[U''(\tilde{x} - \mu)^2] + (\mu - i)E[U''(\tilde{x} - \mu)]$$

and since $(\mu - i)E[U''(\tilde{x} - i)] = (\mu - i)E[U''((\tilde{x} - \mu) + (\mu - i))]$, the entire numerator can also be expressed as:

$$E(U')\{E[U''(\tilde{x} - \mu)^2] + 2(\mu - i)E[U''(\tilde{x} - \mu)] + (\mu - i)^2 E(U'')\}$$

This expression contains a perfect square, so the numerator can also be written as:

$$E(U')\{E[U''((\tilde{x} - \mu) + (\mu - i))^2]\}$$

which is necessarily negative because it is the expected value of a product of terms one of which, U'', is always negative and the other, $[(\tilde{x} - \mu) + (\mu - i)]^2$, is always positive. We have thus shown that:

$$\frac{d}{da}\left[\frac{\text{cov}(U', x)}{E(U')}\right]$$

is negative, which means that the marginal cost of risk is increasing in a for a risk-averse individual. Specifically, when a increases the expression in brackets decreases, that is, it becomes more negative; thus the term that is subtracted from μ is increasing when the gross marginal benefit of an increase in a is evaluated.

Appendix 6

Since the marginal cost of risk equals $-\text{cov}(U',\tilde{x})/E(U')$, we must prove that this term decreases when W_0 increases if A_a is decreasing in W. To this end, we study the sign of:

$$\frac{d}{dW_0}\left[\frac{\text{cov}(U',\tilde{x})}{E(U')}\right] = \frac{E(U')\dfrac{d\text{cov}(\cdot)}{dW_0} - \text{cov}(\cdot)(1+i)E(U'')}{\{E(U')\}^2}$$

$$(A6.1)$$

Now

$$\frac{d}{dW_0}\text{cov}(U',\tilde{x}) = \frac{d}{dW_0}E[(U'-E(U'))(\tilde{x}-\mu)]$$

$$= (1+i)E[(\tilde{x}-\mu)(U''-E(U''))]$$

$$= (1+i)E[(\tilde{x}-\mu)U''(W_f)]$$

Consequently, the numerator N of Equation (A6.1) can be written as:

$$N = (1+i)[E(U')E[(\tilde{x}-\mu)U''] - \text{cov}(U',\tilde{x})E(U'')]$$

Dividing by $(1+i)E(U')$, which does not change the sign, and using the first-order condition (9.6) yields:

$$\text{sgn } N = \text{sgn}\{E[(\tilde{x}-\mu)U''] + (\mu-i)E(U'')\}$$

$$= \text{sgn } E[U''(\tilde{x}-i)]$$

which is positive when A_a is decreasing. It is then easy to show that, under this assumption,

$$\frac{d}{dW_0}\left[-\frac{\text{cov}(U',\tilde{x})}{E(U')}\right] < 0$$

as stated.

Appendix 7

To show that K' is negative we proceed in several steps:

1. Since U' is decreasing in s, the fact that $m < n$ implies, when $a^* > 0$, that:

$$U'[W_0(1 + i) + a^*(m - i)] > U'[W_0(1 + i) + a^*(n - i)] > 0$$

2. The sum of the four integrals between brackets in Equation (9.30) is zero. This follows from Conditions (a) and (b) in (9.28). Specifically, because the expected value of the random variable is constant (see Condition (b)),

$$\int_{m'}^{m} st(s)\, ds + \int_{m}^{i} st(s)\, ds + \int_{i}^{n} st(s)\, ds + \int_{n}^{n'} st(s)\, ds = \int_{m'}^{n'} st(s)\, ds = 0$$

and, similarly, $i \int_{m'}^{n'} t(s)\, ds = 0$ (see Condition (a)).

3. Given that the sum of the four integrals equals zero, the sum of the first two bracketed integrals in Equation (9.30) has the same absolute value as the sum of the last two bracketed integrals in Equation (9.30) but with the opposite sign.

4. The sum of the first two integrals is negative. To see this, it suffices to integrate by parts to write:

$$\int_{m'}^{i} (s - i)t(s)\, ds = [(s - i)T(s)]_{m'}^{i} - \int_{m'}^{i} T(s)\, ds \quad (A7.1)$$

where $T(s) = G(s) - F(s)$ is the integral of $t(s)$. Since $[(s - i)T(s)]_{m'}^{i} = 0$, the right-hand side of Equation (A7.1) is:

$$-\int_{m'}^{i} [G(s) - F(s)]\, ds$$

Since an increase in risk in the sense of Meyer–Ormiston is a special case of an increase in risk in the sense of Rothschild–Stiglitz, the integral condition (Equation (5.1)) implies that the above expression is negative.

It is now only necessary to put the pieces of the puzzle together and to return to Equation (9.30). If the marginal utilities in this expression were equal, K' would be zero. However, since the first expression between the brackets is negative and is multiplied by a larger value of U' than the one that multiplies the other positive expression in brackets, it follows that K' is negative. Since K' exceeds K as well, it must be that $K < 0$.

Appendix 8

We will show here that the existence of an uninsurable risk that is independent of the insurable risk can, under certain conditions, be analysed exactly as an exogenous increase in risk aversion. To do this, we define an 'indirect utility function' V given the characteristics of $\tilde{\varepsilon}$:

$$V[w(x)] = \int U[w(x) + w_0\varepsilon] \, dG(\varepsilon) \tag{A8.1}$$

$V[w(x)]$ is the expected utility conditional on the realisation x of the insurable risk, with:

$$w(x) = w_0(1 + \rho) + L(1 - x) + aL(x - (1 + \lambda)\mu)$$

The insured's problem (10.10) can then be written as:

$$\max \int V[w_0(1 + \rho) + L(1 - x) + aL(x - (1 + \lambda)\mu)] \, dF(x) \tag{A8.2}$$

which has a first-order condition like (10.1), but with the utility function U replaced by the indirect utility function V.

We show that V is a concave transformation of U. Derive:

$$V'(w) = \int U'(w + w_0\varepsilon) \, dG(\varepsilon) = U'[w - \psi(w)] \tag{A8.3}$$

where $\psi(w)$ is the prudence premium associated with the uninsurable risk (Definition (6.3)). This implies that:

$$V''(w) = [1 - \psi'(w)] U''[w - \psi(w)] \tag{A8.4}$$

Thus the absolute risk aversion derived from the indirect utility function equals:

$$-\frac{V''(w)}{V'(w)} = -\frac{U''[w - \psi(w)]}{U'[w - \psi(w)]}[1 - \psi'(w)]$$

$$= A_a[w - \psi(w)][1 - \psi'(w)] \tag{A8.5}$$

Assume that absolute risk aversion is decreasing (Hypothesis 4.1). This implies, by Theorem 6.3, that prudence is positive ($\psi > 0$). Combining this assumption with its implications in terms of prudence implies that:

$$-\frac{V''(w)}{V'(w)} > A_a(w)\,[1 - \psi'(w)] \tag{A8.6}$$

If it is further assumed that prudence is decreasing in wealth ($\psi'(w) < 0$), one finally obtains:

$$-\frac{V''(w)}{V'(w)} > A_a(w) = -\frac{U''(w)}{U'(w)} \tag{A8.7}$$

Using the concept of a concave transformation that was presented in Section 4.1, it follows from Equation (A8.7) that *the indirect utility function V is a concave transformation of U when absolute risk aversion and prudence are decreasing functions of wealth.*

Consequently (A8.2), which describes the problem of an agent with utility function U who faces an uninsurable risk, also describes the problem of an agent *without* an insurable risk but who has a more concave utility function V. Now, we have discussed several times the effect of an increase in risk aversion on the demand for insurance (when we studied changes in w_0, for example): it increases demand unambiguously (Figure 10.3).

By the equivalence of increased risk aversion and the existence of an independent uninsurable risk, we conclude that *the demand for insurance is positively affected by the existence of ε,* given the assumptions stated above. The reader can prove, in the same way, that the demand for risky assets falls.

We conclude with the analysis of a limiting case: if U is quadratic then ψ is zero and $-V''(w)/V'(w) = -U''(w)/U'(w)$. This means that the existence of an independent uninsurable risk does not affect the demand for insurance when utility functions are quadratic.

Appendix 9

In this appendix, we briefly present the form of the competitive equilibrium prices of pure assets when the utility functions are negative exponentials:

$$U_i'(w_{fi}) = \exp(-A_{ai}w_{fi}) \qquad (A9.1)$$

where A_{ai} represents Agent i's constant absolute risk aversion. In this case, condition (14.12) can be rewritten as:

$$p_s \exp[-A_{ai}w_{fi}(s)] = \xi_i \Pi_s \qquad \text{for all } s = 1, ..., S \text{ and } i = 1, ..., n \qquad (A9.2)$$

It follows from this that:

$$w_{fi}(s) = -T_{ai} \ln(\xi_i \Pi_s/p_s) = -T_{ai}[\ln(\xi_i) + \ln(\Pi_s/p_s)] \qquad (A9.3)$$

Summing this equality over all i and using the equilibrium condition (14.11a) yields:

$$w_0(s) = K - T_a \ln(\Pi_s/p_s) \qquad (A9.4)$$

Consequently, the equilibrium price of the pure asset s corresponds to:

$$\Pi_s = p_s K' \exp[-T_a^{-1}w_0(s)] \qquad (A9.5)$$

The value of K' is obtained from the normalisation rule (14.3). It is of no particular interest. In contrast, the combination of Equation (A9.3) and (A9.4) yields, after the logarithm of Π_s/p_s is eliminated, the following rule:

$$w_{fi}(s) = k_i + \frac{T_{ai}}{T_a} w_0(s) \qquad (A9.6)$$

This is the rule for Pareto-efficient sharing of the non-diversifiable risk. It is more difficult to derive the structure of equilibrium prices for pure assets, since the prices Π_s are not linear in w_0, as in the quadratic case. The similarities with the quadratic case are nevertheless important.

Appendix 10

The first-order condition of the programme (14.29) relative to $P(s)$ is

$$0 = \lambda_1 [sg'(q) - P(s)] \frac{\partial q}{\partial P} - \lambda_1 q$$

$$+ \lambda_2 k^{-1} [U_2(w_{02} + P(s)) - U_2(w_{02})] \frac{\partial q}{\partial P}$$

$$+ \lambda_2 \frac{q}{k} U_2'(w_{02} + P(s)) \tag{A10.1}$$

Note that we have abused the notation because the function $q(P, s)$ is not differentiable at $P^c(s)$ (cf. Figure 14.6). This condition is only valid if $P(s)$ is different from $P^c(s)$. Three cases are thus possible.

1. $q^d(P(s), s) > k$. In this case $q(P(s), s) = k$ and $\partial q / \partial P = 0$. Then, it must be that $P(s)$ satisfies the following condition derived from (14.29):

$$U_2'(w_{02} + P(s)) = \frac{\lambda_1 k}{\lambda_2} \tag{A10.2}$$

Define P_{max} by formula (A10.3):

$$U_2'(w_{02} + P_{max}) = \frac{\lambda_1 k}{\lambda_2} \tag{A10.3}$$

This implies that $P(s)$ always equals P_{max} in this first case.

2. $q^d(P(s), s) < k$. In this case $q(P(s), s) = q^d(P(s), s)$ and $\partial q / \partial P = \partial q^d / \partial P$. Then it must be that $P(s)$ satisfies condition (14.26a) with $q^d = q^d(P(s), s)$. Using condition (14.26) as well as the definition of η^d (which is assumed constant), one can rewrite this condition as:

$$\frac{\lambda_1 k}{\lambda_2} = \frac{U_2[w_{02} + P(s)] - U_2(w_{02})}{P(s)} \eta^d + U_2'[w_{02} + P(s)] \tag{A10.4}$$

Define P_{min} by the following formula:

$$\frac{\lambda_1 k}{\lambda_2} = \frac{U_2[w_{02} + P_{min}] - U_2(w_{02})}{P_{min}} \eta^d + U_2'[w_{02} + P_{min}] \tag{A10.5}$$

It follows that at the second-best optimum $P(s) = P_{min}$ in this case.

3. $q^d(P(s), s) = k$. In this case, it is immediate that $P(s) = P^c(s)$. Actually, taking account of the discontinuity in the derivative of $q(P, s)$, a complete proof would demand verification that the two conditions (A10.2) and (A10.4) hold with inequalities when $P(s) = P^c(s)$. In short, this can only occur if $P^c(s)$ lies between the bounds P_{min} and P_{max}.

Condition (14.31) is derived directly from Equations (A10.3) and (A10.5). Since η^d is negative and Type 2 agents are risk averse, it can be easily shown from this condition that P_{min} is smaller than P_{max}. Q.E.D.

To prove condition (14.32) for the quadratic case, it suffices to construct three Taylor series approximations through U_2'' around w_{02} in formula (14.31). In the quadratic case, these approximations are exact. One thus obtains:

$$-\eta_d \frac{U_2'(w_{02})P_{min} + 0.5 P_{min}^2 U_2''(w_{02})}{P_{min}} = (P_{min} - P_{max}) U_2''(w_{02})$$

In other words, after simplification and division by $-U_2''(w_{02})$,

$$-\eta^d(T_{a2}(w_{02}) - 0.5 P_{min}) = (P_{max} - P_{min}) \tag{A10.6}$$

Recall also that, in the quadratic case, $T_a(w) = (\frac{1}{2}\beta) - w$. Consequently, Equation (A10.6) is equivalent to formula (14.32).

Bibliography

At the end of each chapter, we have given the bibliographical references that were directly related to the content of the chapter. The purpose of this list of additional sources is to expand the horizons of readers interested in the various topics indicated below.

Of course, the list of relevant references for each topic is extremely long. We limit ourselves here to a very small number of fundamental references. By optimally using the bibliography at the end of each of these references, the reader can build a very wide set of relevant sources.

1. The 'safety-first' criterion

Besides Arzac, who has already been quoted, let us mention the following articles:

Fishburn P. C. (1977), Mean-risk analysis with risk associated with below-target returns, *American Economic Review*, vol. 67, 116–126.

Holthausen D. M. (1981), A risk-return model with risk and return measured as deviation from a target return, *American Economic Review*, vol. 71, 182–188.

Porter R. B. (1974), Semivariance and stochastic dominance: a comparison, *American Economic Review*, vol. 64, 200–204

It is also worth mentioning that there exists a version of the CAPM if investors use the safety-first criterion. The reference is:

Arzac E. and V. Bawa (1977), Portfolio choice and equilibrium in capital markets with safety-first investors, *Journal of Financial Economics*, vol. 4, 277–288.

2. Stochastic dominance

A very good source for further thinking and additional

references is:

Bawa A. (1975), Optimal rules for ordering uncertain prospects, *Journal of Financial Economics*, vol. 2, 95–121.

We mention the existence of the concept of third-order stochastic dominance, which was not mentioned in the text and which is discussed in:

Whitmore G. (1970), Third order stochastic dominance, *American Economic Review*, vol. 50, 457–459.

Finally, a very recent and highly interesting survey on stochastic dominance was published by H. Levy:

Levy H. (1992), Stochastic dominance and expected utility: survey and analysis, *Management Science*, vol. 38, 555–593.

Besides references to the economics and finance literatures, the reader will find in Levy's survey applications of the economic analysis of risk to the field of agricultural economics. This rich article also contains a description of algorithms that are useful for comparison of distributions in terms of stochastic dominance.

3. Insurance economics

The reader interested in this field now has two compact sources in books edited by G. Dionne and published by Kluwer Academic Press. The exact references are:

Dionne G. (ed.) (1991), *Foundations of Insurance Economics*, Kluwer Academic Press, Boston, Dordrecht and London.
Dionne G. (ed.) (1992), *Contributions to Insurance Economics*, Kluwer Academic Press, Boston, Dordrecht and London.

As the titles indicate, the first book contains reprints of 'founding' articles in the field. The second book is made up of recent contributions to the field and is thus more oriented towards current research topics.

4. The role of futures markets

We start our list with an article we have used intensively in the preparation of the manuscript:

Holthausen D. (1979), Hedging and the competitive firm under price uncertainty, *American Economic Review*, vol. 59, 989–995.

We also mention a text that is very pedagogical and that describes various instruments to cope with commodities risks:

Gardner B. (1977), Commodity options for agriculture, *American Journal of Agricultural Economics*, vol. 59, 986–992.

Finally the reader interested in the topics of both futures markets and multiple sources of risk will find much of interest in:

Briys E., M. Crouhy and H. Schlesinger (1993), Optimal hedging in a futures market with background noise and basis risk, *European Economic Review*, vol. 37, 949–960.

5. Efficiency in risk-sharing

Analyses of risk allocation inside groups can be found in the following two articles:

Eliashberg J. and R. Winkler (1981), Risk sharing and group decision making, *Management Science*, vol. 27, 1221–1235.
Wilson R. (1968), The theory of syndicates, *Econometrica*, vol. 36, 119–132.

A more technical paper using tools from the calculus of variations to analyse risk-sharing applied to insurance with transaction costs is:

Raviv A. (1979), The design of optimal insurance policy, *American Economic Review*, vol. 69, 84–96.

6. Information asymmetry

A rigorous analysis of adverse selection in insurance is given in:

Crocker K. J. and A. Snow (1986), The efficiency effects of categorical discrimination in the insurance industry, *Journal of Political Economy*, vol. 94, 321–344.

A presentation of information asymmetries on financial markets that in some sense competes with that of Kyle can be found in:

Grossman S. and J. Stiglitz (1981), On the impossibility of informationally efficient markets, *American Economic Review*, vol. 70, 393–408.

Author index

Subject index